Methods of Family Research: Biographies of Research Projects

Volume I: Normal Families

METHODS OF FAMILY RESEARCH:
Biographies of Research Projects

Volume I: Normal Families

Edited by

IRVING E. SIGEL
Educational Testing Service

GENE H. BRODY
University of Georgia

1990
LAWRENCE ERLBAUM ASSOCIATES, PUBLISHERS
Hillsdale, New Jersey   Hove and London

Lawrence Erlbaum Associates,Inc., Publishers
365 Broadway
Hillsdale, New Jersey 07642

Library of Congress Cataloging-in-Publication Data

Methods of family research : biographies of research projects / edited
  by Irving E. Sigel, Gene H. Brody.
       p.   cm.
    Includes bibliographical references.
    Contents: v. 1. Normal families.
    ISBN 0-89859-826-5 (v. 1)
    1. Family—Research—Case studies.   I. Sigel, Irving E.
  II. Brody, Gene H.
  HQ518.M47
  306.85′072—dc20   89-16933
                                                                    CIP

Printed in the United States of America
10 9 8 7 6 5 4 3 2 1

Contents

Preface

This is a volume of research journeys—trips along different routes—which, in the long run, plan to arrive at a shared destination, generating knowledge about families. This set of essays is unique. Each describes stages along the research route. Although the penultimate destination may be solving some psychological problems regarding human development and/or family functioning, the move toward that rather vague direction is not always easy; it is as though the traveler packed his or her bag with all of the right stuff and set out in a most efficient and direct route to the goal. That is how research studies are usually described in research journals: No blind alleys, no signs of cogitation, no doubts are reported. All is neat, clean, and efficient. The productions run smoothly and seemingly without effort. Journals rarely report behind-the-scenes details of the origins, of the excitement, and of the disappointments every investigator endures in the course of his or her research journey.

Research designs are built, measures are created, research populations are identified and data are massaged. Misses and near misses occur in reaching conclusions in the inevitable move toward the final goal—publication of the report in a refereed journal. (Of course, many research efforts are aborted and never see the light of day). These trials and tribulations can be avoided to some degree if investigators use designs and measures that have already been established. Now they have a chance to profit from the behind-the-scenes experience of their colleagues. Even replications pose problems in execution because they are subject to errors due to population and social and/or contextual sources of variance.

The amazing thing is that in spite of all of the difficulty and hard work that goes into doing research in this complicated arena of the family, there is a sense of excitement, of mission, and of deep satisfaction in the process of discovery and reporting the new discoveries.

The chapters in this volume are just such exciting journeys. This Introduction is a description of the journey as to how we got the idea of bringing into public view our colleagues' individual behind-the-scenes research trips that we referred to earlier. As we shared our mutual research concerns and interests, we discovered that we also learned not just about our findings, but more importantly, how and why he or I got the results we did and why we elected to do what we did. Even though we were familiar with each other's research, we were unfamiliar with each other's behind-the-scenes activities, and getting to know how things happened added to our understanding of each other's research. If we learned so much from each other in this type of sharing, how much more might be learned from knowing about the journeys of our friends and colleagues? Would it not be great if they each agreed to engage in something like Gene and I had shared and put it into a book—a volume to be shared by all of our colleagues? But, we asked, who is really interested in the struggles of one's peers as they strive to carry out their particular research efforts? Are folks really interested in those details? It is as though one were reading the equivalent of the researchers' *People Magazine*. So, we spoke to some of our colleagues and students and it became patently clear that interest in such a volume was considerable. Why?

First, researchers like to know how and why research decisions are made by their colleagues. For example, why was Scale X used instead of Scale Y since both are okay? Why were home observations used instead of controlled laboratory observations? Is there a tradeoff in each choice? The list could go on and on from, e.g., how to recruit research populations to how to select and/or create new measures. Should creating new measures be the choice of last resort to avoid reinventing the wheel? How does a science develop a cumulative body of knowledge and build progressively? These questions seemed to be of considerable interest and colleagues and graduate students seemed eager to get such information from their fellow researchers.

We shared these ideas with Lawrence Erlbaum who agreed we did have the makings of a useful volume. We proposed two volumes, however, one dealing with research journeys in typical normative populations, the other describing work with clinical populations. Each volume would require different research skills and strategies as well as different ethical and social considerations. For example, while confidentiality is a general rule for all research, patients may also be more concerned with confidentiality of medical or psychometric records—a very sensitive research issue.

Larry Erlbaum accepted our suggestions and we proceeded to recruit authors for the volumes. This was not as difficult as we had anticipated. Virtually everyone we approached accepted the opportunity to write a chapter. To insure that each author would cover essentially the same issues, we constructed an outline which was accepted by most of the writers we approached. The question that most of the authors raised was, "The idea is great, but who is our audience?" We had colleagues and graduate students in mind—colleagues would learn more about the why's and wherefore's of how well-known and experienced investigators work. Graduate students would get a realistic view of research strategies. In this way they would have opportunities to grapple with many central research issues which, we contend, would enhance the quality of their work and perhaps, more important, generate a greater understanding of the vicissitudes of scientific efforts. They would see the excitement and the boredom, the drudgery and the pleasure, the sense of joy when insights evolve.

In a sense, it becomes the joy of discovery—an emotion rarely, if ever, discussed in our too frequently drably written research reports. The only jokes in our literature are when investigators study humans and even then the human is kidded.

Faculty members could use these volumes as case studies of research projects, thereby getting acquainted with the behind-the-scenes maneuvering researchers go through from getting funded to getting published.

Armed with these ideas and with tacit acceptance of the overall idea, we not only recruited the authors, but we also wrote our own chapters and edited the products of our peers.

Our journey to this point was a joint collaborative effort. However, once the manuscripts appeared we decided we would each edit one set of manuscripts although we read them all. (The leadership in editing the volume on the "normal family" fell to Irv Sigel and Gene Brody took the major responsibility for the volume dealing with "clinical research.")

From the outset most of the participants not only liked the idea, but also felt they would enjoy the process of recollecting their research history and reflecting on a particular project. We told the authors to select a single project or a single issue and develop it thoroughly. We asked them not to give us a review of all of their work as they might for an article in *Psychological Bulletin*. This point was made over and over again. Yet it was most difficult for virtually every writer. First drafts were well written literature reviews. Since everyone contributing to the volumes is a well respected and much published author, the chapters were fascinating reading as such, but at first they were not the personal descriptions of journeys. They were objective and distant, even when the personal pronoun "I" was used. It was clear that we, as a professional group, are so programmed that when we write about our work for public consumption, we tend to highlight those points in our trip which advance our cause and overlook the digression, the failures, what "did not work." We have learned our lessons so well. However, that was not our intention for the volumes. We wanted the errors, the details, the doubts. Our colleagues were masters of tact and cooperation. To a person, each one struggled with the assignment. They were good natured (at least to us) about the whole adventure. The major problem we faced was coordinating all of the manuscripts and getting them off on time. Authors' schedules varied and the result was that our timetable had to be reset more than once. We asked the indulgence of the early birds, but their consolation was that their jobs were finished and they could go on to new things.

These papers are not dated. They are tutorial documents reporting in some detail the development of research activities to date. No doubt changes will continue and new directions charted since the writers are prolific in their dedication to their science.

Reading this book should be like reading the travel section of the *New York Times*. There are many different trips described in the style of the authors. This is *not* an integrated thematic volume, tied together in a tight framework. Quite the contrary. Each chapter is a personal tale, its style expressing the individuality of the author. It is this variation that reveals how different researchers are in how they work and in how they structure problems, as well as in their choice of problems. The papers do not follow a rigid sequence. Each chapter stands on its own. However, there is some order that I see in the sequence.

The first three papers share a common interest in the family as a social agency. From the Cowans' description of the process of "becoming," McGillicuddy-DeLisi zeros in on parents' beliefs about family and children. She invites us into her rumination about theory and method through imaginary dialogues with theoreticians and methodologists as they might engage her in solving the complex problems in this area.

My paper demonstrates how a construct, "distancing," evolved from its restricted cognitive developmental context to a model of family interaction.

From these particular family issues we move to a more psycho-social problem that has plagued psychologists for generations — the nature –nurture controversy. Scarr and Weinberg tell us about their wanderings in this complex arena fraught with social and political overtones.

Another set of papers focuses on intrafamilial relationships with emphasis on particular family members. The search for fathers was the major thrust of Ross Parke's research efforts for many years. Brody and Stoneman examined sibling relationships and J. Brooks-Gunn investigated (with broad brush strokes) the complex world of adolescents.

The research paradigm guiding the studies to this point was essentially a psychological model with no attention to the intersect between the biological status of individuals and their psychophysiological state. Gottman sets about seeking lawful relations between marital status and physiological connections.

Hess and Azuma represent a return to the cross-cultural studies, an area that has been neglected for too long. In this decade they had the benefit of the years of struggles social scientists have had working cross-culturally. This paper is an example of a cross-cultural program in which leaders from two very diverse cultures embarked on a joint venture which yielded interesting insights into each other's cultures, not only from the data obtained from respondents, but also from the process of solving research problems in cross-cultural research as they struggled to achieve a coherent and comparable body of knowledge in diverse settings.

Finally, with an overview of the complexities and problems involved in doing family research, the Hoopers share their global perspective on the issues facing all researchers investigating the family. By placing their views in an historical context they articulate the difficulty of doing family research.

We hope that this volume will serve to excite and stimulate the exchange process of descriptions of our research efforts. In this way, we may save ourselves many fruitless hours and come closer to answers to many questions facing us.

Irving E. Sigel
Gene H. Brody

1 Becoming a Family: Research and Intervention

Philip A. Cowan
Carolyn Pape Cowan
University of California, Berkeley

HOW THE BECOMING A FAMILY PROJECT DEVELOPED

For the past 15 years, we have been studying the marriages of men and women as they are forming their families. The most general question we have been addressing is what happens to a husband and wife, and especially to their relationship as a couple, when they become parents. Because we are concerned about the vulnerability of marriages during this major adult transition, one major focus of our work has been the assessment of an intervention in which psychologists trained to work with couples offer small ongoing groups for parents as they make their way from being a couple to becoming a family.

To date, our longitudinal study encompasses two main phases of family formation: the transition to parenthood from pregnancy to 18 months after birth; and the transition from the preschool years until the first child enters elementary school. Just as the views of the parents and children in our study grow as they maneuver these major family events, so too do our perspectives as researchers and clinicians broaden as we explore the findings and tackle the realities of studying developing families. In some ways, we now realize, our move to expand the focus of our investigation from the transition to parenthood to the relationships of parents and children in a three-generational context parallels recent expansion in the field of family study. Thus, we acknowledge at the outset, that to tell about the growth of our thinking and our study design retrospectively implies more order and grand conceptualization than actually existed at the outset. We shall reconstruct our journey into the study of marital and family relationships as honestly and accurately as we can.

1

Typically, research reports begin with a review of the literature, a critical evaluation of the work on a specific topic, and a justification for conducting the study to be reported. On the basis of what has and has not been done, the authors formulate a set of hypotheses and a research design, and then develop appropriate methods and measures designed to test them. This is not the way the Becoming a Family Project evolved.

The stimulus for our wanting to study and work with couples becoming first-time parents was the collision of our own professional and personal experiences in the early 1970s. One of us (PAC) was a developmental/clinical psychologist interested in Piagetian approaches to social-emotional development and in preventive intervention with teachers in schools. One of us (CPC) had been an elementary school teacher, was now active as a parent in the schools, and had undertaken graduate work in clinical and developmental psychology, with a special interest in preventing marital distress. With our three children in grades 2, 4, and 6, we were just beginning to come up for air from an enormously stressful period for a decade-old marriage with three young children and two budding careers. We loved the parenting part, and were immensely challenged by the school and career demands, but the toll these years had taken on our relationship as a couple had been totally unexpected. The dangers of serious marital strain were becoming apparent to us as our friends and neighbors began separating and divorcing at a frightening rate. When we had opportunities to talk with couples close to us, we thought we were hearing a similar refrain. Most of us seemed to be describing—although only in retrospect—a period of years when we had simply put our relationship as a couple ''on the back burner'' while we coped with the extraordinary demands of being parents, workers, and active citizens in our communities. Only recently, as the children moved from center stage in our lives into the formal school systems, had we begun to take stock of what had happened to our marriage.

As we tried to make sense of our lives and those of our friends, we began to think of the transition to parenthood as a vulnerable time for couple relationships. So many things about the ideology of men's and women's work and family roles come into play at this major adult transition. Who does what, and who gives up what, when there are children to be raised seemed to be important ingredients of how parents eventually felt about themselves and their marriages. In addition, many of the couples we met appeared to have been dealing with similar conflicts and strains, yet none of us knew that we were part of a ''trend'' until years later when the separations and divorces became our clues to serious marital strain.

We began to think that the transition to parenthood could be an important time to offer men and women a setting in which mental health professionals might help them focus on strengthening their relationship as a couple while they went about making their dreams of family life a reality. Groups to teach Lamaze and other forms of prepared childbirth had become extremely popular for couples, but they ended when the babies were born—just when the hands-on work of family-making was beginning. .We were not interested in creating another "California group" of the kind that seemed to be sweeping the country in the late 1960s and early '70s. We set out to pilot test and then systematically evaluate our idea of a couples group intervention by including a sample of no-treatment comparison couples in our study. If we followed couples through their actual transition to parenthood, talking with them before, during, and after, we would have an opportunity to do a full-scale evaluation of what happens to men, women, and their marriages as they became parents for the first time. We also realized that parents' before-baby reports about themselves and their marriage would be very helpful in understanding the contributions of the prebaby aspects of parents' individual and marital adaptation to the after-baby quality of their lives.

Our preliminary planning took three forms: talking with expectant and new parents in the larger Bay Area community; searching for previous relevant research; and inviting another couple to work with us on developing a pilot project. Our interviews with couples convinced us that our perception of increased strain in the marriages of new parents was on the mark. The first couples we talked to—recent new parents—were surprisingly open with us about their stress as individuals and as couples. When we discussed our idea of small groups in which couples could talk regularly about these unexpected changes in their lives, they were eager to join, even though they had already made the transition from couple to family.

In the psychological research we first consulted, we found very little work relevant to intervention with couples during the transition to parenthood—or during any other major life change. Caplan (1964) and Rapoport (1963) suggested that major life transitions could be ideal times to provide psychological interventions because they are times of normal crisis that can stimulate development or lead to dysfunction, but we could find no reports of clinical work in that vein. We eventually found Colman and Colman's (1971) account of discussion groups for expectant mothers and Shereshefsky and Yarrow's (1973) study providing individual counseling for women during pregnancy, but we were unable to locate any references to services for expectant fathers or couples before we started our own pilot study in 1973.

As for the larger issues surrounding the transition to parenthood, they seemed not to interest psychologists before the mid-1970s. And, while there was a body of research in sociology that had been discussing the transition for almost 2 decades, we were initially unaware of it. This oversight was not so gently pointed out to us by the dean of family sociologists, Reuben Hill, when we presented our preliminary findings at an NIMH-supported conference on the first child and family formation in 1975 (Miller & Newman, 1978). Needless to report, we have become faithful readers of the sociological literature ever since, and we summarize its essential directions later.

Our first interviews and initial reading had convinced us that our project was worth pursuing, but before we could design a large study we had much work to do to become more familiar with the phenomena associated with the transition to parenthood. In addition to our own experiences and those of the people we knew, we needed to understand the elements in the more general natural history of becoming a family. What differentiated couples who adapted well from those who did not? What did *adapting well* mean for individuals and couples at this particular life stage? And, before we settled on a format for the intervention, we needed to obtain some first-hand experience working with couples who had *not* come seeking psychological help.[1]

We invited our friends and colleagues Lynne and John Coie, who were about to spend a sabbatical year at Berkeley, to join us in developing an intervention study of first-time parents. We welcomed their expertise as individuals and as a couple; Lynne's as an obstetrical nurse, John's as a clinical psychologist with a special interest in children, and theirs as a couple who had recently become a family. We had four tasks: (1) to design an intervention to help couples focus on their experiences of late pregnancy and the early months of new parenthood; (2) to recruit couples to participate in groups and to serve as a comparison sample; (3) to create research tools adequate to describe individual and marital change; and (4) to evaluate the intervention. With only a few modifications, the format for the couples groups and methods of recruitment that we developed for the pilot study became our method of operation in the larger study that we are conducting now.

As our work on the design and measures proceeded, we developed relationships with several interested obstetricians, and with their cooperation, we interviewed all the expectant parents who would agree to talk with us over a 3-month period. Here too, we were amazed at the outpouring of dreams and anxieties by men and women we were meeting for the first time. They dreamed, first and foremost, of the joys that babies can bring. They worried about the delivery, whether the baby would be healthy, whether they would love their babies the way they expected to, whether they could be the kind of parents they were determined to be. What surprised us most was their unanimous interest in groups for couples becoming new parents. Our questions appeared to tap issues that couples rarely talked about, especially for men. Our sense was that couples were as concerned about the statistics on marital breakup as we were; and if we knew something that would help buffer their marriage from strain during this exciting period in their lives, they were willing to learn more about it.

---

[1]Some researchers might argue that we should not design a clinical intervention before we know more about the natural course of the transition to parenthood. Two considerations led us to choose a simultaneous research and intervention approach. First, we may not know enough about the process of becoming a family, but we do know from the high divorce rate that many marriages are in difficulty. We also know that regardless of whether or not parents divorce, marital conflict places children at risk for distress (Emery, 1982; Hetherington & Camara, 1984). Second, we consider the intervention to be an integral part of the research on life transitions, by allowing us to distinguish between correlations and functional interconnections among variables.

We describe the intervention procedures, concepts, and measures in more detail later. Here, we simply note the continuing interplay among self-examination, interviews, reading, discussion with colleagues, and active efforts to design an intervention while developing pilot research. At least in retrospect, the shifting of perspectives from one of these modes to another was absolutely necessary for the ultimate design of the larger study.

Our pilot study (Cowan, Cowan, Coie, & Coie, 1978) examined changes in 16 men and women, half of whom agreed to (1) talk with us and complete questionnaires before and after giving birth, and (2) participate in a 6-month-long couples group led by us. The other half of this small sample (four couples) talked with us and completed questionnaires but they were not asked to participate in a couples group. Based on the results of that small study, we designed the current Becoming a Family Project. In retrospect, we are pleased with how many of the trends from this intensively examined but very small sample have been replicated in the larger study.

Phase 1. Our initial plan for the current study was to complete a short-term longitudinal study of the transition to parenthood from late pregnancy to 18 months after birth, focusing on the impact of having a first child on the couple's marriage. Our first application for research support from NIMH was approved but not funded. The feedback from the reviewers was that we had painted an unnecessarily negative picture of the transition to parenthood. When we rewrote the proposal with what we thought was a more balanced rationale for the proposed study, but with the same research design, the Becoming a Family Project was awarded 3 years of funding beginning in 1979.

Phase 2. As the data and the participants in the study grew, we found ourselves eager to answer a second question: Given that the arrival of the baby affects the relationship between the parents, what impact does the couple relationship have on the early development of the child? We requested further support to follow the couples again, and to add to our ongoing assessment of the marriage an assessment of parent-child interaction and the child's development when the children were preschoolers (3½).

Phase 3. As the family data began to flesh out our picture of what was happening to parents and children during the family formation period, we became excited by the prospect of following the families through the next transition that most would experience—the first child's entrance into elementary school. With continued funding from NIMH, we have been able to study the lives of 96 families over a period of 7 years.

CONCEPTUAL ISSUES

The idea of assessing the quality of couple relationships seemed quite straightforward until we actually set about doing it. We knew that we could obtain a global index of each partner's satisfaction from the widely used Short Marital Adjustment Test (Locke & Wallace, 1959). But what are the essential *ingredients* of marital satisfaction? How do we divide the concept of marital satisfaction into meaningful, measurable domains, so that we can understand *how* the transition to parenthood affects marital quality? We knew from both popular books and professional journals that couple communication was important to examine, but how men and women talk to each other did not seem to provide a sufficient explanation of how both spouses feel about their overall marriage. We believed that each partner's personality style and sense of self could influence the course of discussions between the partners, and that the quality of communication might affect each one's sense of self.

We slowly began to develop what became our *model* of couple relationships—all of the aspects of couple relationships that we needed to know about in order to understand both adaptation and distress in couples' lives. From our own life and from sociological research we knew that the family division of labor—a couple's arrangements to keep the household running, make the family decisions, care for the children, bring in the family income, and so on—is another critical aspect of how the partners feel about their relationship as a couple. This aspect of marriage seemed to be missing from most psychological and psychiatric accounts of functional and dysfunctional families. Yet, the negotiations, or lack of them, around who takes out the garbage, washes the dishes, prepares the meals, or cares for the child, is the real stuff of most couples' daily communication. Frustration in these areas clearly takes a toll on the relationship. We were certain that each partner's ideas about parenting, especially their disagreements about childrearing, would make a difference to the stress experienced by men and women in their role as parents. At first, then, our list of important variables included parents' self-concept, communication, role arrangements, and parenting ideas and stresses.

During the pilot study, it became apparent that we had left out two important aspects of couple life. As psychoanalysts have long claimed, men's and women's relationships with their parents, as they were and as they are, make important contributions to parents' sense of well-being and to their ability to form satisfying marital and parent-child relationships (Benedek, 1959, 1970). In addition, we realized that we had focused only on events and relationships inside the immediate family; outside-the-family stresses and strains on one hand, and sources of support on the other, also contribute to each partner's ability to pay attention to small marital and parenting conflicts before they grow too large to handle.

At this point, we had a long list of what we thought were the ingredients of a satisfying or unsatisfying marriage. We began to see that each of the issues we had named referred to a different level of analysis of family life: (1) individual; (2) couple; (3) parent-child; (4) three generations; and (5) outside-the-family. Our assumption was that events in each of these domains, in interaction, determined each partner's satisfaction with the marriage. How partners feel about themselves may affect the way they play their family roles; conversely, individuals' satisfaction with their family roles may affect how they feel about themselves. Traumatic relationships in husbands' and wives' families of origin make satisfying marriages more difficult to come by (cf. Clulow, 1982), while mutually satisfying marriages have the power to overcome early life difficulties (Rutter, 1983). How smoothly the marital relationship is going can affect men's and women's work involvement and stress on the job, just as the atmosphere on the job, positive or negative, can spill over into family life (Crouter, 1984; Seers, McGee, Serey, & Graen, 1983).

These ideas, not always clearly formulated at the beginning of the study, have been influenced over time by the work of Belsky (1984), Feldman and Nash (1984), Parke and Tinsley (1982), and Heinicke (1984). Our conceptual approach now focuses on a five-domain *structural* model of individual and marital well-being (Cowan & Cowan, 1988). The model is structural in that it refers to the way in which different levels of a family system are related to each other. It provides a set of guidelines concerning the aspects of individual and couple life that we are measuring over time in order to understand how individual and relationship well-being and distress develop in families. With our findings to date, we have begun to describe what we believe to be the *process* by which changes in various family domains interact to produce increases or decreases in each partner's individual, marital, and parenting adaptation.

Our first forays into the research literature left us quite discouraged about finding appropriate questionnaires for pre- and postbirth measures. Because we were asking men and women to tell about the major aspects of their lives, we wanted to pose questions that would be compelling for them. Most questionnaires about marriage have been developed by sociologists studying various aspects and stages of marital life in large samples. Finding some of the items very general—or very dry—we eventually adapted existing questionnaires or developed new ones to test in our pilot study. Because we were unwilling to ask our study participants to answer questions that we found too tedious, dull, or intrusive, we tested all of our questionnaires and interview questions on our research team by using them ourselves to describe our own lives. We describe these measures in more detail following a brief discussion of the research methods and designs that existed in the study of the transition to parenthood before we and a number of other investigators began our longitudinal studies.

EARLIER STUDIES OF THE TRANSITION TO PARENTHOOD

As we have described, we did not begin by reading the sociological research, but over time, our conception of the methodological issues in this field have been shaped by the initial formulations of sociologists and a few psychiatrists whose work was published in the period between the 1950s and the mid-1970s. There were two central questions posed by researchers, each explicitly attacking the myth that becoming a family is a joyous and satisfying time: (1) Does the birth of a first child tend to produce a normal or pathological "crisis" in the lives of new parents?; and (2) Does parenthood have a negative impact on couples' marital satisfaction? Associated with each question was a specific set of methods and research designs. The debate in this research concerned whether the birth of a first child caused individual and marital distress. In our view, limitations inherent in the formulation of this debate, and in the design and methods used, raised serious doubts about the conclusions on both sides of the argument.

Transition as Crisis

There is widespread belief in Erikson's (1950) hypothesis that the psychosocial task demands of each new developmental stage induce intrapsychic conflicts or crises that can stimulate growth or lead to psychological distress. From a very different theoretical perspective, Holmes and Rahe (1967) have also argued that new life events, even very positive ones, tend to stimulate change and stress that may ultimately affect physical and mental health. Two bodies of research, neither of which refers to the other, have explored the crisis-inducing potential of the transition to parenthood.

"Normal Crisis".   Following Reuben Hill's (1949) suggestion that normative life transitions could trigger family crises, E. E. LeMasters (1957) set off what is still an enduring controversy in the sociological literature. In the process of interviews with 57 married couples who had become parents in the 5 years prior to his study, LeMasters, in collaboration with the study participants, developed ratings of the degree of crisis partners experienced during the transition. An astonishing 83% of the couples described extensive or severe crisis within the first year after giving birth to their first child. For 2 decades, other sociologists published rejoinders, all using "more objective" checklists, and all finding a lower incidence of severe distress (Dyer, 1965; Hobbs, 1965; Hobbs & Cole, 1977; Russell, 1974).

The leading figure arguing against the disruptive impact of the transition to parenthood was Daniel Hobbs, who administered a 23-item checklist of "bothersome events" to new parents. In several samples over a period of 10 years, fewer than 20% of Hobbs' couples were rated as experiencing severe or extreme crisis. Jacoby (1969) presented an early critique of Hobbs' checklist method, but his ideas appear to have been ignored. Hobbs' work is still quoted without comment in both sociology and lifespan psychology texts in support of the view that the transition to parenthood may be minimally disequilibrating. We have recently provided another critique of Hobbs' work (Cowan & Cowan, 1988) arguing that:

1. his assessments occurred too early to pick up much couple distress (about 6 months postpartum, during the "baby honeymoon");

2. the checklist method minimizes reports of individual dysfunction that may be revealed in in-depth interviews;

3. the levels of reported crisis were arbitrary cut-off scores defined by the researchers, not by the participants; and

4. even if "only 19%" of the women were described as in crisis on the basis of the checklist and 26% on the basis of an interview, the findings raise serious concerns about the well-being of many new parents.

What concerned us even more than the problem of measurement in this line of research was the exclusive use of retrospective research designs. Men and women were contacted only after the birth of their child. Data concerning the men's and women's prebaby adaptation came exclusively from their memories of events and feelings before they became parents. There appeared to be little concern in the research reports that couples' present level of adaptation might color their remembrance of things past. None of the researchers had actually followed couples from before to after the birth of a baby to assess whether there were alterations in their observed or reported adaptation.

Postpartum Dysfunction.   It seems strange to us, as clinical psychologists, that sociological researchers investigating the possibility of crisis during the transition to parenthood ignored the phenomenon of postpartum psychosis and depression (e.g., Hamilton, 1962). Estimates of the incidence of postpartum dysfunction in women ranges from .01% to 50%: 1 per 1000 (psychosis); 3% (severe distress, but not psychosis); 7–15% (neurotic depression); 17–25% (moderate to mild postpartum depression); and 30–50% ("the blues"), depending on the samples and on the defining criteria for psychosis, neurosis, depression-as-syndrome, and depression-as-symptom (Hamilton, 1962; Pitt, 1980). *There are no epidemiological data documenting the incidence of postpartum depression and other psychological distress for men becoming fathers.* In our view, debates about the "true incidence" of depression in the postpartum period are unproductive; it is evident that at least some new mothers and a few fathers are in acute emotional distress as their families are forming, and in a significant percentage of cases the distress continues over a period of years (Kumar & Robson, 1984).

Research on the transition to parenthood, then, raised the specter of both "normal crisis" and increased risk of mental illness during the family formation period, especially but not exclusively for women. Like sociological research on transition as crisis, the psychiatric research on postpartum psychosis is limited by its assessment of men's and women's psychiatric difficulties only after they have become parents. The data are convincing that new mothers may have higher risk of depression than nonmothers, but without longitudinal studies, we do not know whether the arrival of the baby alters the mother's psychological state or whether prebaby psychiatric distress is the main contributor to a postpartum psychotic outcome. Furthermore, there is unresolved controversy concerning etiology of this disorder, with some theorists attributing it directly to women's biological-hormonal (Yalom et al., 1968) or intrapsychic (Benedek, 1970) disequilibrium, and others assuming that psychotic episodes in the early months of family-making may be a *by-product* of other events occuring in the period before and after childbirth. These indirect explanations locate the causes of women's psychological dysfunction in their relationships with their spouse—either in distress around the division of family labor (Bernard, 1974), or in conflictual or nonsupportive communications with their husbands (Brown & Harris, 1978; Shereshefsky & Yarrow, 1973; Weissman & Klerman, 1977). It seemed to us that there was enough evidence that the early months after childbirth might contribute to increased psychiatric risk, that it was premature to be soothed by Hobbs and Cole's (1977) statement that "initiating parenthood may be slightly difficult, but not sufficiently difficult to warrant calling it a crisis experience for parents whose first child is still an infant" (p. 729).

Impact of the Transition on Marital Satisfaction

Cross-Sectional Studies. Another line of research, also in the sociological tradition, avoided problems of retrospective evaluations of the impact of having a child by selecting cross-sectional samples of couples at different points in the family life cycle. Based on survey-research techniques, with a few global questions devoted to the assessment of marital quality, a number of investigators concluded that marital satisfaction starts to decline after the honeymoon phase— even more for couples who have children—and continues its downward journey over the next 15 years (Glenn & McLanahan, 1982). Some researchers claim to find a U-shaped pattern in which marital satisfaction rises again after children begin to leave home, but others argue that the rise is a result of the fact that older couples appear happier with their marriages only because many of the most dissatisfied couples have now divorced and are no longer included in the older cross-sectional samples (Hudson & Murphy, 1980).

Although cross-sectional research designs eliminate problems inherent in using retrospective data to assess change over time, they introduce biases of their own. Not only is the composition of samples of older couples affected by the cumulative rate of divorce, but each sample is selected from a different cohort. In a study conducted in 1970, for example, couples married for 20 years were originally married in 1950, while couples married for 10 years were married a decade later, a period in which ideology about men's and women's roles was clearly shifting. Thus, in the differences between the two cohorts, the potential contributions of length of marriage and the social changes through which couples live are confounded.

There were three additional problems with the cross-sectional studies we read. First, most of the studies focused on one or two variables at a time. Rossi's (1968) influential review strongly suggested that new mothers were at a disadvantage compared to men in terms of their responsibility for household and childcare tasks, their level of self-esteem, and their overall mental health. She did not have evidence about whether these "outcomes" were in fact interrelated. Second, it was not possible to assess similarities and differences in the impact of the transition to parenthood on husbands and wives because in most studies the data were gathered almost exclusively from women. When men were sampled, they were not the partners of the women in the study, so that there was no way of examining patterns *within* couples as the quality of marriage changed over time.

Finally, cross-sectional designs cannot answer questions about individual differences in adaptation to the transition to parenthood. Even if average ratings of marital satisfaction decline, some couples may remain stable, while others may experience an increase in satisfaction with the quality of their marriage. Only longitudinal data can reveal the proportion of couples in each category. Because we were interested in both the early identification of families at risk and the development of preventive interventions, we needed to assess the consistency or predictability of individual and couple adaptation during family formation. This made it necessary to follow families over time to determine whether those who had difficulty adapting to parenthood were those who were in more distress before the baby arrived.

Longitudinal Studies.   It was clear to us that once we were determined to understand a major change in the structure and function of the family, especially if we were concerned with individual differences as well as group trends, we were committing ourselves to a program of longitudinal research. Four longitudinal studies were available as we began our pilot work. Each lacked several essential ingredients from our point of view, but they suggested that we might be on the right track in our determination to focus on the couple relationship as a key factor in men's and women's adaptation to parenthood. A careful clinical study of women by Wenner, Cohen, Weigert, Kvarnes, Ohaneson, and Fearing (1969) concluded that there is both individual and couple stress and upheaval during pregnancy and at 6 months postpartum, and that "despite our initial assumption that successful adaptation to the intensely personal experience of pregnancy is dependent primarily on the woman's physical and mental health, our clinical impression was that an uncomplicated pregnancy depended to an even greater extent on the success of the marital relationship" (p. 397). This impression was supported by data, but the investigators did not provide independent measures of individual adaptation and marital quality, and they did not assess change in marriage from pre- to postpartum assessments. Meyerowitz and Feldman (1966), following couples over the transition but assessing change in marital satisfaction only retrospectively, reported that satisfaction declined in the first half year of parenthood. Finally, in Shereshefsky and Yarrow's (1973) longitudinal study, independent assessments of marital satisfaction and individual adaptation were done both before and after childbirth, but only for women. The best predictor of mothers' adaptation to parenthood was their level of satisfaction with their marriage in late pregnancy.

Only one short-term longitudinal study of men's entrance to parenthood had been completed by the mid-1970s (Fein, 1976). Fein's sensitive study suggested that "the 'crisis' for men (if there was one) came before the birth (and perhaps immediately after birth—in the first two weeks after the baby came home from the hospital) and that by six weeks after the birth men were adapting to lives as 'family men' without high levels of anxiety, compared to prenatal days'' (p. 343). This optimistic conclusion must be interpreted cautiously in light of the fact that the study ended just 6 weeks after the child's birth. Four factors emerged from Fein's interviews as important to the early postpartum adjustment for men: the health of the baby, support from the families of origin, support at work, and negotiating processes and coherence of roles in the marital relationship. It seemed to us that the time was ripe for a longitudinal study, focusing equally on men and women, and examining how events in many domains of family life contribute to both individual and marital adaptation after the birth of a baby.

THE CASE FOR THE CLINICAL METHOD

In order to describe the assumptions underlying our approach to research we must detour briefly into issues usually addressed in discussions of epistemology or philosophy of science. The central question is whether the methods we use as researchers give us the right to claim that we *know* something, rather than that we believe it to be true. Most psychologists use traditional criteria for determining which methods are deemed to be scientific, based on assumptions from 17th-century physics, and enshrined in British empiricist and logical positivist theories of knowledge. The prevailing assumption in psychological research is that it is both possible and necessary for scientists to be objective observers in the sense that their observations are entirely independent of the frame of reference and the methods used to gather their data. Findings are treated as if they were a *discovery* of relationships existing in nature, by researchers who assume that they function as if they were videotape recorders of connections between stimuli and responses.

There is another quite different point of view of scientific research with its own epistemological and empirical claims to validity. Piaget's (1971) formulation of the clinical method implies that a scientist's search for objectivity can be likened to the quest for the holy grail. Not only is objectivity inherently unattainable, but in the process of searching for it, we miss important information that could help us to understand the meaning of what we observe. Knowledge, in Piaget's view, is not a discovery of what exists, but a *construction* in which the observer always transforms incoming information.

In family research, as in other areas of psychology and social science, there is vigorous debate about the relative merits of various methods of gathering data. Until recently, investigators from most of the disciplines concerned with family life have relied on clinical observations of families in therapy or on self-reports from interviews and questionnaires. A new emphasis on microanalytic observational methods has been stimulated by behavioral approaches to both marital (Gottman, 1979) and family (Patterson, 1983) interaction. The microanalytic observational approach has been justified on the basis of assertions that clinicians' observations are too global and unsystematic, and that self-reports are suspect because people cannot accurately observe what they do or understand why they do it.

We believe that in the polemic among proponents of self-report, global ratings, and microanalytic observational data, an important possibility is being ignored: Each method may contribute important and unique information to our understanding of individual, couple, and family adaptation. Consistent with our intellectual roots in the study of children's cognitive development, we began the Becoming a Family Project with the assumption that the clinical method, as outlined by Piaget (1971) for the study of cognitive development, constitutes an epistemologically valid and useful approach to understanding behavior, relationships, and development in normal families.

P. Cowan (1978, pp. 59—82) has described the essential features of the clinical method as a synthesis of the three major methods of gathering data in psychology—naturalistic observations, tests, and experiments. Although each has been presented as an "objective" method, it is easy to show that the observer always plays a central role in shaping the meaning of the results.

(a) *Naturalistic observations* are designed to collect information about individuals and families with a minimum of experimenter interference. But the observer and the context of the research influence the findings, in that the observer selects what to record and what to ignore, and the presence of the observer (or the video camera) can influence the quality of individual behavior and family interaction.

(b) *Tests* are standardized stimuli, administered in standardized ways, with standardized scoring rules. They range from questionnaires to individually administered intelligence or projective tests, to laboratory problem-solving procedures. Standardization has the advantage of providing a uniform context for the comparison of individuals or families, and is presumed to reduce experimenter bias in the gathering of data, but it is often difficult to assess the *meaning* of the subject's responses. How satisfied with his marriage is a man who checks the midpoint of the marital happiness scale on the Locke-Wallace Short Marital

Adjustment Test? How distressed is a marriage in which partners shout at each other during a problem-solving task in the laboratory? It is important to follow test responses with individualized, non-standard probes designed to understand the participants' interpretations of our questions or laboratory arrangements. Standardization was instituted as one technique for obtaining replicable results— a central requirement for a scientific method. Piaget's own research demonstrates that a theory-guided, systematic but unstandardized, approach can also yield some of the most replicable results in psychology.

(c) Observations and tests can determine whether two or more variables are correlated with each other. *Experiments*—systematic manipulations of experimental conditions—help us to decide whether variables are merely associated or whether they are functionally interconnected. The point we are making here is similar to Kurt Lewin's formulation of action research: "To understand a phenomenon, we must try to change it." The dilemma is that in changing it, we interfere with the naturally-occurring processes affecting what we are studying. There is no method free of *some* form of "bias."

In this tripartite classification of research methods, the interview occupies an intermediate position between naturalistic observations and tests. Unstructured free-form interviews can provide a "naturalistic" situation in which individuals, couples, and families demonstrate how they engage in social interaction with one another and with a nonfamily member, whereas highly structured interviews are virtually identical with individually administered tests.

In the clinical method, researchers, like surveyors, triangulate on what they are trying to observe. First, they attempt to compare their interpretation of the meaning of the stimulus and response with that of the participants in the study. Second, they attempt to integrate data from observations, tests, and experiments. No single perspective is accepted as the standard; the task of the researcher is to create a new and more differentiated synthesis when apparent contradictions arise. In the family field, an excellent example can be found in Levenson and Gottman's investigations of couple interaction (Gottman & Levenson, 1988; Levenson & Gottman, 1983), in which they compare data from physiological measures, observer ratings, and participants' self-reflective reactions to videotapes of their couple interaction. Like the surveyor locating a distant point by measuring from at least two perspectives, the researcher is involved in coordinating and synthesizing various points of view of a phenomenon. Just as data from more than one subject is essential to scientific investigations, the perspective of more than one researcher using more than one method is necessary in order to make sense of the data gathered in any study.

Some researchers advocate multimeasure, multimethod approaches because composite measures yield greater psychometric reliability. Our belief is that the simultaneous consideration of different perspectives is valuable because it may lead to more sophisticated interpretations of the data. In the clinical method, observation and self-report data do not represent competing alternatives, but necessary, complementary sources of data concerning the structure and function of the family. When it appears that self-report and observational data lead to different conclusions, the researcher's task is not to decide which one is correct, but to use data from several sources to clarify and amplify the meaning of results obtained from any single perspective.

We used the clinical method, a synthesis of observational data, tests, and experiments focused on families in the process of development, as the framework for conducting our study. It was central in leading us to (a) try to understand family adaptation *during* a life transition, (b) include intervention as a central part of our research design, (c) employ male-female teams as both group leaders and data-gatherers, (d) examine a relatively small sample with a relatively large selection of methods, and (e) use case conferences, with our separate teams reporting their observations of part of the family, as one way of integrating data from different sources.

The Life-Transition Focus as a Method

We have already described why the study of couples becoming families requires a longitudinal research design. Here we make the point that the *content* of our research focus—marital relationships in the transition to parenthood—can also be seen as a *method* of studying family adaptation. Piaget's clinical method was directed to the understanding of stable stages and periods of transition in individual development. We believe that studying families during periods of change and potential stress can enhance our understanding of the processes involved in development and adaptation because these challenging times highlight people's tendencies to move toward adaptive coping or toward more dysfunctional responses. From the point of view of the researcher, the period of family formation is a "natural experiment" in which we can observe the impact of a major life change on the structure of the family and the quality of family relationships.

The Intervention as a Method of Testing Models

We have indicated that our concern with facilitating adaptation in men and women becoming parents led us to create and evaluate a preventive intervention focused on their relationships as couples. Consistent with the tenets of the clinical method, we also viewed the intervention as a research strategy for testing our theoretical model and our interpretations of correlational data. We have all learned, but often forget, a basic lesson from statistics classes about the meaning of correlation coefficients. The fact that one variable can *explain* variation in the other does not mean that the variables are inextricably linked. If, however, we design an intervention to bolster men's and women's satisfaction with marriage, and we demonstrate that the intervention affects both marital satisfaction *and* adaptation in four additional family domains, then we have made a stronger case for our five-domain theoretical model. If the intervention affects marital satisfaction *without* affecting the other domains (as we found—see below), then we must reconceptualize the meaning of marital satisfaction and the conditions that are necessary to maintain it. In addition to its practical significance, then, the intervention has theoretical importance because it allows us to discriminate between variables that are merely correlated and those that are functionally interconnected.

Couples as Data-Gatherers

The clinical method dictated, in part, our insistence on separate teams of interviewers and assessors at each phase of the study. Not only are observations and ratings more reliable when they are a composite of two or more points of view, but we felt that it was necessary to have two perspectives whenever we attempted to integrate the qualitative and quantitative data from each specific family.

The fact that the teams were always male–female pairs stems less directly from the assumptions of the clinical method than from our clinical intuition and the findings from the pilot study. During our first study, as we have described, all of our interviewing and clinical work in the couples groups was done by two married couples (Cowans and Coies). Having both partners in the researcher couple participate in a discussion appeared to facilitate the involvement of both spouses in the study couples, especially the men. In general, even when expectant and new fathers are involved in being parents they still assume that thinking and talking about family issues is something women do. When a husband and wife are the interviewers or group leaders, both partners get the message that this is a *proper* subject for both men and women. The participants in the study appeared more willing to talk about their own relationship as a couple because they were talking to couples. We were able to capitalize on this finding when the most promising applicants for research assistants turned out to be two married couples, in which three of the four partners were completing graduate work in clinical psychology. The participant couples formed strong relationships with us as they formed their families. We believe that these strong ties led to our small attrition rate as we continued to follow both parents and children over a 7-year period. Of course, it is not always possible to hire married couples as researchers. At a minimum, we believe that male–female interview teams are necessary for the conduct of in-depth family research.

The Case Conference

As the project grew more complex, methodological rigor dictated that data from different aspects of family life be gathered independently. Many of the findings we have reported are based on analyses of both quantitative questionnaire data and qualitative observations, gathered by different teams. More recently, we have begun to use staff case conferences in which we examine a particular family's scores on the self-report instruments along with the more qualitative data from the teams working with the child, the parents and the child, the couple, and the teacher. Each team is blind to the results gathered by the other teams until after the interviews are completed, the questionnaires filled out, and the observations and ratings recorded. Each team presents their data and impressions, and as a group, we attempt to understand how all of the data about the family fit together.

This triangulation process provides a context for interpreting the group trends in the quantitative data. On one hand, we gain confidence in the robustness of our findings when we see how group trends actually operate within individual families—for example, how husbands and wives tend to have more conflict after the birth of a first child. On the other, we are made aware quite forcefully that there are limits in using group trends to describe individual families. The difficulties we have had in our case conferences coordinating data from individual, marital, parent-child, three generational, and school perspectives have forced us to consider an important substantive issue. Family theories and analyses of group data suggest a great deal of coherence and consistency across domains. We expected that when the couple relationship was satisfying, other relationships and individuals in the family would tend to be functioning well. Our case conference discussions indicate that the picture in individual families is more complex than this neat formulation. We have yet to find a family where reports from every domain are all positive or all negative. The "child team" may feel that the child is functioning well on his own, whereas the "parent-child team" expresses concern about the mother's interactions with the son. The "marital team" may report that the spouses have been sweeping their differences under the rug for some time now, and that those differences began to surface in the couple's discussions of their marriage at the recent interview.

Sample Size: Breadth Vs. Depth

From the beginning of this study we knew that we wanted as much information as possible about this time of life from as many couples as possible. Our theoretical model dictated a focus on five domains of family life. The clinical method required multiple sources of data in each domain. In an ideal research situation, we would choose to study a very large number of families with a variety of methods and measures. But, given the realities of our lives, our study design, and funding possibilities, we found that we could follow 96 couples (24 couples in each of four study conditions), which is a large number of couples to study with longitudinal in-depth methods in a family study, but quite small for purposes of statistical analysis. Once the sample is divided by four experimental conditions and gender of first child, there are only a dozen families in each cell, too few cases to provide precise and elegant tests of our multidomain multifactor model. And, in analyzing and reanalyzing data from the same subjects, we increase the risk of obtaining "significant" results by chance. Despite these limitations, we feel that there was no real alternative for this study, which we viewed as an exploratory, hypothesis-forming as well as hypothesis-testing endeavor. If we had reduced the measures to a select few before we had done the research, we risked doing an injustice to the complexity of family life during a major life transition. Our decision was to analyze carefully, to seek converging trends rather than isolated findings, and to report our results with caution. Ultimately, the test of our findings will come from replication, with more focused studies of different samples once the central issues have been identified.

RESEARCH DESIGN: EVALUATING THE INTERVENTIONS

In order to highlight issues of research design and present some results, we are going to reverse what might be a logical sequence; we talk about the impact of intervening with the couples in our study first, and then describe the natural history of the transition to parenthood. We refer only briefly in this section to the measures we used, reserving for the following section a more detailed rationale for the choice of measures and a description of how they show change over time.

Although the couples group, meeting weekly for 6 months, was the major intervention in our study, there were really three different intervention conditions that we examined. First, though we certainly had nothing to do with this part, having a baby can be considered a "natural experiment"—a major intervention in the ongoing life of a couple. Second, as we will show, our assessments involving both interviews and questionnaires constituted another intervention, bringing with it a potential for creating disequilibration in individuals and in their relationships. Finally, the couples group that we designed was an intervention over and above the one that couples arranged for themselves in deciding to introduce an infant into their lives.

In sum, the study followed 24 couples in each of four conditions: (1) late pregnancy pretest with posttests at 6, 18, 42, and 66 months; (2) couples who had not decided about becoming parents, with a pretest and all posttests; (3) no pretest in late pregnancy, but all the posttests; and (4) late pregnancy pretest, followed by a couples group intervention, followed by all the posttests.

Evaluating the Impact of Having a Baby

Almost all research on the transition to parenthood has attempted to evaluate the impact of having a first child by comparing individuals and couples pre- and postpartum and assuming that any changes are attributable to becoming a family. Duncan and Markman (1988) and Belsky and Pensky (in press) point out that we should also expect couples *not* having a baby to change over time, and both cross sectional and longitudinal studies suggest that they do. If we are to measure the impact of the transition to parenthood, then, it is necessary for us to follow couples not having a baby as a control or comparison group over the same period of time. Of the twenty longitudinal studies of transition to parenthood that we are aware of (see Cowan & Cowan, 1988), this comparison had been included in only two (White & Booth, 1985; McHale & Huston, 1985). To remedy this oversight, we recruited 24 couples from the same sources as our expectant parents (gynecologist/obstetricians, a health maintenance organization, a community newsletter); they were of comparable age and length of relationship, and had not yet decided about whether to have a baby. They were not experiencing fertility problems, and had not decided on vasectomies or tubal ligations as permanent methods of birth control.

These initially childless couples helped us to differentiate between systematic marital change over time and change attributable to becoming a family in the earlier phases of marriage. During the first 2 years of the study, 5 of them (19%) became parents, and 4 of them (16%) separated or divorced. Those who remained married and childless showed very few changes in self-concept, role arrangements, communication, parenting ideas, relationships with their own parents, work patterns, social support, and life stress (Cowan et al., 1985). Their satisfaction with marriage also remained relatively stable over that time. By contrast, in new parents, role arrangements became more traditional, conflict increased, work patterns changed, and marital satisfaction declined. The only area in which new parents seemed to be at an advantage was that they described their positive social support as increasing from pregnancy to 6 months postpartum before it declined again 1 year later.

Further, in comparison with childless couples, new fathers and mothers became more different from each other—in their descriptions of themselves and their life together, in their roles, and in their parenting ideology. Increasing differences *within* couples were associated with greater declines in marital satisfaction. The comparison between new parents and nonparents indicates clearly that the first 2 years of the transition to parenthood, on the average, has a disequilibrating impact on couples over and above the sheer passage of time.

We have been concerned about what a negative portrait our research findings and others' paint of what happens in the first 2 years after couples become parents, especially because men and women in our interviews say that having a child is the most exciting and fulfilling event in their lives. Following the parents and childless couples over a 7-year period fleshes out the picture of the impact on marriage of having a baby. Although we have not quite completed the kindergarten assessments, at this point about 19% of the couples who entered the study in pregnancy have separated or divorced. In the initially childless sample, 33% have now had children. Of those remaining childless, the rate of separation and divorce has reached 50%, more than two and one-half times that of the couples with children.

How do we reconcile the different pictures created by short-term and long-term results? In part, they reflect the use of different indices—marital quality and marital stability. During the first 2 years of the study, marital satisfaction remained stable *in those nonparent couples who stayed married.* But having a baby, in the early years at least, appears to be a protective factor affecting the rate of divorce. Our data here are similar to census data reported by Cherlin (1977). The results demonstrate the central importance of including a nonparent comparison group in studies of the early years of family formation.

Assessment as Intervention

Early in our pilot work we were confronted by the fact that our role as experimenters was not neutral. We could see for ourselves, and couples freely told us, that the questionnaires and interviews at the beginning of the study and again after childbirth were functioning as powerful interventions in themselves. Most men and women described how unusual it was for them to discuss their fears, hopes, and difficulties with another couple. It was even more unusual, they reported, to find others who would listen to what they had to say and attempt to understand it without comment, advice, or judgment. Some of the prebirth interviews raised questions and concerns that partners had thought about but not discussed before. Occasionally, our questions raised new issues to which partners subsequently devoted a great deal of thought and emotion.

The questionnaires—and there were many of them—served the same function, helping partners to take a perspective on their lives. Some couples came to refer to the assessments as their "check ups," a way of taking stock of their lives and evaluating with pleasure or with pain how well they were doing or how far they were from reaching their goals. Over the years, we noticed that some partners used our interviews as opportunities to talk together about issues they had not felt secure enough to raise on their own.

We instituted a control condition to evaluate the impact on couples of filling out the questionnaires before the child's birth. We randomly assigned one-third of the expectant couples to a "no-pretest" condition, in which they were interviewed late in pregnancy, but not asked to fill out questionnaires until their babies were 6- and 18-months-old. Assuming that they were comparable to the other expectant couples, we could compare their posttest responses to those of couples who had pretests but no couples group. In this way, we could assess whether completing the initial set of questionnaires had any systematic effect on partners' later responses.

Two findings suggested that when couples did not have an opportunity to complete questionnaires before they gave birth, their after-birth responses were affected. First, 9 of the 24 (37.5%) couples who did not complete pretest questionnaires refused to fill them out at the 6- and 18-month posttests, whereas none of the intervention participants or couples who had been pretested refused to continue to that point in the study. Second, the scores on almost every self-report instrument filled out by the no-pretest controls at 6 months postpartum (their first time) were equivalent to those of the new parents who were filling them out for the second time—with two notable exceptions. Couples who had not completed and discussed the set of questionnaires before having a baby were less satisfied with the "partner" aspect of themselves on *The Pie* (see p. 26) 6 months after birth, and they had lower marital satisfaction scores on the Locke-Wallace Short Marital Adjustment Test than couples who had completed pretest questionnaires.

The fact that the no-pretest couples were equivalent to the other new parents on almost all questionnaire measures suggests that even though 37.5% had left the study, the remaining couples were not a biased subsample. Omitting the pretest had no effects on self-esteem, role arrangements, communication, parenting ideology, life stress, and social support, but it seemed to have an indirect effect on how men and women evaluated their marriage. Or, conversely, the opportunity to fill out the questionnaires before the baby arrived had a positive effect on their feelings about each other. Perhaps, the opportunity to consider the issues raised by each questionnaire and to discuss them with their partners and the interviewers before becoming parents, helped husbands and wives take a perspective on their overall relationship. That is, pretest questionnaires and discussion do not affect behavior and feelings in each specific domain, but they may alter how couples think about their marriage. We return to this point in our discussion of the couples group intervention at the end of the next section.

Evaluating the Impact of the Couples Groups

It is not really possible to assess the impact of the couples group unless participants are randomly assigned to conditions, since initial differences between couples who are willing to volunteer and those who are not may contribute to later differences between the samples. Accordingly, we recruited couples for a "study of couple relationships," and randomly offered a subset of all the expectant parents an opportunity to participate in a couples group that would meet weekly for 6 months. As 85% of the couples accepted, we felt that our selection procedure made it possible to evaluate the effectiveness of the intervention.

In view of what we have already stated, we did not see the couples group simply as part of a treatment vs. no-treatment research design, but as an opportunity to assess what happens to couples when a preventive intervention is added to an assessment procedure and a normative life transition. We have described the groups and the results in detail elsewhere (Cowan & Cowan, 1987a; C. Cowan, 1988), reporting three central findings:

1. The couples groups ended when the infants were about 3-months old. They did not prevent the declines in role satisfaction and increases in conflict shown by couples with no intervention, especially in the period from late preg-

nancy to 6 months after the birth of their first child. However, in the year between the 6- and 18-month postpartum follow-ups, long after the groups had ended, there was no further decline in marital satisfaction for the group participants, whereas the nonintervention couples, especially the men, experienced an even sharper decline in marital satisfaction than they had in the first months after childbirth. It seems as if the couples with the intervention took some time to integrate and use what they had learned from the group experience, and ultimately to experience declines in some aspects of married life without those disappointments being reflected in their overall satisfaction with their relationships as couples.

2. Despite their earlier decline in marital satisfaction (from pregnancy to 6 months after giving birth), none of the group participants separated or divorced during the first 18 months of parenthood, whereas 12.5% of the new parents without the intervention and 16% of the childless couples were living apart at the end of the second year of the study. Preliminary results indicate that the divorce rates are still different at the 3½ year follow-up, but by the time the children enter Kindergarten the separation and divorce rate of intervention and nonintervention couples is very similar—about 19%.

3. We have no assessments of the children or the parent-child interaction until the children are 3½. There were very few differences between intervention and nonintervention families on our parenting style or child outcome measures, no more than one would expect by chance. Thus, despite early positive effects of the intervention on delaying the decline in marital satisfaction at 18 months postpartum, there were no apparent effects on family interaction 2 years later, at least in our preliminary analyses. These findings have led us to plan a new study that will include a ''booster shot'' intervention when the children are two, in hopes of sustaining marital satisfaction and helping it to generalize to parents' interactions with their preschoolers.

The intervention groups, then, ending when the children were only 3-months-old, had a delayed positive effect on the parents' marital satisfaction and marital stability over a 3-year period, and may have had some effect on the quality of parent-child interaction and the child's development in the first 3 years of family formation. No intervention effects should be expected to last forever. Our data suggest that by the time the children were well into their preschool period, and certainly by their entrance to elementary school, their parents could have used one or more booster interventions at selected times to help them sort out their family strains or disagreements and to refocus their attention on their marriage.

The decision of this study does not permit us to identify specific factors in the intervention that served, at the very least, to delay the full force of the negative impact of becoming a family. We have speculated that one of the most powerful ingredients was the chance for couples, usually living far from their families of origin, to normalize the experience, to feel that "we're not crazy," and to avoid the temptation to blame their spouses for the stress that all the parents seemed to be experiencing.

Another possible impact of the couples group bears on our argument that intervention plays a key role in the testing of theoretical models. During late pregnancy, satisfaction with role arrangements was correlated with marital satisfaction. How satisfied each partner was with the "who does what?" of life was intimately connected with his or her positive feelings about the whole marital relationships. But, in our study, role satisfaction declined equally for group and nongroup participants, while their patterns of change in marital satisfaction were quite different. After childbirth, most of the indicators of distress in each domain were correlated with marital dissatisfaction in couples who were *not* in the intervention groups, whereas the correlations with marital distress were low or non-existent in the group participants. The group meetings appear to help couples "unhook" the association between stress or distress in a particular domain and satisfaction with the overall marriage.

This finding tells us something about the nature of marital satisfaction. In general, it seems, there are a number of correlates or "ingredients" associated with positive or negative evaluations of marriage, but these associations are neither necessary nor inevitable. An intervention experience may provide individuals with new ways of thinking about themselves and their relationships that interfere with the connections they usually make between distress in one aspect of life and feelings about the overall marriage.

The finding also tells us something about our five-domain model of family adaptation. We had assumed that events in each of the five domains combined to affect satisfaction in all of the domains. It may be that we need to include a moderator variable describing how individuals *interpret* these events, and how they make, or fail to make, connections among them. A central candidate for such a moderator variable may be the system of beliefs held by family members about their relationships (cf. Sigel, 1985, 1986).

CHOOSING AND CONSTRUCTING MEASURES

There are absolutists who argue that there are right and wrong ways to create measures in psychology, but we are not among them. In our view, measures are generally chosen for a combination of four reasons: (1) an existing measure appears to be appropriate to the research question; (2) an existing measure is well-accepted and will lend credibility to the study by providing reliable anchors for more innovative measures; (3) no existing measure appears to be relevant and so the researcher creates one; and (4) the measure, new or old, fits with the experience, approach, and personal tastes of the researcher. The choices of measures that we made were based on some or all of these four rationales.

In the first phase of our study, we were interested primarily in the impact of becoming a family on the parents' experience of themselves and their marriage. The primary measures we used were previously standardized and newly created self-report questionnaires, supplemented with our own in-depth interviews at each of the assessment periods. In addition, Gertrude Heming (1985, 1987), a member of our research staff, developed an observationally based clinical rating of marital adaptation to be used by the "marital team" (see p. 27), and Jessica Ball (1984) observed and assessed a subset of the couples in a videotaped problem-solving task.

In the second phase of our study, the main question centered around the connections between parents' sense of themselves, their marriage, and their family interaction patterns—and the child's development. At this point, observational measures of family interaction were clearly necessary. In addition to the interviews and self-report test/questionnaires, we invited families to our laboratory playroom for three sessions. In the first visit, one parent brought the child, but once he or she was comfortable, the child spent about 40 minutes with the child team for an individual assessment of cognitive development and personality style. The second session repeated the first with the other parent. For the third session, the whole family interacted together in both play and work tasks. For the parent-child and family interaction sessions, Linda Kastelowitz and Victor Lieberman developed a set of global ratings based on commonly used dimensions of parenting style (warmth, responsiveness, structure, limit setting, anger), and couple interaction (similar to parenting style, but including cooperation and competition *between* the parents). We discuss later our choice to use global ratings completed immediately after the session rather than microanalytic behavioral coding of the videotapes.

What follows here is a brief description of the interviews and tests administered in both phases of the study, along with an outline of the kinds of findings yielded by the measures. In both interviews and questionnaires, we posed questions in which each individual could begin by describing events, situations, or behavior from his or her point of view, and then indicate the discrepancy between the actual state of affairs and some ideal or desired goal. We hypothesized, correctly as it turned out, that these discrepancies between actual and ideal might be indicators of the partners' degree of discontent, discomfort, or distress.

Interviews

At each phase of the study, every couple in the study was interviewed by one researcher couple. Partners were seen together at all times unless they were separated or divorced. Some investigators interview men and women separately in order to avoid having one partner bias the other's answers. We did ask that the questionnaires be filled out independently before being discussed, but we felt that in the interviews, which usually did not provide primary data, we wanted to preserve the study's emphasis on the couple. In addition, we did not want to create a situation in which either partner would reveal secrets that we would not be free to discuss, and we felt that some sense of each partner's reactions to the other's views would give us a sense of the relationship in action.

When the children were 3½ years old, we asked each parent a set of questions from an interview developed in the context of Mary Main's work on attachment between parents and children (Main & Goldwyn, 1984). This body of research focuses on parents' working models of their own upbringing in the past, which are assumed to influence their present relationships with their children. In this case we *did* want to use the interview as primary data and, with strong urging from Main, we considered separate interviews for husbands and wives. Because it would represent a notable shift in the format we had developed over the first 4 years of the study, we ultimately rejected her suggestion of separate interviews. We decided that the problems of using this unexpected variation—for the couple and for our relationship with them—outweighed the potential advantages of separate interviews. As it turned out, this format of asking about the families of origin with both partners present provided many parents with the moving experience of listening to a summing up of how their spouses felt about the relationships with their parents, of why they felt they were the kind of people they were, and of how they thought their own upbringing influenced their marriage and their own style of parenting.

Tests

Self-Concept

(a) Self-esteem. There are any number of personality tests that can be used to provide an opportunity for individuals to describe themselves. Given the length of the battery of questionnaires we were asking couples to fill out, we wanted one that would be relatively brief, that would assess a wide variety of personality domains, and that was not pathologically oriented (like the MMPI) but would yield indices of adjustment and self-esteem. We settled on a widely used instrument, the Adjective Check List, developed by one of our Berkeley colleagues, Harrison Gough, in collaboration with Alfred B. Heilbrun Jr. (1965, 1980). The ACL consists of 300 adjectives, ranging from "absent-minded" to "zany," that individuals can choose as descriptive of themselves. The ACL's added advantage is that it can be used to describe one's ideal self ("Me as I'd like to be"), with the discrepancies between actual and ideal yielding a measure of self-esteem (Gough, Fioravanti, & Lazzari, 1982). We also asked husbands and wives to use the ACL to describe their partners.

The measure of self-esteem derived from the ACL was remarkably stable over time for men and women becoming parents, with no mean change from pregnancy through the 5th year postpartum for fathers or mothers. Individual differences in self-esteem were highly consistent over time, with correlations ranging between .68 and .78 over the course of our study. Low self-esteem in late pregnancy predicted mothers' and fathers' postpartum adaptation at 18 months after the birth of a first child, as measured by their symptoms of depression on the Center for Epidemiological Studies in Depression scale (Radloff, 1977). Self-esteem was also an excellent predictor of adaptation to the parent-child relationship, as measured by the Parenting Stress Index (Abidin, 1980; see below).

(b) Role aspects of self-concept. The Adjective Check List provides an individually focused, context-free description of oneself. The context-independent nature of the ACL may be one reason that self-descriptions remain so stable over the course of the transition to parenthood. We felt that those aspects of the self-concept related more closely to the self in one's major roles like partner, lover, parent, and worker might be more sensitive to the effects of making a major life change. Based on conversations with couples in our pilot intervention group, who saw themselves as having a limited amount of psychological energy to be divided among a number of central pursuits, one of us (CPC) developed *The Pie* (Cowan & Cowan, in press) to represent these aspects of self graphically. Beside a circle 4″ in diameter, each participant is asked to list the main roles in his or her life right now, and to divide the circle so that each section reflects the salience or importance of each aspect of self, not the time spent in the role. Content analysis yielded a coding scheme that included: family roles such as parent and partner/lover; worker and student roles; leisure roles such as artist and gardener; and "core" aspects of the self such as "me" or "myself alone."

In contrast with self-esteem, which remained stable over the course of the transition to parenthood, the self-descriptions on *The Pie* showed systematic and meaningful changes: the parent piece of *The Pie* increased over time; the worker piece increased for men, but decreased for women; and the partner/lover aspect of self grew smaller for both fathers and mothers. In each case, women showed greater changes than men—a larger increase in what we interpret as psychological energy devoted to parent, and a larger decrease in energy devoted to worker and to the marriage. In our view, this graphic representation of changes in psychological energy for various aspects of the self provides an accurate picture of the dilemmas facing new parents. It helps to make sense of the fact that couples tend to place their marital relationship on the "back burner" as they attempt to cope with the demands of a dramatically changed life and a demanding infant.

The data from *The Pie* also illustrate a theme that runs through all of our findings. Men and women becoming parents change in different ways at different rates. We have shown elsewhere (Cowan et al., 1985) that (a) partners having babies become more different from each other over time than partners not having a baby; and (b) the partners who become most different from one another show most increase in conflict and most decline in marital satisfaction over the first 18 months of parenthood.

(c) Adjustment. Unfortunately, we included no direct measures of parents' individual adjustment or psychological symptoms in the pregnancy and 6 months postpartum assessments. At the 18 month follow-up we asked each partner to complete the Center for Epidemiological Study of Depression scale (CES-D; Radloff, 1977), and, in order to obtain a more comprehensive index of symptoms, we administered the Hopkins' Symptom checklist (SCL-90; Derogatis, Lipman, & Covi, 1973) when the children were 3½ and 5½.

Given our initial oversight, we could not assess change in depressive symptoms over the transition to parenthood, but we did have several interesting findings using the CES-D at 18 months postpartum. Heming (1985, 1987) has found that new parents were not at higher risk for depression (CES-D) than were the men and women in the childless control group. She also found that men's and women's depression scores were predictable from scores obtained in the pretest 2 years earlier: parents and nonparents most at risk for depression were those who at pretest were suffering from low self-esteem, lacked an available and satisfying support network, and had recently experienced a high level of stressful life events. Finally, more involvement in work outside the home in the early years of parenthood was a very strong correlate of psychological well-being in mothers.

Role Arrangements

Until recently, psychological studies of marriage have not examined men's and women's division of labor in household tasks, decision-making, and childcare, or each partner's satisfaction with the role arrangements they have established. By contrast, sociological studies, have consistently demonstrated that couples' role arrangements, and especially their satisfaction with them, help explain much of the variance in marital satisfaction (Blood & Wolfe, 1960). Most studies examine role arrangements either by asking about a few general areas of domestic labor or by examining the couple's arrangements in minute-by-minute detail. We opted for an in-between strategy, using a single questionnaire focused on 36 separate items of family work.

The *Who Does What?* (Cowan & Cowan, in press) questionnaire has three subscales of 12 items that ask partners to describe their division of tasks in three areas of family life: (i) *Household and family tasks* including laundry, cooking, care of plants or yard, and car maintenance; (ii) *Family decisions* including plans for vacations, partners' involvement in work outside the family and amount of involvement in the community; and (iii) *Child-related tasks* such as feeding, dressing, bathing, arranging for babysitting, and calling the doctor. The 12 childrearing tasks change somewhat in versions of the scale designed for parents of 6, 18, 42, and 66 month olds, and a separate section asks about general responsibility for childcare during the day, on evenings and weekends, and during the night.

Each item is rated on a 1–9 score for "How it is now" with 1 indicating that the woman does it all, 9 indicating that the man does it all, and 5 showing that partners share the tasks about equally. Partners also rate "How I'd like it to be" on each item. Correlations between husbands' and wives' ratings of their housework and childcare arrangements averaged between .72 and .85 at all assessment periods, although there were smaller discrepancies between husbands and wives on some items like who takes out the garbage or who responds to the infant's cries, and larger discrepancies on who does the shopping, meal preparation, and arranges baby sitters and doctors' appointments. Correlations of partners' perceptions of decision making were lower than those on household and childcare items, probably because the range of ratings on the decision-making items was quite restricted, with many hovering around 5.

Two indices of satisfaction were created. The first was derived from a sum of the absolute discrepancies between ratings of "How it is now" and "How I'd like it to be." The second was a simple rating made after filling out each subsection. The global satisfaction ratings were more consistently correlated with self-esteem, parenting stress, and marital satisfaction than the discrepancy measures (Cowan & Cowan, 1988).

Our first analyses, using totals for household, decision-making, and childcare, revealed that men and women grew more traditional in their division of labor over time, and more traditional in their childcare arrangements than they had predicted in pregnancy—regardless of where they began on the traditional-to-egalitarian continuum (Cowan et al., 1985). More detailed item analyses suggested that this conclusion was too simple (Cowan & Cowan, 1988). From pregnancy to 6 months after birth, men showed significant *increases* in their participation in meal preparation, housecleaning, and food shopping, but that involvement dropped off over the next year, during which fathers became more actively involved in the care of their children. We also found that men's level of involvement with their 18-month-olds was predictable from a combination of variables assessed in pregnancy. In general, though, it was men's and women's *satisfaction* with the role arrangements, not the actual style of arrangements, that was correlated with marital and parenting adaptation after the first child's birth.

Communication. We developed four open-ended questionnaires to elicit each partner's perception of what we believed to be salient aspects of couple communication.

(a) Caring, closeness, and distance. In the first questionnaire, we asked partners what they did to show caring for the other, and what their partners did that felt caring to them. Similarly, we asked which things made partners feel closer or more distant over the past several months and whether there had been a change in their sexual relationship over that time. Abner Boles (1984) created four scores: number of ways of caring, number of things you would like your partner to do for you, positive change in your sexual relationship, and negative change in your sexual relationship. All of these scores were correlated with marital satisfaction in the expected directions.

(b) Problem solving. Again using an open-ended format, we asked partners to choose a problem or disagreement they had experienced recently. Each spouse described the problem independently, indicating how satisfied he or she was with both the process of trying to solve the problem and its resolution. Ball (1984) found that it was not the outcome of problem talk that was correlated with each partner's satisfaction with the marriage but his or her satisfaction with the process, or "feeling on the same side."

(c) Conflict and disagreement. In a questionnaire adapted from Sheldon Starr focused on conflict and disagreement, partners indicated how much conflict they had experienced in the last 6 months on 10 issues that are salient to most couples (division of labor, willingness to discuss their sexual relationship, time alone, relationships with in-laws). They also indicated whether they preferred more, less, or the same amount of conflict about each issue. Almost all respondents (92%) showed a slight increase in conflict during their transition to parenthood, with issues about "who does what?" topping the list.

(d) Feelings. In an open-ended format, we asked each partner to describe their emotional exchanges as a couple. For each of three emotional states (anger, depression, happiness) they were asked "What do you tend to do when you feel _____?", "How does your partner tend to react?", and "What do you tend to do then?" Spouses were then asked the same sequence of questions about times when their partners felt angry, depressed, or very happy. Responses were coded in one of four categories: withdraw ("I just go to another room"), negative approach ("I yell at her"), positive approach ("He asks me what's the matter"), or neutral approach ("We discuss it"). Our preliminary analyses suggest that these self-report data have some differences and some similarities with Gottman's careful observational findings (Gottman, Markman, & Notarius, 1977; Gottman & Levenson, in press), which show that patterns of reciprocated and escalated *anger* correlate with and predict marital dissatisfaction. In these self-report data, anger by one partner in response to the other's *sadness or depression* is a better correlate and predictor of marital distress. In addition, we found that reciprocated *positive* affect, as reported by the partners, is correlated with marital satisfaction at some assessment periods.

Couples complained a great deal about filling out the open-ended questionnaires. Our impression was that the complaints were loudest when the materials touched on aspects of their marriage that were not going well. In an effort to reduce the amount of work, but to preserve the information, C. Cowan created a single, three-page Communication questionnaire that offered a choice of responses, based on the free responses couples had given at earlier assessment periods. Preliminary analyses suggest that staff-coded open-ended responses on the earlier version were highly correlated with responses to the new closed-end version of the Communication questionnaire, which were, in turn, significantly correlated with marital satisfaction for both spouses (r = .56 to .64).

Parent-Child

In the first phase of our study, we were not prepared to do systematic observations of parent-infant interaction in addition to the interventions, interviews, and self-report measures. Although we were interested in what actually happened in the relationships between parents and their children, our primary focus was on the parents and their perceptions of themselves, their marriage, and their relationships with their children.

(a) Attitudes. Gertrude Heming created an Ideas About Parenting (Heming, Cowan, & Cowan, in press) questionnaire, choosing items from scales by Baumrind (1974), Block (1965), and Cohler, Weiss, & Grunebaum (1970). Men and women were asked to indicate the extent of their agreement or disagreement with each item, and also to indicate what they believed their partners' opinion to be. Items factored into four orthogonal scales: idealized parent, discomfort with parent role, authoritarian control; and child centeredness. Perhaps it is fortunate for the children that there was low predictability from their parents' attitudes in late pregnancy to those at 6 months postpartum; both mothers' and fathers' attitudes changed radically once they became parents, although not usually in a systematic direction. The one exception to this generalization is that men and women who had participated in the intervention groups grew less authoritarian in their childrearing attitudes when their children were between 6 and 18 months old, whereas parents who had not been assigned to the intervention groups showed a significant increase in authoritarian-controlling attitudes.

P. Cowan revised the Ideas About Parenting questionnaire for the 42-month follow-up in order to make the items more relevant to older children, and to sample a broader array of theoretically-determined dimensions. Data from this revision are in the process of being analyzed.

(b) Parenting stress. Abidin's 150-item Parenting Stress Index (1980) was chosen as a measure of the stress experienced by men and women in their role as parents. We used the fifth revision, but a new, shorter version is now available. It provides a total stress score and subscales in the Parenting domain, and the Child domain. Although stress scores in the Parent domain remained stable from 6 to 42 months postpartum, parents described the children as increasingly moody and demanding when they were between 6 and 18 months. Fathers and mothers who were most likely to experience a high degree of subjective stress in the parenting role 18 months after childbirth were identifiable from their responses to other questionnaires in late pregnancy (Heming, 1985, 1987). Before their child's birth, they suffered from low self-esteem and greater dissatisfaction with the way their family roles were arranged. They believed early on that they would disagree with their partners on childrearing issues, and experienced both a high degree of life stress and inadequate social support during the transition to parenthood. These results are like many that support our structural model. Adaptation in one domain (parent-child) is related to a combination of the individual, marital, and outside-the-family state of affairs.

Three-Generation Perspective

Each partner filled out the Family Environment Scale (FES, Moos, 1974), a 90-item instrument with 10 scales assessing three domains: Relationship (e.g., cohesion); Personal growth (e.g., interest in intellectual activities); and System maintenance (e.g., organization). The FES was filled out twice at each assessment period, once to describe the family they were creating and once to describe the partner's own family of origin. Because items on this instrument do not differentiate between relationships with mother and with father, we adapted a questionnaire from Grossman, Eichler, and Winickoff (1980), to assess the quality of remembered relationships with each participant's parents, and the quality of the parents' marriage as the adult "child" remembered it. Ratings were also made of parents' current relationship with each of their parents, and between their parents (the grandparents). This latter instrument was administered only at the 18 month follow-up.

Men's and women's descriptions of their families of origin on the FES showed no statistically significant mean changes, and high correlational consistency (.73 - .86) from pregnancy until 18 months after starting their own families. These quantitative data are at variance with our clinical impressions that new parents begin to think about their families of origin in quite different ways after they become parents. Many began to voice more sympathy for what their parents' positions must have been as they faced the dilemmas of rearing their own children.

Several of our findings are consistent with theories of intergenerational transmission, although we cannot be certain of this conclusion in that the data concerning the grandparents' family come entirely from the parents in our study. Men who described their growing up families as more positive in the Relationship domain of the FES (more cohesive and expressive, lower in conflict) tended to become more involved in the care of their 18-month-olds and to have lower parenting stress (Cowan & Cowan, 1987b). Women who remembered more positive relationships with their mothers tended to have more positive relationships with their daughters, as we observed them in interaction (see below), whereas men who remembered more *negative* relationships with their fathers appeared to be making an attempt to compensate for this: they were rated as having warmer, more positive interactions with their sons (Cowan, Cowan, & Heming, 1986). In other words, women tended to carry over the quality of their relationships with their same-sex parent, whereas men seemed to have a compensatory approach as they tried to establish the kind of relationship with their sons that they had wanted with their fathers.

Outside the Family Perspective

(a) Patterns of employment. In the early phase of the study we kept track only of whether each spouse was employed outside the home or went to school, and, if so, for how many hours a week. At the 42-month follow-up we added a job satisfaction measure, and at the 66-month follow-up, in 2 dissertations in progress, Marsha Kline added more extensive questionnaires on the meaning of work and Laurie Leventhal-Belfer asked about child care utilization and decision-making. These additions typify the challenges and dilemmas of longitudinal research. As the study goes on, what is most salient in the parents' lives changes, and thus, new issues become salient to the researchers. It seems important to add new measurement devices, but because they were not administered earlier, they will not yield the kind of change scores that make longitudinal studies so useful. Nevertheless, correlational connections between earlier and later data can be very important in filling out our portrait of current family functioning.

The "real" data on employment patterns are similar to the psychological measures obtained on *The Pie*. In our sample, almost all men and women worked full time before the birth of their first child. Afterwards, most women drastically curtailed their involvement in employment or school, while men's employment hours increased slightly. Because they feel guilty about not bringing in income, women begin to feel reluctant to ask men to participate in household and child care tasks. Men, many of whom want to participate actively in the care of their children, find that their wives are somewhat ambivalent about sharing what has become their major life role; thus, they begin to work away from home for more hours, viewing their work as a direct contribution to providing for the family. These different ways of reconciling men's and women's family–work balance can result in different levels of satisfaction—with self and with partner. We think that differences in employment patterns between new mothers and fathers are a major source of the increasing differences and strain that we find between new parent spouses.

(b) Life stress—Social support balance. The concept and measure of life stress events, originally developed by Holmes and Rahe (1967), has had its share of criticism (e.g., Dohrenwend & Dohrenwend, 1974). The notion of a fixed list of both negative and positive events, given stress ratings by a standardization sample and summed to produce a total score, ignores the difference between positive and negative changes, and the fact that different people may weigh a given life change differently. Although Lazarus and Folkman (1984) argue persuasively that a list of daily hassles provides a more accurate picture of the life events that generate stress, and we would agree, their scale had not been well developed when we started our research. We chose a life-events scale developed by Horowitz, Schaefer, Hiroto, Wilner, and Levin, (1977), with items not only weighted for their potential stress value but also according to how recently they had occurred.

There are many ways of assessing social support, but most of them require extensive interview questions about each person in the network. Instead, Harriet Curtis-Boles on our research staff developed the *Important People* questionnaire, which asks partners to describe four people who are currently important in their lives. With a combination of multiple choice items and rating scales, we obtained information about how frequently and how satisfactorily these people provided support in the form of information, advice, material benefits, and emotional support. A positive support index was created by combining frequency of support with rated satisfaction.

Heming created an index reflecting the balance between life stress and social support from a cross-tabulation of the life stress and social support scores. A high positive balance was ascribed to those in the top third of the sample on positive social support and the bottom third on life stress. For our new parent couples, this balance increased from pregnancy to 6 months after birth and then decreased again during the next year. It was one of the only measures on which new parents were at an advantage compared with nonparents in the first 2 years of the study. Finally, the index was useful as a corrective factor in making predictions (Heming, 1985, 1987). Although prebirth scores accounted for a substantial proportion of the variance in postbirth scores, adding the Life stress–Social support balance index at 18 months almost always improved the accuracy of the predictions. That is, knowing how parents adapted before birth is important to understanding how they adapt later, but knowing the current stress-support balance outside the family makes the picture even more complete.

Observational and Test Measures of Marital Adaptation

(a) Marital adjustment/satisfaction. The Locke-Wallace Short Marital Adjustment Test (Locke & Wallace, 1959) is a well-known self-report instrument commonly used in marital and family research. A newer, psychometrically more elegant Dyadic Adjustment Scale has been created by Spanier (1976), but the Locke–Wallace is shorter and the correlation between the two scales has been found to be extremely high (about .92).

(b) Marital adaptation/dysfunction. This observational assessment of marital function was developed by Gertrude Heming and used by the researcher couple after each interview. From her reading of the family therapy literature, Heming (1985, 1987) created a 5-step scale with detailed descriptions of optimal, mid-range, and dysfunctional couple relationships. This observational index of couple adaptation/dysfunction was moderately but significantly correlated with men's and women's self-reported marital satisfaction at 18 months postpartum, and it could be predicted from a combination of individual and marital self-report scales 2 years earlier during pregnancy.

OBSERVATIONAL AND TEST MEASURES OF FAMILY INTERACTION AND CHILD OUTCOME

We have indicated that in the second phase of the Becoming a Family Project, as our focus shifted to the examination of family factors affecting child development, we needed both observational measures of parent-child and family interaction, and test measures of the child that did not rely exclusively on parent-report or self-report. In this section we describe all of the measurement procedures for examining family interaction and child development, and then present a brief summary of the findings.

Child Tests. We decided early on that we did not want to obtain measures of the children's IQ. We had not contracted with the parents to do so, and we were conscious of how the single IQ number, or even the subtests, are often misunderstood or misused. We wanted to choose measures of development that were theoretically meaningful. Accordingly, our laboratory measures of the child's development at age 3½, and again at 5½ were drawn primarily from Piaget's measures of logic and role-taking (Inhelder & Piaget, 1964; Piaget & Inhelder, 1967/1948), and from Jack and Jeanne Block's (1980) measures of ego resiliency and ego control.

(a) Piagetian tasks. At the 3-year assessment, we gave children toys and shapes to classify, and sticks to be matched with a seriated row presented by the experimenter (Inhelder & Piaget, 1964). We also used two tasks developed by the Blocks to measure children's ability to take the experimenter's point of view, or, in a variation of the ''three mountains task'' (Piaget & Inhelder, 1967/1948), to have the child choose pictures that another observer would see from various compass points around a display, while the child faces the display from the front.

(b) Ego resiliency and ego control. In their two-factor theory (Block & Block, 1980) the Blocks propose that ego development is best described by the child's adaptive resourceful response to challenge (ego resiliency) and his or her ability to control impulses and delay gratification (ego control). We used the same set of four tasks to measure these dimensions that Matas, Arend, and Sroufe (1978) had used in their study, in which they showed that early attachment and early competence predicted the child's ego resiliency and control at 3- and 5-years-of-age. We presented the children with a level-of-aspiration task, in which ego resiliency is assessed by their ability to adjust their predictions in a tower building task to match their actual ability to stack the blocks without having them fall. Ego control is inferred from the height of the child's *predicted* tower. Other tasks included a curiosity box, which the child is free to explore, a Lowenfeld Mosaic test in which the child creates a pattern with colored wooden pieces, and a Motor inhibition test in which the child is asked to walk a line drawn on the floor and then asked to walk the same line as slowly as he or she can. Each task yields a measure of both ego resiliency and ego control.

34

We also asked each child to "build a world" in a sand tray using any of 200 miniatures of people, trees, buildings, and animals. In addition to the scores derived from the Piagetian and ego resiliency and control tasks, Kastelowitz and Lieberman on our staff developed ratings of the child's style of approaching the whole session on dimensions very similar to, or complementary to, the ones we used to summarize the behavior of the parents (see p. 36).

(c) Parent descriptions: Our reliance on laboratory tasks and experimenter observations in a 2-hour visit would not be sufficient to describe the range of children's adaptive and maladaptive behavior. Therefore, at the 42-month-follow-ups we selected two instruments that parents could use to tell us about the child's overall development. First was the Minnesota Child Development Inventory (MCDI, Ireton & Thwing, 1972), which asks parents to check whether their child shows specific developmental skills. The MCDI provides an overall index of development, and subscales of language, motor development, social development, and so on. Second, we used O'Donnell and Van Tuinen's (1979) adaptation of the Quay-Peterson Behavior Problem Checklist to get a sense of the child's emotional-social difficulties.

(d) Teacher descriptions. When the first child entered elementary school, we sought permission from the parents to contact the principal, from whom we requested permission to contact the study child's teacher with an unusual request. We told the teachers about our study, and said that one of the project families had a child in her classroom. To preserve confidentiality and to avoid rater bias, we were asking them to rate all of the children in the class on our adaptation of Earl Schaefer's Classroom Adaptive Behavior Inventory (CABI, 1983). We would pay $40. for each set of classroom ratings, one in the Fall and another in the Spring of Kindergarten year. Almost all of the teachers agreed to cooperate, although several agreed to rate only a limited number of the children in the class.[2]

The 91 items (60 from Schaefer, 31 added by us) factored into four major dimensions: Antisocial; Academic competence; Shy; and Physical Symptoms. The first three factors are almost identical with Schaefer's; the fourth contains a number of the items we added. Scores on each factor were obtained for the study child, relative to the children in his or her class. This avoids the problem of rating biases by teachers, but ignores the fact that some classrooms have more aggressive or more competent children than others (Shephard Kellam, personal communication).

Both parents also filled out a CABI describing their Kindergarten child. The factor structure of the parents' ratings was very similar to that of the teachers' ratings, although the weighting of some items was different. When we compared parents' and teachers' descriptions of the child on the CABI, we found signifi-

---

[2]When teachers were unable to rate all children in their class, we asked for a list of the children, and *we* chose the agreed-upon number, making sure it included the target child.

cant correlations between parents' and teachers' perceptions (averaging .48 for mother-teacher and .35 for father-teacher agreement). These correlations seem low until we remember that most studies find no correspondence between parent and teacher ratings of children.

(e) Additional school-age assessments. During the laboratory assessment of the child at 5½, he or she was administered the Harter Self-Esteem Scale (1978). Later, in a separate session at the child's home, another member of the research team administered the Peabody Individual Achievement Test so that we could have an independent measure of the child's academic skills. Finally, during the home visit, an interview focused on the child's impressions of him or herself, of the family, of school, and of relationships with friends. In addition to a content analysis of the children's responses, we are currently developing a coding system to assess their level of cognitive complexity.

Parent-Child Interaction.   In our application for a second 3 years of grant support, we proposed a study linking parent data from before birth and at 6, 18, and 42 months postpartum, with the quality of parent-child interaction; we hoped to account for the cognitive and personality development in the child and the emergence of behavior problems. We asked for support to buy video equipment to tape the parent-child sessions, which consisted of three types of tasks:

1. One experimenter takes the child out of the room and tells him or her a brief story. After the child returns to the room, the parent, as instructed, asks the child to tell the story (see Pratt, Kerig, Cowan, & Cowan, 1988);

2. The child is presented with four difficult tasks (adapted from Block & Block, 1980). The parent can provide as much or as little help as he or she wishes.

3. The parent and child "build a world together" in a sand tray.

The reviewers supported the grant renewal request but not the purchase of video equipment. They proposed that we simply link the individual parent data with child outcomes, arguing that it would be too time-consuming to become involved in the kind of detailed microanalytic coding of behavior that many family researchers have been adopting. We believed that without some idea of the *mechanisms* involved in linking parent and child characteristics, the study would have limited practical and theoretical utility. We did agree, however, that microanalytic coding would be a costly and time-consuming project, especially since we were not trained in using it.

Our solution was to develop a system of global ratings that observers on our research team would complete at the end of each session. The ratings were developed by Kastelowitz and Lieberman from two sources. First, an extensive literature review identified a number of dimensions considered important by previous investigators of family socialization (warmth, pleasure, anger, creativity, clarity, structure, limit-setting, granting of autonomy). Second, Kastelowitz and Lieberman used as guidelines rating scales developed for similar tasks by Jack and Jeanne Block (1980), as modified by Donald Rahe at the University of Minnesota. We found that the scales could be rated reliably in both parent-child and whole-family sessions, and that they factored into six "scales"; the most important of these scales for our purposes was one that included warmth, responsiveness, structure, and limit setting. In our view, this combination represented the style of parenting described by Diana Baumrind (1979, in press) as authoritative (in contrast with authoritarian, permissive, or disengaged). Our choice of the global rating approach, then, was governed by issues of practicality and familiarity with methods. The empirical question was whether the global ratings would be useful in understanding concurrent and future adaptation of the child.

Whole-Family Interaction.   When the first child was 3½, we limited the "whole-family" sessions to the nuclear triad, even if there were infant brothers and/or sisters, as there were in 42% of the families. By the time this round of visits was complete, we had learned that a number of parents in the study felt that we were missing an important aspect of their family interaction by not including the second child. Thus, at the Kindergarten year assessments, we included all children in the family in the family visit, regardless of age.

The Kindergarten year assessment included tasks comparable to those in the preschool visits, a family drawing, and a task in which the Kindergartner attempted to teach the younger sibling a task that had been presented to him or her 2 years earlier by the parents.

Our team rated father-child and mother-child interaction as observed in the parent-child sessions, with each rater focusing on one parent-child dyad. In addition, both observers rated the couple as they interacted in planning and carrying out the tasks—on dimensions of warmth, anger, cooperation-competition, conflict, and clarity of communication. With the collaboration of Prof. Yona Teichman and Dr. Nancy Miller, we are now working on a rating of "the family." Using the videotaped family visits, we examine and rate the behaviors and styles of individuals, dyads, and the triad on both the structured and unstructured tasks. We are currently attempting to answer the question of whether each level of analysis contributes *uniquely* to our understanding of individual and family adaptation.

Issues of Data Reduction

It should be clear by now that we have followed the multimethod, multimeasure, multidomain ideal of family research, perhaps to excess. To the self-report measures of both parents in pregnancy and after birth, we added observational ratings of parenting and coparenting styles, and laboratory, parent, teacher, and self-descriptions of the child's development and adjustment. Exploratory correlational analyses of partial samples at the 42-month assessment gave us the information that we seemed to be on the right track. Analyses of the full data set for that period and a partial data set for the Kindergarten year are in progress now (see Cowan, Cowan, Heming, & Miller in press).

We have already described factor analyses of individual instruments as one way of reducing data, but if each instrument or procedure yields several scores, we still have a mountain of data concerning each of the five domains of our model of family adaptation. Our general strategy has been to do a large number of correlations on an exploratory sample—guided by our model—and then to create composite measures based on a variety of instruments or procedures within each domain. Unlike the pure research model that we were taught, with specific tests of specific hypotheses, there is an interplay between guiding principles and data analysis in our approach. We cannot test our hypotheses until we learn the meaning of the responses to some of our instruments and the meaning of the rating scales.

Recently, in analyzing the family data and its relation to child outcome, we have been influenced by theoretical models of risk and protective factors described by Rutter (1983) and by Sameroff, Seifer, and Zax (1982). Risk factors in evidence *before* a new transition make subsequent adaptation less likely and distress more likely. For example, when parents have low self-esteem or marital distress before they become parents, not only is it more likely that they will have low self-esteem and marital satisfaction in the postpartum period, but they are also at greater risk for parenting stress and depression. In other words, there may be an impact across domains. We can also look at the other end of the continuum, with events *in each domain* serving as protective factors that make adaptation more likely and distress less likely. Individuals with high self-esteem and more satisfying role arrangements may cope better with stressful life events. Our working hypothesis is that adaptation (whatever the domain) is the product of risk factors and protective factors operating in all of the domains.

Preliminary analyses of our data have been guided by the schematic representation in Fig. 1.1. Marital satisfaction when the first child is 3½ is not correlated directly with any of our child outcome measures at that time or 2 years later. We have constructed and tested a theoretical path model using simple correlations, hierarchical multiple regressions, and Latent Variable Path Analyses with Partial Least Squares ("soft modeling"—Falk, 1987; Wold, 1982). We expected and found a line of associations from the status of (a) the individual parents and their marriage, parenting ideology, family of origin, life stress, and social support *in pregnancy,* and (b) characteristics of the birth and the child *at 18 months postpartum,* to (c) marital satisfaction, and (d) depression at *42 and 66 months postpartum.* Parents' individual and marital adaptation, in turn, are related to (e)

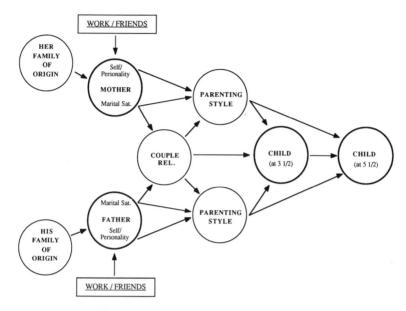

FIG. 1.1. A five domain model of family adaptation with a focus on the child's development.

each parent's style of interacting with the child (parenting ratings), and to (f) how the parents interact with each other while the child is present (coparenting ratings). Finally, parenting and coparenting styles are related concurrently and predictively to (g) child developmental outcomes, as assessed in our laboratory, and as described by both parents and teachers during the child's Kindergarten year (Cowan, Cowan, Heming, & Miller, in press).

The correlations between individual characteristics, the marital relationship, the parent-child relationships and child development cannot be interpreted as stemming primarily from the child. Parents' marital satisfaction and self-esteem when their children were 3½ was highly predictable from the state of the marriage and views of the self 4 years earlier, before the children were born (r = .65 and .78). These prebirth data are essential for interpreting the direction of effects in studies of family interaction.

Risk Ratings.   The findings so far have been exciting but overwhelming. We believe that it is imperative to reduce the data so that we are not examining hundreds of individual correlations. Our most recent efforts in this direction have been to create 5 "risk indices," with each one summarizing data from a different family domain:

1. Individual risk—a composite of low self-esteem, high symptoms, and low scores on an adult development index;
2. Couple risk—a composite of self-report and observer ratings of couple interaction;
3. Parenting risk—a composite of parent report (e.g., Parenting Stress) and observer ratings of parent-child interaction;
4. Family of origin risk—grandparents divorced, grandparents alcoholic, family of origin interaction perceived as negative;
5. Outside the family risk—high life stress, low social support, low job satisfaction.

Each of these risk indices was correlated with *different* child outcomes when the child was 3½. Authoritative parenting style was most clearly related to the child's scores on classification, seriation, and role-taking (20% of the variance). Mothers' and fathers' individual adjustment and parenting style were related to the children's scores on the Minnesota Child Development Index (40% of the variance). Couple risk and fathers' lack of authoritativeness, especially for boys, was related to the children's internalizing and externalizing problems (30%).

Finally, we have begun to test the hypothesis that the parents' adaptation to the transition to parenthood predicts their child's adaptation to school *almost 4 years later*. We created a change score index of the amount of decline in parents' self-esteem or marital satisfaction between pregnancy and 18 months after birth. Parents with *less decline* in self-esteem during the transition were more authoritative in the parent-child interaction sessions 6 years later ($r = .42$ fathers; .30 mothers). Similarly, parents who showed smaller earlier declines in marital satisfaction tended to have sons rated by their Kindergarten teachers as less shy (.59 for fathers; .54 for mothers) and daughters rated as more academically competent (.45 for fathers; .47 for mothers) as they made their transitions to elementary school. There is a strong belief that adaptation during earlier family life transitions foreshadows adaptation during later transitions, but this hypothesis is rarely given an empirical test.

In sum, these preliminary data lend support to the 5-domain model we have been developing, and to the variety of self-report and observational measures we have chosen. A substantial and meaningful proportion of the child's academic and social adaptation to Kindergarten can be predicted from a combination of the parents' individual adaptation, parenting style, and interaction as a couple, with some of the predictors reaching back to the time before the child was born. Later risk indices, too, are predictable from our prebirth assessments of the parents. Of course, the prebirth data do not explain *all* of the variance in later parent child outcomes. The nature of the child makes a difference, external circumstances and stressors change, and parents themselves develop and grow. What our data suggest is that the quality of the parent-child relationship has its roots in the kind of individuals that parents are, the families they grew up in, the quality of their relationship as a couple, and how they arrange the nonfamily aspects of their lives. We see increasing evidence for this view of parenting in our study and in others (e.g., Brody, Pellegrini & Sigel, 1986; Goldberg & Easterbrooks, 1984).

Connections Between Global and Micro Levels of Analysis

As part of the clinical method approach to taking multiple perspectives on the same events, Prof. Michael Pratt has been working with us to examine the relation between our global ratings of parenting style, and more microanalytic examinations of parent-child interaction. In one study (Pratt et al., 1988), he has shown that parents who are more authoritative in their parenting (based on a composite of global ratings) are more likely to use "scaffolding" techniques in teaching their children. That is, parents move in at an appropriate level when the child has difficulty, and then reduce their support when the child succeeds. This is one example of the fact that measurement techniques using different levels of analysis can be complementary, and can help to enrich the meanings of constructs that the measures are designed to assess.

FINE TUNING OUR RESEARCH METHODS

Like proud parents, we are highly pleased with our research offspring, even though it has not always turned out the way we expected in the beginning. Some aspects of the study have changed, either because our views have expanded, or because we began to ask new questions as we followed the families over time. In a few cases, we made changes by including measures and procedures that we had simply not considered in the beginning; in others, we developed new ways of coding observations and scoring already collected questionnaires. Especially in longitudinal studies, however, not everything is fixable by adding new measures and procedures. As we attempt to evaluate the study in hindsight, there are a few things that we would change if we were planning the study based on what we know now.

1. *Interview data.* We are impressed with how the questions in our interviews proceed in logical order and seem to provide a stimulus for each partner, in the presence of the other, to do a serious evaluation of couple and family life. These interviews have been invaluable to us as a way of maintaining relationships with the families in the study, and as a source of general hypotheses about how individuals and couples cope with becoming a family. Although we now wish that we had been able to precode more responses so that they would be accessible

immediately for data analysis, this level of structuring was difficult to do before we knew the territory.

2. *Adult development data.* From the beginning, we built in a number of ways to capture parents' individual characteristics—age, race, education, work, and personality characteristics. As the study progresses we feel a need for a more differentiated assessment of each man's and woman's level of development. It seems to us that when men and women have a well-articulated positive sense of themselves, when they demonstrate competence in their ability to solve problems and take a perspective on their life, and when they are able to balance individuality and mutuality in their relationships, they are better able to deal with the disequilibration of becoming a family. All of these characteristics have been used as definers of maturity (Allport, 1961) and adult development (P. Cowan, 1988). Recently, in her dissertation, Elaine Ransom has begun to conceptualize ways of coding some of our interviews to construct indices that would reflect individual differences in developmental level. We have also begun to construct an adult development index from a combination of autonomy, affiliation, and adjustment scales from the Adjective Check List.

3. *The family as a unit.* We have not done too badly in our attempts to assess individuals and dyadic relationships in this study. But, as we have continued to mine the data, we have felt the need to develop better ways of conceptualizing the complexity of "the family." Juanita Dimas, Nancy Miller, Joanna Self, and Kristina Whitney, under the direction of Yona Teichman of Tel Aviv University, have been attempting to develop a coding manual that would provide information about individuals, dyads, and the whole family, based on our videotaped observations of the family sessions at the 42 and 66 month follow-ups.

We have found this task to be more difficult than we had expected for a variety of conceptual and methodological reasons. We were brought up to accept the assumption of family therapists—that the whole family is different than the sum of its parts, and that characteristics of the system may be more useful than descriptions of individual personalities in understanding adaptation and dysfunction. But we have been experiencing great difficulty as we attempt to construct codes to capture characteristics of *the family* as distinct from its individuals or dyads (P. Cowan, 1987). It makes conceptual sense to describe a family as "enmeshed," but our primarily "nonclinical" families do not tend to show a pattern in which all of the dyads appear to be enmeshed. Instead, if one relationship—usually, but not always the mother-child—is enmeshed, the other two (father-child, father-mother) appear to be disengaged. How, then, are we to describe *the family?*

Part of our disequilibration, we believe comes from the fact that we *expected* to be able to characterize the whole family, but we sometimes get contradictory information from individual and dyadic domains. In our future analyses we will be testing the hypothesis that individual, dyadic, and family-level data will each add unique variance to our understanding of adaptation or dysfunction in any of the 5 domains of the family structure.

4. The farther along the family lifespan we move in our study, the more we realize that we need to know about how employment and family adaptation intersect for parents of young children. At this time of life there are strongly competing demands for men's and women's time and energy as they try to be "good enough" parents and partners, while forging ahead with their jobs or careers. Marsha Kline is completing a dissertation looking at parents' work patterns at home and at the office, and at how these patterns interact with intrapsychic and interpersonal stress to produce individual and marital well-being. Because we had not gathered detailed employment data in the early assessments, this substudy made it necessary to go back to the couples and ask their help in providing more detail about their work histories, their income, and their conflict and strain about juggling work at home and on the job. Inevitably, issues of employment-family role strains raise questions about the availability, quality, and attractiveness of child care facilities. In another dissertation based on our project, Laurie Leventhal-Belfer has created a retrospective examination of the connection between couples' decision-making about child care and their satisfaction with childcare arrangements, and satisfaction with their marriage.

5. *Keeping subjects.* A primary concern in any longitudinal study is maintaining contact with the participants, and enlisting their cooperation at each follow-up. As they have more children, enter new phases of their careers, move away, and separate or divorce, some men and women feel less attachment to our project, and less investment in it. We have used several simple procedures to keep track of people (asking them for names of relatives who will know where they are) and to maintain their ties with the project (newsletters and published articles). We held a reception for all families at the beginning of the 42 month follow-ups where they met the whole research team, heard about our latest findings, and met many other families in the study for the first time. By then, a large number of families had moved away and were not available for visits to our laboratory playroom. In the next follow-ups, we built in a relatively small amount of travel funds in the grant to cover some of the transportation and one day's stay in Berkeley, and were able to entice an additional 16% of the original sample to return to our lab at the Kindergarten assessment.

The main difficulty in maintaining the cooperation of the couples is the amount of work filling out questionnaires. The questionnaires are providing rich and meaningful data, but most parents have now completed them five times since their pregnancy. A few families (10%) have refused to continue, and some have expressed the wish to talk with us without having to do "the homework." In retrospect, it might have been better to reduce what we asked of the couples, but we would have had to sacrifice the depth of information we have been gathering.

This is an example of the choices and tradeoffs involved in doing this kind of research.

The fact that more than 20% of the couples in our study have divorced (both parents and nonparents) has also affected our ability to maintain continuity, but not as much as we feared. In most cases, we have been able to obtain data from at least one of the parents, and occasionally from the parent's new partner.

6. *A sampling issue.* While our sample represented a wide range in terms of age, socioeconomic status, race, and place of residence in communities surrounding the San Francisco Bay Area, it was by no means a random sample of the population of couples having babies in the years between 1979 and 1982. Subsequent conversations with Shepard Kellam, a family epidemiologist at Johns Hopkins School of Mental Hygiene, have made us more aware of the possibility of selecting a research sample from a more clearly defined population. If we could begin the study again, we might start with county marriage records (though not all of our couples were married) and a more systematic survey of Bay Area obstetricians and doctors who deliver babies, so that we would know more about how far our results can be generalized.

7. *A final design issue.* As we reported earlier, we initially included a control sample of expectant couples in the study who did not receive the pretest questionnaires, so that we could evaluate the impact of completing the questionnaires on the couples' adaptation to parenthood. This control group did allow us to conclude that questionnaires could be considered an important intervention in themselves, over and above the impact of having a baby and participating in a couples group. However, these couples that we asked *less* from tended to drop out of the study at a much higher rate than the couples from whom we asked more. And, for our predictive equations from the pregnancy period, we lost a sample of 48 individuals (24 men and 24 women) for whom we had no prebaby data. While the inclusion of these couples made for a more elegant research design, following them was a very labor-intensive endeavor, with very little additional yield in terms of results. In future studies, we might simply assume that every assessment constitutes an intervention, without attempting to assess the magnitude of this intervention effect.

A PERSONAL CONCLUSION

In this chapter we have described the Becoming a Family Project and its origins, our orientation to the clinical method of studying families, some results, and some analyses in progress. Consistent with the clinical method, we have argued that the personal and theoretical perspectives of the researchers shape the ways in which questions are asked, data are gathered, and results are interpreted. Coming back full circle to the fact that this project began with own personal concerns, we should not fail to mention that just as researchers affect the conduct and results of their investigations, involvement in a project like this one has a marked impact on the researchers.

In our own case, in the early years of the study we were a couple with school-aged children, leading groups of couples with newborns, supervising researcher-couples who were not yet parents, who, in turn, were working with the families in our study. We decided early on that we needed clinical consultation to keep track of which couple issues belonged to whom. We met twice a month for 2 years with Dr. Hilde Burton in immensely helpful sessions that covered all of the levels of the study—personal, professional, conceptual, and clinical. This consultation, along with our continuing attempts in subsequent years to understand how couple relationships work, has had a tremendously positive impact on the way we work and live together.

We have also observed a significant impact of participating in this study on the researchers who have worked with us. Two of the original couples who co-led groups began the study as childless couples, but both had become parents before they completed their degrees and left the project. We take comfort in the fact that their close observation of the difficulties that many couples experienced were balanced by the many examples of the wonders and joys of becoming parents.

Others who have worked with the families in our study, whether or not they became parents, have had an unparalleled opportunity to observe a panorama of men, women, and children as they struggle to make families that meet their needs. Most of our research assistants have been clinical psychology graduate students, with an occupational tendency to focus on individual pathology. Working with the nonclinical families in our study has given all of us an unparalleled view of the wide range that constitutes normal family processes, and the many ways that families find to support the development of their members.

This project is clinically oriented in ways that go beyond the use of the clinical method. While we welcome the fact that the couples group intervention is useful for testing theoretical models, we are also committed to the application of knowledge and the creation of interventions that might alleviate or prevent distress early in the lives of young families. The results of the study so far indicate that we have not yet discovered a permanent inoculation against marital stress and dysfunction in new parents, but we have found promising positive early effects on their marital satisfaction and stability. There is now enough basic research documenting the disequilibration of this life transition for family members and the possibility of identifying individuals and couples at risk for later individual and marital distress. We believe that it is now possible to design interventions that can strengthen couple relationships during the transition to parenthood. The couples who participated in the intervention in this study feel strongly that the groups have helped their adjustment to becoming families and many have said that ''every couple should have one.''

We are hopeful that this approach of working with both partners in the couple can be expanded to other major family life transitions.[3] Wherever we talk about this project, members of the audience ask "Where's the group for parents of adolescents?" or "Why isn't there such a group for parents with aging parents?" It seems clear to us that now is not an easy time to be a parent of children of any age. We hope that all family researchers, however *basic* their orientation to research, will keep one eye on the implications of their work so that it can ultimately be useful to the families who make such a central contribution to our studies.

ACKNOWLEDGMENT

This study has been supported throughout by NIMH grant MH 31109. We also want to acknowledge major contributions to the longitudinal study by members of the research team: Gertrude Heming served as data manager throughout the study, and Dena Cowan, Barbara Epperson, Beth Schoenberger, and Marc Schulz, processed the immense data set. Ellen Garrett, William S. Coysh, Harriet Curtis-Boles, and Abner Boles III were the other two couples who followed the families over time and led intervention groups; Laura Mason Gordon and David Gordon interviewed couples in the last three years. Sacha Bunge, Michael Blum, Julia Levine, David Chavez, Marc Schulz, and Joanna Cowan worked with the children in the study; Linda Kastelowitz, Victor Lieberman, Marsha Kline, and Charles Soulé worked with the parents and children together. Laurie Leventhal-Belfer and Elaine Ransom collected the teachers' ratings; and Rachel Conrad, Juanita Dimas, Patricia Kerig, Julia Levine, Nancy Miller, Joanna Self, and Kristina Whitney rated videotaped family interaction. We are indebted to Nancy Miller who served as a Postdoctoral fellow with us from 1986–88, and to our colleagues Michael Pratt and Yona Teichman whose collaboration from afar has proved invaluable.

---

[3]The intervention results have spawned two other pilot intervention projects, in which we have trained other graduate students in clinical psychology to work with couples in groups. In both cases, couples groups co-led by graduate student couples have been offered to men and women at other stages of married life considered to be stressful for couple relationships. In the first, graduate student couples who had recently moved to the campus community met weekly for 4 months; in the second, parents of preschool children in the cities surrounding the university community discussed how their parenting and marital issues are intertwined. In both cases, we adapted questionnaires from the Becoming a Family Project study, using the participants' responses both as a stimulus for discussion in the couples groups, and for an initial look at how these men and women describe their lives as couples. Our ongoing supervision of these new mental health professional couples keeps us testing our hypothesis that life transitions are an ideal time to do preventive work on relationships; the participants' reactions keep us convinced that nonclinic couples can certainly use some assistance in keeping their relationships satisfying.

REFERENCES

Abidin, R. (1980). *Parent education and intervention handbook.* Springfield, IL: C. C. Thomas.

Allport, G. (1961). *Pattern and growth in personality.* New York: Holt, Rinehart & Winston.

Ball, F. L. J. (1984). *Understanding and satisfaction in marital problem solving: A hermeneutic inquiry.* Unpublished doctoral dissertation, University of California, Berkeley.

Baumrind, D. (1974). *Ethical judgment and parent attitude questionnaire.* Unpublished research report. Institute of Human Development. University of California, Berkeley.

Baumrind, D. (1979). The development of instrumental competence through socialization. In A. D. Pick (Ed.), *Minnesota symposia on child psychology* (Vol. 7). Minneapolis: University of Minnesota Press.

Baumrind, D. (in press.) Effective parenting during the early adolescent transition. In P. A. Cowan & M. E. Hetherington (Eds.), *Advances in family research* (Vol. 2). Hillsdale, NJ: Lawrence Erlbaum Associates.

Belsky, J. (1984). The determinants of parenting: A process model. *Child Development, 55,* 83–96.

Belsky, J., & Pensky, E. (in press). Developmental history, personality, and family relationships: Toward an emergent family system. In R. Hinde & J. Stevenson-Hinde (Eds.), *The interrelationship of family relationships.,* London: Cambridge University Press.

Benedek, T. (1959). Parenthood as a developmental phase. *Journal of the American Psychoanalytic Association, 7,* 389–417.

Block, J. (1965). *The child-rearing practices report.* Berkeley, CA: Institute of Human Development.

Benedek, T. (1970). Parenthood during the life cycle. In E. J. Anthony & T. Benedek (Eds.), *Parenthood: Its psychology and psychopathology.* Boston: Little, Brown.

Bernard, J. (1974). *The future of marriage.* New York: World.

Block, J. H., & Block, J. (1980). The role of ego-control and ego-resiliency in the organization of behavior. In W. A. Collins (Ed.), *Minnesota symposia on child psychology* (Vol. 13). Hillsdale, NJ: Lawrence Erlbaum Associates.

Blood, R. O., & Wolfe, D. M. (1960). *Husbands and wives: The dynamics of married living.* Glencoe, IL: The Free Press.

Boles, A. (1984). *Predictors and correlates of marital satisfaction during the transition to parenthood.* Unpublished doctoral dissertation, University of California, Berkeley.

Brody, G. H., Pilligrini, A. D., & Sigel, I. (1986). Marital quality and mother-child and father-child interactions with school-aged children. *Developmental Psychology, 22,* 291–296.

Brown, G. W., & Harris, T. (1978). *Social origins of depression: A study of psychiatric disorder in women.* New York: The Free Press.

Caplan, G. (1964). *Principles of preventive psychiatry.* New York: Basic Books.

Cherlin, A. (1977). The effect of children on marital dissolution. *Demography, 14,* 264–272.

Clulow, C. F. (1982). *To have and to hold: Marriage, the first baby and preparing couples for parenthood.* Aberdeen: Aberdeen University Press.

Colman, A. D., & Colman, L. L. (1971). *Pregnancy: The psychological experience.* New York: Herder & Herder.

Cohler, B. J., Weiss, J. L., & Grunebaum, H. V. (1970). Child-care attitude and emotional disturbance in mothers of young children. *Genetic Psychology Monographs, 82,* 3–42.

Cowan, C. P. (1988). Working with men becoming fathers: The impact of a couples group intervention. In P. Bronstein & C. P. Cowan (Eds.), *Fatherhood today: Men's changing role in the family.* New York: Wiley.

Cowan, C. P., & Cowan, P. A. (1987a). Men's involvement in parenthood: Identifying the antecedents and understanding the barriers. In P. Berman & F. Pedersen (Eds.), *Men's transition to parenthood.* Hillsdale, NJ: Lawrence Erlbaum Associates.

Cowan, C. P., & Cowan, P. A. (1987b). A preventive intervention for couples becoming parents. In C. F. Z. Boukydis (Ed.), *Research on support for parents and infants in the postnatal period*. Norwood, NJ: Ablex.

Cowan, C. P., & Cowan, P. A. (1988). Who does what when partners become parents: Implications for men, women, and marriage. *Marriage & Family Review, 13*, 1 & 2. Special issue on the transition to parenthood.

Cowan, C. P., Cowan, P. A., Coie, L., & Coie, J. D. (1978). Becoming a family: The impact of a first child's birth on the couple's relationship. In W. B. Miller & L. F. Newman (eds.), *The first child and family formatiohn*. Chapel Hill, NC: Carolina Population Center.

Cowan, C. P., Cowan, P. A., Heming, G., Garrett, E., Coysh, W. S., Curtis-Boles, H., & Boles, A. J. (1985, December). Transitions to parenthood: His, hers, and theirs. *Journal of Family Issues, 6*, 451–481.

Cowan, C. P., Cowan, P. A., Heming, G., & Miller, N. B. (in press). Becoming a family: marriage, parenting, and child development. In P. A. Cowan & E. M. Hetherington (Eds.), *Advances in family research* (Vol. 2). Hillsdale, NJ: Lawrence Erlbaum Associates.

Cowan, P. A. (1978). *Piaget: With feeling*. New York: Holt, Rinehart & Winston.

Cowan, P. A. (1987). The need for theoretical and methodological integrations in family research. *Family Psychology, 1*, 48–50.

Cowan, P. A. (1988). Becoming a father: A time of change, an opportunity for development. In P. Bronstein & C. P. Cowan (Eds.), *Fatherhood today: Men's changing role in the family*. New York: Wiley.

Cowan, P. A. & Cowan, C. P. (in press). The Pie. In J. Touliatos, B. F. Perlmutter, & M. A. Straus (Eds.), *Handbook of Family Measurement Techniques*. Newbury Park: Sage.

Cowan, P. A. & Cowan, C. P. (in press). "Who Does What?" In J. Touliatos, B. F. Perlmutter, M. A. Straus (Eds.), *Handbook of Family Measurement Techniques*. Newbury Park: Sage.

Cowan, P. A., Cowan, C. P., & Heming, G. (1986, April). Risks to the marriage when partners become parents: Implications for family development. Paper presented to American Psychiatry Association, Washington, D.C.

Crouter, A. C. (1984). Spillover from family to work: The neglected side of the work-family interface. *Human Relations, 37*, 425–442.

Derogatis, L. R., Lipman, R. S., & Covi, L. (1973). SCL-90: An outpatient psychiatric rating scale-Preliminary report. *Psychopharmacology Bulletin, 9*, 1–25.

Dohrenwend, B. S., & Dohrenwend., B. F. (Eds.). (1974). *Stressful life events: Their nature and effects*. New York: Wiley.

Duncan, S. W., & Markman, H. J. (1988). Intervention programs for the transition to parenthood: Current status from a preventive perspective. In G. Y. Michaels & W. A. Goldberg. *Transition to parenthood: Current theory and research*. Cambridge, England: Cambridge University Press.

Dyer, E. (1965). Parenthood as crisis: A re-study. *Marriage and Family Living, 25*, 196–201.

Emery, R. E. (1982). Interparental conflict and the children of discord and divorce. *Psychological Bulletin, 92*, 310–330.

Erikson, E. (1950). *Childhood and society*. New York: W. W. Norton.

Falk, F. (1987). *A primer for soft modeling*. Berkeley, Institute of Human Development.

Fein, R. (1976). Men's entrance to parenthood. *Family Coordinator, 25*, 341–348.

Feldman, S. S., & Nash, S. C. (1984). The transition from expectancy to parenthood: Impact of the firstborn child on men and women. *Sex Roles, 11*, 84–96.

Glenn, N. D., & McLanahan, S. (1982). Children and marital happiness: A further specification of the relationship. *Journal of Marriage and the Family, 44*, 63–72.

Goldberg, W. A., & Easterbrooks, M. A. (1984). Role of marital quality in toddler development. *Developmental Psychology, 20*, 504–514.

Gottman, J. M. (1979). *Marital interaction: Experimental investigations*. New York: Academic Press.

Gottman, J. M., & Levinson, R. W. (1988). The social psychophysiology of marriage. In P. Noller & M. A. Fitzpatrick (Eds.), *Perspectives on marital interaction.* San Diego, CA: College Hill Press.

Gottman, J., Markman, H., & Notarius, C. (1977). The topography of marital conflict: A sequential analysis of verbal and nonverbal behavior. *Journal of Marriage and the Family, 39,* 461–477.

Gough, H. G., Fioravanti, M., & Lazzari, R. (1982). Some implications of self versus ideal congruence on the revised adjective check list. *Journal of Consulting Psychology, 44,* 1214–1220.

Gough, H. G., & Heilbrun, A. B., Jr. (1965, 1980). *The adjective check list manual.* Palo Alto: Consulting Psychologists Press.

Grossman, F., Eichler, L., & Winickoff, S. (1980). *Pregnancy, birth, and parenthood.* San Francisco: Jossey-Bass.

Hamilton, J. A. (1962). *Postpartum psychiatric problems.* St. Louis: Mosby.

Harter, S. (1978). *Perceived competence scale for children.* Manual. Colorado seminary: University of Denver.

Heinicke, C. (1984). Impact of prebirth parent personality and marital functioning on family development: A Framework and suggestions for further study. *Developmental Psychology, 20,* 1044–1053.

Heming, G. (1979). *Ideas about parenting. An instrument developed for the Becoming a Family Project.* Department of Psychology, University of California, Berkeley.

Heming, G. (1985). *Predicting adaptation in the transition to parenthood.* Unpublished doctoral dissertation, University of California, Berkeley.

Heming, G. (1987, April). *Predicting adaptation during the transition to parenthood.* Paper presented at the Society for Research in Child Development, Baltimore.

Heming, G., Cowan, P. A., & Cowan, C. P. (in press). Ideas About Parenting. In J. Touliatos, B. F. Perlmutter, & M. A. Straus (Eds.), *Handbook of Family Measurement Techniques.* Newbury Park: Sage.

Hetherington, E. M., & Camara, K. A. (1984). Families in transition: The process of dissolution and reconstitution. In R. D. Parke (Ed.), *Review of child development research: The family* (Vol VII). Chicago: University of Chicago Press.

Hill, R. (Ed.). (1949). *Families under stress.* New York: Harper.

Hobbs, D. F., Jr. (1965). Parenthood as crisis: A third study. *Journal of Marriage and the Family, 27,* 367–372.

Hobbs, D., & Cole, S. (1977). Transition to parenthood: A decade replication. *Journal of Marriage and the Family, 38,* 723–731.

Holmes, T. H., & Rahe, R. H. (1967). The social adjustment rating scale. *Journal of Psychosomatic Research, 11,* 213–218.

Horowitz, M., Schaefer, C., Hiroto, D., Wilner, N., & Levin, B. (1977). Life event questionnaire for measuring presumptive stress. *Psychosomatic Medicine, 39,* 413–431.

Hudson, W. W., & Murphy, G. J. (1980). The non-linear relationship between marital satisfaction and stages of the family life cycle: An artifact of Type I errors? *Journal of Marriage and the Family, 42,* 263–267.

Inhelder, B., & Piaget, J. (1964). *The early growth of logic in the child: Classification and seriation.* New York: Harper and Row.

Ireton, H. R., & Thwing, E. J. (1972). *Minnesota Child Development Inventory Manual.* Minneapolis: Interpretive Scoring Systems.

Jacoby, A. P. (1969). Transition to parenthood: A reassessment. *Journal of Marriage and the Family, 31,* 720–727.

Kumar, R., & Robson, K. M. (1984). A prospective study of emotional disorders in childbearing women. *British Journal of Psychiatry. 144,* 35–47.

Lazarus, R., & Folkman, S. (1984). *Stress, appraisal, and coping.* New York: Springer.

Levenson, R. W., & Gottman, J. M. (1983). Marital interaction: Physiological linkage and affective exchange. *Journal of Personality and Social Psychology, 45,* 587–597.

LeMasters, E. E. (1957). Parenthood as crisis. *Marriage and Family Living, 19,* 352–355.

Locke, H., & Wallace, K. (1959). Short marital adjustment and prediction tests: Their reliability and validity. *Marriage and Family Living, 21,* 251–255.

Main, M., & Goldwyn, R. (1984). Predicting rejection of her infant from mothers' representation of her own experience: Implications for the abused-abusing intergenerational cycle. *Child Abuse and Neglect, 8,* 203–217.

Matas, L., Arend, R. A., & Sroufe, L. A. (1978). Continuity and adaptation in the second year: The relationship between quality of attachment and later competence. *Child Development, 49,* 547–56.

McHale, S. M., & Huston, T. L. (1985). The effect of the transition to parenthood on the marriage relationship. *Journal of Family Issues, 6,* 409–433.

Meyerowitz, J. H., & Feldman, H. (1966). Transition to parenthood. *Psychiatric Research Reports, 4,* 78–84.

Miller, W. B., & Newman, L. F. (Eds.). (1978). *The first child and family formation.* Chapel Hill: Carolina Population Center.

Moos, R. H. (1974). *Family Environment Scale.* Palo Alto: Consulting Psychologists Press, Inc.

O'Donnell, J. P., & Van Tuinen, M. V. (1979). Behavior problems of preschool children: Dimensions and congenital correlates. *Journal of Abnormal Child Psychology, 7,* 61–75.

Parke, R. D., & Tinsley, B. (1982). The early environment of the at-risk infant: Expanding the social context. In D. D. Bricker (Ed.), *Intervention with at-risk and handicapped infants.* Baltimore: University Park Press.

Patterson, G. (1983). Stress: A change agent for family process. In N. Garmezy & M. Rutter (Eds.), *Stress, coping, and development in children* (pp. 235–64). New York: McGraw-Hill.

Piaget, J. (1971). *Genetic epistemology.* New York: W. W. Norton.

Piaget, J., & Inhelder, B. (1967/1948). *The child's conception of space.* New York: Norton.

Pitt, B. (1980). Depression and childbirth. In E. S. Paykel (Ed.), *Handbook of affective disorders.* New York: Guilford Press.

Pratt, M., Kerig, P., Cowan, P. A., & Cowan, C. P. (1988). Mothers and fathers teaching three year-olds: Authoritative Parenting and adult scaffolding of young children's learning. *Developmental Psychology, 24,* No. 6, 832–839.

Radloff, L. (1977). Sex differences in depression: The effects of occupation and marital status. *Sex Roles, 1,* 249–265.

Rapoport, R. (1963). Normal crises, family structure and mental health. *Family Process, 2,* I, March.

Rossi, A. (1968). Transition to parenthood. *Journal of Marriage and the Family, 30,* 26–39.

Russell, C. (1974). Transition to parenthood: Problems and gratifications. *Journal of Marriage and the Family, 36,* 294–302.

Rutter, M. (1983). Stress, coping and development: Some issues and some questions. In N. Garmezy & M. Rutter (Eds.), *Stress, coping and development in children* (pp. 1–42). New York: McGraw-Hill.

Sameroff, A. J., Seifer, R., & Zax, M. (1982). Early development of children at risk for emotional disorder. *Monographs of the Society for Research in Child Development, 47,* (7, Serial No. 199).

Schaefer, E. S. (1983). *Classroom Behavior Inventory.* Unpublished instrument. University of North Carolina at Chapel Hill.

Seers, A., McGee, G. W., Serey, T. T., & Graen, G. B. (1983). The interaction of job stress and social support: A strong inference investigation. *Academy of Management Review, 26,* 273–284.

Shereshefsky, P., & Yarrow. L. J. (Eds.). (1973). *Psychological aspects of a first pregnancy and early postnatal adaptation.* New York: Raven Press.

Sigel, I. E. (Ed.). (1985). *Parental belief systems: The psychological consequences for children.* Hillsdale, NJ: Lawrence Erlbaum Associates.

Sigel, I. E. (1986). Reflections on the belief-behavior connection: Lessons learned from a research program on parental belief systems and teaching strategies. In R. D. Ashmore & D. M. Brodzinsky (Eds.), *Thinking about the family: Views of parents and children* (pp. 35–65). Hillsdale, NJ: Lawrence Erlbaum Associates.

Spanier, G. B. (1976). Measuring dyadic adjustment: New scales for assessing the quality of marriage and similar dyads. *Journal of Marriage and the Family, 38,* 15–28.

Weissman, M. M., & Klerman, G. L. (1977). Sex differences and the epidemiology of depression. *Archives of General Psychiatry, 34,* 98–112.

Wenner, N. K., Cohen, M. B., Weigert, E. V., Kvarnes, R. G., Ohaneson, E. M., & Fearing, J. M. (1969). Emotional problems in pregnancy. *Psychiatry, 32,* 389–410.

White, L. K., & Booth, A. (1985). The transition to parenthood and marital quality. *Journal of Family Issues, 6,* 435–50.

Wold, H. (1982). Systems under indirect observation using PLS. In C. Fornell (Ed.), *A second generation of multivariate analysis,* (pp. 325–347). New York: Praeger.

Yalom, I. D., Lunde, D. T., Moos, R. H., & Hamburg, D. A. (1968). "Postpartum blues" syndrome. *Archives of General Psychiatry. 18,* 17–27.

2 Parental Beliefs within the Family Context: Development of a Research Program

Ann V. McGillicuddy-De Lisi
Lafayette College

This book was initially described to me as a collection of autobiographies of a research idea. Autobiographies are most appealing when they include personal letters and pictures that depict the life of the central character. There was no diary, no photo album and no collection of yellowed letters tied with a ribbon that could be used to illustrate the life of this research program on parental beliefs, so I decided to create some of these personal momentos. Figures depicting the size and shape of the project at various stages of development are included to show both continuities and discontinuities in the development of the project. I also created an imaginary correspondence with several writers who influenced the evolution of my ideas about what beliefs are, what function they serve for parents, the nature of their impact on children, and ways to assess and analyze these beliefs within the context of a family system framework. These letters and figures are my own constructions, formed from an application of the work of these writers to the domain of parental beliefs. The goal of this fictional dialogue with influential psychologists is to present the underpinnings of this research program within its theoretical and chronological context, rather than to provide a veridical account of the individual's own writings.

Institute for Research in Child Development
Educational Testing Service
Princeton, NJ 08541

Dear Dr. McGillicuddy-De Lisi,

Jim Johnson and I each enjoyed our meetings with you last month. I think that our interests coincide with your own research interests. It appears that the position we anticipated is indeed becoming a reality. The purpose of this letter is to formally offer this position to you.

I would like to review some of the events that led to this opening and provide an overview of the research project you will be directing if you accept the position. Jim and I had written a grant proposal to study the effects of family size, birth spacing and birth order on the development of children's representational competence. It didn't look like it was going to funded and Jim is on postdoctoral funds that run out soon, so he accepted a faculty position at the University of Wisconsin. Then the Office of Population Research funded the project for two years (NICHD Grant R01 HD 10686). I am already overextended in the practical and empirical aspects of running an experimental nursery school. We therefore need someone to direct this two-year research project.

You will recall that the proposal was pretty straightforward. As you are aware, it has been reported that children from larger families with less time between births do not perform as well as children from smaller families with greater birth spacing on many tests (Zajonc & Markus, 1975). We think that this is because parents in these two types of families treat their children differently. The research you will be conducting will describe exactly how these parents in different family constellations differ from one another in the ways they teach and manage their children. The ideas about ways parents might teach their children differently as a result of family constellation are derived from the distancing model (Sigel, 1971).

Parental distancing strategies, which are defined largely as inquiry strategies at this point, require time and patience in comparison to didactic teaching approaches. Parents with lots of young children, closely spaced in age and therefore placing similar demands upon the parents in the types and amounts of attention they demand, are less able to use these inquiry-based distancing strategies than parents with an only child or parents with children who vary greatly in age as a result of birth spacing. Parents with an only child or with large differences in the ages of the children do not have as many demands to deal with regarding the children. As a result, they are free, in a sense, to ask their children lots of questions and gradually guide the children to discover answers for themselves rather than provide them with information in a more efficacious and directive manner.

These distancing strategies have been theoretically linked to children's abilities to reconstruct past events, anticipate outcomes and attend to transformations of phenomena. There is an experimental nursery school at ETS that is not be directly related to this project, but it is based on distancing theory too. The children who have been assigned to teachers who have been trained to use distancing strategies perform better on tests of these abilities at the end of the year. Relating this to a family rather than school environment, we reason that if some parents spontaneously use these strategies on a day-to-day basis with their children, then their children should have developed these abilities, called representational abilities, to a greater degree than children of parents who don't use these distancing strategies.

We hope that you will accept this position, which will involve nearly all aspects of directing the project. We need to get underway as soon as possible because some measures need to be developed, others must be refined and a research staff formed.

I would appreciate an answer within a week. If you have any questions, please let me know.

Sincerely,

Irving E. Sigel, Ph.D.
Senior Research Scientist

THE FIRST FAMILY PROJECT: EFFECTS OF FAMILY CONSTELLATION

Initial Research Goals and Design.   A nice design had been constructed by Jim Johnson and Irv Sigel in which parents from three different family constellations would be interviewed about their childrearing strategies and observed teaching their children. The children would be assessed using a series of representational ability tasks, some of which had been used with the nursery school population at ETS. The focus of the research at this point was observation of parent-child dyads in teaching situations and assessment of children's abilities. We hoped to demonstrate that a relationship existed between the parents' behavior in the laboratory teaching situation and the children's performance on an independent assessment of representational ability. The idea was that parents who evidenced a distancing style in the lab were more likely to have exposed their children to these strategies at home, thus facilitating the development of representational competence in their children. The purpose of the interview was to demonstrate that parents with larger, more closely spaced families felt constrained in the types of teaching strategies they used. We planned to ask them what they thought they should do in certain hypothetical situations with a child, and what they would really do, and why. Thus, an interview was originally included to provide information confirming the notion of practical constraints on parents with varying family constellations.

Development of Parental Interview: The Discovery of Parental Beliefs

Jim Johnson had begun developing an interview to assess childrearing strategies parents preferred, and constraints that affected whether they used those strategies or not. This interview originally consisted of 20 vignettes involving a parent and a child engaged in a critical incident. The initial measure required parents to rank each of nine options as best to worst ways to handle each situation. Next, parents were interviewed. For each vignette, they were asked to describe the best way to handle the situation and what they would hope to accomplish with that strategy.

Parents were then asked what they might really do in such a situation with their own child, and why. Finally, the parent was asked what they would do if their initial strategy failed to resolve the situation, and rationales regarding their choice were again elicited. These pilot studies revealed two surprising findings. First, parents didn't do what they said they would. It's difficult to believe now that we were surprised, but we had attributed earlier reports of failures to find a link between parental reports and observations of behavior to poor measures and lack of a theoretical framework for classifying behaviors (cf. Fishbein & Ajzen, 1975; Shaefer, 1971). The second finding that surprised us was that parents with all types of families gave lots of different reasons for their behaviors, but these reasons seemed to stem from their view of what children are like, and what makes them change, rather than practical considerations directly tied to family constellation and pressures on the parents.

We were not happy. We were "ready" to run subjects! Advertisements had been placed in the newspaper soliciting volunteer families. Ten thousand fliers had been distributed through local labor unions, pediatricians offices, apartment rental offices and library reading hours in an attempt to find 120 children with little or no preschool experience so we could be sure that the parents, and not "outside influences," were primarily responsible for their children's intellectual development. And we were back at the drawing board with respect to this interview.

At an informal gathering at ETS, we were bemoaning the lack of reliability and validity of parent measures when Walter Emmerich, the Director of the Child Development Institute at ETS at the time, commiserated with us. He noted that parental reports probably correspond with their behaviors when the setting of the behavioral observation directly corresponds to the hypothetical situation, in every minute detail, that is posed to the parent as a stimulus for the self-report.

That was such a depressing thought. How could one ever conduct any (ecologically) valid research with a constraint like that? One would have to use a "stooge" as the child, and ensure that the actor behave in exact accordance with the interview items, or else the interview would need to take place after the behavioral interaction, replicating the events observed during the interpersonal interaction with the interview. Or each subject would be exposed to different conditions. Finally, this notion of creating interview and observational assessments that presented extremely similar contexts was simply rejected. Parents are viewed as mere respondents to stimuli within such an approach, and the pilot interviews indicated rich interplays of parental cognitions about development and attributions about children behavior. It was an in depth analysis of these interviews that led us to become more general and to increase the range of contexts of development that we would assess, rather than become more specific in our assessment of the reasons for parents' behaviors.

Eventually we came to see the reasons given by parents as beliefs, constructed by the parents out of their experiences as children being parented and their experiences as parents, as well as other life experiences. This conceptualization led to more questions and complex issues concerning the nature of parents' cognitions, the nature of the relationship to parental childrearing practices, the factors that influence parental beliefs, the translation of these beliefs into childrearing practices, and the processes through which these beliefs affect the child. These became the major conceptual issues of my next 10 years of research on the family and are the subject of the remainder of this chapter.

IDEAS ABOUT BELIEFS AND BELIEFS ABOUT IDEAS: A REFORMULATION OF EFFECTS OF FAMILY CONSTELLATION

Within the model of the effects of family constellation on children that we were developing, it was assumed that these ideas that parents held about children were going to act as mediating factors between descriptive characteristics of the family and parental teaching behaviors. Beliefs about children were seen, rather globally, as a source of parental childrearing practices and as the result of experiences with children. A constructivist perspective was particularly appealing. This was in part due to the nature of my graduate training, which has since been described to me as "Orthodox Piaget." It is indeed difficult to imagine children who have constructed logical operations, number, movement and speed, time, etc., growing into adults who no longer organize their experiences and engage in reflective abstraction! It seemed sensible to think of parents, when faced with the task of teaching and managing their children, to be very practical and create some type of approach that made sense to the individual parent, and that fit with their everyday experience with the child and what they were trying to accomplish. In 1978 very few developmental researchers were writing and conducting studies from the perspective of parents as thinking, organizing individuals with a set of cognitions guiding their childrearing practices. We turned to social and personality psychology for ideas about beliefs. Our conceptualization was influenced by Harvey, Hunt, and Schroder's (1961) conceptual systems, Heider's (1958) beliefs, Kelley's (1972) attributions, Weiner's feedback (1979), Kohn's (1969) values and Kelly's (1955) personal constructs. Irv Sigel (1986) has written that he was influenced by Polanyi (1958), Pepper (1967) and Scheibe (1970) in an account of reflections on the belief-behavior connection. Because my discussions with Irv influenced my own thinking, these authors indirectly affected the conceptualizations of beliefs that eventually became incorporated into the research project to follow.

    None of these perspectives alone quite captures the essence of what we meant by parental "constructions of the child." We began the process of defining these beliefs, as we came to call them, with a two pronged attack. First, we attempted to differentiate our view of beliefs from each of the theoretical systems noted above, thinking that we would end up with a distillate that held certain features in common with each approach, but was not really identical with any single orientation. For example, we tried to describe how our notion of beliefs was different from and similar to a value or an attribution.

January 5, 1979

Dear Dr. Kohn,

I am very interested in your focus on the goals of parents, as opposed to the strategies that parents say they will or actually do implement. This is appealing because I agree that there doesn't have to be a direct one-to-one correspondence between what parents think and what parents do. That is, there are probably lots of different ways that a value, or in the case of our own research, beliefs, can be expressed in behavior during a parent-child interaction.

I do have trouble developing some ideas about the process through which these parental ideas are translated into parenting strategies. In addition, I think that it is important to link these ideas to outcomes in the child in some manner. That is, the values are important because they ultimately affect the child. I am interested in how you think that these values impact the child, although I am aware that you do not focus directly on child outcomes. Since you are also not interested in assessing specific behaviors during parent-child interactions, can I assume that you think that values can be transmitted and have an impact in more subtle ways, or that the effect is not contained in a single isolated behavior, but in a pattern over time?

I wonder how these values differ, theoretically and practically, from beliefs about what children are like and how they develop. Do beliefs form the basis for values or vice versa? Or does each system affect the other directly? Is it possible that values and beliefs arise and develop independently from one another? Could it be that values have some affective component that charges them, while beliefs are somewhat more cognitive, or philosophical, and removed from the everyday life of the individual in a sense that is not true with values? Values, as you write about them, seem to have their origin, or are at least intertwined with, the daily life, goals and salient events of the person's life. In addition, values seem to be more closely related to what the parent wants the child to end up with, while beliefs are focused on how the child gets from one level to another. If these distinctions are real, what are the implications for the impact of values and beliefs on the individual's life, on the interactions of others with whom that individual shares a major part of daily living and what is the relationship of values to beliefs?

I enjoy reading your ideas and have found your work helpful in formulating my own notions about what parents think and why they differ from one another. We expect that beliefs will vary with the educational background and occupational status of the parents in our own research. In part this prediction has been affected by your work on social class differences in values, although we are not focused directly on issues like conformity.

Sincerely,
Ann V. McGillicuddy-De Lisi

As the imaginary correspondence indicates, this view of beliefs is in direct contradiction with Rokeach's (1968) position that attitudes and values can be interpreted as beliefs. Our early attempts to define beliefs asserted that

> It must be noted that a belief system differs from attitudes and from attribution systems . . . it is not limited to a single object nor is it defined as a predisposition to act . . . (and does not) emphasize inferences of cause-effect. . . . to a particular class of events or singular outcomes. (McGillicuddy-De Lisi et al., 1979, pp. 93–94)

In this process we tried to tackle the question of how beliefs, as we conceived them, were related to attributions, values, etc. For example, beliefs were viewed as general cognitive constructs that parents held to be true. Attributions, values, and attitudes stemmed from these beliefs, and perhaps affect the translation of a belief into a particular behavior in a particular situation or in response to a child behavior. We spent considerable time discussing issues such as whether there was an affective component to beliefs and whether beliefs were formed after a behavior occurred or the belief existed first, with the behavior stemming from the belief. Most of the questions we asked within this approach to definitions could not be addressed with a research methodology, but we felt that it was necessary to clarify such relationships within our own minds before making predictions about how these ideas called beliefs operated within the social context of the family. And of course, we were enjoying this process of working out an approach to parental cognitions that was free of the constraints imposed by the scientific method.

Models of the Role of Beliefs within the Family. There was a research project to conduct that had posed specific questions which had to be answered, however. As a result, a second approach to defining beliefs within the context of the family was under way at the same time as the more theoretical discussions and open-ended interviews were conducted. This approach involved a description of the manner in which beliefs might operate within the context of the family. This was quite different from the more philosophical questions we were asking in our discussions of ''What is a belief?'' but I am certain that these two approaches to definition affected each other. The second approach consisted largely of drawing diagrams depicting relationships and processes within the family, some of which are reproduced in Figs. 2.1–2.4. The focus of these diagrams was to explain the variability in parental practices that occurs with descriptive characteristics of the family such as number of children, and to depict the process of influence between parent and child.

We began with the notion that beliefs were a source of the parent's childrearing practices, as is depicted in Fig. 2.1. If attributions, values, beliefs and/or personal constructs could be used to explain the nature of adults' social interac-

FIG. 2.1.   The role of parental
beliefs in childrearing.

tions with other adults, it seemed reasonable to propose that the same processes
operate with respect to social interactions between adults and children. As a
result of these considerations, we began to incorporate beliefs into the distancing
model we were trying to test, assuming that certain beliefs were the source of
parental teaching strategies such as distancing behaviors. These teaching behaviors, in turn, were postulated to influence the course of the child's cognitive
development through the stimulation of representational thought.

Before attempting to delineate the nature of the belief-behavior process more
fully, we turned to the question of the origins of beliefs. As already indicated, the
constructivist perspective had a particular theoretical appeal because the parent
was viewed as actively building and modifying ideas about children and development on the basis of information from experience. The notion of beliefs about
children began to form within Kelly's theory of constructive alternativism.

Dear George,

Your last letter certainly gave me a lot to think about. Following your suggestion, I have been rereading *The Psychology of Personal Constructs* (Kelly,
1955) recently. If I understand what you are saying, people create ideas (constructs) about other people, interpersonal interactions and maybe even the world on
the basis of their interactions with people. The constructs that an individual holds to
be true at any moment must therefore be a reflection of the experiences that the
individual has had and the way that she has organized those experiences.

These personal constructs are used to forecast events and behaviors of others,
and actual results are compared to those predictions and constructs. This gives your
system somewhat of a developmental flavor, in my construction of it, since the
constructs and the organization are open to change as experiences that are discre-
pent with prior predictions are encountered. I would like to know what determines
how open these constructs are to change. Are there individual differences in the
permeability of these constructs, and if so, what is the source of these variations in
openness to change?

In addition, you have described these personal constructs as being psychologically consistent with one another, as opposed to logically consistent. I am not sure
exactly what this means, what the implications are for trying to classify people as
fitting a particular theoretical framework, and how the personal constructs are
interrelated within a larger organization of beliefs. But it is an appealing idea. The
parents we have been talking with seem to have some beliefs that are in logical

opposition to other beliefs, and they seem to have no difficulty holding these contradictory ideas simultaneously.

Do you think that systems of cognitions about the world are idiosyncratic? I don't. But I think they must be individualistic and this is what you mean by *personal* construct. What is it that prevents them from being idiosyncratic and removed from a "reality" that is shared by individuals? Piaget used the notion of logical necessity for children's constructions of reality, but this does not seem suitable for personal constructs. Can we find some kind of structure underlying the different personal constructs that people create to predict and interpret events around them? Do these structures differ across individuals or are there constraints that we are not addressing?

I think that we can view the parent as a theorist who tests the results of her behaviors against the predictions based on beliefs about what children are like, and, most importantly, the beliefs might be challenged as a result of disconfirmation. What types of experiences could form the basis for the construction and subsequent modifications of these beliefs? This is a very important question for a study of the effects of family constellation, because a parent's experience with children could provide the content from which the beliefs are built. For example, a person who has had experience parenting three children has had different opportunities to try out different strategies and note the results, as compared with a parent of an only child. In addition, the parent with three children has already parented the oldest child through the preschool years and has had the opportunity to see subsequent developmental stages and outcomes, as compared to the parent of an only child. Differences between mothers and fathers, between people with different educational levels, between people with experience parenting more versus fewer children are some of the factors that could be considered within this view of beliefs.

You have been very helpful in our effort to conceptualize the ways parents regard their children and why parents from different families might be different from one another. I hope some of these ideas make sense to you.

Sincerely,

Ann

Figure 2.2 presents some of the additions to the model that resulted as parents in our pilot program told us why they would behave in certain ways and where their ideas about children came from. A multitude of experiences could affect the nature and content of parental beliefs. Some of the factors that we considered were the parent's experience as a child in a family, ideas and childrearing strategies of friends, feedback from schools about their own child, the teacher models that they were exposed to as students, the types of books and television programs that they used and expert advice, such as books and meetings with pediatricians, educators, etc. In addition, many factors within the family seemed important, such as observations of their own children, the beliefs of their spouses

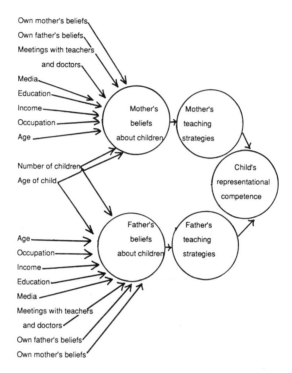

FIG. 2.2.   Sources and effects of beliefs.

and the beliefs of their parents and in-laws. As can be noted in Fig. 2.2, this complicated the left side of the model depicted in Fig. 2.1 to a great degree.

This consideration of sources of beliefs led us to posit mutual influences between parent and child, since the behavior and ability of the child could be viewed both as affecting the nature of the parent's beliefs and as being affected by the parent's childrearing practices (see Fig. 2.3). This bidirectional influence would lead to great difficulty in testing the model, and we were not sure how much of the model we would be able to test. Once we began to conceptualize the family as a system of mutual influences (McGillicuddy-De Lisi, 1980) in which the child is a source of parental beliefs and is affected by parental practices, it was necessary to consider alternative ways in which family members could influence one another. We were influenced by Bell's (1968) writings concerning children's impact on parents at this point and by Rubin Hill's (Hill & Mattlessich, 1979) view of developing families (see Fig. 2.3).

We decided to create a model of a family frozen for a moment in time, although we conceived of the family as a dynamic and developing entity as family members and their relationship mature and change. But at this point, our

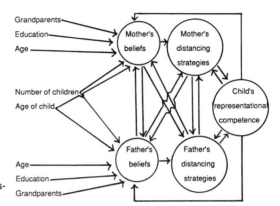

FIG. 2.3. The family as a system of mutual influences.

aim was to seek ways to analyze parts of the model after decisions were made about what to measure. For example, we thought that the beliefs of the parents of the mothers and fathers (i.e., the grandparents of the target children) we were studying were an important source of the parent's beliefs (see Fig. 2.3). But it would be impractical to try to assess those "grandparental" beliefs. On the other hand, the interest in the manner in which family members influence one another led us to the literature on family systems, and ultimately caused us to include observations of the parents with older children in the family as well as with the target child. Although the theoretical formulations in this area were based on studies of special populations, such as families of alcoholics and schizophrenics (e.g., Bowen, 1978; Minuchin, 1974; Satir, 1964), many of the concepts of family interaction and the notion of the relationship between members of the family affecting interactions with other members of the family influenced our model. For example, the interactions of the mother with the oldest child could be an important source of her beliefs about children. Such a possibility is depicted in Fig. 2.4. These beliefs, formed on the basis of interactions with the first child, are then the source of her interactions with her secondborn child. The resulting interactions with the secondborn child could lead to further modifications of her beliefs, which would impact the interactions she has with her firstborn and her secondborn children. Another instance of the manner in which one relationship affects others in the family might occur if the father observes the manner in which the mother handles a situation in which she is teaching the child a concept or a social norm. If the mother's behavior is discrepant with strategies that are be generated by the father's beliefs, his beliefs and subsequent behavior with the child, and with others in the family, will be altered. Thus, there are several processes through which beliefs operate within the family system to produce an effect on the nature of interactions between family members.

At this point, we had some ideas about the ways we thought that beliefs

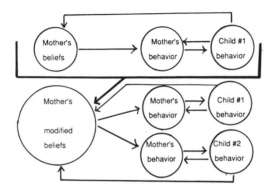

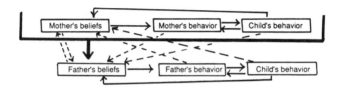

FIG. 2.4.   Sources of beliefs within the family.

operate within the family. The next task was to develop a way of assessing those beliefs that was consistent with our formulation of beliefs as a construction of the child.

ASSESSMENT OF BELIEFS

June 1, 1978

Dear Jim,

I think that we made the right decision in focusing on the content of beliefs in terms of processes of development, rather than use the ''This I Believe'' or the ''Role Construct Repertory'' tests. I am not completely happy with the way that we decided to assess beliefs and the manner in which they are theoretically tied to parental behaviors, though. If I had known that Schaefer and Edgerton (1986) were developing a scale that measured childrearing and education beliefs, that would have been a good possibility for use in our own project. It looks somewhat similar to what we are after in terms of the type of beliefs in processes of change that occur in children.

There are three other areas in which we made the right choices, too, I think. The first two relate to the observations and the third to beliefs. First, my confidence in the results of the study will be much higher as a result of including laboratory observations of parental teaching behaviors during two different tasks. If we have missed the boat with these ideas about how beliefs operate within the context of the family or if we have not assessed them in the best manner, at least there should be a relationship between observed behaviors of parents and children's representational thinking scores. Hopefully, we will at least be able to describe how these families are different from one another in terms of teaching strategies or styles of parents. The use of two different tasks should provide us with some information concerning the interplay of task demands or context on the belief-behavior connection and the way situational factors influence parental teaching.

Second, we have stacked the deck against ourselves, in a sense, by trying to tie the parents' behaviors to child outcomes that are assessed independently rather than during the parent-child interaction. I like taking this conservative approach. Barring a genetic link in intelligence (which we are not able to address), any relationship between parental behaviors and child outcomes that is obtained should be due to the history of the child's experience with the parent, rather than to a particular behavior that worked on this particular day in this particular setting with one particular task.

I was torn, as you know, about the issue of the lab versus more natural settings for the observations, but I think the lab was the best choice for this project. We get so much variability among parents and I do think, now, that even the accomodations that the parents make to the laboratory setting reflect some aspect of their parenting style, as well as reflect beliefs. And without the control over the task and situation I would be more wary of the findings. Some comparison of laboratory and home observations under a variety of conditions must be done, though. Inspection of the observational data already reveal great differences in parental teaching strategies across the paperfolding and story tasks, which has converted me to a belief in the salience of the context in determining parent behaviors. I must write to Roxanne Croft et al. (1976) and thank her for showing us her paperfolding procedure. It's giving us some great data.

Third, I think we made the right choice with the interview format for assessment of parental beliefs about child development states and processes (the "construction of the child" interview). Sameroff gave us some good advice when he wrote about the difficulty of creating questionnaires highly specific to behaviors (Sameroff et al., 1982). Conducting and scoring the interviews is really a pain in the neck, though. It takes so long to get the data, and then about three times longer to score it from the audiotapes. But without the tapes we missed an awful lot of the developmental processes parents talked about. For example, parents don't come right out and say that children learn through positive reinforcement. Instead they say that the consequences that followed a particular behavior lead the child to try that behavior again. Plus, we have to do periodic interrater reliability checks to make sure that we are all still in agreement about the definition of each construct. But the information seems so rich, as compared to a simpler "check off" method that is supposed to indicate what the parent thinks about the nature of childhood and development.

The responses that parents give us over the variety of teaching, social and discipline domains seem too "eclectic" to try to fit them into theories as

Sutherland (1983) is doing or into stages that vary in complexity of thought as Sameroff and Feil (1983) are working on now, but we do seem to be getting something more general, more philosophical, than an expectation or a childrearing goal. This is important if we are going to address the issue of where these beliefs come from and why parents change. I want to develop some ideas concerning how these beliefs about children exist within a larger system of "models of humanity" or even what the universe is like. The single major problem with our current assessment is that the beliefs in each developmental construct are assessed separately from one another. Our conceptualization definitely leans more towards a systems approach. The assessment doesn't match that level. Hopefully, we can use some statistical procedure like factor analysis to look for some properties of systems or interrelationships.

In some ways I think that the study of parents' cognitions is important in it's own right. For example, we should know how parents think and organize their world, why (and if) they change—all the developmental questions. But when I put on my "family research" hat, I ask what difference do all these parental beliefs make unless there is some tie to the overt behavior, or some way to link these beliefs to outcomes in the child. Like family law, in some ways our focus must ultimately be upon what is good for the child.

I hope that we get the money to do the new analyses that will address some of the questions about the linkages among parental cognitions, behaviors and child outcomes. I have so many questions to ask of these data now that they are collected. But I'll write more about that as the data are analyzed.

I hope that the winters are still enjoyable. Say hello to the family. I was so happy to hear that entry into parenthood is not a crisis after all, at least in your case. We are getting pretty excited about the imminent arrival of our own firstborn. Somehow it is not real, yet, in spite of the fact that this huge balloon precedes my entry into the room, by several seconds now!

Ann

Although there was some work on beliefs, constructs, values, and attributions in the literature when we began collecting data in 1977, none of the measures that we examined (ranging from the "This I Believe Test" to Likert-type causal attributions of performance) captured the essence of beliefs about developmental processes that we felt were a major source of parenting strategies. Since we had discovered these notions of parent's beliefs in the course of interviews, we decided to construct our measure of beliefs from the protocols of the parents of children enrolled in the nursery school program at ETS.

You may recall that the original interview was designed to get parents to tell us what strategy they thought a parent should use (the answer was clear to us. . . . Distancing!), what they would really do, with all the constraints of their own family, and what they would try next if that failed. These interviews began with 20 vignettes that presented a child and parent interacting over a critical incident, such as wondering if a cereal spoon would float in the bathtub. During the pilot testing, the interviews were extremely open-ended and that's when parents told us about their ideas concerning where children's knowledge of principles like flotation comes from. We listened to these audiotapes and transcribed parents' descriptions of these processes. We asked research assistants from other projects to group the protocols that described similar processes. Then four research associates assigned to this project labeled and defined those 47 groups of processes that were created by the research assistants. These labels, definitions and examples of actual protocols were compiled into a scoring manual. It was a lengthy process. This practice of working backwards from parent data to create stimulus items and a scoring system for use with later samples worked well in spite of the large investment of time and pilot testing. The process of finding the definitions within actual protocols improved the system's validity and applicability to other data sets in the long run.

Of course, we knew that we could not count on obtaining such rich protocols as a matter of course from an open-ended discussion of floating spoons, thrown blocks, and other incidents that were raised in the parent discussions, so a series of 22 probes that focused on issues that had been raised during these pilot interviews were devised and inserted into the interviews. The interviews presented 12 vignettes selected from the original twenty items that had been used in pilot testing. The final procedure involved discussion of what parents thought was the best way to handle each situation first (which was *not* considered part of the assessment of the parents' beliefs, i.e., their "construction of the child," but rather an assessment of strategy preferences), followed by a few questions designed to tap beliefs about developmental states and processes. These probes were pilot tested on a group of parents who varied in education and income level to ensure that a wide range of responses that fit our coding categories would be obtained with the new structured format and a more heterogeneous group of parents. We found that parents were more comfortable answering questions about children's acquisition of knowledge and skills when these questions were tied in some way to a specific incident such as those presented in the hypothetical situations. We also felt that this gave all the parents the same stimulus base to respond to, increasing our control over the experience of the subjects more than an unstructured interview would have allowed.

Each reference that a parent made to one of the 47 constructs was coded on a 3-point intensity scale and these scores were summed across the 22 probes. This scoring system yielded interval data which was desirable in relation to the range and power of statistical analyses to be applied to the data. There was serious consideration given to categorizing parents into theoretical perspectives based on the patterns of references to constructs. This was especially appealing in a few cases where the parents' protocols could have been translations of writings of Skinner, Gesell, or Piaget for a popular magazine. But we encountered some difficulties with this procedure early during the scoring process because many parents would refer to diverse processes such as positive reinforcement, abstraction, and modeling to explain different phenomena. These types of patterns are what led to theoretical questions regarding how the constructs might be interrelated so as to be psychologically consistent with one another, as well as issues concerning the origins of such beliefs and their relationship to context, values, attributions and some aspects of personality that might be related to openness of the beliefs to change. Finally, the practical consideration of using interval versus categorical data and the difficulty of classification led to the decision to use frequency scores assigned to individual constructs.

This created a new problem in that the data set for this project was tremendous. Each of 240 parents had been assigned scores for 47 belief variables, over 100 frequency scores pertaining to references to preferred communication strategies, childrearing goals, constraints (we had not completely abandoned our initial hypotheses!) and childrearing orientation gleened from the interview involving the 12 vignettes, and another 100 frequency scores for both verbal and nonverbal behaviors observed during each of two parent-child interactions. There was another corpus of data pertaining to the children's performance on the seven assessments of representational competence. The first thing we did was try to reduce our data base! Descriptive and correlational analyses led us to drop or combine many of the original 47 belief variables into 16. For some analyses, we reduced the data base further by using principal component scores. Next, the problem of data analysis.

DATA ANALYSIS

A summary of the design is presented in Table 2.1. There were some minor problems with this design. For example, the three family constellation groups

TABLE 2.1
Design of the First Family Research Project

	Number of Families in Each Group Family Constellation[1]		
	One-Child	Three Children	
Social Class[2]		Near Spacing	Far Spacing[3]
Working Class	20	20	20
Middle Class	20	20	20

[1]The target child was a 3-4 year old child in all families and was secondborn in the 3-child families. Half of the target children in each group were boys and half were girls.
[2]Defined by education and income level of parents.
[3]Near Spacing = fewer than 3 years birth spacing between the firstborn and secondborn; Far Spacing = greater than 3 years birth spacing.

consisted of a one-child family and three-child families in which the target child was the secondborn. This did not allow for a comparison of only children with firstborn or lastborns, controlling for age. The decision about family constellation groups was based on the consideration that social class had been frequently found in interaction effects with family constellation (see Marjoribanks, 1979). Thus, it was very important to include some SES indicator in the design. Second, the confluence model proposed by Zajonc and Markus (1975) was making a big splash in the family constellation literature (and rightfully so, looking at the fit between predictions and subsequent SAT scores). Zajonc (1976) was quite clear about the importance of birth interval in creating different intellectual environments that affect the developing child. Thus, it was critical to include a comparison of families that varied in this area while other aspects, such as educational level of the parents, sex and age of the children were controlled through sampling if we were to describe exactly what was going on in families that affect the intellectual status of the children. It was a Herculean task to identify 120 families with children who did not go to preschool programs, with mothers who did not work outside of the home and who varied in educational level of the parents and in sex, spacing, and birth order of the children in exactly the manner required by this design. Inclusion of first and lastborns was therefore not possible. On the whole, the design was a good one, and we used variations of it in subsequent studies which will be described later in the chapter.

Given the research design, certain analyses were obvious. The original proposed research involved relatively simple comparisons of the groups on the relevant factors. Not surprisingly, social class was related to almost everything, even when amount of parental verbalization was covaried. The family constellation factors were somewhat disappointing, but there were some relationships between family size and parents' and children's behaviors (see Sigel, 1982). We conducted a series of regression analyses in which we forced descriptive characteristics into the analyses first, then allowed belief scores to enter. This was an effort to establish whether the belief scores could predict parent teaching behaviors above and beyond what was associated with factors like social class and number of children. The results were promising, although the pattern appears to differ for mothers and fathers (McGillicuddy-De Lisi, 1982a).

But in our minds, the research project had become transformed. We wanted to know how each of the family members influenced one another and how these beliefs worked into the picture of family members influencing one in the manner depicted in Figs. 2.1 through 2.4.

We wrote a new grant proposal that focused on these issues and we were fortunate to receive new funding from NICHD to pursue these questions regarding the interrelationships among family constellation factors, parental beliefs, parental behaviors and child outcomes. The most exciting project we undertook was a path analysis of the model depicted in Fig. 2.5 (McGillicuddy-De Lisi, 1982b).

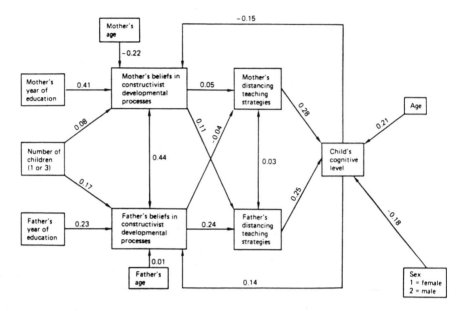

FIG. 2.5.   Results of path analysis of family influences. Reprinted with permission from McGillicuddy-DeLisi (1982). Parental beliefs about developmental processes. *Human Development, 25,* 192–200. Reproduced by permission S. Karger/A. G. Basel.

April 22, 1980

Dear Dr. McGillicuddy-De Lisi,

I received your inquiry and the path model which you sent upon Don Rock's suggestion. I will advise you first and foremost that it is prudent to make predictions concerning causality on the basis of a theory. If you base your approach on an a priori substantive model based on the interpretation of distancing theory (and the temporal nature of the measures, i.e., the mother's education preceded and is likely to have affected her beliefs about children rather than vice versa), the final model of family influences will be more likely to yield interpretable results than a model based on strictly exploratory procedures designed to meet statistical criteria, such as stepwise regressions. In the same vein, it is easy to be seduced into using models that are created with a specific sample by fitting variables and equations to the data according to the usual least squares statistical criteria. While the results of one analysis might be stronger with the latter approach, the liklihood of replicating the results with subsequent data sets will be higher with a model posed on a substantiative and/or logical basis.

If I understand correctly, you have created a nonrecusive model. It is true that reciprocal influences are most often found in real life phenomena. It is, of course, difficult to tease apart bidirectional influences, especially with nonexperimental data. The fact that estimation procedures become more complicated for feedback loops such as the one posited between children's intellectual level and mothers' beliefs should not lead researchers such as yourself to ignore the possibility of such real-life situations.

One of the problems in estimating nonrecursive models in which a mother affects the child's development and the child's ability, in turn, influences what the mother does when interacting with her child, is that the models tend to be underidentified and no unique solution can be found as a result. The simplest way to think of this is to consider a variable that affects parental beliefs but not children's representational scores and a variable that is primarily linked to children's ability, but not to parental beliefs.

Unknown path coefficients can be estimated using either the two stage least squares procedures or the full information maximum liklihood procedure. While I was at ETS I developed both the theory and the numerical techniques for an efficient solution to the latter model. You are fortunate that Don Rock is assisting you because he has had extensive experience in the application of such procedures.

Good luck with your research. I am glad that Don talked you into simplifying the model. I had heard that he wallpapered his office with the path model that had been developed during the course of this research project (only kidding!)

If you ever come to Europe, look me up. I hope everyone at ETS is doing well and working hard with the LISREL model.

Sincerely,

K. Jöreskog
(see Jöreskog, 1973; Jöreskog & Van Thillo, 1972)

As the results of the path analysis indicated, some of the hypotheses concerning the origins and the relationships within the family were not supported (McGillicuddy-De Lisi, 1982b). While many of the results were consistent with predictions, it is these unexpected results which led to new questions and subsequent research. For example, the relationship between beliefs in constructivist developmental processes were related to distancing behaviors in fathers, but not in mothers. Mothers' distancing behaviors, but not the teaching behaviors of fathers, were related to children's representational abilities. Education was an important predictor of beliefs for mothers and for fathers, but the relationship was much stronger for mothers. Number of children in the family, which represented experience as a parent in my view, was related to beliefs about child development processes for fathers but not for mothers. Age of the parent was important in predicting the mother's beliefs, but not the fathers.

There were several questions to be addressed with subsequent research. Why did the descriptive characteristics that we had proposed as an effect on beliefs differ for mothers and for fathers? Are beliefs constructed out of experiences, and if so, what are the factors that affect how these beliefs are modified? Why did the belief-behavior patterns differ for mothers and fathers? How do these beliefs come to be grouped? These questions address three issues: Where do beliefs come from, what happens to them throughout the parenting years, and what factors influence the translation of beliefs into behaviors.

THE ORIGINS OF BELIEFS AND CHANGES IN BELIEFS: A CONSTRUCTIVIST MODEL

It appeared that experiences of the mother before parenting (e.g., age and educa-tion) were important in determining her beliefs about child development, but experience as a parent was important for the father, as indicated by the rela-tionship between number of children and beliefs. Perhaps this pattern is a result of socialization factors. That is, females may think about children, parenthood and be focused upon developmental issues as they pass though their own devel-opmental phases prior to parenthood. The socialization of males may not include these aspects of adult roles until after parenthood is achieved. Or some uniden-tified factor may influence males to develop belief systems that are more open to modification as a result of experience obtained during parenting. Or the experi-ences that give rise to change may simply differ for males and females because the nature of their adult experiences differ. That is, women may talk about children more than men do. Men may talk about how to learn on the job more than women do. Thus, the origins of beliefs about children may differ in timing and/or in the types of experience that provide the structure of the belief system.

The different pattern of relationships between beliefs and behaviors obtained for fathers and mothers cannot be as readily explained by different socialization experiences or different forms of the beliefs, however. We feared that this pattern was due to the nature of our sample. The families consisted of mothers who did not work outside of the home and who were the primary caregivers for their children. These children attended preschool and/or playgroups less than 10 hours per week. As a result, the 120 mothers we studied had extensive and intensive knowledge of their individual children. Fathers were the breadwinners and had considerably less experience with their children. These characteristics of the family may have produced the different pattern of results with respect to belief-behavior relationships. In the absence of detailed knowledge about their own child's ability level, responses, and characteristic behavior during teaching situations, perhaps fathers were more likely to rely on their notions of what a 4-year-old in general is capable of, whereas mothers did not have to rely on their beliefs about children's development. That is, these mothers might have been so "tuned in" to their children as a result of their experience with the child that they did not use ideas about what a 4-year-old is like cognitively and how they aquire concepts. She knows exactly how to get the best performance out of her own child given the child's mood, ability, the context, and the task demands. Thus, she responds to these external characteristics more than to her own ideas about children.

Stolz (1967) reported that the relationship between ideas and actions was greater for fathers than for mothers. There was also the possibility that mothers and fathers each construct their beliefs on the basis of their experience with children, but that they construct them in different manners. For example, mothers may observe their own children, compare their children to other children, talk to other parents, while fathers may use experience such as teacher models they have been exposed to, notions of ability adopted form the workplace, trying out strategies and noting the results. In some senses, the results of our first study indicated that the origins of beliefs may vary, in that the educational experience and the parenting experience (indicated by number of children) had differential effects for different individuals. This suggested to us that we should try to replicate the study with a different set of families, families in which the mother might work outside of the home and the father, or other caregivers, gain as much experience and knowledge of the child.

SUBSEQUENT STUDIES OF BELIEFS WITHIN THE FAMILY CONTEXT

As we examined a series of different explanations for the pattern of effects, we thought that it might be helpful to assess beliefs of different ethnic groups in order to examine the origins of beliefs and the role of experience in the formation of beliefs. We were beginning to question the constructivist perspective, and were trying to find parents who had had different experiences or exposure to different ideas about children in our search for the origin of differences among parents. It was exciting when we heard that Goodnow (1981) was doing cross-cultural work and was finding a relationship between parents' ideas about the child's age and behavior and ethnic background. Differences in developmental timetables that occured in different cultural groups suggested to us that given different experiences, different values and different emphases, people interpreted development differently. We decided to take these comparisons one step further and compare families who did and did not have an atypically developing child. We chose communication handicapped (CH) children to define the area of atypical development.

This decision was influenced by a variety of factors. First, the series of studies on deaf children conducted by Furth and his colleagues in the 1960s suggested this approach (see Furth, 1969). I recalled that these studies had been undertaken as part of an effort to understand the thought-language relationship. These children had no experience with language and their conceptual development was compared to that of hearing children to examine the influence of language experience on development of thinking. A similar approach seemed possible in that we could compare parents who had experience with an atypically developing child to parents who had not had such an experience. In this manner, we could examine the role of experience as parent on the construction of beliefs about developmental processes. In addition, we could investigate whether the belief-behavior relationship is affected by the differences among the children.

Second, I was becoming familiar with the literature on communication handicaps because of the developmental pattern of my 3-year-old son's speech. After his birth, I discovered that I had contracted German measles during my pregnancy. I had read that many children who escape the major health disabilities associated with rubella, which he apparently had, later evidence language problems. No-one aside from myself, my husband and the babysitter could understand my son at age 2 years. At age 3, his speech was judged to be 90% unintelligible by a speech pathologist and he began speech therapy. This may sound odd to many readers, but my son was very verbal. That is, he was a chatterbox—he talked all the time. This made his lack of intelligibility even more marked than if had he withdrawn verbally. He was extremely ingenious in communicating his needs and thoughts when he was not understood and, of course (note that I am biased by the fact of my motherhood in this instance) he was (and is) very smart.

It was difficult, even with Project Child Find and PL 92-142, which mandated identification and service for exceptional children, to get him assessed and in a treatment that I thought was acceptable for such a young child. I wondered how the other mothers that I saw and spoke with at various referrals were dealing with these and similar issues. Did they think that their nonarticulate children were intelligent? Did they believe that their children were learning in the same manner and at the same rate as other children? Did their beliefs suggest that the parents should continue to talk with the child who could not be understood or who failed to respond verbally? What about distancing? Could parents be expected to use inquiry and verbal discovery-based strategies with children who could not respond verbally, could not be understood when they did speak, and/or became frustrated when asked questions? The parents that I spoke with, and commiserated with, and complained with, and shared information with, and offered support to, in many waiting rooms sometimes seemed to be just like parents of any 4-year-old and sometimes seemed to be quite different. I was interested in how their beliefs might be affected by the experience of parenting a communication handicapped child. In addition, I felt that these families might be helped by meeting with other parents and sharing ideas/beliefs. I felt that way myself.

Finally, parents were likely to show changes in beliefs if what they were doing did not work well with the child. This seemed especially applicable to families dealing with a child who has a communication handicap. Within a constructivist perspective, parents of children with normally developing intelligence but a handicap in the area of speech were likely to experience challenges to their beliefs concerning the origins of intelligence and would be open to changes and new strategies for teaching children. Related to this, the first 2 years of development for a CH child are similar to those that most parents would observe. Therefore, the parents could be expected to have constructed beliefs on the basis of their experience with "normal development" during the first several years, and as the communication handicap became apparent, discrepancies in experiences with CH versus nonhandicapped children could be expected. Thus, if parents' beliefs are affected by their experience with their children, some differences in beliefs about development might be observed when one compared parents who had a CH child to parents who did not.

In addition, if parent education/intervention programs were warranted to encourage parents to continue to stimulate their children verbally and through discovery-based strategies, intervention at the level of beliefs rather than the level of behaviors would be advantageous to the development of teaching strategies that could change to fit the developing child, versus simple training in distancing. Distancing behaviors are essentially verbal behaviors, and it would be a natural reaction to lessened verbal facility to reduce the amount and level of demand of one's communications with a communication handicapped child. Although many CH children in fact have developed very fine receptive language, the lack of productive facility often affects their social interactions and the manner in which others speak to them. Because the verbal inquiry strategies that require the child to anticipate, reconstruct, and attend to transformations tend to enhance the development of representational thought, and parents might be less likely to evidence such strategies with CH children, there was the possibility that CH children were at risk with respect to the development of these abilities. Within distancing theory, the communication handicapped child who is not questioned, not challenged, not stimulated verbally, is in double jeopardy because the representational skills enhanced through parent-child interaction will be neglected due to a lack of verbal responsiveness on the part of the child.

Research Goals and Design. We began two research projects, each dealing with 120 families, half of which included a child who had been diagnosed as communication handicapped. Although the CH children by definition should have normal levels of intelligence, intelligence tests were administered by our staff in order to relate scores to the parents' beliefs and behaviors (as well as to use for screening children we felt had been misdiagnosed). Both studies involved interviews to assess beliefs and observations to assess teaching strategies. The two studies were different in three important ways, though.

First, one study included 3.5–4.5-year-old target children, while the other focused on children age 5–7 years old. In this manner, we could assess the impact of the child's age, albeit cross-sectionally, on the parents' beliefs and behaviors. This was important, because the processes of the parents' construction, as well as the content, could change with the child's age and the different issues that are relevant to parents of 4- versus 6-year-olds. We felt that the processes of construction of beliefs would be similar, i.e., the experience of the parent would be tantamount, but that the content of beliefs would change with the child's age. These predictions were based in part on the findings of the first study, which indicated that factors in the mother's background, such as age and education (indicators of life experiences before the onset of parenthood) had important impact on beliefs about child development after the children reached the age of four years. However, important changes occur in children during 4- to 6-years-of-age. For example, the influence of peers increases and children become engaged in many new activities that involve the aquisition of knowledge, information, and skills. Thus, the content, i.e., the processes that parents use to account for change in their children, could vary dramatically over this age span. In addition, the children themselves have changed dramatically over these years in terms of representational abilities. Within most developmental theories, the preschool to early school years are marked by a shift in representational abilities in particular. Parental beliefs about development and the way they deal with their children could be altered as the parent accommodates to these changes in the child's level of functioning. This could be especially important in the case of the CH child, who does not evidence this shift as noticeably through verbal interactions. Therefore, the two projects differed in the focus on the child's age to investigate the impact of these factors on parental beliefs and practices.

Second, the focus of one study was upon parents as teachers of the CH child (Office of Education Grant G007902000). That is, we wanted to see how the handicap affected the parents as teachers of their own children, in terms of beliefs and behaviors, and then how the children's representational abilities in a variety of areas were developing in relation to the parent's style. This was the closer of the two projects to the initial family constellation project in terms of goals, except that the focus was upon describing areas of representational thinking in which the CH children showed deficits or strengths and how those deficits/strengths were related to the parent-child interaction. The parents were not seen as the cause of these deficits, but rather as reactive, although we thought that the child's problems might be exacerbated because of the importance of communication in social interactions.

The second project (NIMH Grant R01-MH32301) focused on how the family was affected by the CH child. That is, we were interested in how siblings interacted with the child and how the marital relationship might be affected, as well as in how parents' beliefs and teaching behaviors were influenced by the presence of the CH child. This project was the result of our developing awareness of the family as a system in which each member influences the family as a whole, each member and also the relationships between other members of the family.

The information obtained through these research projects has not been fully explored, but the findings with respect to beliefs were disappointing. With the exception of a stronger belief that children learn through negative feedback as a result of their own actions for parents of CH children than for parents of nonhandicapped children, there were few differences in parental beliefs about developmental processes. We are not sure why this is the case, but we have postulated that perhaps parents view the atypically developing child as different to the degree that most ideas about how development occurs are not affected. We did ask parents of CH children how they think their own child developed the same ideas and skills, but we accepted responses that indicated there was no difference from other children rather than probing for a specific account of the process. As a result, we do not have much information in ways that parents might view the processes as different. We should have taken care to avoid a comparison with other children, but we had simply added three short probes to the end of an already lengthy interview to assess how they thought their child was different from other children.

Parents' behaviors with the children did vary with age and with the communicative status of the child. In fact, the levels of distancing demands used by parents and the child's performance on a variety of tests were related, suggesting a match between parents' distancing and children's representational abilities (McGillicuddy-De Lisi, De Lisi, Flaugher, & Sigel, 1987: Pellegrini, McGillicuddy-De Lisi, Sigel, & Brody, 1986). This relationship was hypothesized to reflect bidirectional influences. That is, parents seem to be flexible and smart enough to adapt their strategies to fit the level of performance their children are capable of, and parents who demand more of their children in terms of distancing strategies have probably enhanced the development of representational abilities in their children.

Although many predictions were supported, several notions and hypotheses regarding belief-behavior relationships were not fully supported by the findings. Throughout this research program on families, assumptions and hypotheses have been challenged and reformulated, unfamiliar literatures from sociology, clinical psychology, and social psychology have been explored, new measures have been developed, revised, tested, then revised again, pragmatic choices as well as those derived from theory led to particular methodologies, and my own predilictions as an investigator have undergone careful scrutiny. Like the initial study, the results of the studies of families with children evidencing communication handicaps did not provide clear evidence concerning the interplay between specific knowledge of one's own child, beliefs about developmental processes in general and parenting behaviors. But once again, each new finding has opened up a new avenue of inquiry for those who are interested in clarifying the complexity of adult's thinking about children and developmental processes. Some of these areas are summarized below.

CURRENT AND FUTURE RESEARCH CONCERNING
BELIEFS

As this chapter was going to press, an excellent review of the literature on parental beliefs was published in *Child Development* (Miller, 1988). Four areas for future research were discussed. These are:

1. exploratory investigations of parents' implicit theories (or developmental issues) that are unrestrained by explicit psychological theories,

2. questions concerning the interrelationships among different aspects of beliefs, with greater focus on a fuller network of beliefs,

3. longitudinal studies and direct measurement of differences/changes in experiences to broaden the scope of possible influences of beliefs as well as increase precision in relating determinants to particular beliefs, and

4. suggestions for specifying the relationship between beliefs and behaviors.

Many of the questions and unresolved issues raised in this chapter can be subsumed under these four areas and are therefore not addressed here. However, reflections concerning the patterns of findings in the research program and experience in interviewing over 200 parents and scoring countless other protocols has led to a few specific speculations and research questions, in addition to these important ones raised by Miller. These can be summarized as questions concerning (1) the role of beliefs for individuals, (2) the nature of change in adult cognition, and (3) intergenerational relationships in beliefs.

In addition, there are many questions raised in the letters to my "mentors" that have gone unanswered, such as the role of affect in beliefs, the relationships among beliefs, values, attributions, philosophical models of humanity, the process and structure of interrelating beliefs that are in logical contradiction, the personal versus cultural bases on beliefs, etc. At this point, however, the discussion focuses only on the three questions posed earlier.

The Role of Beliefs.   Much of my attention to beliefs has been focused on the role of beliefs in the *family,* as opposed to the function that beliefs play for an individual. For example, beliefs were presented as a mediating factor through which parental experiences with one child in the family creates new behaviors towards another child in the family (see McGillicuddy-De Lisi, 1980). For the individual, beliefs were simply viewed as the origins of behaviors and the filter through which one own and others' behaviors are interpreted. The finding that mothers' beliefs were not as strongly and systematically related to teaching strategies as fathers' beliefs is one example of individual differences in beliefs that needs further investigation. The lack of a relationship between maternal beliefs that the child is an active constructor of reality and distancing teaching strategies is especially problematic given the strong theoretical linkage between such beliefs and behaviors.

One possible explanation is that beliefs and behaviors are indeed related but there are problems in measurement that make it difficult to accurately assess that relationship. Given that an association was obtained for fathers but not for mothers, perhaps a different kind of belief (beliefs about specific abilities relevant to the task or teaching goals, for example) is the source of behaviors for mothers. Or perhaps beliefs and behaviors relate for some other domain (didactic-control strategies as opposed to teaching strategies). It has been argued that the obtained relationship was weaker for mothers than for fathers because the mothers had specific knowledge concerning their child's ability and did not have to rely on beliefs about development in general to teach their own child (McGillicuddy-De Lisi, 1982a). Because we had other questions to answer as well as this one, we conducted another large-scale study of atypically developing children, rather than simply investigating the relationship between beliefs and behaviors in mothers and in fathers with their own child versus a child who is a stranger (I still wonder why no one has done that relatively simple study), or obtain information regarding specific abilities of the child from the parent.

The well-formed ideas about children, including the "constructivistic" perspective that we had hypothesized would lead to distancing strategies, make it difficult to reject the notion that mothers hold beliefs to be true about children's development. A principal component analysis supported this view, and in fact revealed a first principal component that was remarkably similar to that obtained with data from the fathers. Why would mothers have such beliefs if they were not a way of organizing and interpreting information about children? What function did these beliefs serve? The problems of assessment that diminish the relationship to behaviors should be similar for fathers and mothers. It seemed possible that beliefs may not function in the same manner for all individuals, or that an overarching framework may vary, creating differences in structure while the content (e.g., "Children are active") may not vary. This line of reasoning began to develop as the factors related to origins of beliefs were analyzed. Recall that the first study of family constellation effects suggested that the origins of beliefs might differ for mothers and fathers. Mothers may develop ideas about children, development, and parenting, at least in our culture, long before they become parents. Part of the socialization process for girls is to focus them upon nurturance, childrearing, and hence child development issues. For males, ideas about childrearing may not be realized as important until after parenthood is attained, and thus there may be little usefulness or practical demand for cognition about children and/or development.

In addition to these considerations, recall that the relationships between maternal beliefs and distancing strategies were low and nonsignificant for the most part in the two studies involving CH children. This was true for the comparison families with nonhandicapped children, too. These samples were very different in terms of ability of the child and parental teaching behaviors, but not in terms of beliefs about development. Further, Comfort (1987) has reported minimal relationships between maternal perceptions of the child and play behavior with the child, with moderate relationships between beliefs and play behaviors for fathers. Perhaps it is not simply that the belief-behavior relationship is different for men and for women. It is possible that the nature and function of beliefs, as well as the origins, differ for men and women, presumably because of different socialization experiences.

The literature on women's views of themselves, mothering, and development has several suggestions to offer in this regard (see Belenky & Bond, 1987; Belenky, Clinchy, Goldberger, & Tarule, 1986; Brabeck, 1983; Gilligan, 1982; Kittay & Meyers, 1987; Trebilcot, 1983). Extending these writings to cognitions about child development, it is possible that men approach children and childrearing in a rule-oriented manner, relying on principles of development that are held to be universal. This rational, impersonal, and objective view of the child is analogous to the individualistic, autonomous view of justice that has been presented as an approach to moral development. Women's approaches to the child, to development and to the childrearing function, may be relational, empathic and perhaps even intuitive. That is, women's beliefs concerning child development processes may not arise from a view of the child so much as from a view of the relationship of the child to the adult, within the context of parenting responsibility and function. If this is true, the particular content of the beliefs would indeed be well-formed and similar across men and women, but the practical application of those beliefs might follow a quite different path than a system of beliefs based on principles or guidelines for behavior that are held to be universal. The relationship between the child and the parent is, in effect, part of the belief system itself for mothers. In both cases, the beliefs are constructed out experiences, but the framework to which those experiences are assimilated may be fundamentally different for men and for women.

This view needs further elaboration before specific predictions can be tested. For example, a reasonable case could be made that mothers respond to teaching situations in terms of these relational views of child performance within the context of a parent-and child-create-the-learning process-together relationship, but a different connection between beliefs and behaviors might hold for discipline situations. The relationship between beliefs and behaviors may be less variable across contexts for fathers, e.g., the-parent-as-teacher and child-as-learner. The mother's view of the relationship, as well as her view of the child, may be involved in the function of maternal beliefs, while the stronger relationship of paternal beliefs and behaviors may be a reflection of a different relatively straightforward functions of beliefs. For fathers, beliefs may be a source of strategies. For mothers, beliefs and behaviors may be embedded in the relationship with the child.

An issue related to the notion individual differences in the function of beliefs is that of context. Parent behaviors have been shown to vary considerably with the nature of the task (Sigel, 1982), mothers and fathers seem to teach sons and daughters differently (McGillicuddy-De Lisi, 1988), and parents' vary strategies with task demands and ability of the child (Pellegrini et al., 1986). There has been some suggestion that obtained relationships between beliefs and behaviors could be enhanced if an attempt was made to assess beliefs that relate directly to behaviors to be assessed, in essence controlling the context (e.g., Sigel, 1986). This is probably true. On the other hand, our conceptualizations of beliefs, and our research concerning the function of beliefs, must address how beliefs about children arise in a variety of contexts and how they apply to a variety of contexts. This is true in the sense of relationships between mother and child that have been discussed, but also in relation to different types of activities (e.g., stories, model building), different age children (preschool, school age), different childrearing contexts (e.g., teaching, discipline) as well as the various cultural and affective factors studied by others (e.g., Goodnow et al., 1985). How do we move from the specific interaction between parent and child to the level of beliefs, internal to the parent and general in form, and then back to the social interaction again? The processes and constraints upon beliefs as well as a description of the content and structure, will be necessary for an understanding of the function of beliefs for the individual.

The Nature of Change. The theoretical underpinnings of the research on parental beliefs clearly stem from a constructivistic perspective. As such, the parents' experiences in a wide variety of contexts, but especially in the course of interactions with the child, form the basis for the particular beliefs the parent will use to organize and interpret information. It is particularly troubling that parents of communication handicapped children do not differ as a group from parents of nonhandicapped children. Under what circumstances, if any, are adult cognitions about children open to change? The social psychological literature suggests that experiences that are extremely discrepant with attitudes or expectations are most likely to produce change. Sameroff and Feil (1986) propose that parents are most open to change when there is a practical need for it—when there is a problem with the child that is not resolved or understood. Adult development literature suggests that nonnormative experiences are a likely source of change during adulthood, with dialectical approaches going so far as to predict growth out of contradiction and conflict. Within each of these approaches, one might expect that parents who observed their children developing physical concepts, social skills, and social cognitions in the absence of communicative competency would react to that information and therefore differ from parents who had not had that experience. Atypical communication ability might not have fit this assumption as well as anticipated. We do not abandon the notion that differential experiences will lead to change in adult cognitions about children, but suspect that one must be very specific in formulating types of experiences that could lead to changes.

Some laboratory experiments in which information is maniplated concerning their own child's performance on a particular task after a particular belief has been assessed could clarify this issue. It seems likely that a focus on beliefs concerning the role of communication/speech in development in several areas would have yielded differences between the parent. Thus, changes in beliefs may be constrained to particular areas affected directly by experience, rather than a realignment or new integration of constructs when a discrepant experience creates a change in a particular area of the belief system.

Intergenerational Relationships among Beliefs.   There can be little doubt, on the basis of both theoretical grounds and empirical studies (Goodnow et al., 1985) that cultural frameworks for childrearing exist and influence behavior. When parents were asked to report the source of their own beliefs, the overwhelming response related to the parent's own upbringing and many referred directly to beliefs of their own parents (McGillicuddy-De Lisi, 1982a). An emphasis on construction of beliefs on the basis of experience does not preclude the transmission of beliefs from one generation to the next. The question of interest is how these beliefs of prior generations, which may or may not be articulated, are conveyed to the developing parent and how these experiences from "prior parents" are integrated with one's own experiences and existing structure of beliefs.

This issue may become especially important as we intensify our investigations of the function of beliefs for the individual. Since women may construct the basis of their belief systems at a different point in the lifespan than men, when different developmental processes are operating (e.g., normative versus nonnormative experiences, sex-role socialization, etc.), there may be a more powerful pressure for intergenerational similarity in women's beliefs. This could hold true even when there are major sociocultural events affecting cohorts differently, as evidenced by shifts in "expert" opinion. For example, it has been suggested that girls are developing notions about children and mothering during childhood socialization, while they acquiring a sense of self and gender identity. They may be more likely to adopt available beliefs, which are those of their mothers and significant others in the child's life. If men, on the other hand, do not construct or acquire such beliefs until adulthood as a result of socialization pressures focusing on other areas during childhood, they may be more dependent on sources of information available as adult socialization, such as pediatrician's advice, "How to" books, etc. As a result, men are also more likely to be open to changes in the cultural norms. For men, less intrafamilial transmission of beliefs may occur and there is more potential for extrafamilial impact on the developing beliefs. Thus, the construction of beliefs may in fact be a reflection of a complex interplay of factors that are melded together differently depending upon sociocultural events, gender, socialization, and individual experiences.

CONCLUSION

Dear Parents,

It has been great talking with you over the past 12 years. When you first volunteered to participate in these studies you were told that we wanted to hear *your* ideas about children, rather than those of the experts, because we believe that you are the experts. You are the ones who teach children and discipline them and finally send them on their way to raise their own children. And it has been true that you were experts. You taught us a lot about parents' ideas about children and why people behave the way they do. You showed us the best way to teach children in different contexts and you told us what is important to parenting.

Most importantly, though, you taught us to listen to you. We were often surprised at some of the ideas you had, and the reasons behind them. You taught us to take our own ideas and thoughts and put them aside for a moment or two and ask new questions as these surprises arose. You taught us to be learners with you, experiencing children and parenting through the countless experiences you shared with us. You taught us to keep asking questions. And that is what made this small study of effects of family size on children's problem-solving abilities grow into an evolving program of research that has been so rewarding.

Thank you,

Ann V. McGillicuddy-De Lisi

P.S. Want to participate in a follow-up study?

REFERENCES

Belenky, M. F., Clinchy, B. M., Goldberger, N. R., & Tarule, J. M. (1986). *Women's ways of knowing: The development of self, voice and mind.* New York: Basic.

Belenky, M. F., & Bond, L. (1987). *Conceptions of mind and parenting strategies.* Poster presented at the Biennial Meeting of the Society for Research in Child Development, Baltimore, MD.

Bell, R. Q. (1968). A reinterpretation of the direction of effects in studies of socialization. *Psychological Review, 75,* 81–95.

Brabeck, M. (1983). Moral judgment: Theory and research on differences between males and females. *Developmental Review, 3,* 274–291.

Bowen, M. (1978). *Family therapy in clinical practice.* New York: Aronson.

Comfort, M. (1987). *Differential relationships of parental perceptions to maternal and paternal involvement in play with young high risk and handicapped children.* Poster presented at the Biennial Meeting of the Society for Research in Child Development, Baltimore, MD.

Croft, R., Stern, S., Siegelbaum, H., & Goodman, D. (1976). *Manual for description and functional analysis of continuous didactic interactions.* Rochester, NY: University of Rochester.

Fishbein, M., & Ajzen, I. (1975). *Belief, attitude, intentions and behavior: An introduction to theory and research.* Reading, MA: Addison-Wesley.

Furth, H. G. (1969). *Thinking without language: Psychological implications of deafness.* New York: Free Press.

Gilligan, C. *In a different voice: Psychological theory and women's development.* Cambridge, MA: Harvard University Press.

Goodnow, J. J. (1981). Everyday ideas about cognitive development. In H. Tajfel (Ed.), *Social cognition: Perspectives on everyday understanding.* New York: Academic Press.

Goodnow, J. J., Knight, R. & Cashmore, J. (1985). Adult social cognition: Implications of parents ideas for approaches to development. In M. Perlmutter (Ed.) *Social Cognition: Minnesota symposia on child development* (Vol. 18, pp. 287–234). Hillsdale, NJ: Lawrence Erlbaum Associates.

Harvey, O. J., Hunt, D. E., & Schroder, H. M. (1961). *Conceptual systems and personality organization.* New York: Wiley.

Heider, F. (1958). *The psychology of interpersonal relations.* New York: Wiley.

Hill, R., & Mattessich, P. (1979). Family development theory and life span development. In P. B. Baltes & O. B. Brim (Eds.), *Life-span development and behavior* (Vol. 2). New York: Academic Press.

Jöreskog, K. G. (1973). A general method for estimating a linear structural equation system. In A. S. Goldberger & O. D. Duncan (Eds.), *Structural equation models in the social sciences.* New York: Seminar Press.

Jöreskog, K. G., & Van Thillo, M. (1972). LISREL; A general computer model program for estimating a linear structural equation system involving multiple indicators of unmeasured variables. *Research Bulletin* RB-72-56. Princeton, NJ: Educational Testing Service.

Kelley, H. H. (1972). Attribution in social interaction. In E. E. Jones, D. E. Kanouse, H. H. Kelley, R. E. Nisbett, S. Valins & B. Weiner (Eds.), *Attribution: Perceiving the causes of behavior.* Morristown, NJ: General Learning Press.

Kelly, G. A. (1955). *The psychology of personal constructs* (Vols. 1 & 2). New York: Norton.

Kittay, E. F., & Meyers, D. T. (1987). *Women and moral theory.* Totowa, NJ: Rowman & Littlefield.

Kohn, M. L. (1969). *Class and conformity: A study in values.* Homewood, IL: Dorsey Press.

Marjoribanks, K. (1979). *Families and their learning environments: An empirical analysis.* London: Routledge & Kegan Paul.

McGillicuddy-De Lisi, A. V. (1980). The role of parental beliefs in the family as a system of mutual influences. *Family Relations, 29,* 317–323.

McGillicuddy-De Lisi, A. V. (1982a). The relationship between parents' beliefs about development and family constellation, socioeconomic status and parents' teaching strategies. In L. M. Laosa & I. E. Sigel (Eds.), *Families as learning environments for children.* New York: Plenum.

McGillicuddy-De Lisi, A. V. (1982b). Parental beliefs about developmental processes. *Human Development, 25,* 192–200.

McGillicuddy-De Lisi, A. V. (1988). Sex differences in parental teaching behaviors. *Merrill-Palmer Quarterly, 34,* 147–162.

McGillicuddy-De Lisi, A. V., De Lisi, R., Flaugher, J., & Sigel, I. E. (1987). Familial influences in planning (pp. 395–427). In E. Scholnick, S. Frichman & R. R. Cocking (Eds.), *Blueprints for thinking: The growth of cognitive planning skills.* Cambridge, England: Cambridge University Press.

McGillicuddy-De Lisi, A. V., Sigel, I. E., & Johnson, J. E. (1979). The family as a system of mutual influences: The impact of parental beliefs and distancing behaviors on children's representational thinking. In M. L. Lewis & L. A. Rosenblum (Eds.), *The child and its family: The genesis of behavior* (pp. 91–105). New York: Plenum.

Miller, S. A. (1988). Parents' beliefs about children's cognitive development. *Child Development, 59,* 259–285.

Minuchin, S. (1974). *Families and family therapy.* Cambridge MA: Harvard University Press.

Pellegrini, A. D., McGillicuddy-De Lisi, A., Sigel, I. E., & Brody, G. H. (1986). The effects of children's communicative status and task on parents' teaching strategies. *Contemporary Educational Psychology, 11,* 240–252.

Pepper, S. R. (1967). *World hypotheses: A study in evidence.* Berkeley, CA: University of California Press. (Originally published 1972)

Polanyi, M. (1958). *Personal knowledge.* Chicago: University of Chicago Press.

Rokeach, M. (1968). *Beliefs, attitudes and values.* San Francisco: Jossey-Bass.

Sameroff, A. J., & Fiel, L. A. (1986). Parental concepts of development. In I. E. Sigel (Ed.), *Parental belief systems* (pp. 83–105). Hillsdale, NJ: Lawrence Erlbaum Associates

Sameroff, A. J., Seifer, R., & Elias, P. K. (1982). Socio-cultural variability in infant temperament ratings. *Child Development, 53,* 164–173.

Satir, V. (1964). *Conjoint Family Therapy.* Palo Alto: Science and Behavior Books.

Schaefer, E. S. (1971). Development of hierarchical, configurational models for parent behavior and child behavior. In J. P. Hill (Ed.)., *Minnesota Symposium on Child Psychology* (Vol. 5). Minneapolis: University of Minnesota Press.

Schaefer, E. S., & Edgerton, M. (1986). Parent and child correlates of parental modernity. In I. E. Sigel (Ed.), *Parental belief systems: The psychological consequences for children* (pp. 287–318). Hillsdale, NJ: Erlbaum.

Scheibe, K. E. (1970). *Beliefs and values.* New York: Holt, Rinehart & Winston.

Sigel, I. E. (1971). Language of the disadvantaged: The distancing hypothesis. In C. S. Lavatelli (Ed.), *Language training in early childhood education.* Urbana: University of Illinois Press.

Sigel, I. E. (1982). The relationship between parental distancing strategies and the child's cognitive behavior. In L. M. Laosa & I. E. Sigel (Eds.), *Families as learning environments for children* (pp. 47–86). New York: Plenum.

Sigel, I. E. (1986). Reflections on the belief-between connection: Lessons learned from a research program on parental belief systems and teaching strategies. In R. D. Ashmore & D. M. Brodzinsky (Eds.), *Thinking about the family: Views on parents and children* (pp. 35–65). Hillsdale, NJ: Lawrence Erlbaum Associates.

Stolz, L. M. (1967). *Influences on parent behavior.* Palo Alto, CA: Stanford University Press.

Sutherland, K. (1983). Parents' beliefs about child socialization: A study of parenting models. In I. E. Sigel & L. M. Laosa (Eds.), *Changing Families* (pp. 137–166). New York: Plenum.

Trebilcot, J. (1983). *Mothering: Essays in feminist theory.* Totowa, NJ: Rowman & Allanheld.

Weiner, B. (1979). A theory of motivation for some classroom experiences. *Journal of Educational Psychology, 71,* 3–25.

Zajonc, R. (1976). Family configuration and intelligence. *Science, 192,* 227–236.

Zajonc, R. B., & Markus, G. B. (1975). Birth order and intellectual development. *Psychological Review, 82,* 74–88.

3 Journeys in Serendipity: The Development of the Distancing Model

Irving E. Sigel
Educational Testing Service

The story I am about to tell describes the origins and development of a theory that began with three simple events. These experiences formed the basis of a research program to investigate the development of *representational competence,* that is, the ability to understand that events can be transformed from one symbolic system to another and be represented by signs or symbols. This essay is a biographical sketch of my research as it grew from three serendipitous experiences to a mini-theory called *Distancing theory—The Development of Representational Competence.*

The story began when I was investigating the development of classification skills in young children. I was testing an 8-year-old girl to whom I presented a group of familiar three-dimensional objects (e.g., vehicles, furniture). I asked her to place the objects in as many piles as she wished on the basis of similarity or belongingness. She put them into a number of piles as requested. Then I asked her the reason for each grouping. She labeled one group, "metal." I was impressed and surprised because no child had given that response. I asked her to tell me what a metal was. She said, "silver." "Are there any other metal things here on the table?," I asked. "No," she said, "only the silvery white things are metal." (There were other metal objects in the array). I then realized that her definition of the concept "metal" was restricted to but one attribute which was not an essential criterion for metal, but not an exclusive one. This minimal response gave me pause. I do not know what grabbed my attention that time because when testing children I usually accepted the labels they used, taking for granted that the label implied understanding of the term. I suddenly realized that the girl did not understand the concept "metal," even though she used the term correctly in that context. I concluded: *Correct usage does not mean understanding.*

A second related serendipitous finding came to mind. It had occurred several years earlier while I was investigating abstraction ability in young elementary school children for my dissertation (Sigel, 1953). The purposes of that study were to determine age differences in children's classification of everyday familiar materials and to determine whether these differences, if any, would vary as a function of the symbolic level of presentation.

Three-dimensional objects, pictures, and words were presented to the child with instructions to classify them in anyway he or she wished. It was found that children of average mental ability, between the ages of 8 and 11, categorized the materials similarly, irrespective of their symbolic form. But, there were age-related differences in the type of categorizations used (Sigel, 1953). The surprising event occurred when the children were given a group of objects, identically colored, but varied in meaning (e.g., a reading lamp, a table, a ladder, and a horse—all colored red), and I asked (while pointing to the objects), "How do they go together?" Most of the children, irrespective of age, failed the task. They did not acknowledge the color as a relevant categorical attribute. After recording each response I asked each child to tell me of all the tasks I had given them, which one was the most difficult. Virtually every child said "When you put all those *red* things together and wanted to know why." "Why did you not say *red?,*" I asked. "Oh, that was too obvious; that is not what you meant." I asked myself if it was the diverse meaning of the objects that precluded a coherent classification, or how the children interpreted my instructions (Sigel, 1953, 1954).

David Bearison and I decided to study the potency of meaning of an item relative to other physical attributes as determinants of classification behavior. In this experiment, color and/or form were less frequently chosen compared to meaning of the object (Bearison & Sigel, 1968). We concluded that *meaning* of an object transcended its physical characteristics as criteria for classification.

Serendipity number 3 occurred when I tested poverty-level Black children in their neighborhood school to select pictures for a cognitive style task. I presented the children with black and white *pictures* of familiar scenes, objects, and people since, as I already mentioned, I had found that children did not differentially categorize words, pictures, or objects. So, I used pictures of familiar instances, and to make certain they knew what the pictures were, I asked them to label the pictures. They had no difficulty giving the correct name for the items in the pictures. But, lo and behold the children in this school had considerable difficulty categorizing the pictures. They created chain responses relating each item to another, but not unified by a theme. the organization was primitive, thematically indicating that the children were able to grasp relationships between individual items only. These tended to be stories reflective of the child's own experiences (e.g., "You put the spoon in the cup and you drink out of the cup.''). The fact that children could label each picture, yet not identify a concept around which to build a group, puzzled me since in my dissertation children had no difficulty sorting pictures of familiar items (Sigel, 1953). I decided to repeat my dissertation to determine whether these findings were due to difficulty classifying in general, or whether the difficulty was related to working with pictures. Further, I wanted to know if they did have difficulty whether it was due to social class differences or to the age of the children. The children in the original study were 7-years-of-age and older and from lower middle-class White families (Sigel, 1954), whereas the children in this pilot work were 5- and 6-years-of-age and from low-income Black families. To test for class differences I first selected two groups of Black children (middle-class and lower-class), all kindergarten age. The materials were a set of three-dimensional life-sized objects and a set of colored, life-sized pictures of these objects. I chose simple, everyday familiar items, such as a cup, spoon, top, and pencil. These items comprised four classes: writing items, kitchen items, smoking items, and toys. The photographs taken of these objects were the best possible match in color and size. Each child was given two classification tasks—an object and a picture condition in a counterbalanced sequence. The items were placed on a table and the child was asked to label them. Then each child was asked to put those that were alike, or belonged together, in one pile and those that belonged together in a different way in another pile. They could have as many piles as they wished. It was found that there was no significant discrepancy in the way middle-class children grouped pictures or objects. They created the same number of groupings and also labeled their groupings similarly. This finding is consistent with the original study.

The low-income children, on the other hand, had no difficulty in grouping the three-dimensional objects, but they did have difficulty grouping the pictures. There was a *discrepancy* between their grouping responses with the three-dimensional materials and the pictures for the low-income children. Are the social class differences robust (Sigel, Anderson, & Shapiro, 1966)?

To test the robustness of these findings, I decided to do a large-scale study with middle-class White and Black children as well as lower-class White and Black children participating. I still could not believe that the picture-object discrepancy was valid since pictures are such pervasive stimuli to which all children are exposed. Yet, how do I explain the findings? Perhaps the problem is just understanding about classification. For these reasons I needed this more large-scale study. I added a condition to test out whether manipulating the objects (active) to form groups differed from recognition situation (passive) where the objects were grouped and the child had to label the groups. The difference between active construction and a passive recognition should reflect differences in understanding. In each passive group presented to the child, highly diverse items were used. It was hypothesized that the passive condition would be a stringent test of understanding as the child had to recognize similarity in the face of diversity (Sigel & McBane, 1967). Using a discrepancy score between picture and object grouping, we found that middle-class children revealed minimal discrepancy compared to the maximal discrepancy score for low-income Black groups. This discrepancy was found for the active and for the passive conditions. The lower-class children did less well with the passive sort (Sigel & McBane, 1967). This was indeed a confirmation of the previous work (Sigel et al., 1966).

These results were also counterintuitive. Hochberg and Brooks (1962) reported that by the age of 18 months children could understand pictures, even though they had never been exposed to them before. My interpretation was that these authors confused *recognition* of a representation with *understanding* of representation. For the task that I used it was necessary for the children to understand that a picture is a representation of the object and hence shares meaning. Hence the picture and its referent are equivalent for classification purposes in spite of their differences in symbolic level. The problem was particularly perplexing since I used pictures of items known to the children such as kitchen objects (e.g., cup, spoon) and smoking things (e.g., cigarette, matches, pipe), all familiar objects. Also, it should be recalled, the children could label each object, whether presented in a picture form or in a three-dimensional life-sized form. Thus, knowing the name of the objects did not facilitate this grouping. The problem seemed to be the children's difficulty in conceptualizing the objects and their picture-referent as members of the same class. One could argue that their difficulty in grouping was independent of the stimuli. They could not understand the task. However, this was not the case. They could group three-dimensional objects. The children did group the three-dimensional objects by use, such as: "My mother smokes with these" or "You use matches to light a cigarette." But, they did not perform equally well with pictures.

I interpreted the children's performance as not conserving the meaning of the object in the picture. They were not able to hold two ideas in mind—that pictures and objects are in fact different, and yet similar. For these children a picture of a cup and its three-dimensional referent are not members of the same class—cups. They did not *conserve the meaning,* which is, I contend, a *prerequisite* for picture comprehension.

The question was, "Why the difficulty?" This question haunted me for a long time. It was a finding that I could not explain, nor could I find any explanations in the literature. I dismissed cultural studies that reported similar findings (Hudson, 1967; Jahoda, 1966; Serpell, 1976) because the children in my studies were native-born American children, exposed to television and a host of modern phenomena and, *they were in school.* Teachers did not recognize the problem because they assumed that pictures were primitive representations which children could identify. *The teachers also confused identification and recognition of pictures with understanding.* The results I obtained in the previous studies were truly robust (Sigel & McBane, 1967). What in the experience of these children, I asked, accounted for this difficulty?

All of this thinking is, of course, based on the conviction that the problem is worth all the attention. I believed it was an important question, in spite of the lack of interest among educators and cognitive and developmental psychologists. The problem of picture comprehension was studied by those interested in artistic development (Gombrich, 1969), and those interested in visual literacy (Randhawa & Coffman, 1978). Most of these folks were not in the mainstream of developmental or cognitive research. Of course there were those like Gibson (1966) who investigated pictures as perceptual problems (Hagen, 1974) or a cultural phenomenon (Serpell, 1976). I felt very much alone in arguing that picture comprehension is an important cognitive achievement for all children and not one to be taken for granted. Since pictures are representations, I contend that understanding of how picture comprehension develops would provide a window to our understanding of representational thinking involving signs and symbols. The reliability of the picture-object discrepancy provided the empirical justification for continuing this research.

How do these three apparently discrepant serendipitous events coalesce into a single conceptual framework? The conceptual answers are unfolded during the course of this chapter. To anticipate, let me describe the relationships among picture comprehension, categorization behavior, and concept definition.

Pictures represent objects, events, persons, or ideas. They contain critical features which signal their referents. Understanding of *picture meaning* requires grasping this concept. Concepts and classifications overlap in their meaning and in the fact each of them is also a representation. A *concept* is usually represented in words. A *classification* is an organization of instances bound by some common characteristic represented by the classifier. The basic connection is that each of these components involves understanding of the principle of *representation.* So, the primary goal of my research program was a search for the ontogenesis of *representational* competence—how humans come to know the representational rule (Sigel, 1979b).

THE SEARCH FOR ANSWERS

The results of all of the previous work confirmed that the difficulties which low-income Black and White children have in classification of pictures as compared to three-dimensional objects is a deficit in functioning. The question is *why,* because, as I indicated, the findings are counterintuitive. There is one source of difficulty from my perspective—something about the socialization of these children. Is there anything about how they interact with their parents or significant others that may account for the difficulty I noted? Of course, I was not sure what particular experiential factors accounted for the finding. I knew it had nothing to do with the role of the examiner, with the conditions in which the children were tested, or with the rapprochement the children had with the examiner. they did manage the tasks when the objects were used. It must have something to do with the materials, with the nature of the picture? So, I thought, "Let us go into the home and see how pictures are used, how parents talk with their children about pictures and about things in general." I had also noted at this time that Piaget discussed the significance of children's understanding of anticipation and hindsight as ingredients in representational competence (Inhelder & Piaget, 1964). So, I had thought that we might ask parents how they involve their children in planning or anticipation and hindsight or reconstructive memory (my interpretation of hindsight) in daily interactions.

The results of such interviews of parents would shed light on the environmental factors contributing to the children's difficulty, and perhaps provide insights for intervention programs. There was no question in my mind that children should not be entering school or 1st grade without first understanding how to interpret pictures and know that they are representations. After all, many of the materials used in the classroom, including the reading primer, are in picture form, and children are expected to understand these materials. For as I said before, the phenomenon I identified had not been identified before, and perhaps the difficulties that these children were having in school were based on an inadequate foundation in pictorial comprehension which in turn reflected a more general cognitive deficit.

A large number of home interviews were conducted with "poverty-level families" in the Detroit area. The home interviews confirmed what I had suspected. Low-income families (both Black and White) tended to spend little time engaging their children in dialogue. they also spent little time in planning and using previous experiences as guides to the present. There seemed to be a lot of present orientation. They did not read to their children and seldom engaged them in mutual or shared play. In other words, they did not do much to activate their children's representational competence. In some ways the parents interacted with their children in the same way that some of the teachers did, didactically, providing little opportunity for conversation, storytelling, planning and those activities we come to refer to as "building representational competence."

Rationale and Procedure for Intervention. How does one teach children to become aware of the nature of pictures as representational stimuli? There are a number of choices: for example, ask them to memorize names as they see pictures, give them exercises in naming pictures, etc. The choice depends on one's theoretical orientation. Being in the camp of Werner (Werner, 1948; Werner & Kaplan, 1963) and Piaget (1962), I developed teaching sessions for the children in which they could have opportunities to construct their own experiences (Sigel & Olmsted, 1970a, 1970b). The way to facilitate this, I concluded, was by using questioning strategies, the type which Piaget used in his Method Clinique (see Sigel & Cocking, 1979). Further, opportunities for imaginative play and verbalization involve imagination and language labeling.

Coming from a Piagetian orientation, I was also sure that cognitive development required experiences that would induce cognitive conflict (Piaget, 1950). These parents did not do this. It became clear that one source of the child's difficulty emanated from the limited home experiences involving engagement, anticipation, reconstruction, and transcendence of the immediate into signs and symbols. These understandings involved understanding the representational rule, which in turn is prerequisite for problem-finding or problem-solving.

Initial Training Studies

Two intervention studies were undertaken. Basically, in each of them the procedures involved engaging children in a discussion about objects and/or pictures, asking them to enumerate the characteristics and functions of the objects. It also involved role playing, didactic teaching, and a control condition. By counterbalancing the picture or object training condition we could test out which experiences with pictures or with objects made a difference in the children's eventual ability to categorize pictures and objects equivalently. In the initial study we discovered that the only conditions that contributed to reducing the picture-object discrepancy were engaging children in a discussion of object characteristics, followed by creating object groups, and repeating this process with pictures. Posttests with objects and pictures revealed a decrease, but not a significant one, in the picture-object discrepancy (Sigel & McBane, 1967).

On the basis of these results, Pat Olmsted and I zeroed-in on training children in small groups to come to the understanding that the objects and the pictures are representations of the objects. We undertook this study in the public schools, convinced that by using teachers as our experimenters we would create a more natural school environment and perhaps could teach the children that pictures were, in fact, representations of objects. Pat Olmsted and I designed the study using:

Six training conditions, three of which deal with classification training and three with non-classification procedures. For the classification training, the three conditions vary in type of material to be used: (1) the use of objects alone; (2) the presentation of three-dimensional objects, followed by a series of pictures of these objects—for the first two weeks of training the children dealt with three-dimensional objects, and for the second 2 weeks they dealt with representations of these objects; and (3) the use of pictures alone.

With regard to the other training conditions, we established appropriate control or contrast groups: children who received no classification training but who did work with the teacher, and children who had no small group experience at all. In each of the three classification conditions, small groups of 4 to 6 children worked with the teacher who was trained by us and who employed training procedures. The time spent with each group of children was approximately 20 minutes a day for a total of 20 school days.

One month after the conclusion of our training, the children were retested. It was found that those children in the classification training program showed the following significant changes: (1) they improved in grouping; (2) they provided more articulate verbal labels for their groupings; and (3) they used a variety of bases for grouping, such as color, form, some structural responses, relational responses, and categorical responses. The training influenced the child's capability, then, not only in grouping but also in the variety of criteria employed for grouping. Of particular significance, and in a way a surprise and disappointment, however, was the fact that there was no increase in the child's ability to employ representational materials. There was no differential effect as a function of the media used in the classification training: use of objects or pictures made no difference. Further, the discrepancy in capability in sorting objects as compared to pictures in the pretest session did not differ significantly from the same relationship in the posttest session. Thus our training did not have any particular impact on the child's capability in dealing with representational material.

Eight months later, when the children were reexamined, the experimental group did not differ significantly from the control group in frequency of grouping on single dimensions. The control group increased in their ability to group whereas the experimental group stayed at the same level. One significant difference did persist: the classification training group employed more multiple criteria as bases for grouping than the nonclassification training group. For example, the classification training group used such rationales for their groupings as: "These are big and they are green," or "These are big, and we use them." They offered significantly more of these multiple responses which still, however, were not conjunctive, but serial.

Thus we were prompted to ask two questions: (1) What is the effect of these training situations if they do not persist over time and the control group catches up? (2) Why was there no shift toward increased capability in dealing with representations? In examining the question of why there was no continued discrepancy between experimental and control groups, one could ask if it is reasonable to expect continued progress unless the environment provides continued reinforcement or support. We are convinced on empirical grounds that short-term training programs are ineffective in inducing long-term gains unless there is something in the environment to reinforce these accomplishments. The argument, perhaps, is best expressed in medical terms, where immunity through immunization procedures in many cases is short-lived, unless booster shots are given. So with enrichment. Gains that are made, then, can only be retained and built upon provided the environment continues the necessary and sufficient conditions for development. The fact that the classification-trained children did not regress suggests the training was not superficially assimilated, but was maintained. The fact that other groups improved suggests that children achieve grouping skills in any case. This raises an interesting question. Are we accelerating the children and merely providing what they would acquire in the course of their usual educational experience? We do not accept this reasoning yet, for a number of questions relative to the sensitivity of our test, the lack of breadth of our posttest, and so on, need further study before we can accept the idea of premature acceleration being solely responsible for this finding.

As to the second question of why there was no change in representational skills, one of the conclusions we came to after studying the content of the training sessions was that descriptive aspects were too heavily emphasized by the teacher. There was minimal emphasis of inferencing, or on the realization that objects can be presented in many ways. Could it be, then, that we were accentuating the use of perceptual skills and putting little emphasis on the representational nature of the perceived? In effect, we may have been supporting the tendency of these children to be very literal instead of enabling them to deal with representations.

Crude as our techniques were, and admittedly superficial, they have helped to identify the problem. Having observed these children in play, in schoolrooms, and in testing situations, we are persuaded that the impoverished children, as compared to middle-class children, lack experiences that focus on the unseen, on the significance of representation: their experiences tend to emphasize the here and now. The significance of work in this area rests on the conviction that adequate mastery of our educational requirements, such as arithmetic and reading, requires the ability of the child to deal with representations. After all, we live in an environment of symbols and signs, and only perhaps when deprived children can enter the world of signs and symbols as equals will they be able to participate profitably in the educational enterprise.

In view of our conviction that this kind of competence is necessary, it is incumbent on us to reexamine our training procedures and to look toward other means by which such acquisitions can be facilitated. (Sigel & Olmsted, 1970a, pp. 54–56)

Pat Olmsted and I reported the findings to the administrative personnel from the Board of Education. We were certain that we had something important to tell the curriculum people. After we presented our findings, however, the kindergarten supervisor said that she had learned nothing from this experiment since in our study we did what classroom teachers do all of the time. When we pointed out that the control group did the worst of all, and that group had been taught with the standard kindergarten, the supervisor walked out. Ironically, the teachers were impressed with our findings and said that they would alter their strategies from then on. This experience demonstrated how difficult it is for research to penetrate a system already entrenched.

The training results, coupled with two other studies in which the teaching strategies were instrumental in creating change among the students, supported the notion that the use of inquiry strategies and open-ended questions, properly structured, could have important cognitive impact on young children (Sigel, Roeper, & Hooper, 1966; Griffiths, Shantz, & Sigel, 1967).[1]

---

[1]This study was a conservation training study which involved preschool gifted children. One of the experimental conditions was similar to the one used in the intervention study, that is, dialoguing, asking questions, and leading the children to construct their own reality. The results were in the predicted direction.

SUMMARY

To this point it becomes clear that the use of inquiry-like strategies do engage children and do seem to make a difference in their understanding of some aspects of representation. However, the effects of dialoguing were more pronounced for the middle-class children in the conservation studies (Sigel et al., 1966). The change in the representational competence of the low-income children was not significant, but there were training effects for their labeling and naming of objects, their ability to use multiple criteria, and in constructing groupings.

So, I was left with the perplexing question of why the children continued to have difficulty in transcending the obvious differences in the stimuli (pictures vs. objects), and continued to have difficulty in classification tasks with pictures. In general the following specific questions persisted:

1. Do children need more experience in inferencing and in the realization that objects can be attended to differently even though they are presented in pictorial modes?

2. Do low-income children have difficulty in discriminating, scanning and generalizing when they have to transcend the ongoing, immediate environment?

3. What are the kinds of experiences that will enhance their representation since the failure to achieve continued growth in representational competence was found?

I could not get a handle on the phenomenon. The behavioral data were robust. The intransigence was consistent. Of course, I could attribute the difficulty these children had to intelligence or some other such general and nonspecific concept. What I sought was an explanation.

The search for the connections between dialoguing as in the training studies (Shantz & Sigel, 1967; Sigel & Olmsted, 1970a, 1970b; Sigel et al., 1966) and the development of representational competence required the development of a theory. As we shall see, rereading and rethinking of Piaget (1962) and Werner (1948) helped. Above all, analysis of the task demands when categorizing pictures as compared to objects conjointly led me to developing what came to be called *Distancing Theory*. The arrival of the name, however, had its own unique history as I shall now relate.

Identifying the Central Construct. The discovery of the name *Distancing Theory* came serendipitously. I had been invited to Teachers College, Columbia University, to give a colloquium to a group of graduate students and faculty interested in mental retardation. I had planned to talk about the picture-object discrepancy in categorization behavior of young children from impoverished families. I had struggled to find a name for the hypothesis that I was generating.

The plane I took from Detroit to New York was a French Caravel, a jet that had a very steep ascent. Looking out of the window as the plane rose, I noticed how all of the objects on the ground were getting smaller and smaller in a *real* sense. I was seeing them as smaller. I realized that those objects below were not getting smaller. They were still the same size. It was just that I was going further away. The awareness of the discrepancy between what I saw and what I knew them to be (the fact that the objects do not change in spite of my retinal image) is referred to as *object constancy*. I knew of the object constancy construct, but I had never thought about its implications as a cognitive process related to understanding pictures. To me, the critical aspect of this experience was that in spite of the apparent shift in retinal size from a cognitive perspective, I was aware that the change in appearance was not a change in the meaning of the object. I was, in fact, distant from the object, and in spite of the distance I did transform the visual experience into a representation and I *knew* the object's state. I had decided to call the phenomenon *Distancing*. *Distancing* described an inner mental activity because I separated myself mentally or physically from the concrete visual experiences. While I was being physically separated from the objects I was observing by the airplane, two things were going on simultaneously: (1) I was aware of the decrease in the size of the objects I was observing on the ground; and (2) I was aware that the objects on the ground were not really changing in size. The contradiction between my visual experience during the changing physical state (movement) and my knowledge (object constancy) was not disturbing because I *knew* (inner mental representation) that there was a relationship between size of the retinal image and the physical distance, and I *knew* that objects do not shrink just because my retinal image changes. The objects were represented in my mind, just like a picture of an original painting. This analysis provided a cognitive explanation of the object constancy construct. These thoughts percolated while I was thinking of my speech. In addition, I realized that when I see a picture I *also* separate myself virtually automatically from the physical appearance and know that the picture is someone's representation of reality, just as in the airplane experience. I also realized that this is an example of *rule-governed behavior* since it happened with no deliberate, conscious activity. The rule I know is that objects can be *represented* in forms alternate to their three-dimensional appearance and still retain their identify. Now the question was, if this is a rule, how do I learn it? No one has taught me the rule directly. I must have come to it from some type of experience. I could not accept the idea that the rule is innate. The rule is learned. But, what kinds of learning experiences are involved? I was pondering this question when I arrived in New York and went to Teachers College to meet my host, Brian Sutton-Smith. We went for a walk and I presented him with my most recent thoughts about the picture-object discrepancy and the distancing concept. In the course our conversation I recounted my experience on the airplane, and without further awareness he corroborated that I had a hypothesis; namely, that "distancing" experiences influence the development of representational competence. Specifically, I came to the decision that it is the creation of distance between the person and the object psychologically or physically that requires the individual to represent an experience, and in that process distances self from the here and now. The experience is transformed—it becomes a representation. Open-ended questions exemplify the process. For example, they "demand" a response and the answer is not embedded in the question. It has to be constructed by the responder. It is in the head of the responder. The open-ended question forces the individual to engage in an active search for a response. This process of construction is done through re-presentation of previous experience or anticipation of intentions. Such experiences lead to the development of *representational competence*. This was a big conceptual leap.

There were still many question of *the how, the what*, and *the why* that needed to be formulated, and, of course, addressed. But at the time I felt that I was on the right track. Brian-Sutton Smith's concurrence was reassuring. I tried these ideas out at the colloquium and it seemed to work. The audience resonated to the description, perhaps because they felt the experience which I was describing was initially valid. The ideas were never articulated this way to them. I believed I had the germ of the idea.

From that point on, I became literally obsessed with the *Distancing* construct, and began to formulate the distancing hypothesis as generic to the ontogenesis of representational competence. A number of questions just poured out, such as: What creates the distance?; Does it have to be physical distance or can there be mental distance?; What is the source of representation?; Do we learn to represent? These questions, and many others, were addressed in my first paper on this particular topic (Sigel, 1970). I was invited to the Miami Symposium on the Prediction of Behavior and was asked to talk on any subject I wished relative to cognitive development. In the preparation of this seminal paper I was able to put together the previous experiments and formulate a tighter conception of the distancing hypothesis and lay out some questions for further study. The conceptual system is described as follows:

> Acquisition of representational competence is hypothesized as a function of life experiences that create temporal and/or spatial and/or psychological distance between self and object. "Distancing" is proposed as the concept to denote behaviors or events that separate the child cognitively from the immediate behavioral environment.
>
> The behaviors or events in question are those that require the child to attend to or react in terms of the nonpresent (future or past) or the nonpalpable (abstract language). Distancing stimuli can emanate from persons or events, e.g., the mother and child discussing an anticipated birthday party or the child searching his toy chest for a particular favorite toy.
>
> The child adapts to these situations by developing and utilizing representation. It is in this sense that representation is viewed as adaptive.
>
> Distance is expressed in the stimuli themselves. For example, a cutout picture of

a chair is closer to the chair, or less distal, than is the word chair, simply because the latter contains no overlap of any kind with the actual reality of the chair. A photograph, for example, may be more distal than the cutout, since the cutout contains some notion of dimension or depth in its physical form, whereas the picture (photograph) only represents depth through particular visual cues. . . .

The set of events that are hypothesized as significant determinants for the development of representation are distancing ones—where distal stimuli may or may not be employed. As we shall see, the point of view of this paper stresses the role of distancing experiences for the child, with the distal media furnishing some of the communication modalities. For example, a parent may describe in very vivid language an anticipated event, e.g., a trip; or a parent in preparing a child for a hospitalization experience might employ a picture book depicting hospital events to be experienced. These types of communications probably stimulate the child to image, to anticipate, in effect, to represent the nonpresent events.

The distance may be temporal, as between a past event and a present recall; spatial, as with a picture or image and the pictured or the imaged; in its modality, the name of the object; or in degree of detail, a sketch of an object and the object itself.

Distancing is a way to characterize differentiation of the subjective from the objective, the self from others, ideas from actions. Representational competence is hypothesized as the resultant of experiences creating such distance.

The foregoing statements are based on the assumption that man has the generic capability to respond to distancing by creating representations of reality; the actualization of representational competence depends on the distancing experiences as part of the broader culture as well as the particular life history. (Sigel, 1970, pp. 111–113).

After I wrote this paper, I became concerned about the term *Distancing* because it had a familiar ring to it, and sure enough, I realized this was the same term that Werner and Kaplan used in their book (Werner & Kaplan, 1963). I realized that this is an example of how the unconscious words (sources of ideas) are often forgotten and reappear with the author believing he intended it. So too for me. However, just to be sure of the ownership of the term, I went to the Werner and Kaplan volume to check it out, and sure enough, they used the term *distancing*. Their use of the concept was quite different from mine. Yet, there was some similarity in that they wrote of separation in a metaphorical sense between the object and the word, whereas I used the term to reflect a generalized transformational process. I realized how Werner had influenced me and I had expanded and transformed his idea into something else. Perhaps this is what happens when we integrate our reading and develop our own system.

The challenge now was to continue studying the relationship between *Distancing* and representational competence. Among the choices were the creation of experimental situations, such as those characteristic in experimental child psychology. These would be similar to the training studies. I rejected this idea on the basis of my previous experience with training studies. It will be recalled that the outcomes of these studies were short-lived. I concluded that immersing poor Black children in a school setting would be the method of choice if long-term effects were to be achieved.

I realized, then, as I do now, that opting for a school program instead of a laboratory experiment precludes precise testing of the *Distancing Hypothesis* because it is difficult to control the teacher's use of distancing strategies. There are a number of other factors that could confound the results, such as effects of peers, frequency of teacher-child interaction, influence of management techniques, the role of curriculum materials, etc. Nevertheless, I concluded that developing a school program would be worthwhile because the more general notion of distancing could be tested in an environment that would provide an intensive experience over a relatively long time. There was a tradeoff between precise fragmented interactions where treatment effects can be clearly identified, such as in an experiment, and the school-based treatment where more global effects might emerge. I opted for the school-based approach.

The choice of school-based intervention, if it worked, would allow for broad applicability and hence could have useful social implications. So, I proceed to the next phase of the test of the distancing hypothesis at the State University of New York at Buffalo.

The research program I had been developing pointed in the same direction—identifying the phenomena of representational thinking and the search for answers. It will be recalled that the picture-object discrepancy studies followed the conservation studies (Griffiths et al., 1967; Roeper & Sigel, 1966; Sigel et al., 1966). All of these studies demonstrated the utility of the inquiry discussion method as a way of enhancing children's cognitive growth and so this approach became central to subsequent educational programming.

THE DISTANCING PROGRAM MOVES TO BUFFALO

With funds from the Office of Economic Opportunity, a preschool program was established for 2½-year-olds. The rationale for selecting children of that age was because, in Piaget's terms, this is the period of transition between the sensorimotor to the preoperational phase. It is, fundamentally, the shift to representational thinking (Piaget, 1962). Thus it seems to be a developmentally appropriate time to engage the children in ways to help them imagine and engage in figurative thinking in a systematic way, to come to understand that various media are available to express similar ideas, and to engage in planning, reconstructing experiences and transforming their ideas into language. Their language competence would be enhanced, along with their understanding of symbols and representations. Guided by teachers using distancing strategies the children should make significant cognitive gains.

Empirical support for the idea came from a study by Golden and Birns (1968) who reported that differences in cognitive functioning (representational competence) between middle- and lower-class children occurred after the age of 2½. Establishing an educational program directed at this age group, I hypothesized, could alter the trajectory of the children's intellectual growth.

The original notion was to select a different group of children (about 20) each year to participate in the program for one year only. Then a new group would participate the following year. This would give us a larger sample. Twenty-two children were recruited for the program initially. We could not employ random assignment since there were no available programs for children of this age. There were day care centers; we were *not* a day care center. Matching children by criterion other than age was difficult for this population. Family structure varied. We would not control for intellectual level. Two- to 2½-year-old, toilet-trained boys and girls were enrolled, all at the poverty level. This was determined by the fact that they all lived in housing projects where a means test determined eligibility. The selection of children was a compromise. We could not create the research design so often described in our research texts. There was no choice if I wanted to test the efficacy of the distancing model with a group that would probably end up in the usual course of events with limited representational competence.

Yet, the experience of engaging in this type of work is challenging and highly informative. Not only does one discover the limits of social science research strategies, but one also gets to appreciate the range of individual differences that exist among these groups. The stereotype we often have of the Black poor is just that—a stereotype. In the 3 years of the grant, then, 60 children would have gone through the program. However, as we planned the group's future, George Forman, Ada Secrist, and I looked around at the preschool programs for children in the city and discovered that there were none that provided the services that we did (transportation, a breakfast snack, and intellectual stimulation). We then decided to keep the initial group until it was time for them to enter kindergarten. Thus the cross-sectional study became a longitudinal one. In this way we could follow the same children for 3 years.

However, this posed a serious research problem. Could we find control groups? Or, more appropriately, could we find contrast groups? This issue is very important in research of this type. When random assignment is not possible, and even when finding enough individuals to form equivalent groups for control purposes is difficult, what is one to do? We could have dropped the project or tried to set up our own day care program (we were not funded at that level) or make the best of it and compromise. We decided to compromise. We decided to combine the procedures: The experimental group would be the ongoing core group, but each year we would look at a sample of children who were in other centers, but who shared the comparable demographic characteristics of the experimental groups. There were day care centers in Buffalo that enrolled welfare mothers or mothers from single families whose educational and occupational levels were comparable to the children in the experimental group. We had also hoped to find children in these centers who would be continuing so that we could have a longitudinal sample. This proved to be very difficult because the families moved or transferred to other centers. Sometimes, even if they stayed in the same Center, their attendance would be very irregular. I suppose that if we had the funds to struggle with this problem we would have been able to work it out. We did not have funds for such extra efforts, so we compromised and did yearly analyses using a cross-sectional group.

The idea of using a school set up as an analogue to an experimental situation seemed, at the outset, very reasonable. Then it became evident that there was considerable slippage between the traditional experimental design with tight controls and the schoolroom situation. In a school setting the treatment can be applied equally to every child and there can be no independence of effects since children can influence each other in unexpected ways. The experimental paradigm became our research metaphor. We used the experimental concept as our model and guide to provide a way to formalize the approach.

What were the requirements to create an experimental school? There had to be an articulated theory that could be communicated to the teachers. They had to know it in order to become "free agents," i.e., they could spontaneously know what to do when it was not in a script and yet be consistent with the theory. Theory has to be transformed into practice, in this case I did it by defining distancing strategies, identifying them and demonstrating when some would be used and under what conditions. Because the distancing strategies I had identified did not include *all* possible strategies, I had to define which types of interactions should be used to be consistent with the theory.

Then, of course, there was the curriculum to develop. What tasks would be used? How would they be organized? How would the day be arranged? All of these matters had to be resolved. Since representational competence was an intended outcome, tasks requiring representational thinking had to be created. Further, they had to be developmentally arranged for the children as they got older. However, because there was no previous school-like arrangement, and because all we had available was the results of some experimental studies, it became clear that we would have to create our own curriculum while at the same time meeting with the children. The result was that at times we were not too far ahead in our program planning.

To help structure the program for teachers, there were six major objectives underlying the program:

1. The child must be challenged to think in the nonpresent;

2. the child must be given opportunities to search for alternative actions when unable to solve a problem;

3. the child must come to recognize that every object is made up of more than one property;

4. the child must have opportunities to be aware of temporal and physical relations among objects, events, and people. These principles formed the basis for curriculum development and were congruent with the concept of representation as developed in distancing theory;

5. The child should come to know that ideas, objects, and events can be presented in various media or symbols, and, most important, there is an equivalence principle operating; and

6. the child must engage in reconstruction of anticipation experiences as well as transcend the immediate present.

The way the teacher carried out these principles was through her choice of appropriate *distancing strategies*. The interaction of the strategies with the materials was believed to be the basis for developing representational competence.

The curriculum focused on planning for daily activities using representational material and consciously articulating the meaning of representation. Games involving memory, searching for objects, transforming, and other imaginative activities were constructed. The program was held five mornings a week from 8:30 A.M. to 11:30 A.M. The children were given a breakfast snack and a midmorning snack, but no lunch was served (see Sigel, Secrist, & Forman [1973], for details).

The determination of the effectiveness of the program had to be done through valid measurements. I eschewed IQ assessment as relevant since determination of program effectiveness required testing the distancing hypothesis relative to representational competence. The specific components of representational competence had to be assessed. As no test battery encompassing the competence of interest existed, I had to construct one. This is not an uncommon problem. Rather than just using a given battery of tests, e.g., the Stanford Binet, my colleagues and I searched through the literature. We chose those which in our judgment assessed those that were judged to assess representational competence. A battery of 25 tasks was assembled to measure the cognitive areas involving anticipation, prediction of outcomes of action, reconstruction of the past, understanding of symbols and pictures. See Sigel et al. (1973) for a complete list.

How could we validate these tasks? Was it legitimate to take them out of the context of their original set? These methods questions are frequent since very often tasks do not exist in the form in which an investigator wishes. For want of a better procedure, we defined each variable we sought to measure and then reviewed existing batteries, selecting out the subtests that met our definition. Independent judgments were made by each of us. In effect, we worked with judgments to establish construct validity.

One of the key considerations was to select tests with high ceilings. Four test batteries were constructed. There was some overlap of the tasks to take the age of the child into account.

The results were complex and cannot be described in detail. In general, however, we noted significant changes in the major areas of concern. The children in the experimental program showed significant gains in fluency and comprehension of language, in planning, and reconstruction of previous experiences in contrast to children in day care centers. However, differences in developmental rate were found for boys and girls. Overall, significant developmental changes were found when the performance of children in our program was compared to the performance of children in other day care centers. In general, the children in the experimental program did gain more than might have been expected by chance (Sigel, 1973b).

The results which are complex in nature, were, however, encouraging. They demonstrated that intervention beginning at age 2½ did make a difference, at least at age 5.

The main thrust of the preschool program was to test the ontogenesis of representational competence as mediated by distancing strategies. The findings from all sources were positive, supporting the Distancing Model (Cataldo, 1978; Sigel, 1974).

Each year the teachers in our program reviewed the children's test scores. The results were used as the basis for modifying those aspects of the program which needed strengthening. During the third year of the program the children were given tests to determine their number knowledge. The teachers were shocked at how poorly the children had done and questioned the validity of the scores. From their knowledge of the children they were convinced that the tasks underestimated the children's knowledge. I observed the children myself in their daily routines in the classroom to look for evidence not only of number knowledge, but also for other areas of interest as measured by the test battery. In other words, I was engaged in a validity check, seeking corroboration of test performance in the classroom. What I found amazed me. The teachers were right. The children did understand more number and language concepts than assessed in our psychometric battery. One day I decided to check out my observation a bit more systematically. When the children were sitting around the table having juice the teacher asked them to pass crackers from one to the other stating the exact amount, e.g., "Andre give Jane 4 crackers." Andre would respond correctly. This type of activity became a game with the questions becoming increasingly complex. Not only did we engage in this type of activity to check for understanding of number, but also for prepositions and memory for commands. I was surprised at how often the children revealed greater knowledge in the classroom than when being examined by a familiar, competent examiner. These observations led to the writing of the essay, "When do we know what a child knows?" (Sigel, 1974).

The issues raised in that paper are still with all of us who work with young children. In fact, I would ask if we are obtaining valid assessments of children's competence—a problem endemic to all standardized tests, especially when the items are decontextualized. Is the problem to find valid procedures using appropriate contexts to assess children's cognitive status? For example, is asking the child to pass a particular number of crackers while sitting around the juice table equivalent to asking him or her to give the examiner a number of blocks from an array presented to him or her in a testing situation.

This experience is another serendipitous event that gave me pause and influenced the way I view assessment procedures. Let me return to the main trend of the narrative.

A Major Follow-Up Study.   The late Dr. Christine Cataldo decided to follow up the children in elementary school for her dissertation. The children were now in the 2nd grade. It was found that the children from my program were doing better compared to the control group. Details of the procedure are described in Cataldo (1978) and Sigel (1987). Unfortunately, we could not follow them up into their later years in school.

Of particular interest was the fact that the children continued to be highly verbal, curious, and innovative. These were anticipated outcomes. However, these characteristics were not encouraged, but rather punished in the public school. The public school experience was a negative influence, in essence, depressing positive outcomes. For the first time, I came to wonder what I was doing to children if I provided them with a wonderful preschool experience and then had no way of maintaining the program. Perhaps I should have gotten the parents to assume some responsibility and support for the children's intellectual development. However, the parents were basically intimidated by the public school teachers. Hence they did not complain or interfere. More important, they did not value curiosity or intellectual aggressiveness, values intrinsic to our program. On the contrary. They valued obedience to authority, doing what one was told to do, and not fighting. Why? Basically, they wanted their children to learn how to stay out of trouble. From the viewpoint of the parents, low-income Black children were vulnerable to aggressive acts by police, teachers, and Whites in general. Keeping a low profile was the safest course of action. In fact, one of the reasons the parents accepted, and even advocated, physical punishment was because in that way they believed the children would learn how to behave in public, on the street, on the playground, and in the classroom. The parents wanted their children to do well in school, and for them this meant mastering the basics: reading, writing, and arithmetic—no frills. The conflict was between the general intellectual orientation, a basic value in my program, versus skill development and survival. The parents believed that they were teaching children how to survive in a cruel, oppressive, prejudiced world.

The experience was a powerful one for me and led me to have many second thoughts about intervention with the so-called "underclass," and the moral responsibility of researchers working with these families, especially in building up expectations of the outcome of these experiences (Sigel, 1973a).

THE MOVE TO EDUCATIONAL TESTING SERVICE:
ANOTHER EDUCATIONAL PROGRAM

In 1973 I was invited to come to Educational Testing Service to set up a similar program. In this case, Samuel Messick, the Vice President of Research, and Walter Emmerich, were interested in the model that we had developed in Buffalo. This was another opportunity to test the distancing hypothesis. But why? Did not the Buffalo project test it already? I felt that the Buffalo project did show that an educational program based on Distancing theory, at least for poor children, did have a positive effect on intellectual and socioemotional development (Sigel et al., 1973). The fact that these children developed differently cognitively from their peers in other preschool programs did demonstrate something important.

The general belief at the time I came to ETS was that working with middle-class children would not be a good test of Distancing theory. These children did not *need* the same type of educational programming we had used in Buffalo. After all, these children came from privileged homes and their privilege was having many opportunities available to them for cognitive stimulation and enrichment.

Ironically, it was my early work with middle-class White and Black parents that convinced me that although middle-class families were privileged, privilege did not mean that the children were, in fact, stimulated intellectually. The idea that providing a child with rich experiences, such as visiting a museum, is ipso facto stimulating, but misses a crucial point. The experience of that child in that context is enriched when the parent interacts with him or her in such a way as to enable the experience to become meaningful. Too often these so-called enriched experiences are not involving for the child, as little interaction occurs between parent and child about the event. Even if there was interaction, what kind was it? Are parents didactic and authoritative or do they engage children as active participants in the process of exploration? We know from the literature that when parents are authoritarian and do not allow children an opportunity to think for themselves, then these children are less competent than the children who have a more active exchange of ideas and are encouraged to reflect about their experiences. Thus parental style may be more important than class status.

In 1973, Rod Cocking and I came to ETS to set up the program, with Rod covering the research and evaluation aspects. We began the process of building the preschool program on the Buffalo experience. Because we had only one classroom, we decided to set up a program for two groups of 3- and 4-year-old boys and girls (one group came in the morning; the other in the afternoon); one group would be exposed to the distancing model, the other to a traditional preschool program. Our sample came from the local area since parents had to provide their own transportation.

The logic of the program and design was similar to the Buffalo project except for greater opportunities to improve the design in terms of sample selection, social class, and methods of assessment.

The ETS Preschool Program

The teachers were oriented in the same way as they were at Buffalo. The focus was on using distancing strategies and teaching situations requiring representational competence (see Copple, Sigel, & Saunders (1979/1984) for a detailed description of the program). The focus here was on the program's contribution of the distancing hypothesis. The Buffalo experience provided a basis for developing more precise procedures for assessing teachers' distancing behaviors and children's representational competence. An observational schedule was constructed by Freda Rosner. Distancing strategies were carefully defined (Rosner, 1978) on the basis of the cognitive demands inherent in the statement, e.g., demands to sequence, to infer, to describe, etc. In addition to content of the "demand," utterances were coded in terms of structure, e.g., question or statement. Questions were further categorized in terms of open or closed. Finally, the strategies were set in a hierarchy defined by degree of "demand" to represent.

The cognitive tasks were selected to assess anticipation, reconstruction, associative memory, and transformation of ongoing experiences into equivalent symbol systems.

The results of the nursery school program were very instructive. They did show that children do profit from distancing experiences. The children in the experimental group did better on prediction tests, use of language, temporal terms, and drawing (Cocking, 1984; Cocking & Copple, 1979; Sigel, 1979a). I now felt that distancing behaviors were identifiable and did have the expected enhancement of representational competence.

The next question in my search for ontogenesis representation led me to the family, the crucible for cognitive development.

The Shift to Family Studies

Jim Johnson, while doing postdoctoral work at ETS, and I submitted a proposal to NICHHD to study distancing behaviors in families. In the interim Jim left for Wisconsin and Ann McGillicuddy-DeLisi joined me in the first of three major research projects, each focusing on distancing strategies, but in different family contexts. The first, following the program guidelines of NICHHD, focused on variations in parental distancing behaviors among different family constellations and social classes. In addition to identification of the effects of distancing, attention was paid to determinants of such behavior (see McGuillicuddy-DeLisi chapter for the development of those ideas). The family model in the grant involved three interdependent components: parent constructions ↔ parent distancing behaviors ↔ children's representational competence. The argument was that number and spacing of children, as well as parents' social backgrounds, would influence parent construct and parent distancing strategies.

A number of critical decisions had to be made in spite of the fact that we did present a detailed proposal. The decisions involved determining how to assess parent distancing strategies, parent constructs and establishing reliable outcome measures. The proposal set the rationales and guidelines we had to get down to a construction of the measure. The assessment of distancing strategies posed less of a problem because I could build on the nursery school studies. The dependent measures assessing representational competence were also extensions or modifications of previous work in the preschool projects.

Decisions About Assessing Parent Constructs of Children Eventuated in an Interview.   The major decision had to do with assessing distancing strategies. They could be identified through the interview—that is, using strategies as a window to parent constructions of children's learning. For example, asking parents how children learn about a task and following it up by a request for how he or she (the parent) would teach the tasks could yield the strategies the parent would use. Such an approach is useful as it provides specific ties to parents' strategies. I believed that such a method would not be as subject to mnemonic distortions or impressive descriptions as compared to asking about teaching strategies with no context. The final decision was to do both, recognizing the value of each. Because constructs are nonobservable events, there is no other way to get at them except through some self-report measure. Asking parents for their constructs and correlated strategies in face-to-face interviews and observing them teaching their children would provide the opportunity to determine consistency between behavior and self-report.

An initial decision had to be made regarding how and where to observe the parent-child interactions. Initially I had opted for home observations, using an approach similar to the nursery school. Home visits would be made at appropriate times and observers would record parent-child interactions in a familiar environment. The problem with this approach was that home settings would vary, yielding noncomparable data. Further, frequency of distancing strategies would be subject to sources of error. If, on the other hand, as Ann McGillicuddy-DeLisi suggested, a laboratory-type approach was used in which parents were asked to teach children a task, the context would be comparable for all parents and how they interacted in the laboratory would be more a function of parents' choices and not exigencies of the context. Of course, it could be argued that the laboratory is an artificial environment and the parents would not be behaving naturally. Nevertheless in spite of the environmental constraints, I agreed with Ann that there are decided advantages to the laboratory approach and so we proceeded to create a laboratory set-up.

Once the decision to use parent-child observations was made, a number of critical choices had to be made. Working within time and funding constraints of a grant, opportunities for extensive piloting of the variety of procedures were limited and decisions regarding research procedures had to be made relatively quickly. The first problem was creating a social interaction situation that would provide opportunities for parents to use distancing strategies in a natural way. Further, how many interaction tasks should we use? Many studies use just one and generalize from that. So, on we moved to making a number of decisions such as: number and kind of tasks, social interactions, the length of the observation, the social context, i.e., dyadic or triadic? Our guide for all of these choices was the theory—the tasks should allow for opportunities for parent distancing in a natural type social context. To test the distancing model it would make sense to use a structural task and an unstructured one. In this way, a broader sample of parent teaching behaviors would be observed analogous to what parents do in everyday life. Now, what type of task? By chance, Dr. Arnold Sameroff, a fellow developmental psychologist, told me about an origami task developed by Croft, Stern, Siegelbaum, and Goodman (1976). The advantage was that it was novel, the difficulty level could be systematically increased relative to age of child, and there were opportunities for parents to use distancing strategies.

Once the decision to observe in the laboratory was made, we then had to make choices about how to create the physical set-up. On the basis of my experience with observations in the preschool, it became patently clear that it would be impossible to get an accurate fix on the *behavior* the parents used to teach their children a task by recording on the spot. I wanted to get as much detail of the verbal observation between participants. Videotaping became the recording method of choice. This is a tradeoff in that videotaping requires labor-intensive coding so it is time consuming and expensive. Fortunately, our grant support enabled us to go this route. We decided to observe parent-child dyads because we wanted to get at how each parent interacted. We would have liked to use triads, but we could not afford it. We did, however, observe siblings of the target children interacting with each other and with each parent. Our hunch was that these arrangements were probably the most frequent in the family.

Parents and children were observed in a small room with one-way mirrors through which their interactions were videotaped. Two tasks were used—paper-folding (origami) and a story. The paper-folding task involved parents teaching their children how to create a design. This was followed by a story-reading task in which parents were asked to teach the children a story. Each of these methods came about through much discussion and pilot testing to make sure the tasks would provide adequate frequencies of distancing types of behaviors since we planned to use regression and path analyses. We planned these during the course of designing the study. I believe this is critical in research design and reduces analysis problems later on. All of our pilot work did support our decision.

Now that everything was recorded on tape, the next step involved decisions about coding. Again distancing theory had to guide our decision on how and what to code. Because we already coded teacher distancing strategies, we had the broad outline of the system (Rosner, 1978; Sigel & Cocking, 1977b). But those codes were done live and on the spot. In this way they omitted a lot of verbalizations. It is not possible to do detailed coding that way. Having the material on videotapes, however, allows for a detailed coding of content and structure of the verbalizations. For this effort an elaborate and detailed coding system was developed (Sigel & Flaugher, 1980). We also coded each utterance of the parent and the child sequentially. Coding the interactions in such detail allows for a number of data analysis options. The choices range from frequency counts to sequential analyses. In the studies we published we used frequency counts.

A final decision was how much of the observation would be coded. Parents varied in the length of time they needed to complete the paper-folding and the story tasks. We discovered that coding each utterance of the parent and the child was overwhelming so we took a sample of interactions—2 minutes at the beginning, 1 minute in the middle, and 2 minutes at the end. Thus our time sample was 5 minutes long, indicating how the parent intervened, maintained the activity, and concluded it.

The distancing behaviors that parents used were the same types we found among teachers. The differences we found between parents and teachers were in frequency, not types of distancing behaviors and no new ones were identified. We concluded that there is a finite number of these distancing behaviors. Distancing strategies are categorized by mental operational demands (MODs) in the message for the child to separate self (mentally) from the ongoing present, as well as to transform the message into some representation. Cognitive demands can vary from minimal demands to represent (directive) to maximal demands (inference). We identified three levels of demands using a conceptual analysis. These levels are identified in Table 3.1. Statistical analysis later confirmed our logical categorization.[2]

It will be noted that the levels vary from close-ended questions or statements to high level ones which include questions or statements asking the respondent to infer, to identify causal connections, and the like. The basic argument is that children who experience such distancing from the ongoing present, develop cognitive structures that enable them to deal with representational thinking.

Implicit in such learning is the *representational rule.* It can be argued that just experiencing distancing interactions is a sufficiently potent experience to warrant achievement of the rule. Using these distancing strategies as our predictors, we found that parents' use of low-level distancing strategies, that is, close-ended questions, or commands, or imperatives, correlated negatively with children's performance on virtually every cognitive task (i.e., planning, remembering, predicting, and verbal and performance IQ). These findings were consistent for

---

[2]Dr. Anthony Pellegrini of the University of Georgia reported that a factor analysis of the strategies confirmed our logical reduction.

TABLE 3.1
Types of Distancing Strategies Categorized by Levels

High-Level Distancing	Medium-Level Distancing	Low-Level Distancing
evaluate consequence	sequence	label
evaluate competence	reproduce	produce information
evaluate affect	describe similarities	describe, define
evaluate effort and/or performance	describe differences	describe--interpretation
evaluate necessary and/or sufficient	infer similarities	demonstrate
infer cause-effect	infer differences	observe
infer affect	symmetrical classifying	
generalize	asymmetrical classifying	
transform	enumerating	
plan	synthesizing within classifying	
confirmation of a plan		
conclude		
propose alternatives		
resolve conflict		

Note. Three main groupings are used based on the level of the distancing demand upon the child.

111

each of our studies (Sigel, 1979a; Sigel, McGillicuddy-DeLisi, Flaugher, & Rock, 1983; Sigel, McGillicuddy-DeLisi, & Johnson, 1980). This is just as the theory had predicted (Sigel & Cocking, 1977a).

In addition to the findings relative to distancing strategies, we examined assessments of the parents' beliefs or constructs (see McGillicuddy-DeLisi, this volume). The model we developed, and which continues to guide our work to date, is that beliefs influence strategies and strategies influence child outcomes. The model is an interactive one of mutual influences. Distancing strategies were then conduits or mediators of parent beliefs (McGillicuddy-DeLisi, 1982; Sigel, 1981).

I was impressed with the findings from these early explorations. However, too often developmental research stops at this level and it is assumed that what follows is consistent with the past. However, that perspective is contradicted by developmental theory from any "school of thought." Development is an on-going life process, where change is endemic to existence. So, I ask, what about the role of beliefs and/or distancing strategies? Do parents use the same types of distancing strategies when the children are older? If so, do they have the same effect on the children?

The Distancing Model, 1988

The purpose of the follow-up study was to determine the relationship between parental beliefs and behaviors at Time 1, when the children were between the ages of 3½ and 5, and Time 2, 5 years later. A related question has to do with the consistency of parental beliefs and behaviors over time. The issues in this study can be reduced to questions of stability and change in parents' beliefs and practices (especially distancing behavior) and the stability and consistency of outcomes. For example, we found low-level distancing strategies relating negatively to verbal IQ. Is this a finding that depends on the age of the child, or to put it another way, do low-level distancing strategies have the same effect irrespective of age? Questions of this type are rarely asked in developmental research. The accepted view is that relationships of the type described here are general and independent of context, age of participants, or domains involved. Ironically, there is no rational base for such reasoning. Quite the contrary, there is reason to expect that with changes in conditions, relationships among variables may change. If the earlier relationships are obtained in this later study, then that strengthens the generality of the distancing model.

The sample was made up of 80 families from our previous samples: 40 with a communication handicapped child and 40 with a noncommunication handicapped child. The samples were matched pairs—matched for social class and sex. The dependent measures that were chosen were school achievement in both reading and mathematics since performance in these two knowledge domains requires representational competence.

On the basis of our earlier studies I concluded that children who grow up in homes where parents use distancing will have developed a positive sense of self as problem solvers and as independent thinkers. This type of analysis would extend the significance of the distancing from just a cognitive model to a cognitive-affective model. I feel this is a more realistic way to conceptualize the issues since cognition does not function in isolation (Sigel, 1984). These feelings of thought would spill over into their social and personal sense of self-worth. We used the Harter Scale to Assess these factors (Harter, 1985).

Although this follow-up study was designed to be as close in method to our earlier ones as possible, we were faced with the fact that the children were older, therefore we had to modify our procedures. In addition, we had learned from our past experiences and so were able to tighten up the interview procedures both in terms of structure and coding.

Before reporting on those changes, I want to share an experience that demonstrated the value of taking parents into our research as partners, not just in data collection, but also in developing our procedures. In this way we could get feedback on how our intended respondent might respond.

I had hoped that we could short cut the interview procedure by building a questionnaire on the basis of previous interviews. My colleagues and I developed the questionnaire in the format of previous interviews. Rather than pretest the interview on a one-to-one basis, I decided to adopt the focus group strategy—a marketing research technique. A group of mothers comparable in age and social background to those in our sample were invited to come to ETS for a discussion. We had two groups of seven mothers each. We told them exactly what we wanted—a critical analysis of the questionnaire with no holds barred. After they filled out the questionnaire we got into the critique phase. It was an enlightening experience. First, each mother reported the questionnaire was not the way to get at her views. All the questionnaire gets, according to our informants, is *their* reaction to *our* views, not *their* views. Second, questionnaires are too restrictive, providing no opportunity to clarify meanings or to challenge the items—the usual respondent's critique. Finally, they would prefer an interview where they would have the opportunity to state their opinions, qualify their responses, and above all, acquaint us with life with their child at home. After 2 hours of discussion we shifted briefly to a discussion of a teaching task. Remember we were discussing teaching 8- to 12-year-olds. After much discussion the procedure of teaching child to tie knots came up as an idea. The mothers thought it would work.

A second focus group meeting was held and they agreed with much of what the first group had said and recommended. On the basis of their suggestions and what we had learned from previous experience, we structured our interview to enable us to get at beliefs and behaviors within four specific knowledge domains. Such information would prove valuable in determining whether beliefs and practices are general or tied to specific content areas, thus demonstrating that parent and child interactions are not of one cloth, but interact with the setting and the task.

This latter point was evident in our developing the knowledge domain areas in the interview. The idea of knot-tying as a replacement for the origami task and a family dilemma as a replacement for the story-telling task are familiar to the children and parents. I was extremely satisfied with the focus group approach and they certainly influenced our choices by holding a mirror to our activities, a painful, but useful procedure.

We decided to go with an interview. The interview was made up of 11 scoreable vignettes involving problems or issues in four domains: physical knowledge, intrapsychic knowledge, moral knowledge, and social knowledge. Factor analysis of these vignettes yielded three factors: physical knowledge, intrapsychic knowledge and moral-social knowledge. These domains held for beliefs as well as for strategies. For each vignette, the parent provided a strategy regarding the problem. Then he or she was asked, ''How do you think your child 'learns' about, e.g., fire?'' Distancing strategies were used most often in the areas of physical knowledge and moral-social knowledge, whereas positive and negative feedback were the strategies of choice of the intrapsychic and moral-social knowledge domain. The finding that strategies vary with the problem speaks loudly and clearly to the notion that parents' strategies are domain-dependent and generalizations about parental behaviors have to be qualified. Ignoring the context of the problem to be dealt with misleads us about parents' attitudes, beliefs, strategies, etc.

Do distancing behaviors relate to academic achievement? The answer is, *yes*. Distancing behaviors predict to children's achievement in mathematics and reading. However, a significant fact is that the predictions are different for boys and girls. Often the correlations between distancing and math achievement are negative for girls, but not for boys. Why this is the case is an open question. There are many possible speculations, but being merely speculative, I will leave that for some future investigators.

Summary

We have come a long way with the Distancing theory model. Our family studies, involving mostly preschool children, reaffirmed our findings and our theory that distancing strategies do relate to children's intellectual and social characteristics, especially those involving abstract thinking, mathematical reasoning and reading. These results, albeit with parental interview data about older children, are entirely consistent with our earlier reports. Thus the Distancing Hypothesis is no longer a hypothesis, but in my view, it is now a model for studying the ontogenesis of representational competence.

What is also of particular interest is that we discovered relationships between beliefs and behaviors. It is quite clear that parents who believe children learn through their thinking, reasoning, and the like use distancing strategies quite consistently. However, parents who have other beliefs do not use such strategies. Of course, this summary is an oversimplification of the results, but of particular interest is the overarching consistency of relationships (Sigel, Stinson, & Flaugher, 1988).

With all of this empirical support, let me conclude with a discussion of where the Distancing theory is now.

The Current Status of the Distancing Hypothesis

Actually, what started as a hypothesis has been transformed into distancing theory. The data from all of the studies point to the same set of conclusions—to wit, teacher's or parent's use of distancing strategies does relate to children's intellectual functioning. Low-level strategies relate negatively to cognitive outcomes whereas high-level strategies relate poitively. The consistency of our research results indicates that the initial distancing hypothesis was supported. In general, the cognitive demands on children to transcend the ongoing, reconstruct past events, and plan or anticipate outcomes do relate to representational competence. Studies focusing on modification of categorization behavior (Sigel & Olmsted, 1970b), picture comprehension (Sigel, 1978), conservation (Sigel et al., 1966), representational competence in educational settings (Cocking & Sigel, 1979; Sigel, 1986; Sigel et al., 1973) and in family settings—concurrently (Sigel, 1982) and long-term (Sigel, 1986), demonstrate that distancing strategies do play a significant role in children's cognitive development.

These results are indeed rewarding, particularly because they were obtained in different settings with different populations. However, much more remains to be done to provide greater understanding of the phenomenon. Consequently, I am broadening my conceptualization of distancing, taking into account its dialogical aspects in a social context. Because distancing strategies have been studied as verbal phenomenon intrinsic to social interaction, a social process perspective immediately becomes relevant in order to help understand, and eventually explain, what there is about distancing strategies that influences children's development.

Two types of studies need to be done: naturalistic and experimental. Naturalistic observation of discourse in various social contexts with different age, sex and social groups can help elucidate the degree to which the distancing phenomena functions: What are the constraints and facilitators for effectiveness? For example, a discourse analysis of our parent-child interaction dialogues revealed that the effectiveness of the distancing strategy depends on the number of turns in the dialogue (Zahaykevich, Sigel, & Rock, 1985). The more turns, the better. Further, work examining sequential interactions may provide additional information regarding the specific social factors that mediate the influence of the strategies, e.g., age, sex, and power relationships among the participants, length of the dialogue. Naturalistic observations, however, do not allow for testing specific hypotheses since the occurrence of certain classes of events are not predictable. If number of turns, for example, are at issue, there is no way in a naturalistic setting to create that. There are a number of questions dealing with the structure and message of the strategies.

Although naturalistic studies can provide valuable insights regarding the relationships of distancing behaviors and the development of representational competence, it could also be valuable to study the phenomena with an experimental paradigm. It seems possible to test for effects of types of distancing behaviors in various types of groups differing in age, sex or kinship composition. Through such controlled procedures, I believe we can test for the effects of particular discourse patterns. No doubt other issues can be addressed with experimental paradigms, e.g., understanding of signs, symbols, etc.

What began as a simple idea has developed into a theory. This is not the place to spell it out in detail. What I have shown is the development of an idea of how through various research efforts it has been transformed from a singular hypothesis to a conceptualization of a particular class of social interactions.

Although the distancing hypothesis virtually was developed in the context of social development with little or no thought of its relevance for family research, the work done during the past 10 years has shown quite clearly that the theory as it has developed is indeed appropriate for family research because the kind of development involved in distancing is embedded in family communication. Not only do parents communicate via distancing strategies to their children, but to each other, and children use such strategies between themselves and with their parents. What will vary within and between families is the frequency and type of strategies used and how patterns of each communication change over time (McGillicuddy-DeLisi & Sigel, in press). From my point of view, distancing theory incorporated into the broader aspects of family research should enrich our understanding of the family as a socialization agent (Sigel, Dreyer, & McGillicuddy-DeLisi, 1984).

ACKNOWLEDGMENTS

Funding for the research reported here was supported in part by the United States Office of Economic Opportunity Head Start Subcontract No. 1410 to Michigan State University, Office of Economic Opportunity Grant No. CG8547 to the State University of New York at Buffalo, National Institute of Child Health and Human Development Grant No. R01-HD10686 to Educational Testing Service, National Institute of Mental Health Grant No. R01-MH32301 to Educational Testing Service, National Institute of Mental Health Grant No. R01-MH40103 to Educational Testing Service, Bureau of Education of the Handicapped Grant No.

G007902000 to Educational Testing Service and the National Foundation March of Dimes Grant No. 6-416 to Educational Testing Service.

The journey I have described brought me in touch with many people who have helped me change the ideas expressed here. Special thanks to Rodney R. Cocking whose insightful questions forced me to sharpen my ideas, to Ann McGilli-cuddy-DeLisi for her skill in transforming theory into operations, to Jim Johnson who demonstrated that it all makes sense, and to Jan Flaugher who managed to keep our family projects on track. I also wish to acknowledge the contributions over the years of the following: David Brodzinsky, Carol Copple, Walter Emmerich, George Forman, James Johnson, Ruth Saunders, Ada Secrist, Carolyn Shantz, Brian Vandenberg, and Frederick Verdonik.

A special note of appreciation to Linda Kozelski for her invaluable technical and editorial assistance in bringing this manuscript to completion.

REFERENCES

Bearison, D. J., & Sigel, I. E. (1968). Hierarchical attributes for categorization. *Perceptual and Motor Skills, 27,* 147–153.

Cataldo, C. Z. (1978). A follow-up study of early intervention (Doctoral dissertation, State University of New York at Buffalo, 1977). *Dissertation Abstracts International, 39,* 657-A.

Cocking, R. R. (1984). Dimensions of early language learning and relationships with higher-order cognitive skills. In W. E. Fthenakes (Ed.), *Current topics in child development and education* (pp. 277–324). Düsseldorf: Schwann.

Cocking, R. R., & Copple, C. E. (1979). Change through exposure to others: A study of children's verbalizations as they draw. In M. K. Poulsen & G. I. Lubin (Eds.), *Proceedings of the Eighth Annual Conference on Piagetian Theory and the Helping Professions* (Vol. 2, pp. 124–132). Los Angeles, CA: University of Southern California.

Cocking, R. C., & Sigel, I. E. (1979). The concept of décalàge as it applies to representational thinking. In N. R. Smith & M. B. Franklin (Eds.), *Symbolic functioning in childhood* (pp. 67–83). Hillsdale, NJ: Lawrence Erlbaum Associates.

Copple, C., Sigel, I. E., & Saunders, R. (1984). *Educating the young thinker: Classroom strategies for cognitive growth.* Hillsdale, NJ: Lawrence Erlbaum Associates. (Original work published 1979).

Croft, R., Stern, S., Siegelbaum, H., & Goodman, D. (1976). *Manual for description and functional analysis of continuous didactic interactions.* New York: University of Rochester.

Gibson, J. J. (1966). *The senses considered as perceptual systems.* Boston: Houghton Mifflin.

Golden, M., & Birns, B. (1968). Social class and cognitive development in infancy. *Merrill-Palmer Quarterly, 14,* 139–149.

Gombrich, E. H. (1969). *Art and illusion: A study in the psychology of pictorial representation* (Bollingen Series XXXV.5). Princeton, NJ: Princeton University Press.

Griffiths, J. A., Shantz, C. U., & Sigel, I. E. (1967). A methodological problem in conservation studies: The use of relational terms. *Child Development, 38,* 841–848.

Hagan, M. A. (1974). Picture perception: Toward a theoretical model. *Psychological Bulletin, 81,* 471–497.

Harter, S. (1985). *Manual for the self-perception profile for children.* Denver: University of Colorado.

Hochberg, J., & Brooks, V. (1962). Pictorial recognition as an unlearned ability: A study of one child's performance. *American Journal of Psychology, 75,* 624–628.

Hudson, E. (1967). The study of the problem of pictorial perception among unacculturated groups. *International Journal of Psychology, 2,* 89–107.

Inhelder, B., & Piaget, J. (1964). *The early growth of logic in the child.* New York: Harper & Row.

Jahoda, G. (1966). Geometric illusions and environment: A study in Ghana. *British Journal of Psychology, 57,* 193–199.

McGillicuddy-DeLisi, A. V. (1982). The relationship between parents' beliefs about development and family constellation, socioeconomic status, and parents' teaching strategies. In L. M. Laosa & I. E. Sigel (Eds.), *Families as learning environments for children* (pp. 261–299). New York: Plenum.

McGillicuddy-DeLisi, A. V., & Sigel, I. E. (1989). Family environment and children's representational thinking. In S. Silvern (Ed.), *Development of literacy* (Vol. 6). Greenwich, CT: JAI Press.

Piaget, J. (1950). *The psychology of intelligence.* London: Routledge & Kegan Paul.

Piaget, J. (1962). *Play, dreams and imitation in childhood.* New York: Norton.

Randhawa, B. S., & Coffman, E. (1978). The development of pictorial comprehension. In B. S. Randhawa & E. Coffman (Eds.), *Visual learning, thinking and communication* (pp. 93–111). New York: Academic Press.

Roeper, A., & Sigel, I. E. (1966). Finding the clue to children's thought processes. *Young Children, 21,* 335–349.

Rosner, F. C. (1978). An ecological study of teacher distancing behaviors as a function of program context and time (Doctoral dissertation, Temple University, 1978). *Dissertation Abstracts International, 39,* 760A.

Serpell, R. (1976). *Culture's influence on behavior.* London: Methuen.

Shantz, C. U., & Sigel, I. E. (1967). *Logical operations and concepts of conservation in children: A training study* (Final Report on Project No. 6-8463). Washington, DC: Office of Education, Bureau of Research.

Sigel, I. E. (1953). Developmental trends in the abstraction ability of children. *Child Development, 24(2),* 131–144.

Sigel, I. E. (1954). The dominance of meaning. *The Journal of Genetic Psychology, 85,* 201–207.

Sigel, I. E. (1970). The distancing hypothesis: A causal hypothesis for the acquisition of representational thought. In M. R. Jones (Ed.), *Miami Symposium on the Prediction of Behavior, 1968: Effect of early experiences* (pp. 99–118). Coral Gables, FL: University of Miami Press.

Sigel, I. E. (1973a, June). *Contributions of psycho-educational intervention programs in understanding of preschool children.* Paper presented at the Burg Wartenstein Symposium No. 57, "Cultural and Social Influences in Infancy and Early Childhood," New York.

Sigel, I. E. (1973b). Intervention at age 2. In R. Piret (Ed.), *The Proceedings of the XVIIth International Congress of the International Association of Applied Psychology* (Vol. 2, pp. 1155–1164). Brussels, Belgium: EDITEST.

Sigel, I. E. (1974). When do we know what a child knows? *Human Development, 17,* 201–217.

Sigel, I. E. (1978). The development of pictorial comprehension. In B. S. Randhawa & W. E. Coffman (Eds.), *Visual learning, thinking, and communication* (pp. 93–111). New York: Academic Press.

Sigel, I. E. (1979a). On becoming a thinker: A psychoeducational model. *Educational Psychologist, 14,* 70–78.

Sigel, I. E. (1979b). Piaget and education: A dialectic. In F. B. Murray (Ed.), *The impact of Piagetian theory: On education, philosophy, psychiatry, and psychology* (pp. 209–223). Baltimore, MD: University Park Press.

Sigel, I. E. (1981). Social experience in the development of representational thought: Distancing theory. In I. E. Sigel, D. M. Brodzinsky, & R. M. Golinkoff (Eds.), *New directions in Piagetian theory and practice* (pp. 203–217). Hillsdale, NJ: Lawrence Erlbaum Associates.

Sigel, I. E. (1982). The relationship between parental distancing strategies and the child's cognitive behavior. In L. M. Laosa & I. E. Sigel (Eds.), *Families as learning environments for children* (pp. 47–86). New York: Plenum.

Sigel, I. E. (1984). Reflections on action theory and distancing theory. *Human Development, 27,* 188–193.

Sigel, I. E. (1986). Early social experience and the development of representational competence. In W. Fowler (Ed.), *Early experience and the development of competence* (pp. 49–65). New Directions for Child Development, No. 32. San Francisco: Jossey-Bass.

Sigel, I. E. (1987). Educating the young thinker: A distancing model of preschool education. In J. L. Roopnarine & J. E. Johnson (Eds.), *Approaches to early childhood education* (pp. 237–252). Columbus, OH: Merrill.

Sigel, I. E., Anderson, L. M., & Shapiro, H. (1966). Categorization behavior of lower and middle class Negro preschool children: Differences in dealing with representation of familiar objects. *Journal of Negro Education, 35,* 218–229.

Sigel, I. E., & Cocking, R. R. (1977a). Cognition and communication: A dialectic paradigm for development. In M. Lewis & L. A. Rosenblum (Eds.), *The origins of behavior: Vol. 5. Interaction, conversation, and the development of language* (pp. 207–226). New York: Wiley.

Sigel, I. E., & Cocking, R. R. (1977b). *Cognitive development from childhood to adolescence: A constructivist perspective.* New York: Holt, Rinehart & Winston.

Sigel, I. E., & Cocking, R. R. (1979). A cybernetic approach to psychological testing of children. *Cybernetics forum, 9,* 46–50.

Sigel, I. E., Dreyer, A., & McGillicuddy-DeLisi, A. (1984). Psychological perspectives of the family. In R. D. Parke (Ed.), *Review of child development research* (Vol. 7, pp. 42–79). Chicago: University of Chicago Press.

Sigel, I. E., & Flaugher, J. (1980). *Parent-child interaction observation schedule (PCI).* Princeton, NJ: Educational Testing Service.

Sigel, I. E., & McBane, B. (1967). Cognitive competence and level of symbolization among five-year-old children. In J. Hellmuth (Ed.), *The disadvantaged child* (Vol. 1, pp. 433–453). Seattle, WA: Special Child Publications of the Seattle Sequin School.

Sigel, I. E., McGillicuddy-DeLisi, A. V., Flaugher, J., & Rock, D. A. (1983). *Parents as teachers of their own learning disabled children* (ETS RR 83-21). Princeton, NJ: Educational Testing Service.

Sigel, I. E., McGillicuddy-DeLisi, A. V., & Johnson, J. E. (1980). *Parental distancing, beliefs and children's representational competence within the family context* (ETS RR 80-21). Princeton, NJ: Educational Testing Service.

Sigel, I. E., & Olmsted P. (1970a). The development of classification and representational competence. In A. J. Biemiller (Ed.), *Problems in the teaching of young children* (pp. 49–67). Ontario, Canada: The Ontario Institute for Studies in Education.

Sigel, I. E., & Olmsted, P. (1970b). Modification of cognitive skills among lower-class black children. In J. Hellmuth (Ed.), *The disadvantaged child* (Vol. 3, pp. 300–338). New York: Brunner-Mazel.

Sigel, I. E., Roeper, A., & Hooper, F. H. (1966). A training procedure for acquisition of Piaget's conservation of quantity: A pilot study and its replication. *The British Journal of Educational Psychology, 36,* 301–311.

Sigel, I. E., Secrist, A., & Forman, G. (1973). Psycho-educational intervention beginning at age two: Reflections and outcomes. In J. C. Stanley (Ed.), *Compensatory education for children, ages two to eight: Recent studies of educational intervention.* Baltimore, MD: Johns Hopkins University Press.

Sigel, I. E., Stinson, E. T., & Flaugher, J. (1988, June). *Family processes and school achievement.* Paper presented at the Third Annual Summer Institute, Hilton Head, SC.

Werner, H. (1948). *Comparative psychology of mental development* (rev. ed.). Chicago: Follett.

Werner, H., & Kaplan, B. (1963). *Symbol formation: An organismic developmental approach to language and the expression of thought.* New York: Wiley.

Zahaykevich, M., Sigel, I. E., & Rock, D. A. (1985). *A model of parental speech acts and child cognitive development.* Unpublished manuscript, Educational Testing Service.

4 The Nature-Nurture Problem Revisited: The Minnesota Adoption Studies[1]

Sandra Scarr
University of Virginia

Richard A. Weinberg
University of Minnesota

MAJOR CONCEPTUAL ISSUES

The role, indeed the very existence, of genetic differences in human behavior has long been a matter of heated debate in the social sciences. Each generation of scientists rediscovers the nature-nurture problem. Throughout intellectual history, although the social, political, and religious contexts have varied, the question has remained about the same: "To what extent are genes *and* environments important variables in accounting for the development of human behavior?" The question seems to remain unanswered despite an expanded knowledge base in the fields of behavioral genetics and psychology, an increased repertoire of methodologies in research design and statistical analyses, and the availability of populations appropriate for studying the problem. Counterbalancing these advances is a plethora of value and moral issues rooted in the rich soil of the social-political and judicial arenas (Weinberg, 1983).

In the past 2 decades, the writings of Jensen (1973), Lewontin (1970), Herrnstein (1973), and Kamin (1974) have generated an overheated emotional climate. Strong public opinion has been sparked, accompanied by uncontrolled polemics. The controversy has been stoked by questioning the authenticity of Sir Cyril Burt's data, long considered a cornerstone of hereditarian arguments, and by increasingly vigorous interest in sociobiology and its emphasis on the evolutionary roots and adaptive nature of complex social behavior. Charges of racism, genocide, and antifeminism have been made against psychologists, ethologists,

---

[1]This chapter is based in part on studies reported earlier in the *American Psychologist, Child Development,* and *Human Nature.*

121

anthropologists, and others who have embraced sociobiological perspectives. In their extremes, hereditarian arguments have been used both to defend notions of racial inferiority and supremacy in various domains of human behavior (e.g., intellectual ability) and to attack compensatory education programs such as Head Start and other intervention programs as naive, untenable exploitations of federal funds. "Pure" environmentalists have offered a rationale for developing specific intervention programs and general social policies that guarantee major changes in an individuals' behavior presumed to be genetically determined by hereditarians. Environmentalism, run amok, has provided the basis for Pygmalion schemes that promise geniuses in every home and scholars in every classroom.

Like master chess players, advocates from the hereditarian and environmentalist camps have played a rigorous game—accepting theoretical and mathematical assumptions as reasonable when they support an argument, rejecting methodological strategies and research designs as inappropriate when they challenge a position, and shaping data to fit their own particular views. Clad in ideological armor, the combatants have hurled scientific rhetoric and ad hominem insults; while the battlefield remains cluttered, no clear victory has been won by either side. Indeed, undiluted polar positions have characterized discussions of the sources of individual differences in behavior. This "either-or" philosophy must create confusion for many members of the psychological community, whose primary interest is fostering an individual's development by creating optimal environments. If intellectual ability, cognitive skills, school achievement, personality characteristics, and other parameters of behavior are predetermined by genetic blueprints, then what role can environments play in the development of the individual? More specifically, can an environment contribute to the development of a child's behavior? Can the level of an individual's performance be altered as the result of childrearing, instruction, and interventions? Are there limits to the impact of such interventions?

It is in the context of these issues that our program of research evolved. Coming from different academic and professional backgrounds, we joined forces in 1971 to embark on a 15-year collaboration, 2 major studies and their follow-ups, and over 30 joint publications.

In this chapter we share that odyssey—the kinds of questions we individually posed which led us to this research program, the conceptual model that has guided our research design, the plan for our research, what we have found, and what we think it all means. It is hoped that this insider's view of a research enterprise will help the reader see the personal, subjective side of even the most basic, objective, efforts in science.

Sandra Scarr: What's a Nice Girl Like You Doing In a Place Like This?

"My interest in the possibility of genetic behavioral differences began, when as an undergraduate, I was told there were none. The social science view of the time was that genetics might set limits on species but that each individual within the species was endowed with everything that was important to develop into a beggar, king, attorney, or con artist.

My own observation of human behavior made me curious about their certainty in this matter, especially since I could find no evidence for this view. It seemed to me important to understand human differences rather than to stifle research for fear of unpopular results. I joined the American Civil Liberties Union in my senior year in college, to assure myself and others that an interest in genetic differences did not necessarily go with antidemocratic politics.

In graduate school, I decided to have a closer look at human individuality by doing a doctoral dissertation with Irving Gottesman on genetic variability in motivation. Even then, I was struck by the behavioral individuality of my own first child (compared to my friends' children) and by the resistance among professors of psychology to such ideas.

After moving to the University of Pennsylvania in 1966, a quick glance at the local scene told me that the most interesting question of practical import was, "Why do Black children do so poorly in school and on intellectual tests?" This question had been addressed in hundreds of studies that merely charted the intellectual differences between Blacks and Whites at many age levels and in many locales. There must be, I thought, more analytically powerful ways to get at the causes of these differences in performance.

Two logically possible hypotheses had been offered to explain why Black children do poorly in school and badly on tests: sociocultural disadvantage and racial genetic differences. The advocates of both views asserted their positions with vehemence, but there were no critical tests of either hypothesis.

Thus, in 1967, I began a program of research that continues today, employing five previously unused strategies to study the sources of racial differences in intellectual performance:

1. studies of individual differences within the U.S. Black population by the twin method;

2. the study of genetic markers of degrees of African ancestry and their relation to intellectual differences with the U.S. Black population;

3. the study of transracial adoption by which socially classified Black children are reared in the cultural environment sampled by the tests and the school;

4. cross-cultural studies in which Black children are or are not socially disadvantaged, and

5. educational intervention programs with young children to test ideas about reaction range and malleability.

Evidence against a racial genetic hypothesis and for the importance of genetic individual variability has come from all five sources.

The implications I have drawn from these five lines of research on racial and social class differences are that Black and White children do not differ much, if they have reasonable opportunities to learn the culture of the tests and the schools, but that social class differences among Whites are largely due to genetic differences. Among Blacks, the correlation of social class indicators with IQ test scores are about half of those for Whites, a suggestion that mobility by individual attributes has been historically limited, thereby limiting the contemporary association between genetic differences and social stratification among Blacks.

Individual differences, I find, are predominantly genetic within any group that is reasonably nurtured. Deliberate interventions to improve children's intellectual and academic performance are most effective for those who have little contact with the knowledge and skills to be tested or used in schools. Educational interventions to improve the performance of children who are not considerably disadvantaged have little effect. Framed in the reaction range concept, malleability is a property of organisms within the range of species-normal environments, and development is not so plastic as to be shoved around by any but the most severe environments."

Richard A. Weinberg: Does What We Do Really Make a Difference?

"I received my doctorate in 1968, trained in school psychology with a strong focus on child development. Like most school psychologists, influenced by the writings of the 1960s—Jerome Bruner, B. F. Skinner, J. McVicker Hunt, and Benjamin Bloom, I was a strong advocate of educational interventions and programs that would "make a difference." In fact, my doctoral thesis was a study aimed at modifying children's conceptual tempos using behavioral techniques. As a clinician, I wanted to believe that interventions in the form of alternative curricula, therapeutic programs, and remedial efforts were time well spent. At Teachers College, Columbia University, my first teaching position, I expanded my interests in the early education enterprise and watched the unfolding of the Head Start program, a major early childhood intervention effort and national social experiment (Weinberg, 1979). Then, in 1969, Arthur Jensen published his controversial critique of compensatory education programs and rekindled the nature-nurture controversy in a contemporary context of racial unrest and the quest for civil rights. Jensen's paper (Jensen, 1969) and the responses that followed had a profound impact on me. I had been working with some groups of Black parents and children in Harlem and the Morningside Heights areas of New York. Certainly, I saw individual differences among the children in terms of ability, personality, and attitudes, but these differences appeared also among the advantaged White parents and children who were applicants to a prestigious girls' school for which I consulted. Two different cultures and socioeconomic climates were represented in my experiences, but personally I could not see how *racial* differences and Jensen's account could explain the variance within and between these populations.

Sandra Scarr and I joined the faculty at the University of Minnesota in 1970 and quickly came to share views that represented an appreciation of individual differences and a thirst to know more about why Black children and White children had such disparate school records, why children within the same families could appear so different, and what limits were set by genetic endowment for altering human behavior.''

A Conceptual Framework

We joined forces—a developmental behavior geneticist and a developmental school psychologist—to address the nature-nurture problem, taking advantage of the time and place to pursue behavior genetics research.

In developing a conceptual framework for studying the nature-nurture problem, we agreed on some basic assumptions and beliefs. Initially, we acknowledged that the social sciences have been plagued by the controversy over nature *and* nurture, because of a misconception that the conjunction was "or." At the core of the controversy is the idea that genetic variation *fixes* individual and group differences in human behavior. Opponents of the idea believe that genetic differences are antithetical to malleability or change in behavior. A common error underlying this belief is a failure to distinguish environmental and genetic sources of individual differences in behavior from the necessary roles of both genes and environments in behavioral development. One cannot assess the relative impact of heredity or environment in behavioral domains because everyone must have both a viable gene complement and an environment in which the genes can be expressed over development.

Behavioral differences among individuals, on the other hand, can arise in any population from genetic differences, from variations among their environments, or both. Imagine a population of genetically identical clones who are reared in family environments that vary from working to upper-middle class. Any behavioral differences among the clones would necessarily arise from developing within those different environments. Next, imagine a genetically diverse human population reared in laboratory cages. All members experience exactly the same environments. Naturally, all differences among those individuals are accounted for by their genetic variability. Notice, however, that in the two fantasies the organisms all have *both* genes *and* environments for development (Scarr & Weinberg, 1980). Because nearly all families share both genes and environments, it is usually impossible to know why individuals are similar or different from one another.

RESEARCH METHODS

The Adoption Model

The adoption of children with biological backgrounds that are different from both their adopting parents and each other provides an opportunity to evaluate the impact of environments on children's development. If differences among the child-rearing environments provided by families determine differences in children's development, then the differences among adopted children ought to be correlated with differences among their adoptive families. Theoretically, regressions of adopted-child outcomes on adoptive-family characteristics will provide genetically unbiased estimates of true environmental effects in the population from which they are drawn.

Unfortunately, adoptive families are selected by agencies for being above average in many virtues, including socioeconomic status. Children in adoptive families are reared in nondeprived, nonabusive environments. However, the fact that the SES range of adoptive families usually includes at least two-thirds of the U.S. White population makes results of adoption studies compelling.

Comparisons of adopted and birth relatives assume that the greater behavioral similarity usually found among birth relatives is a result of their greater genetic similarity. Critics of the adoption model assert to the contrary that important biases can creep into comparisons of genetically related and unrelated families through parental and child expectations of greater similarity among birth than adopted relatives. Fortunately for the adoption model, knowledge of adoptive or biological relatedness does not constitute a bias in comparisons of measured behavioral differences in birth and adoptive families, because there appear to be no correlations between perceived and actual similarities in intelligence or personality (Scarr, Scarf, & Weinberg, 1980).

The Minnesota Adoption Studies

Following in the tradition of Alice M. Leahy (1935), who conducted a pioneering adoption study in Minnesota, we launched two large adoption studies in 1973 for two quite different purposes. The Transracial Adoption Study was carried out in Minnesota to test the hypothesis that Black and interracial children reared by White families (in the culture of the tests and the schools) would perform on IQ tests and school achievement measures as well as other adopted children (Scarr & Weinberg, 1976). A second investigation, the Adolescent Adoption Study, was conceived to assess the cumulative impact of differences in family environments on children's development at the end of the child-rearing period (Scarr & Weinberg, 1978; Scarr & Yee, 1980). In both studies, we examined the levels of intellectual and personality development, as well as the degree of resemblance among family members, by comparing adoptive and birth relatives.

Why choose the adoption model? There are alternative methods or designs for studying the effects of environments and human genetic endowment on psychological development—studies of identical and fraternal twins reared together and apart or studies of families including members of varying degrees of resemblances: siblings, cousins, etc. However, Minnesota has been in the forefront of adoption and that is where we were in 1971! The interest and cooperation of

the State Department of Public Welfare Adoption Unit and two large agencies—
Lutheran Social Service and Children's Home Society made the study *feasible*. It
is easy to conceptualize a research program on paper but the lack of accessibility
and cooperation of appropriate subject samples can be a major stumbling block.

Also, the adoption method is generally recognized as the most powerful
human behavioral genetic design because it includes genetically related and
unrelated family members reared together and natural parents and their adopted
children reared apart. Thus, the impact of heredity and the influence of family
environment can be separated (Plomin, 1986).

OUR PROGRAM OF RESEARCH: 1973–1976

In our two large-scale studies of adoption in Minnesota, one of White adolescents,
the other of Black and interracial children adopted into White homes, we interviewed hundreds of children and their parents; we gave comparable tests for
intelligence, interests, and attitudes to both generations (see Table 4.1); our
interviews and tests covered a great deal of information other than IQ. Most
important, we were able to assess the relative effects of heredity and environment
because we could compare birth and adopted children within the same family,
compare adopted children with their birth and their adoptive parents, and explore
the origins of differences between children who grow up in similar environments.

Procedures

Early on, we decided to see families with young children (i.e., Transracial
Adoption Study) in their homes, because many of the preschool-age children
could be intimidated by coming to the University. We wanted to assess their best
performance and adaptations. Most data were collected directly from the adoptive families. Some data on the natural parents and the children's preadoption
histories were obtained from the adoption records. Achievement and aptitude
scores were supplied by school districts for all school-age children to whom such
tests had been administered.

Choosing measures to be included in the extensive battery was difficult.
Quickly, we decided that both parents and all children in the family over 4-years-
of-age would be administered an age appropriate IQ test (*Wechsler Adult Intel-
ligence Scale (WAIS), Wechsler Intelligence Scale for Children (WISC)*, or
Stanford-Binet (S-B). Table 4.1 gives a list of the measures administered in the
Transracial Adoption Study. Personality measures included the *Junior Eysenck
Personality Inventory* for the children over 8-years-of-age and the *Eysenck Per-
sonality Inventory* for older children and the parents. Fathers completed the
Rotter Locus of Control and mothers, the *Parent Attitude Research Instrument*.
Standardized measures were chosen for several reasons. First, we had confi-

TABLE 4.1

The Data Bank for the Minnesota Adoption Studies

Data Bank--Transracial Adoption Study	Data Bank--Adolescent Adoption Study
1. Adoption Record Abstract for each adoptee including: --birthdate --number and dates of preadoption placements --evaluation of the quality of preadoption placements (rated by our research team) --date of placement in adoptive home --natural parents' age at child's birth, educational level, race, and occupation of mother, and if available, IQ	1. Adoption Record Abstract for each adoptee including: --birthdate --number and dates of preadoption palcements --evaluation of the quality of preadoption placements (rated by our research team) --date of placement in adoptive home --natural parents' age at child's birth, educational level, race, and occupation of mother, and if available, IQ
2. Adoptive Family Demographics and detailed personal interview with mother	2. Adoptive Family Demographics and detailed personal interview with mother
3. Family Index--questionnaire on home life and family life style	3. Family Index--questionnaire on home life and family life style
4. School aptitude and achievement test data on children (gathered for all school-age children)	4. School aptitude and achievement test data on children (gathered for all school-age children)
5. Cognitive Measures: Raven's Matrices (age appropriate) Stanford-Binet, WISC, or WAIS (age-appropriate)	5. Cognitive Measures: Wechsler Adult Intelligence Scale (short form)
6. Personality Measures: Junior Eysenck Personality Inventory (for older children) Eysenck Personality Inventory (parents) Rotter Locus of Control (completed by father) Parental Attitude Research Instrument (completed by mother)	6. Personality Measures: Eysenck Personality Inventory (parents) Differential Personality Questionnaire (DPQ) (Form 9) Activities Preference Questionnaire (APQ) (1973 version)
	7. Attitudes: (F-Scale
	8. Vocational Interests: Strong-Campbell

dence that their reliabilities would be high when administered by well-trained examiners. Reliable measurements are crucial to the success of any study and too seldom appreciated in developmental research. Second, we had confidence in their validity. In our opinion, the *Wechsler* tests and the *Stanford-Binet* provide broad samples of knowledge and skills that fall squarely in the domain we call intelligence. We do not claim that other measures do not also sample intellectual ability, but that the measures we chose are efficient and valid samples of knowledge and skills that are central to commonly accepted definitions of intelligence. The personality measures represent the two major factors that can be extracted from nearly all personality tests: introversion and anxiety or neuroticism.

Third, previous research has shown these measures of intelligence and personality to have far-flung implications for all kinds of personal and social functioning. That is, they have a "web" of interrelationships with many aspects of an individual's adjustment in everyday life. Experimental measures cannot claim the long history of research that enriches the interpretation of results.

Clearly, the selection of appropriate examiners for a family study is a critical aspect of the design. We chose a team of graduate students who had completed at least a year-long course in psychoeducational assessment and who had participated in a training session on assessment for this study. Among the 21 examiners were 6 males and 15 females, including 2 Blacks. Testers were assigned randomly to members of the family. The tests and interviews were administered in the family homes during two visits.

Over the 3 years that we collected data, our team of examiners became a closely knit group. At regular meetings of the team, essential for maintaining an esprit de corps and quality control, we shared perspectives on the study, our research methods, and the relationships with the families. One amusing anecdote comes to mind. The nosey neighbors of a participating family were amazed at the arrival one evening of 5 examiners (it was a larger family!), with suitcases in tow (test kits). They were even more shocked when the group returned a week later!

In light of the cost of seeing a large sample of families in their homes, in the Adolescent Adoption Study, we decided to bring families to the University. During a 3- to 4-hour session, we administered an abbreviated version of the WAIS which consists of four subtests (vocabulary, arithmetic, block design, and picture arrangement). The combination of these four subtests has been shown to correlate above .90 with the full-scale test score and is generally accepted as a shortened version of the adult test (Doppelt, 1956). All of the test protocols were scored by an experienced psychometrician who was unaware of the respondent's adoptive status. The *California F-Scale* (a measure of social attitudes, especially authoritarianism) and the *Strong-Campbell Interest Inventory* (a measure of vocational interests) were also administered to parents and children in the Adolescent Adoption Study. In the personality domain, three measures were administered: *The Eysenck Personality Inventory* (in its adult and junior forms) measuring Extraversion and Neuroticism, the *Differential Personality Question-*

naire (Form 9), with scales on social closeness, social potency, and impulsiveness, and the *Activities Preference Questionnaire* (1973 version), focusing on trait anxiety. Interestingly, the State Department of Welfare was not supportive of using the *Minnesota Multiphasic Personality Inventory* (MMPI) because of the content of its items.

The Results of the Studies

Some of our findings were expected. Others surprised us. In general, we found no evidence of genetic differences in IQ between Blacks and Whites; strong evidence of genetic origins of intellectual differences among individuals within each race; strong evidence of a genetic component in individual differences in some attitudes having to do with prejudice and authoritarianism; and good evidence of a genetic component in some vocational and personal interests.

Let us consider the studies in greater detail.

The Adolescent Adoption Study.   For the White adolescent adoption study, we selected two groups of families that had at least two children in late adolescence: 120 birth families that had had children of their own and 115 adoptive families that had adopted two or more unrelated children as infants. The children in both sets of households were close in age, the average being 18½.

We found the adoptive families through the Minnesota Department of Public Welfare, which sent letters on our behalf to families who had adopted children between 1953 and 1959 (and who were thus at the ages we wanted for our study). To make sure our final sample of volunteers was representative of adoptive parents, we compared the participants with nonparticipants on critical characteristics. We found no differences between them in age, income, education, or occupational status at the time of adoption. Next we recruited a comparable sample of birth families through newspaper articles and advertisements, by word of mouth, and from the adoptive families themselves. The 120 families we eventually chose did indeed match the adoptive families in income (both groups averaged about $25,000 a year), education (generally at least two years of college for mothers and fathers), occupation (typically teacher and social worker), and IQ (an average of 117 for fathers and 113 for mothers). In short, both the birth and adoptive families were well above the national American average in socioeconomic status and intellectual ability. It is also significant that some families had incomes of $11,000; that some mothers and fathers were secretaries and electricians; that some parents had gone to work right after high school; and that some parents had IQs in the 90s—in other words, the sample was varied.

In contrast, the birth parents of the adopted children were of average intelligence, as we inferred from their educational levels. Further, a survey of 3600 unmarried mothers in Minnesota between 1948 and 1952, where IQ tests were required for all women who gave up children for adoption, found that their average IQ was right on the national mean: 100. Although our group of mothers had had their children between 1953 and 1959, there is no reason to think that they would differ from the intellectually average generation that preceded them. What did we find?

The Sample and IQ Data

The adolescents in this study had spent an average of 18 years in their families— 194 adopted children in 115 adoptive families and a comparison group of 237 biological children in 120 other families. All of the adoptees were placed in their families in the first year of life, the median being 2-months-of-age. From 1975 to 1977 both groups of children were 16–22 years old. Both samples of parents were of similar SES, from working to upper-middle class, and of similar IQ levels on the WAIS. The IQ scores of parents in both adoptive and biological families averaged 115, approximately 1 SD above the population mean. The biological children scored, on the average, an IQ of 113, and the adopted children 7 points lower at 106. The parent-child IQ correlations in the biological families were what we were led to expect from other studies—about .40 when corrected for the restricted range of the parents' scores. The biological mid-parent-child correlation was .52. The adoptive parent-child correlations were about .13; the adoptive midparent-child correlation was only .14.

The adopted children's IQ scores were more closely correlated with the educational levels of their birth mothers (.28) and fathers (.43) than with those of their adoptive mothers (.09) and fathers (.11). In fact, adopted children's IQ scores were as highly correlated with their natural parents' education as were those of the adolescents in the biological sample (.17 with mothers and .26, with fathers) (Scarr & Weinberg, 1980).

The IQ correlation of the biologically related siblings was .35. However, the IQ correlation of adopted children reared together for 18 years was zero! These White adolescents reared together from infancy did not resemble their genetically unrelated siblings.

In support of the IQ results were the standardized test data, collected from many different school districts and uncontaminated by biases that might have inadvertently influenced testing in our studies. Most important, they represent a "real-life" criterion of intellectual achievement. The effects of being reared in the same family, neighborhood, and school are negligible unless one is genetically related to one's brother or sister. The correlations of the biological siblings were modest but statistically different from zero, whereas the aptitude and achievement scores of the adopted siblings were virtually unrelated.

Our interpretation of these results (Scarr & Weinberg, 1978) is that older adolescents are largely liberated from their families' influences and have made choices and pursued courses that are in keeping with their own talents and interests. Thus, the unrelated siblings have grown less and less alike. This hypothesis cannot be tested fully without longitudinal data on adopted siblings; to date all of the other adoption studies sampled much younger children, at the average age of 7 or 8. We can think of no other explanation for the markedly low correlations between the adopted siblings at the end of the child-rearing period, in contrast to the several studies of younger adopted siblings, who are embarrassingly similar.

Beyond IQ: F-Scale

In the Adolescent Adoption Study we expected that genetic background would be important in accounting for intellectual differences but that it would have nothing to do with political or social attitudes. To demonstrate our point, you will recall we included in the test battery a 20-item version of the California F-Scale, a set of questions that measure a person's degree of authoritarianism, rigidity of belief, and prejudice. People taking the test indicate on a scale of 1 to 7 how much they agree or disagree with such statements as ''What youth needs most is strict discipline, rugged determination, and the will to work and fight for family and country,'' and ''One of the most important things children should learn is when to disobey authorities.''

Confident that our F-Scale would measure the effects of environment, we were utterly astonished by our findings. The attitudes captured by the authoritarianism test appear to be transmitted genetically from parents to children, just as verbal ability and intelligence are.

We make this remarkable statement because we found no correlation between the authoritarian attitudes of the adopted children and those of their parents or siblings, even though the adoptees had been exposed to their parents' attitudes since infancy. The parents' attitudes and those of the adopted children, in other words, were as different as if the adults and teenagers had been randomly paired on a street corner. But we found a highly significant correlation between the authoritarian attitudes of biological children and parents. Whether both were highly authoritarian or both were antiauthoritarian, their attitudes tended to be very similar.

All the strong correlations of attitudes toward authority occurred between birth relatives—fathers and children, mothers and children, brothers and sisters. Among adoptive relatives, the only significant correlation, the only predictably shared attitude, occurred between fathers and adoptive daughters. The reason for this exception we do not know.

One possible explanation for the similarities between birth relatives and the differences between adoptive relatives was that mothers and fathers of adopted children disagreed on their attitudes toward authority, whereas the parents of birth children shared similar attitudes. In that case, adopted children would have a choice of two opinions and values, one set being less authoritarian than the other. Not so. Husbands and wives in both kinds of families tended to share their political and social attitudes.

Another possibility for these results was that adoptive parents, knowing that their children were not "their own," somehow treated them differently from the way parents treat birth-related children. But if this were so, we would still expect to find the correlations between adoptive siblings to be similar to the correlations between birth siblings. They are not.

Perhaps, we thought, the finding reflected an artificial problem in the samples. For instance, more adoptive families than birth families came from small towns and rural areas. But then we would have been hard-pressed to explain why the authoritarianism patterns consistently distinguished adopted children from birth ones, and other personality traits did not. On tests of introversion, neuroticism, and some forms of anxiety, parent-child correlations within adoptive and birth families were similar.

We then looked at the comparable table of correlations of IQ scores. The patterns were amazingly similar to those for authoritarianism, including that baffling father-adoptive daughter resemblance in the adoptive families—which we are beginning facetiously to call the Electra phenomenon. Something unique about authoritarianism and IQ was afoot.

To track it down, we took a closer look at the relationship of intelligence to the F-Scale. One measure we used was the vocabulary subtest of the *Wechsler Adult Intelligence Scale;* the other was the *Raven Standard Progressive Matrices,* a nonverbal measure of intellectual ability. At this point the pieces of the puzzle began to fit.

Scores for authoritarianism turned out to be negatively correlated with verbal ability—the higher one's score on the *WAIS* vocabulary subtest, the lower the F-Scale score (the correlation for all participants in the study was −0.42, which is strong). In other words, the most articulate, verbal family members were the least authoritarian, the vice versa. But the relationship between the nonverbal IQ measure and authoritarianism was much weaker (Scarr & Weinberg, 1981).

These results suggest to us that F-Scale scores are similar in birth but not in adoptive families because the F-Scale measures intellectual skills that are partly heritable. Many of those skills have to do with thinking and reasoning ability. The similarity of scores in birth families was largely a result of the intellectual similarity of genetic relatives. Adopted children barely resembled their adoptive parents in F-Scale scores, and what little similarity there was could be ascribed to their similar vocabulary scores.

Previous studies had also found that authoritarianism was more characteristic of lower-class than of middle-class people, but psychologists assumed that this reflected the powerlessness and poorer circumstances of the working class. Our results require another interpretation. Differences in social class of the adoptive families were not related to the expected differences in authoritarianism and IQ: Although the adoptive parents varied in intelligence, education, occupation, and income (to be sure, none was truly poor), their adopted children were no more or less authoritarian because of their class backgrounds.

In our view, the only adequate explanation of the link between low IQ and high authoritarianism begins with a person's mental abilities. Scores on the F-Scale are the results of moral-reasoning ability that in turn reflects the general level of verbal intelligence. We believe that moral decisions and authoritarian views are not learned by rote or by imitation of one's parents, teachers, and friends; instead, they represent conclusions that a person reaches by applying mental skills to social and political experiences, and through schooling that teaches abstract concepts that broaden one's perspective.

The F-Scale is a set of complex intellectual judgments about the world, examples of opinions that people have accepted or rejected about politics and values. IQ tests also contain items that tap everyday, commonsense judgments about social problems precisely to see how people use intellectual abilities to solve daily dilemmas. Consequently, in a way it is not surprising that the F-Scale should correlate with some of the broad measures of intellectual functioning that IQ tests represent.

Vocational Interests

Developmental psychologists and parents believe that children acquire ambitions and interests by modeling themselves after their parents. Typically, boys model themselves after their fathers, girls after their mothers; some children, for unknown reason, imitate their parents of the opposite sex. If the modeling theory were true, adoptive and birth children would be equally likely to resemble their parents.

But we found evidence for a genetic contribution to vocational interests. In association with Harold Grotevant, we gave our White adolescents and parents a reliable test on this question, the *Strong-Campbell Interest Inventory*. This inventory includes John L. Holland's model of vocational interests, which classifies people according to their scores on six "styles":

1. realistic (practical, aggressive persons who enjoy working outdoors and with their hands);
2. investigative (scientifically oriented persons);
3. artistic (self-expressive and creative persons);
4. social (humanistic or religious persons who wish to help others);
5. enterprising (persons who like to sell, dominate, lead); and
6. conventional (persons who prefer highly ordered verbal or numerical work).

People are scored on this test not only according to the style they most prefer but also according to how they score on each of the six types. The result is a profile of interests for each individual.

Once again, our expectation that children would model themselves after their parents was not fulfilled. On the average, adoptive family members no more resembled one another in interests than parents and children paired randomly from the outside world. For all their similarity to their adoptive parents, the adopted children of teachers and engineers could have grown up with cattle ranchers or plumbers (Grotevant, Scarr, & Weinberg, 1977).

We looked at the interest profiles of each family member in comparison with every other family member—mothers with sons and daughters, fathers with sons and daughters, siblings with one another. Of the 24 possible correlations (each of the six interest scales by mother, father, daughter, son), only two were significant for the adoptive family pairs, and one of those would have been expected just by chance. In the birth family pairs, fully 15 correlations were significant. For example, birth fathers and sons resembled one another most on social interests; mothers and daughters, on investigative interests; fathers and daughters on artistic interests; and mothers and sons, on realistic interests. Further, scores of birth siblings were strongly correlated on five of the six scales, but scores of adoptive siblings were correlated on only one scale.

The fact that birth parents and children shared the same specific interests and disinterests, whereas their adoptive counterparts did not, suggests that there is a small but reliable hereditary influence in people's professional ambitions. In most families, the interests of the parents were not alike, even after 20 years of marriage; but the birth siblings were the most alike—as a genetic explanation would predict. Also, these siblings resembled one another more than they resembled their parents, because the children were raised in the same place and time.

Personality

Finally, in the personality domain, we expected biological relatives to be moderately similar and adoptive relatives to be less so. Indeed, these expectations were fulfilled. The median correlations for parents and their birth children on the scales tapping introversion-extraversion and neuroticism was .15 and for adoptive parents and their adoptive children, .04 (Scarr, Webber, Weinberg, & Wittig, 1981).

There is evidence for genetic differences in interests and personality. There is little evidence that environmental differences among families account for variability in these psychological domains. However, most of the variance in personality and interests is not accounted for by either genetic or environmental differences among families. Most of the variance lies in individual experiences— that is, environmental differences among individuals in the same family.

Some of the differences in results between intellectual and personality measures may lie in the lower reliabilities of the latter. Family correlations for personality measures may be lower than those for abilities because of lower reliabilities. Given that the reliabilities of personality measures used in this study range in the .70s to .80s, however, family members could be much more similar than they are. It must be that the unique genotypes and experiences of individuals shape the development of personality and interest patterns.

The Transracial Adoption Study. The unique and controversial nature of our second study, the transracial adoption project, warrants an especially detailed discussion of its rationale and goals.

Rationale

It is well known that Black children reared by their own families achieve IQ scores that average about a standard deviation (15 points) below Whites (Jensen, 1973; Loehlin, Lindzey, & Spuhler, 1975). This finding is at the heart of a continuing controversy in the educational arena. Studies (e.g., Cleary, Humphreys, Kendrick, & Wesman, 1975) confirm the hypothesis that low IQ scores predict poor school performance, regardless of race. Thus, more Black children than White children fail to achieve academically and to earn the credentials required by higher occupational status, with its concomitant social prestige and economic security (Husen, 1974; Jencks, 1972).

In an attempt to remedy the alarming rate of school failure, compensatory educational programs, which were directed particularly at Black children, were introduced in the 1960s. At the same time, but for different reasons, a more intensive intervention began: the adoption of Black children by White families. Whereas compensatory educational programs involve the child for a few hours per day, we believed that transracial adoption alters the entire social ecology of the child. Transracial adoption is the human analog of the cross-fostering design, commonly used in animal behavior genetics research (e.g., Manosevitz, Lindzey, & Thiessen, 1969). The study of transracial adoption can yield estimates of biological and sociocultural effects on the IQ test performance of cross-fostered children.

We realized that the results of a transracial or cross-fostering study would require careful interpretation. Black children reared in White homes are socially labeled as Black and therefore may suffer racial discrimination. Because of the unmeasured effects of racism, poor IQ test performance by Black children in White homes cannot be uncritically interpreted as a result of genetic limitations. In addition, equal performance by Black and other adoptees cannot be interpreted as an indication of the *same* range of reaction for all groups. Again, the unknown effects of racism may inhibit the intellectual development of the Black adoptees. However, equally high IQs for Black and other adoptees would imply that IQ performance is considerably malleable. These issues were of special concern to the site visitors from the National Institute of Child Health and Human Development, our funding agency. The political climate of the early 1970s was clearly not supportive of research on heated racial issues.

Upper-middle-class White families have an excellent reputation for rearing children who perform well on IQ tests and in school. When such families adopt White children, the adoptees have been found to score above average on IQ tests, but not as highly as the birth offspring of the same and similar families (Burks, 1928; Freeman, Holzinger, & Mitchell, 1928; Leahy, 1935; Munsinger, 1975b; Skodak & Skeels, 1949).

If Black children have genetically limited intellectual potential, as some have claimed (Jensen, 1973; Shockley, 1971, 1972), their IQ performance would fall below that of other children reared in White upper-middle-class homes. On the other hand, if Black children have a range of reaction similar to other adoptees, their IQ scores would have a similar distribution. The concept, range of reaction, refers to the fact that genotypes do not usually specify a single phenotype. Rather, genotypes specify a range of phenotypic responses that the organism can make to a variety of environmental conditions.

Minnesota was especially in the forefront of *transracial adoption*. Although the Black population of the state is small (.9% in 1970), there were too many Black and interracial children (with one Black and one White or other racial group parent) available for adoption and too few Black families to absorb them. Minority group children—Black, American Indian, Korean, and Vietnamese— have consequently been adopted by White families in large numbers. Furthermore, in recent years, many non-White children have been adopted from other states.

The support for interracial adoption changed dramatically in the late 1950s and early 1960s because of the efforts of public and private agencies and the pioneering White adoptive parents. Several agency and parent organizations were formed to promote the adoption of Black and interracial Black children. The most influential organization was the Open Door Society of Minnesota, formed in 1966 by adoptive parents of socially classified[2] Black children. The founding president of the Open Door Society was a leading columnist on one of the Minneapolis daily newspapers who frequently wrote about his multiracial family. The intellectual and social climate of Minnesota is to this day generally conducive to liberal and humanitarian movements such as interracial adoption.

Goals of the Study and the Sample

We posed four major questions in the study regarding the development of intellectual skills:

---

[2]In the United States, individuals with visible signs of African ancestry are socially labeled or classified as Black.

1. What is the estimated reaction range for IQ scores of Black/interracial children reared in Black environments or in White adoptive homes?

2. Do interracial children perform at higher levels on IQ tests than do children with two Black parents; that is, does the degree of White ancestry affect IQ scores?

3. How do the IQ scores of socially classified Black children reared in White homes compare to those of other adopted children and birth White children within the same families; that is, do different racial groups, when exposed to similar environments, have similar distributions of IQ scores?

4. How well do socially classified Black children reared in White families perform in school?

For the Black adoption study, we recruited 101 families (from 136 families eligible to participate) consisting of 176 adopted children (130 who had one or two Black parents; 25 White; 21 others including Asian, North American Indian, and Latin American Indian children) and 145 birth White children. Like our other sample of adoptive parents, these families were above average in income and education, stability and mental health, and interest in children. The birth parents of these adoptees were about average intellectually and educationally, as we determined from the adoption records.

The sample of families lived within a 150-mile radius of the Twin Cities metropolitan area. Although nearly all of the children were adopted in Minnesota, 68 were born outside of the state. Through interstate cooperation, the child placement agencies arranged for the adoption of many non-White children from other states.

The birth children in our studies had the benefits of both genes and environment; the adopted children were born to intellectually average parents but raised in intellectually enriched homes. To make environmental conditions as similar as possible, we most often limited our analyses to the children who had been adopted in the first year of life—most during the first 3 months.

Answering the Questions

The first question considered *whether socially classified Black children reared in economically advantaged White homes would score above those reared in Black environments.*

The average IQ score of Black and interracial children, adopted by advantaged White families, was found to be 106. Early-adopted Black and interracial children performed at an even higher level. This mean represents an increase of 1 standard deviation above the average IQ of 90 usually achieved by Black children reared in their own homes in the North Central region. Furthermore, in the Minneapolis public school district, the average performance of 4th-grade children on the *Gates-MacGinities* vocabulary test at a school with 87% Black and interracial enrollment in 1973 was about the 21st national percentile, which translates to an IQ equivalent of about 90.

Since 68 of the 130 Black children were known to have one White parent and only 29 were known to have had two Black parents (the remainder were of other mixed or unknown parentage), it may seem misleading to compare the adoptees to Black children in the general population. Even if all of the Black children were interracial offspring, we thought a strong genetic hypothesis should not predict that they would score well above the White population average. Nor should they score as highly as White adoptees. In fact, the Black and interracial children of this sample scored as highly on IQ tests as did White adoptees in previous studies with large samples (Burks, 1928; Horn, Loehlin, & Willerman, 1979; Leahy, 1935).

In other words, the range of reaction of socially classified Black children's IQ scores from average (Black) to advantaged (White) environments was at least 1 standard deviation. Conservatively, if we consider only the adopted children with two Black parents (and late and less favorable adoptive experiences), the IQ reaction range was at least 10 points between these environments. If we consider the early-adopted group, the IQ range was as large as 20 points. The level of school achievements among the Black and interracial adoptees was further evidence of their above-average performance on standard intellectual measures.

The dramatic increase in the IQ mean and an additional finding that placement and adoptive family characteristics accounted for a major portion of the IQ differences among the socially classified Black children strongly suggested that the IQ scores of these children are environmentally malleable.

We reasoned that the substantial increase in test performance of the Black and interracial adoptees is because their rearing environments are culturally relevant to the tests and to the school. Amid the IQ controversy, some have argued that standardized measures are inappropriate for children whose cultural background is different from that of the tests. While the rejection of IQ tests as predictors of academic success, on the basis of their cultural bias, is untenable (Jensen, 1974), we strongly believe that the tests and the schools share a common culture to which Black children are not as fully acculturated as are White children. However, the socially classified Black children in this study were fully exposed to the culture of the tests and the school, although they were still socially defined as Black.

The second question concerned a comparison of the IQ scores of children whose parents were both Black with Black children of interracial parentage. The interracial children scored about 12 points higher than those with two Black parents, but this difference was associated with large differences in maternal education and preplacement history. The part correlations suggested that variation in the race of mothers accounted for 3% of the children's IQ variance, but even this percentage of variance probably includes some additional and unmeasured environmental differences between the groups.

For example, Black mothers are known to be at greater risk than White mothers for nutritional deficiencies, maternal death, infant mortality, and other reproductive casualties (Scarr-Salapatek & Williams, 1973). The prematurity rate among Black mothers is more than double that of Whites. These risks are often found to be associated with poverty and long-term developmental problems among the children. The interracial children, all but two of whom have White mothers were less likely to have suffered any of these problems.

The third question asked for comparisons among the IQ scores of Black/ interracial, Asian/Indian adoptees, and the birth children of the adoptive families. There were significant differences in IQ scores among the groups. The socially classified Black children scored on the average between the White and Asian/Indian adoptees, but these results were confounded with placement variables. Among the early adoptees, there were too few White and Asian/Indian children to make meaningful comparisons. The Black/interracial early adoptees, however, performed at IQ 110, on the average.

Compared to adopted children in previous studies, the average IQ of 110 for the 99 early adopted Black/interracial children compares well with the 112.6 reported by Leahy (1935, p. 285) for White adoptees in professional families, with the IQ 108 of the Texas White adoptees from a private adoption home, and with the 106 of the adopted adolescents reported in our other study.

The above-average IQ level of adopted children, reported in all adoption studies, reflects both their better-than-average environments and the elimination of severely retarded children from the pool of potential adoptees. Although Munsinger's (1975a) review concluded that adoptive family environments have little or no impact on the intellectual development of adoptees, past studies have not adequately tested this hypothesis. Because children who are selected for adoption are not grossly defective, their predicted IQ level is slightly above that of the general population. In this study, however, the adopted *Black/interracial* children could not have been predicted to have average IQ scores above the mean of the *White* population unless adoptive family environments have considerable impact.

The birth children of the adoptive families scored above the average of the Black/interracial early adoptees. Not only have the birth children been in their families since birth, but their natural parents are considerably brighter than those of the adopted children, regardless of race.

A fourth question focused on the school achievement of the Black/interracial adoptees and the birth children in the adoptive families. Black/interracial adoptees were found to score slightly above average on school-administered achievement and aptitude tests, as predicted by their IQ scores. The natural children of the adoptive families scored higher than the socially classified Black adoptees on school achievement measures, a finding which is congruent with their higher IQ scores. The school achievement data provided validation for our IQ assessment.

Implications of the Findings

What are the implications of these results for developmental plasticity? First, it is clear from the IQ scores of the transracially adopted children that they, like other adoptees, were responsive to the rearing environments in adoptive families, which as a group provided intellectual stimulation and exposure to the skills and knowledge sampled on IQ tests. The mean IQ scores of both samples of adoptees were above the average of agemates, primarily because they benefited from their rearing environments.

Second, individual adoptees differed in their responses to the environmental advantages of adoptive families. Those with natural parents of higher educational levels, and by implication higher intellectual abilities, were more responsive to the rearing environments of adoptive families than were those with natural parents of more limited intellectual skills. Children adopted into families of adoptive parents at and above the average educational and IQ levels of adoptive parents scored higher on the *WAIS* than children of comparable natural mothers adopted into families with less bright adoptive parents. The adolescents whose natural mothers and adoptive parents were both below average scored 10.4 IQ points below those whose natural mothers and adoptive parents were both above average.

Individual differences among the adopted children at both younger and older ages were related to intellectual variation among adoptive parents and their biological parents, even though the average IQ of adoptees most likely exceeded that of their natural parents. Human beings are not infinitely plastic; malleability does not mean that given the same environment, all individuals will end up alike.

At present we are conducting a 10-year follow-up study of the transracially adopted children, who are now ages 14 to 22. Their intellectual and academic achievements, their personality and social adjustments, and their personal stories are all of interest to our understanding of what families can (and cannot) do for children.

USING TWO STATISTICAL METHODS: FINE-TUNING

Our two studies showed that in *advantaged* environments, differences between children in ability are largely due to differences in genetic programming. We reached this conclusion by using two statistical methods. First, we put all the factors that might have something to do with intelligence (such as qualities of the parents and the children's home life) into an equation that told us the relative importance of each factor in predicting a child's IQ.

In the first set of equations, we tried father's education and occupation, mother's education, and family income as predictors of the differences in the children's IQs. These factors had a mild impact on differences in the birth children's scores, but hardly any impact on the adoptee's scores. When we added parental IQ, however, we got an enormous effect in predicting the birth children's scores—but differences in adoptive parents' IQs had virtually no effect on the scores of the adoptees. The power of adding parental IQ to the equation must reflect the genetic contribution of the birth parents to their children's intelligence.

In contrast, the best predictor of IQ differences in adopted children was the education of their birth mothers (and, when we had the information, of their birth fathers). The education of the birth mothers was more closely related to IQ differences in their children than the same information about the adoptive parents—the adults with whom these children grew up. In both groups of adoptees, the Black children and the White adolescents, the birth parents best accounted for the children's differences in IQ.

Our second method was to study the correlations of scores between related and unrelated family members. In the transracial adoption study, children reared in the same family and who were still under the major influence of their parents scored at similar levels on IQ tests whether genetically related to each other or not. That is, the IQ correlations of adopted siblings were as high as those of the birth siblings reared together.

However, more evidence of genetic effects came from the White adoption study when we correlated IQs for all pairs of adoptive and natural relatives. Whether we used the overall IQs or the scores on the four subtests of the IQ tests (e.g., vocabulary, arithmetic), the correlations between biological family members were statistically significant, whereas the correlations between adopted children and their unrelated parents and siblings were weak or negligible. The only scores that were significant between the adoptees and other family members were in vocabulary. This is not surprising, as people who live together tend to talk together. Vocabulary abilities are the most amenable to the influence of environment. But we thought the lack of correlations between adopted children and their adoptive parents—with whom they had lived since infancy—must point to the influence of genetic factors on intellectual abilities.

METHODOLOGICAL AND DESIGN RECOMMENDATIONS: PROPOSING AN EVOLVING THEORY OF BEHAVIORAL DEVELOPMENT

We have interpreted the results of the two studies to mean that younger children, regardless of their genetic relatedness, resemble each other intellectually because they share a similar rearing environment. Older adolescents, on the other hand, resemble one another only if they share genes. Our interpretation is that older children escape the influences of the family and are freer to select their own environments. Parental influences are diluted by the more varied mix of adolescent experiences.

We also note that differences among family environments in the humane range have little or no effect on the children's intellectual or personal outcomes at late adolescence. Yet, no characteristic measured is more than 60% genetically variable in this range of environments. The remaining variance occurs within the shared environments of siblings; that is, a major portion of the differences among ordinary people arise from differences in the experiences of children *within* the same families (and their correlated experiences in neighborhoods, communities, and so forth).

The results of the two studies led us to reconsider theories of development and to formulate some research strategies that have seldom been tried. Because theory must precede investigations, let us first review the theory of genotype ⟶ environment effects that has indeed evolved from our work (Scarr & McCartney, 1983).

Individual Differences in Experience

Each of us encounters the world in different ways. We are individually different in the ways we process information from the environment, which makes our experiences individually tailored to our interests, personality, and talents. Human beings are also developmentally different in their ability to process information from the environment. Preschool children do not glean the same information from a football game as older children or adults. Preschoolers may wonder why grown men are mauling each other, while adults accept the rules of the competition and forget to ask why players are rewarded for being so aggressive toward one another. Each of us at every developmental stage gains different information from the same environments, because we attend to some aspects of our environments and ignore other opportunities for experience. Each individual also processes information against a background of previously different experiences—not different environments but different experiences gleaned from those environments.

These differences in experience—both developmental changes and individual differences—are likely to be caused by genetic differences. Across development, different genes are turned on and off, creating maturational changes in the organization of behavior, as well as maturational changes in patterns of physical growth. Genetic differences among individuals are similarly responsible for determining what experiences people do and do not have in their environments. What is attended to and what is ignored are events that are correlated with individual differences in interests, personality, and talents. Thus, it seems that individual and developmental differences in behavior are more a function of genetic differences in individuals' patterns of development than of differences in the *opportunities* in most environments.

In other papers (Scarr & McCartney, 1983; Scarr & Weinberg, 1983), we proposed a theory of environmental effects on human development that emphasizes the role of the genotype in determining not only which environments are experienced by individuals, but also which environments individuals seek for themselves. To show how this theory addresses the process of becoming an individual, the theory was used to account for seemingly anomalous findings from deprivation, adoption, twin, and intervention studies.

In evolutionary theory the two essential concepts are selection and variation. Through selection the human genome has evolved to program human development. Phenotypic variation is the raw material on which selection works. Genetic variation must be associated with phenotypic variation, or there could be no evolution. Therefore, it follows from evolutionary theory that individual differences depend in part upon genotypic differences.

Genetic differences prompt differences in which environments are experienced and what effects they may have. In this view the genotype, in both its species specificity and its individual variability, largely determines environmental effects on development, because the genotype determines the organism's responsiveness to environmental opportunities.

Development depends on both a genetic program and a suitable environment for the expression of the human, species-typical program for development. But *differences* among people can arise from both genetic and environmental differences. The process by which differences arise is better described as genotype ⟶ environment effects. The genotype determines the *responsiveness* of the person to those environmental opportunities.

One can distinguish here between environments to which a person is exposed and environments that are actively experienced or "grasped" by the person. Individuals simply do not learn the same material, given equal exposure. In addition, individuals *prefer* to spend time in different settings. Given leisure time, some people gravitate to the sports field or the television set, others to libraries, still others to concerts, films, self-help groups, gardening, horse races, butterfly collecting, and so forth. The environments they choose from the vast array of possibilities are determined in part by their individual personalities, interests, and talents. The development of the *Strong-Campbell Interest Inventory* (Campbell, 1974) is based on the idea that different personalities are more and less satisfied with different occupations. The *Holland Scales* (Holland, 1966) are even more explicit about the connection between personality and the nature of the work environment. Any theory of individuality must take into account the selective nature of experience and the compatibilities and incompatibilities of persons and environments.

An Evolving Theory of Behavioral Development

Plomin, DeFries, and Loehlin (1977) described three kinds of genotype ⟶ environment correlations that we believe form the basis for a developmental theory. We believe that the Plomin group's model, relating genotypes and environments is superior to either strict environment or genetic models to account for development. The theory of genotype ⟶ environment effects we proposed has three propositions:

1. The process by which children develop is best described by three kinds of genotype ⟶ environment effects: a *passive* kind whereby the genetically related parents provide a rearing environment that is correlated with the genotype of the child (sometimes positively and sometimes negatively); an *evocative* kind whereby the child receives responses from others that are influenced by his genotype; and an *active* kind that represents the child's selective attention to and learning from aspects of his environment that are influenced by his genotype, and indirectly correlated with those of his biological relatives.

2. The relative importance of the three kinds of genotype ⟶ environment effects changes with development. The influence of the passive kind declines from infancy to adolescence, and the importance of the active kind increases over the same period.

3. The degree to which experience is influenced by individual genotypes increases with development and the shift from passive to active genotype ⟶ environment effects, as individuals select their own experiences.

The first, *passive* genotype ⟶ environment effects, arise in biologically related families and renders all of the research literature on parent-child socialization uninterpretable. Because parents provide both genes and environments for their biological offspring, the child's environment is necessarily correlated with her genes, because her genes are correlated with her parents' genes, and the parents' genes are correlated with the rearing environment they provide. It is impossible to know *what* about the parents' rearing environment for the child determines *what* about the child's behavior, because of the confounding effect of genetic transmission of the same characteristics from parent to child. Not only can we *not* interpret the direction of effects in parent-child interaction, as Bell (1968) argued, we also cannot interpret the *cause* of those effects in biologically related families.

An example of a positive passive kind of genotype ⟶ environment correlation can be found in social skills. Parents who are very sociable, who enjoy and need social activity, will expose their child to more social situations than parents who are socially inept and isolated. The child of sociable parents is likely to become more socially skilled, for both genetic and environmental reasons. The children's rearing environment is positively correlated with the parents' genotypes and therefore related to the children's genotypes as well.

An example of a negative passive genotype ⟶ environment correlation can also be found in sociability. Parents who are socially skilled, faced with a child who is a social isolate, may exert more pressure and do more training than they would with a socially more adept offspring. The more enriched environment for the less able child represents a negative genotype ⟶ environment effect (see also Plomin et al., 1977). There is, thus, an unreliable, but not random, connection between genotypes and environments when parents provide the opportunities for experience.

The second kind of genotype ⟶ environment effect is called *evocative,* because it represents the different responses that different genotypes evoke from the social and physical environments. Responses to the person further shape development in ways that correlate with the genotype. Examples of such evocative effects can be found in the research of Lytton (1980) and the review of Maccoby (1980). Smiley, active babies receive more social stimulation than fussy, difficult infants (Wachs & Gandour, 1983). Cooperative, attentive preschoolers receive more pleasant and instructional interactions from the adults around them than uncooperative, distractible children. Individual differences in responses evoked can also be found in the physical attractiveness; people who are considered attractive by others receive more positive attention, are thought to be more pleasant, desirable companions, and so forth (Berscheid & Walster, 1974).

The third kind of genotype ⟶ environment effect is the *active,* niche-picking or niche-building sort. People seek out environments they find compatible and stimulating. We all select from the surrounding environment some aspects to which to respond, learn about, or ignore. Our selections are correlated with motivational, personality, and intellectual aspects of our genotypes. The active genotype ⟶ environment effect, we argue, is the most powerful connection between people and their environments and the most direct expression of the genotype in experience.

Examples of active genotype ⟶ environment effects can be found in the selective efforts of individuals in sports, scholarship, relationships—in life. Once experiences occur, they naturally lead to further experiences.

The relative importance of the three kinds of genotype ⟶ environment effects changes over development from infancy to adolescence. In infancy much of the environment that reaches the child is provided by adults. When those adults are genetically related to the child, the environment they provide in general is positively related to their own characteristics and their own genotypes. Although infants are active in structuring their experiences by selectively attending to what is offered, they cannot do as much seeking out and niche-building as older children; thus, *passive* genotype ⟶ environment effects are more important for infants and young children than they are for older children, who can extend their experiences beyond the family's influences and create their own environments to a much greater extent. Thus, the effects of passive genotype ⟶ environment effects wane when the child has many extrafamilial opportunities.

In addition, parents can provide environments that are negatively related to the child's genotype, as illustrated earlier in social opportunities. Although parents' genotypes usually affect the environment they provide for their biological offspring, it is sometimes positive and sometimes negative and therefore, not as direct a product of the young child's genotype as later environments will be. Thus, as stated in proposition 3, genotype ⟶ environment effects increase with development, as active replace passive forms. Genotype ⟶ environment effects of the *evocative* sort persist throughout life, as we elicit responses from others based on many personal, genotype-related characteristics from appearance to personality and intellect. Those responses from others reinforce and extend the directions our development has taken. High intelligence and adaptive skills in children from very disadvantaged backgrounds, for example, evokes approval and support from school personnel who might otherwise despair of the child's chances in life (Garmezy, 1983). In adulthood, personality and intellectual differences evoke different responses in others.

The expected degree of environmental similarity for a pair of relatives can be thought of as the product of a person's own genotype ⟶ environment path and the genetic correlation of the pair. On the assumption that individuals' environments are equally influenced by their own genotypes, the similarity in the environments of two individuals becomes a function of their genetic correlation.

This model can be used to describe the process by which biological siblings come to be more similar than adopted siblings. The environment of one biological sib is correlated to the genotype of the other as one-half the coefficient of the siblings' environment to her own genotype, because the genetic correlation is approximately 0.50. There is virtually no correlation in intellectual or personality characteristics between parents and unrelated children adopted into the same household, so that their genetic correlation is effectively zero. And thus their resemblances in behavioral characteristics are also predicted to be low because they will not evoke from others similar responses nor choose similar aspects of their environments to which to respond. This model describes very well the findings from family studies, including our own.

Research Strategies for the Future

The theory we propose can be tested in several ways. First, studies of parental treatment of more than one child would be informative about passive genotype ⟶ environmental effects. In general, we expect the rearing environment provided for the children in a family to differ in ways that are related to each child's characteristics. Do parents treat all of their children alike, as so many studies of one child per family seem to imply? Can parents be authoritative with one child and permissive with another? One theory predicts that parents will respond to individual differences in their children, in keeping with Lytton's (1980) research on families with twins. If parent treatment of their children is not related to children's talents, interests, and personalities, the theory is wrong.

Second, studies of responses that individuals evoke from others would test our

ideas about evocative genotype environment effects. The social psychology literature on attractiveness (Berscheid & Walster, 1974), for example, would seem to
support our view that some personal characteristics evoke differential responses
from others. Similarly, teachers' responses to children with high versus low
intelligence, hyperactivity versus acceptable levels of energy, and so forth provide some evidence for our theory. If others do not respond differentially to
individual characteristics for which there is genetic variability, then the theory is
wrong.

Third, active niche-building is being studied by the Laboratory of Comparative Human Cognition in their naturalistic observations of children's adaptations to problem-solving situations. Our theory predicts that children select and
build niches that are correlated with their talents, interests, and personality
characteristics. If not, the theory is wrong.

Fourth, longitudinal studies of adopted children, such as the ongoing work of
Plomin and colleagues, can provide valuable evidence of the changing influences
of family environments on children. The theory predicts that children's characteristics will be more related to characteristics of the adoptive parents and other
adopted siblings in earlier than later development. If adopted children are as
similar to their adoptive parents and each other in late adolescence as they were
in early childhood, that aspect of the theory is wrong.

Fifth, studies of older adolescents and adults who were adopted in infancy and
others who were born into their families can provide evidence on the long-term
effects of passive genotype ⟶ environment effects within the families. Both
evocative and active kinds of genotype ⟶ environment effects can be traced
through the similarities and dissimilarities of the two kinds of siblings.

In these ways and others, the theory can be tested. It can fail to account for
results obtained, or it can account for the diverse results more adequately than
other theories. Given the various results of family studies presented in this paper,
we believe that its predictions will be fulfilled. At least, we hope it will encourage more developmentalists to study more than one child per family, genetically
unrelated families, and individual differences in experience.

So What?

We have found evidence of genetic sources of variability for all of the psychological characteristics we have studied, from early childhood to the end of the childrearing period. The same studies also provide evidence for the malleability of
development—the responsiveness of genotypes to differences in their environments. We think that developmentalists ought to be concerned with individual
differences in development under similar rearing conditions, as well as the average level of development expressed under varying environmental conditions. An
evolutionary view incorporates both perspectives, because individuals vary genetically in their responses to diverse rearing conditions.

Thus, the view we have embraced is a middle-of-the-road, interactionist perspective that highlights the roles that genes *and* environments play in determining human development and behavior. As a personal observation we can affirm that by staking ground between two well-armed, ideological forces, one becomes an easy target in the crossfire of bitter accusations, conceptual challenges, and verbal assaults that are hurled in defense of respective positions in the field.

The conclusion that our genetic heritage contributes to the complex accounting of variation in our performance is not pessimistic and does not bode evil for social and educational policy. The position we have taken has been summarized as follows:

> Social policy should be determined by political and ethical values. . . . Once social policy has been determined, however, research can be useful. Governments can do a better job of designing effective intervention programs if people know which variations in the environment make a difference and which do not. The *average level* of a culture's environment determines the average level of achievement: by providing good schools, nutrition, health care, and psychological services, a society can raise the overall level of health and attainment for the whole population. Resources spent in these areas should eliminate conditions that have definite deleterious effects on individual development.
>
> But governments will never turn their entire populations into geniuses, or altruists, or entrepreneurs, or whatever their philosophy is. Biological diversity is a fact of life, and respect for individual differences derives from the genetic perspective. (Scarr & Weinberg, 1978, p. 36)

Those of us who devote our professional efforts to the mental health enterprise can appreciate individual differences and accept the challenge to create those environments that effectively "match" a child's abilities and talents. We can attempt to provide the necessary full range of environments that will facilitate optimal psychological outcomes for every child. We can invest our resources in changing those circumstances that clearly leave deleterious effects on development.

ACKNOWLEDGMENT

Funding of the research projects discussed in this chapter was provided by the William T. Grant Foundation and National Institute of Child Health and Human Development (HD-08016).

REFERENCES

Bell, R. Q. (1968). A reinterpretation of the direction of effects in studies of socialization. *Psychological Review, 75,* 81–95.

Berscheid, E., & Walster, E. (1974). Physical attractiveness. In L. Berkowitz (Ed.), *Advances in experimental social psychology*. New York: Academic Press.

Burks, B. S. (1928). The relative influence of nature and nurture upon mental development: A comparative study of foster parent-foster child and true parent-true child resemblance. *Twenty-seventh Yearbook of the National Society for the Study of Education*, 219–316.

Campbell, D. P. (1974). *Manual for the Strong-Campbell Interest Inventory T325 (Mergd Form)*. Palo Alto, CA: Stanford University Press.

Cleary, T. A., Humphreys, L. G., Kendrick, S. A., & Wesman, A. (1975). Educational uses of tests with disadvantaged students. *American Psychologist, 30*, 15–41.

Doppelt, J. E. (1956). Estimating the full scale on the Wechsler Adult Intelligence Scale from scores on four subtests. *Journal of Consulting Psychology, 20*, 63–66.

Freeman, F. N., Holzinger, K. J., & Mitchell, B. C. (1928). The influence of environment on the intelligence, school achievement and conduct of foster children. *Yearbook of the National Society for the Study of Education, 27*, 101–217.

Garmezy, N. (1983). Stress-resistant children: The search for protective factors. In J. E. Stevenson (Ed.), *Recent Research in Developmental Psychopathology*. Journal of Child Psychology and Psychiatry Book Supplement No. 4. Oxford: Pergamon Press.

Grotevant, H. D., Scarr, S., & Weinberg, R. A. (1977). Patterns of interest similarity in adoptive and biological families. *Journal of Personality and Social Psychology, 35*, 667–676.

Herrnstein, R. (1973). *IQ in the meritocracy*. Boston: Atlantic, Little, Brown.

Holland, J. L. (1966). *The psychology of vocational choices: A theory of careers*. Aaltham, MA: Ginn.

Horn, J. M., Loehlin, J. C., & Willerman, L. (1979). Intellectual resemblance among adoptive and biological relatives: The Texas adoption project. *Behavior Genetics*, 177–207.

Husen, T. (1974). *Talent, equality, and meritocracy*. The Hague: Martinue Nijhoff.

Jencks, C. (1972). *Inequality: A reassessment of the effects of family and schooling in America*. New York: Basic Books.

Jensen, A. R. (1969). How much can we boost IQ and scholastic achievement? *Harvard Educational Review, 39*, 1–123.

Jensen, A. R. (1973). *Educability and group differences*. New York: Basic Books.

Jensen, A. R. (1974). How biased are culture-loaded tests? *Genetic Psychology Monographs, 90*, 185–244.

Kamin, L. J. (1974). *The science and politics of IQ*. Hillsdale, NJ: Lawrence Erlbaum Associates.

Leahy, A. M. (1935). Nature-nurture and intelligence. *Genetic Psychology Monographs, 17*, 235–307.

Lewontin, R. C. (1970). Race and intelligence. *Bulletin of the Atomic Scientists, 26*, 2–8.

Loehlin, J., Lindzey, G., & Spuhler, J. N. (1975). *Race differences in intelligence*. San Francisco, CA: Freeman.

Lytton, H. (1980). *Parent-child interaction: The socialization process observed in twin and single families*. New York: Plenum Press.

Maccoby, E. E. (1980). *Social development*. New York: Harcourt, Brace, Jovanovich.

Manosevitz, M., Lindzey, G., & Thiessen, D. (Eds.). (1969). *Behavioral genetics*. New York: Appleton-Century-Crofts.

Munsinger, H. (1975a). The adopted child's IQ: A critical review. *Psychological Bulletin, 82*, 623–659.

Munsinger, H. (1975b). Children's resemblance to their biological and adoptive parents in two ethnic groups. *Behavior Genetics, 5*, 239–254.

Plomin, R. (1986). *Development, genetics, and psychology*. London: Lawrence Erlbaum Associates.

Plomin, R., DeFries, J. C., & Loehlin, J. C. (1977). Genotype-environment interaction and correlation in the analysis of human behavior. *Psychological Bulletin, 84*, 309–322.

Scarr, S., & McCartney, K. (1983). How people make their own environments: A theory of genotype → environment effects. *Child Development, 54,* 424–435.

Scarr, S., Scarf, E., & Weinberg, R. A. (1980). Perceived and actual similarities in biological and adoptive families: Does perceived similarity bias genetic influence? *Behavior Genetics, 10,* 445–458.

Scarr, S., Webber, P. L., Weinberg, R. A., & Wittig, M. A. (1981). Personality resemblance among adolescents and their parents in biologically-related and adoptive families. *Journal of Personality and Social Psychology, 40,* 885–898.

Scarr, S., & Weinberg, R. A. (1976). IQ test performance of black children adopted by white families. *American Psychologist, 31,* 726–739.

Scarr, S., & Weinberg, R. A. (1978). The influence of "family background" on intellectual attainment. *American Sociological Review, 43,* 674–692.

Scarr, S., & Weinberg, R. A. (1980). Calling all camps! The war is over—A reply to "The non-influence of 'family background' on intellectual attainment: A critique of Scarr and Weinberg." *Amertican Sociological Review, 45,* 859–864.

Scarr, S., & Weinberg, R. A. (1981). The transmission of authoritarianism in families: Genetic resemblance in social-political attitudes? In S. Scarr (Ed.), *IQ: Race, social class and individual differences.* Hillsdale, NJ: Lawrence Erlbaum Associates.

Scarr, S., & Weinberg, R. A. (1983). The Minnesota Adoption Studies: Genetic differences and malleability. *Child Development, 54,* 260–268.

Scarr-Salapatek, S., & Williams, M. L. (1973). The effects of early stimulation on low-birth-weight infants. *Child Development, 44,* 94–101.

Scarr, S., & Yee, D. (1980). Heritability and educational policy: Genetic and environmental effects on IQ, aptitude, and achievement. *Educational Psychologist, 15(1),* 1–22.

Shockley, W. (1971). Morals, mathematics, and the moral obligation to diagnose the origin of Negro IQ deficits. *Review of Educational Research, 41,* 369–377.

Shockley, W. (1972). Dysgenics, geneticity, raciology: A challenge to the intellectual responsibility of educators. *Phi Delta Kappan, 53,* 297–307.

Skodak, M., & Skeels, H. M. (1949). A final follow-up on one hundred adopted children. *Journal of Genetic Psychology, 75,* 85–125.

Wachs, T. D., & Gandour, M. J. (1983). Temperament, environment, and six-month cognitive-intellectual development: A test of the organismic specificity hypothesis. *International Journal of Behavior Development, 6(2),* 135–152.

Weinberg, R. A. (1979). Early childhood education and intervention: Establishing an American tradition. *American Psychologist, 34,* 912–916.

Weinberg, R. A. (1983). A case of a misplaced conjunction: Nature or nurture? *Journal of School Psychology, 21,* 9–12.

5

In Search of Fathers: A Narrative of An Empirical Journey

Ross D. Parke
University of Illinois at Champaign-Urbana

This is the story of a journey that is not yet finished. The modest goal of this endeavor was to outline the role that fathers might play in infancy and early childhood. My search began in 1970 and nearly 20 years later the task is still not complete. As is the case of any attempt to reconstruct retrospectively, my account is by definition incomplete, selective, and probably distorted. It is perhaps ironic that the primary methods that are used in the series of investigations that comprise my ongoing research are observational, and I chose this approach deliberately to avoid some of the problems and pitfalls inherent in the "reconstruction through retrospection" methodology (e.g., Sears, Maccoby, & Levin, 1957) that characterized research on child-rearing practices for many years. So with this caveat as my guide we begin.

THE STATE OF THE ART IN THE STUDY OF FATHERS IN THE EARLY 1970S

People differ in how they select research topics. In selecting the topic of the father-infant relationship, I considered several factors. As argued later, the topic was theoretically important since it would provide a corrective to the field's long-standing focus on the mother-infant relationship as the basis for later social development. In addition, I was attracted to the topic because I viewed it as an issue of social as well as scientific relevance. In the early 1970s there were beginning to be serious re-examinations and re-evaluations of women's and men's roles in both the family and the workplace. I hoped that this debate could be placed on a firmer empirical foundation through systematic investigation of

153

the father's role in infancy and early childhood. Moreover, I am attracted to topics that have been neglected or ignored by previous researchers or approached in ways that still leave plenty of room for making a contribution. My assessment of the field in the late 1960s was that the study of fathers was a topic awaiting to be examined in a convincing and useful way. Most of the current research on early social development involved only mothers. The research on fathers was of two brands—both of which had serious limitations. To a large degree, the study of fatherhood was assessed indirectly, mainly by the examination of the effects of father absence. This was a natural outgrowth of the large number of father absent families during the second world war—a clear reminder that scientific problems throughout the history of child development research are often driven by secular changes and historically timed events (Sears, 1975). However, these studies of father absence were not an adequate substitute for research that directly assessed father roles. Several limitations of this research tradition can be noted (see Herzog & Sudia, 1973; Pedersen, 1976). First, comparison groups of father-present children are often not carefully matched with the father-absent samples. Second, as Herzog and Sudia note, the causative agent that produces behavioral problems is often incorrectly viewed as the absent father, but in fact may be due to other factors associated with the father-absent situation. The stress and lowered socioeconomic conditions often linked with father-absent families may, in fact, be the critical factor rather than father absence per se. Third, the impact of father-absence varies as a function of factors such as the child's age at departure, the sex of child, as well as the reason for the father's absence (Hetherington & Deur, 1971). Often these factors were not considered, thus limiting the value of the research findings. Moreover, this is a deficit oriented approach to families and yields little information about the effects of specific types of paternal influence on family functioning. The most central limitation was stated well by Pederson (1976) who noted that "this research paradigm is inherently incapable of providing a direct test of father influence" (p. 460). However, there was a second strand of father research that merits mention, namely the work on paternal child-rearing attitudes (Tasch, 1952). While this is an important aspect of paternal roles, the methodological limitations associated with the reliance on verbal reports as substitutes for assessment of actual behavior clearly limited the value of this approach. As a number of writers have noted there are often large discrepancies between attitudes and behavior which makes it necessary to independently assess both attitudes and behavior (Parke, 1978b; Yarrow, Burton, & Campbell, 1968). It was clear that a different approach was necessary in order to understand the father's role in infancy.

It was more than limitations in prior approaches that led to my interest in the father's role in infancy. The most critical turning point was the shift in theoretical paradigms for the study of early social development. Up until the late 1950s or early 1960s the most influential paradigm had been psychoanalysis, which emphasizes the feeding situation as the critical context for the development of social responsiveness and the mother as the primary object of infant attachment. Although the influence of the original theory waned, the translation of psychoanalytic theory into the drive-reduction language of learning theory extended the life of the assumption of the centrality of both the feeding situation and the mother for early social development (Sears et al., 1957). According to this revised view, the mother, as a result of being paired with drive-reducing feeding activity, acquires positive secondary-reinforcement properties and consequently is valued by the infant in her own right. Because father was typically less involved in feeding activities, his role in infant development was minimized. Although the assumptions of drive-reduction theory were replaced by an ethological-evolutionary analysis, Bowlby (1969) similarly presented an attachment theory of early social development that, like his predecessors, stressed the primary role of the mother in the development of social responsiveness. In fact, much of the research in infancy in the 1960s focused on the development of the mother-infant interaction system and specifically on the ways in which the infant's attachment to the mother develops (Ainsworth, 1967, 1973).

The stage was set for a reemergence of the father's role in infancy by the general decline of secondary-drive theory (Hunt, 1961; White, 1959). Specifically, Harlow's (1958) classic demonstration via surrogate mother experiments that the feeding situation was not the critical context for attachment development, combined with the emerging evidence that social and sensory stimulatory activities were important determinants of infant social development (Brackbill, 1958; Rheingold, 1956), led to a revival of interest in the role of noncaretaking socializing agents—including fathers. Another landmark event was Schaffer and Emerson's (1964) demonstration that human infants showed "attachment" to individuals, such as fathers, who never participated in routine caretaking activities. They found that the amount of social stimulation and the responsiveness of the social agent to the infant's behaviors were important determinants of attachment. Fathers, of course, are just as capable of providing these important ingredients for early social development as mothers. Therefore, by the mid 1960s, theoretical shifts finally legitimized the active investigation of the father's role in early infant social development. This revised view of social development was summarized in my earliest writing on infancy when Richard Walters and I wrote a paper on "The role of the distance receptors in the development of social responsiveness" (Walters & Parke, 1965). These theoretical shifts and the priming of my interest in infant social development through this early writing laid the groundwork for my first excursions into the study of fathers and infants.

EARLY WORK: FATHER-NEWBORN INTERACTION

Methodological Considerations. The methodological strategy that we adopted in our earliest studies of fathers represented a radical departure from the favored approach of the social learning tradition in which I had been trained and worked (Bandura & Walters, 1963; Parke, 1967, 1969, 1970). However, by the early 1970s there were signs of dissatisfaction with the main methodological strategies that characterized this approach. There was an increasing concern about the limited ecological validity of the laboratory paradigm, the sine qua non of the social learning theorist. I was particularly influenced by Baldwin (1967) who accused child development researchers, particularly social learning theorists, of building a ''mythology of childhood'' in which a set of effects obtained in the laboratory is assumed to actually take place in naturalistic socialization contexts and be an accurate account of how the child is socialized. As a result there was confusion between necessary and sufficient causality: The laboratory experiments may tell us only that certain variables are potential contributors to the child's development. However, the extent to which these processes are, in fact, necessary or are actual contributors to socialization is left unanswered (Parke, 1972, 1976). Others expressed similar concerns about the heavy reliance on the laboratory experiment (Bronfenbrenner, 1974; Hartup, 1973) and set the stage for broadening of my own choice of methodological strategies. In an effort to take these concerns about ecological validity seriously, I embarked on a series of studies that differed in terms of method and design from the previous experimental laboratory work than I had done (Parke, 1967, 1970). My assessment of our knowledge of father behavior with infants indicated that a good deal of descriptive work was a necessary first step before any more process oriented experimental work was undertaken. This led to my earliest studies of fathers and infants. This work can be characterized in three ways that contrast with the earlier orientation: (1) direct observation, (2) naturalistic context, and (3) nonexperimental approach.

Observations of Fathers and Newborn Infants. A series of observational studies by my associates and I was conducted in order to describe—in behavioral terms—the nature of father's interaction with his newborn infant. In the first study we observed the behavior of fathers in the family triad of mother, father, and infant for a 10 minute period in the hospital during the first 3 days following delivery (Parke, O'Leary, & West, 1972). A time-sampling procedure was used in which 40 intervals of 15 sec duration were scored for the following behavior for each parent: holds, changes position, looks, smiles, vocalizes, touches, kisses, explores, imitates, feeds, hands over to other parent.

The results indicated that fathers were just as involved as mothers and that mothers and fathers did not differ on the majority of the measures. In fact, fathers tended to hold the infant more than mothers and rock the infant in their arms more than mothers. Fathers, in short, in a context where participation was voluntary, were just as involved as mothers in interaction with their infants.

However, there are a variety of questions that I raised about this study that limited its generality. First, the context was unique, since the mother and father were together, and possibly the higher degree of father-infant interaction observed was due to the supporting presence of the mother. Moreover, the sample of fathers was unique in ways that may have contributed to their high degree of interaction with their infants. Over half of the fathers had attended Lamaze childbirth classes, and with one exception, all fathers were present during the delivery of the child. Both of these factors may have increased the fathers later involvement with their infants. Finally, these fathers were well educated and middle class, and their high degree of involvement may be more common in middle-class groups. It was simply unclear whether lower-class fathers would show similar degrees of interest and involvement.

To overcome the limitations of the original study, a group of lower-class fathers who neither participated in childbirth classes nor were present during delivery were observed in two contexts: (1) alone with their infant (dyad), and (2) in the presence of the mother (triad) (Parke & O'Leary, 1976). This study permitted a much more stringent test of father-infant involvement and permitted wider generalization of the previous findings. Moreover we were becoming aware of the potential importance of contextual factors and this gave us the opportunity to compare father behavior in two settings: dyadic and triadic. As in the earlier study, the father was a very interested and active participant. In fact, in the family triad, the father was more likely to hold and visually attend to the infant than the mother. Nor was the mother's presence necessary for the father's active involvement; the father was an active interactor in both settings—alone and with his wife. However, we discovered that context was a significant modifier of parental behavior. Mothers and to a lesser extent fathers reduced the rate of occurrence for most categories of behavior directed toward the baby when they were with their spouse in the family triad than when alone with the infant in the dyad. Parental behaviors such as touching, holding, rocking, imitating, and vocalizing decreased when a second adult was present. This reduction of activity in a triadic rather than a dyadic-context was later termed a "second-order effect" (Bronfenbrenner, 1979) and has been found in both the laboratory (Lamb, 1979) and at home (Belsky, 1979; Clarke-Stewart, 1978; Pedersen, Anderson, & Cain, 1980) with infants of varying ages (see Table 5.1)

In this early work with O'Leary, I found that not all behaviors followed this pattern (Parke & O'Leary, 1976). Some behaviors such as smiling at the baby and exploring the baby (counting toes, checking fontanels) increased in the presence of the spouse. This increase in affective and exploratory behavior in the presence of the spouse underscored the uniqueness of the family triad. Our hypothesis was that parents verbally stimulate each other by focusing the partners attention on aspects of the baby's behavior which, in turn, elicits either positive affect directed toward the baby or exploration and checking on an aspect of infant behavior noted by the spouse. It was an early clue that parents may affect the infant indirectly by altering the behavior of the spouse as well as by direct contact. This issue of alternative pathways of influence was explored formally in a later paper with Power and Gottman (Parke, Power, & Gottman, 1979).

Finally, fathers in our early studies were just as nurturant as mothers. For

TABLE 5.1
Mean Frequency of Parent Behavior

	Mother and Father Present		Mother Alone	Father Alone
	Mother	Father		
Hold arms	7.7	21.6	25.8	25.8
Hold lap	2.7	4.1	5.9	7.2
Hand over	.7	.71	--	--
Change position	3.6	8.1	13.3	11.3
Look	38.7	39.3	38.0	38.6
Vocalize	4.0	11.9	10.4	12.8
Smile	9.2	7.7	3.7	4.8
Rock	1.6	5.6	7.4	13.7
Walk	.2	.4	.3	.9
Touch	9.2	12.3	17.7	17.6
Explore	2.6	3.3	1.0	1.8
Kiss	.2	.3	.4	.2
Imitate	.0	.2	.1	1.0
Feed	2.9	8.2	17.0	9.8

Adapted from Parke and O'Leary (1976).

example, in the first study with O'Leary and West (Parke et al., 1972) they touched, looked, vocalized, and kissed their newborn offspring just as often as mothers did. In the second study with O'Leary, an even more striking picture emerged with the father showing more nurturant behavior in the triadic context than the mother and only slightly less when alone with the baby. There was only a single nurturant behavior—smiling—in which the mother surpassed the father in both studies.

Although there were few differences in the nurturant and stimulatory activities of the parents, fathers did play a less active role in caretaking activities than mothers. In the Parke and O'Leary study (1976) in which all infants were bottle-fed, fathers fed significantly less than mothers when they were alone with the baby. Additional support for these mother-father differences comes from another study of father-newborn interaction that involved a detailed examination of early parent-infant interaction in a feeding context (Parke & Sawin, 1975). Comparisons of the frequencies and durations of specific caretaking activities of mothers and fathers while alone with their infants in a feeding context indicate that mothers spend more time engaged in feeding the infant and in related caretaking activities, such as wiping the baby's face, than do fathers. These findings suggest that parental role allocation begins in the earliest days of life.

These findings are consistent with the more general proposition that pregnancy and birth of a first child, in particular, are occasions for a shift toward a more traditional division of roles. Cowan, Cowan, Coie, and Coie, (1978) studied couples between late pregnancy up to 6 months after the birth of a first child. They found that couples tended to adopt more traditional roles with mothers engaging in more housework and baby care than fathers. Of particular interest is the fact that these patterns held regardless of whether their initial role division was traditional or equalitarian.

In Search of Competence.   However, the lesser degree of father involvement in feeding does not imply that fathers are less competent than mothers to care for the newborn infant. Competence can be measured in a variety of ways, but our approach was to measure the parent's sensitivity to infant cues in the feeding context. Our decision to define competence in this way stemmed from our view that feeding was a social as well as an instrumental task and therefore it was important to measure the interactive features of feeding. Our thinking was clearly shaped by earlier analyses of feeding that focused on the social and stimulatory in contrast to the psychoanalytic and Hullian views of feeding as principally a biologically based drive-reduction system (Harlow, 1958; Walters & Parke, 1965). Success in caretaking, to a large degree, is dependent on the parents' ability to correctly "read" or interpret the infant's behavior so that their own behavior can be regulated in order to achieve some interaction goal. To illustrate, in the feeding context, the aim of the parent is to facilitate the food intake of the infant. The infant, in turn, by a variety of behaviors, such as sucking or coughing, provides the caretaker with feedback concerning the effectiveness and/or ineffectiveness of the parent's current behavior in maintaining the food intake process. In this context, one approach to the competence issue involves an examination of the degree to which the caretaker modifies his/her behavior in response to infant cues. Parke and Sawin (1975, 1976) found that the father's sensitivity to an auditory distress signal in the feeding context—sneeze, spit-up, cough—was just as marked as the mother's. Using a conditional probability analysis they showed that fathers, like mothers, adjusted their behavior by momentarily ceasing their feeding activity, looking more closely to check on the infant, and vocalizing to their infant. The only difference concerned the greater cautiousness of the fathers, who were more likely than the mothers to inhibit their touching in the presence of this signal. The implication of this analysis is clear: in spite of the fact that they may spend less time overall, fathers are as sensitive as mothers to infant cues and as responsive to them in the feeding context.

Moreover, the amount of milk consumed by the infants with their mothers and fathers was very similar (1.3 versus 1.2 oz with mothers and fathers, respectively). In short, fathers and mothers are not only similar in their sensitivity but are equally successful in feeding the infant based on the amount of milk consumed by the infant. Invoking a competence/performance distinction, fathers may not necessarily be frequent contributors to infant feeding, but when called upon they have the competence to execute these tasks effectively.

Moreover, fathers are just as responsive as mothers to other infant cues, such as vocalizations and mouth movements. Both mothers and fathers increased their rate of positive vocalizations following an infant vocal sound; in addition, both parents touched and looked more closely at the infant after hearing infant vo-calizations. However, mothers and fathers differ in the behaviors that they show in response to this type of infant elicitor. Upon vocalization, fathers are more likely than mothers to increase their vocalization rate. Mothers, on the other hand, are more likely to react to infant vocalization with touching than fathers. Possibly fathers are more cautious than mothers in their use of tactile stimulation during feeding owing to their concern about disrupting infant feeding behavior. A further demonstration of the modifying impact of the infant's behavior on his caregivers—fathers as well as mothers comes from an examination of the impact of infant mouth movement: Parents of both sexes increase their vocalizing, touching, and stimulation of feeding activity in response to mouth movements. These data indicate that fathers and mothers both react to the newborn infant's cues in a contingent and functional manner even though they differ in their specific response patterns.

The interaction patterns in the newborn period are clearly reciprocal. While our focus in the Parke and Sawin (1975, 1976) study was on the role of infant cues as elicitors of parent behavior, in a later study (Parke & Sawin, 1977) we showed that parent vocalizations can modify newborn infant behavior, such as infant vocalizations. Interaction between fathers and infants—even in the new-born period—is clearly bidirectional in quality with both parents and infants mutually regulating each other's behavior in the course of interaction (Parke, 1979b).

These advances in our understanding of the reciprocal nature of father-infant interaction were driven mainly by conceptual concerns. We were well aware of the bidirectionality issue from the earlier paper by Bell (1968), but our progress in actually demonstrating these effects came about, in part, due to meth-odological, statistical, and technological advances. In spite of the headaches due to breakdowns, failed batteries, and other problems associated with a new de-vice, the use of Datamytes—a portable memory-laden keyboard that permitted collection of sequential data—was a significant factor in alerting us to the re-ciprocal nature of father-infant interaction. This device yielded the data in a form that permitted Sawin and I to undertake the conditional probability analyses that led to these insights. Advances in technology and conceptual progress often go hand in hand. It clearly did for us in our studies of the mutual influence of fathers and infants.

The Importance of Context.   Our research suggests that parents are more similar than different, at least up to this point in our narrative. However, the choice of settings or contexts may often exert a powerful influence on the researcher's ability to detect differences between individuals. The significance of context for illuminating individual differences in parental interactive style is schematically summarized in Fig. 5.1. As this figure shows, the structural re-straints imposed by the demands of context and the goals of the interaction will

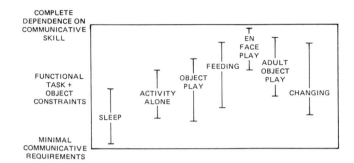

FIG. 5.1. Relative communicative requirements of different infant activities. From Brazelton et al. (1975).

play an important role in determining the variability in behavioral outcome. Our research had focused solely on the feeding context and the portrait of similarities between mothers and fathers may have been due in part to the apparent competence of parents of either sex but also due to the situational constraints imposed by our choice of the feeding context. This led us to reorient our search from the questions of competence and overlap of parental roles to the uniqueness of parental roles.

We were seriously concerned that we had missed important aspects of the father-child relationship by restricting our observations to young infants and to the feeding situation. Research reports were beginning to appear that confirmed folklore, namely that the fathers role may be primarily as a playmate. For example, Kotelchuck (1976) found that fathers spent a greater percentage of their time with their infants in play than mothers did who in turn spent more time, as expected, in caregiving than fathers. In view of the fact that fathers play a great deal, it seems reasonable not only to explore this context but to examine the ways in which fathers and mothers differed in their styles of play as well. In view of our contextual argument, we hoped that the play setting would also lead to more insights about mother-father differences than the earlier studies of feeding interaction. These considerations led us to select a less structured context—free play—for our next set of studies.

Early Studies of Parent-Infant Play

In collaboration with Power, I conducted a series of descriptive play studies in both the lab and home settings (Power & Parke, 1982, 1983, 1986). Briefly, these studies involved 8–13 month-old infants interacting either in a lab playroom or at home with their mothers and fathers. In the lab studies, parents were told that we were "interested in the ways in which mothers and fathers played with their infants"; they were provided with toys and were instructed to use these toys in play with their infants. In the home studies, natural interchanges between parents and infants were videotaped. To illustrate, I will discuss a study with Power in which we observed 8-month-old infants and their parents in our lab playroom (Power & Parke, 1982).

In addition to our search for mother-father differences in play style, we were also interested in exploring different ways of coding play interaction that would help illuminate the ongoing debate in our own laboratory as well as in other labs concerning the choice between molecular and molar levels of coding (Parke, 1978b, 1979a). It was our view that multiple levels of analysis (molar and molecular) are often necessary to describe interaction patterns adequately (see also Cairns & Green, 1979; Hinde, 1976; Sackett, 1978). Therefore, a primary purpose of this phase of our work was to develop an observational system that could codify molar units of parent-infant play interaction while also providing a detailed description of the context and structure of these interactions. This kind of analysis was employed because of our belief that units of social interaction corresponding to extended sequences of social behaviors might be more meaningful in describing the nature of social interaction than would discrete, molecular units that correspond to the occurrence of individual social behaviors. Without the use of molar units, it is often impossible to specify the behavioral context in which a given behavior occurs (Hinde, 1976; Sroufe & Waters, 1977). This is important, as the behavioral context often gives the molecular behavior its meaning. Sroufe and Waters (1977) provide some examples:

> The same behavior may act as a member of class X in one context, class Y in another. For example, most babies turn away when their nose is wiped. Such a response is of limited interest and would not predict turning away when picked up in the course of seeking contact. The latter has a radically different meaning, and tallying the two responses together is certain to obscure results. Contact seeking mixed with squirming to get down, pushing away, or general petulance has a different meaning than relaxed molding to the caregiver (though both would contribute to total scores for time in contact). Looking at the mother, when combined with bounding and smiling upon the caregiver's entrance, has different significance (positive greeting) than mere looking sometime later. (pp. 1188–1189)

These examples clearly illustrate why larger units are often necessary to capture the meaning of various social interchanges (Patterson & Moore, 1979; Sackett, 1978). Therefore, a central problem in coding social interaction is the relationship between levels of analysis; specifically, this requires the articulation of how molecular behaviors relate to specific molar units (Hartup, 1979).

In this study, units at two levels were utilized. Specifically, molar units which we termed play bouts were identified; these corresponded to extended sequences of parent and infant behaviors that occurred frequently during the play interactions. In addition, molecular behaviors such as "smile," "touch," and "vocalize" served as the smaller units within these molar bouts were coded. Thus, through simultaneous use of both molar and molecular units, the structure of the parent-infant play interactions could be described more adequately.

Two sets of findings merit comment. First, we were able to identify several distinctive types of parent-infant interaction bouts. These are presented in Table 5.2; these account for 88% of the play interactions observed. Comparison of the structure of the bouts indicated that they fell into three general categories of bouts in which the parent attempted to (1) focus or otherwise manipulate the infant's attention or level of affective arousal (attention/arousal-regulating bouts), (2) influence or direct the infant's motor exploration of a toy (exploratory bouts), or (3) engage the infant in face-to-face social interaction (communicative bouts).

Moreover, as we had anticipated, the types of bouts revealed sex of parent differences as well. Fathers spent more time in toy touching bouts in which they physically stimulated their infants with the toy. In addition, fathers, especially fathers of boys spent more time engaged in lifting bouts, which involves lifting tossing and shaking the baby. Mothers, on the other hand engaged in more distance-receptor oriented activities such as watching bouts. In this type of play bout the parent presents a toy, and makes it salient for the baby by moving or making a noise with the toy. These stylistic differences between mothers and fathers are commonly found (Parke, 1981; Parke & Tinsley, 1981 for reviews).

Just as we had found that sequential analytic techniques were useful for illuminating father competence in feeding in our earlier studies (Parke & Sawin, 1976, 1980), we applied lag sequential analyses (Sackett, 1979) to our play data in order to determine if there were differences in the competence of mothers and fathers in their execution of different kinds of play. These sequential analyses revealed that fathers were more likely than mothers to engage in extended physical no-toy play interactions with their infants. Fathers often alternated between physical and communicative, no-toy play while mothers generally terminated play after becoming physical. In other words fathers were more competent than mothers in maintaining physical play bouts with their infants. On the other hand, mothers appeared more skillful at engaging in extended, successful sequences of exploratory behavior. This is indicated primarily by the sequences involving unsuccessful exploratory play. Mothers often followed unsuccessful exploratory play with successful exploratory play, i.e., they were able to change the nature of play in order to engage the baby in this type of activity. Fathers, on the other hand, who engaged in unsuccessful exploratory play often terminated play or persisted in the unsuccessful exploratory activity. Finally, mothers often shifted from attention regulating play to successful exploratory play; fathers, in contrast, often shifted to physical no-toy play after failures to focus their infant's attention on a toy. These sequential analyses revealed clear stylistic differences in mother and father play styles.

Moreover, analyses of the bouts served to generate hypotheses concerning the functions that different types of play activities might serve. Power and I (Power & Parke, 1982) suggested that:

TABLE 5.2

Descriptions of Bout Structure: Laboratory Study

Bout	Parent Verbalizations	Infant Affect[a]	Percentage
Attention/arousal-regulating bouts			
Watching — Parent presents toy → Make toy salient (make noise, move) → Present toy	--	0	11
Toy touching — Parent presents toy → Move toy with toy [Touch[b]] → Present toy	--	0	10
Minor physical — Parent touches, tickles, bounces, or shakes infant	nonverbal	0	16
Exploratory bouts			
Grasping — Parent presents toy → Infant reaches → Infant grasps toy → parent vocalizes	Attention directing Information: objects	0	25
Retrieving — Parent presents toy out of reach → Infant crawls and reaches → Infant grasps toy	Commands Information: objects	0	12
Communicative bouts			
Face — Parent positions face in front of infant's face → Eye contact → Infant looks away → Parent moves own face away	Information: parent/ infant	+	11
Lifting — Parent lifts infant in air → Parent positions infant in face-to-face orientation → Face bout → parent shakes infant → Parent lowers to lap	Information: parent/ infant	+	3

[a]Two symbols are used to indicate the predominant level of infant affective involvement: 0 for predominantly neutral affect and + for predominantly negative affect. From Power and Parke (1982).

The fact that father-infant play was more physical than mother-infant play (especially for fathers of boys) indicates that fathers may play an important role in their infants' social development. This is suggested because the descriptive analysis of the physical bouts (especially the lifting bouts) showed that these bouts often serve as contexts for a wide range of communicative and affectively charged social interactions between parents and their infants. Therefore, through such interactions fathers may play an important role in facilitating the development of communicative skills and the formation of social relationships. (p. 160)

Another implication of the physical play between fathers and their infants is suggested by the earlier work of Harlow and his colleagues (Suomi & Harlow, 1971). In this research, infant monkeys who were deprived of opportunities for physical interaction with either peer or adult monkeys showed serious deficits in their ability to regulate physical social exchanges, particularly aggression. Therefore, we might expect that early physical play may be important both as an antecedent of later peer-peer play and in the regulation of agonistic and aggressive interactions.

Finally, because the results of the sequential analyses indicated that mothers were more successful than fathers in engaging their infants in extended sequences of toy play (and thereby played a greater role in structuring their infants' early environmental exploration), it is hypothesized that mother-infant play may have its greatest influence in the realm of early cognitive development.

These observational analyses were useful in our research program not only for revealing differences in maternal and paternal interactional style, but in generating further hypotheses that, in turn, could be evaluated directly.

THE IMPLICATIONS OF PHYSICAL PLAY FOR CHILDREN'S SOCIAL DEVELOPMENT

The next step in our research program was to address the issue of the impact of these variations in mother and father play styles on children's social behavior. We set out to explore some of the links between play interaction in the family and social relationships with peers. We moved up the developmental ladder from infancy to preschool-age children in order to be able to adequately capture the nature of children's peer competence. Our first step was to determine whether the stylistic differences in play that we found in infancy were still present between preschoolers and their parents. Unless it was clear that these differences were still evident, this age choice would have been unwise. To find out, we deviated from our usual observational strategy and used a telephone survey approach. The decision to use a telephone survey reflected our conviction that different methodological strategies are useful at different stages of a research project. The survey provided a relatively economical way of evaluating the wisdom of our decision to move up to the preschool age period. This served as a guide concerning the wisdom of investing the time and resources necessary to carry out an observational study. From our point of view it is not a substitute for doing the actual observational work. We telephoned 390 randomly selected intact families and asked the parents to report the frequency of physical play with their children of different ages (1 year to early adolescence) over the last 24-hour period. Our findings yielded two insights: (1) mothers and fathers continued to differ in expected ways in their frequencies of physical play across age with fathers being more physically playful than mothers, and (2) physical play was still relatively common between parents and their children in the preschool period (MacDonald & Parke, 1986). This gave us greater confidence in our choice of the preschool-age period as the time period for testing our hypothesis concerning the possible implications of parent-child play for children's social development. Next we turn to a series of observational studies aimed at evaluating this general hypothesis.

Parent-Child Play and Children's Peer Competence: Overview of the Paradigm

In order to explore the relationships between parent-child play and peer relationships a two-step paradigm had been developed and employed across a number of investigations that are described in the next section of this narrative. Briefly, in the first phase of this paradigm, mothers and fathers on separate occasions are observed interacting with their 3–5 year-old children in semistructured play sessions. In all studies, a 10-minute period of physical play is included, in which parents are specifically instructed to play in a physical manner with their children. Parents are given examples such as tickling, tumbling, wrestling, or playing horsey. In light of our interest in physical play, it was necessary to insure through instructions that we would elicit this type of play from all parent-child dyads. Often this physical play session is preceded by a free play session of similar length or a briefer warm up session in which parents can play "as they normally do." It was our assumption that we could capture "typical" or "representative" parent-child play by this opportunity to choose their own type of play. These sessions have been conducted in either the home or the laboratory and videotaped for later analysis. We chose to observe the families in their homes in order to provide greater ecological validity for our findings on the assumption that parents would be more relaxed in their familiar home environments. On the other hand, quality of lighting and sound often reduces the quality of videotaped productions. In other studies we have used a laboratory playroom setting to insure better quality productions. Our experience indicates that the context does not alter the general pattern of the findings. This is largely due to the fact that the sessions are structured by instructions concerning the type of activity that is required. There will obviously be home–lab differences when less structured activities are being observed. For purposes of examining interactive processes in structured situations, the lab–home choice appears to be of less concern. The type of question and the type of interactive task determines whether or not context is important. These types of play sessions differ from unstructured naturalistic observations of parent-child interaction and were specifically selected in order to (1) standardize the nature of playful interaction across families, and (2) to insure a sufficiently high level of play interaction to permit detection of individual differences across parent-child dyads. In the second phase, measures of peer interactive competence are secured. These have varied across studies in this series and include (1) teacher assessment of peer competence, and (2) sociometric ratings by peers. The particular features of the paradigm that are used in each study are noted.

In Search of Parent-Child Interaction Processes

In our initial study (MacDonald & Parke, 1984), we observed 13 boys and 14 girls ranging in age from 3- to 5-years-of-age interacting with their mothers and fathers. Each dyad was observed for 10 minutes of free play and 10 minutes of physical play in their homes. Mother-child and father-child observations were carried out on separate occasions.

The videotapes were scored for a variety of physical and verbal behaviors as indicated below:

1. Physical play: The number of 10-second epochs in which the parent and child engaged in physical play together. Physical play included a wide range of active play styles characterized by wrestling, tickling, swinging the child in the air, and so on, but was not restricted to these specific activities, and included physically active parent-child interactions that did not correspond readily to any of the usual categories of physical play.

2. Positive affect of the child with the parent: Each 10-second epoch was rated on a 4-point scale, with a rating of 1 indicating neutral affect; 2, low-level laughter; 3, moderate laughter; and 4, intense laughter. A child's total positive affect score was the sum of his or her ratings for each 10-minute session (i.e., 60 epochs). Negative affect was too infrequent to merit scoring.

3. Directiveness: Instances in which a parent issues a command to the child.

4. Parental engagement: Number of epochs in which the parent was actively participating in the child's activity as opposed to merely observing the activity.

5. Number of verbal interchanges: This category was arrived at by counting the number of times the parent spoke to the child. An interchange was bounded on both sides either by a statement by the child or by a pause of at least 5 seconds.

The following parental behaviors were scored each time they occurred, regardless of how many times they occurred within an epoch: directiveness, ending pausing, and verbal interchanges. Because the remaining behaviors often occurred for a considerable time, they were scored if an instance occurred during a 10-second epoch. These included physical play and engagement. Reliability was calculated as the quotient of the number of agreements divided by the number of agreements plus disagreements. Reliability was above .90 for all these behaviors.

To provide indices of peer interactive competence, two types of teaching assessments were secured: (1) teacher rankings of the children in their nursery school class according to the frequency and extensiveness with which they were sought out as playmates by other children. This measure is an index of peer popularity and has been shown to relate well to extensive peer observations (Connolly & Doyle, 1981). (2) The teachers completed the California Q-Sort (Baumrind, 1968) which involved rating the child on a variety of social and personal characteristics.

In order to determine how mothers' and fathers' behavior related to their children's peer relationships, correlations between the observational data from the parent-child play and the two measures of peer interactive competence—the teacher popularity rankings and the teacher Q-sort data—were calculated.

Parent Behavior and Teacher Rankings of Popularity.   Table 5.3 shows the correlations between parental variables and the teacher rankings of popularity. For boys, both maternal and paternal behaviors were related to teacher popularity rankings. Boys whose mothers were engaging, directive, verbally stimulating, and who elicited positive affect during play were rated as popular. Paternal engagement was also positively correlated with popularity, but paternal directiveness was negatively related to the teacher ratings. Girls' popularity rankings were positively correlated with paternal physical play and affect during play and negatively related to paternal directiveness and verbal interchanges. The correlations between the rankings of the girls and mother-daughter interaction showed a positive relationship between maternal directiveness and social popularity. As physical play and directiveness are highly correlated, partial correlations were calculated controlling for directiveness. These revealed that for boys paternal physical play, engagement, and the affect of the child with the father in the second session showed higher associations with teacher popularity rankings with directiveness controlled and revealed a higher correlation between first-session physical play for both sexes of parents and teacher rankings for girls.

In summary, popular boys have mothers and fathers who are engaging and elicit positive affect during play, mothers who are verbally stimulating, and fathers who are low in directiveness but physically playful. Girls whose teachers rated them as popular have physically playful and affect-eliciting but nondirective fathers, and directive mothers.

Parent Behavior and Teacher Q-Sort Items.   The teacher Q-Sort items provided a more detailed picture of the specific aspects of children's social behavior

TABLE 5.3
Correlations Between Parental Variables and Teacher Rankings of Popularity[a]

	Fathers		Mothers	
	Session 1	Session 2	Session 1	Session 2
Boys				
physical play		(.56)**		
Affect of child with parent		(.41)*	.52**(.61)**	.42(.45)*
Parental directiveness	-.43*	-.37*	.51**	
Parental engagement	.46**(.65)**	.37*(.55)**	.53**(.32)	.62**(.61)**
Ending pauses			.62**(.57)**	.41*(.40)*
Verbal interchanges			.43*(.43)*	.63**(.67)**
Girls				
Physical play	.36*(.40)*	.71***(.76)***	(.45)*	
Affect of child with parent		.47**(.40)*		.40*
Parental directiveness		-.56**	-.58**	.37*
Parental engagement	(-.42)*			
Ending pauses		.36*(.43)*	.38*(.57)**	
Verbal interchanges	-.40*(-.41)*			

*p < .10
**p < .05
***p < .01

[a]From MacDonald and Parke (1984). Reprinted with permission.

that were associated with parental interactions. Using the prior analyses as a guide, only those parental variables that were most highly correlated with teacher popularity scores were analyzed. For boys, these variables were *paternal engagement* and *physical play,* controlling for directiveness, as well as paternal directiveness and maternal verbal interchange, while for girls these were *paternal directiveness.* Paternal engagement and physical play as well as maternal verbal interchange were generally positively associated with desirable attributes such as helpfulness, leadership, involvement, and clear communication skills and negatively associated with undesirable attributes such as being apprehensive, being unable to get along with others, and an unwillingness to share. In addition, these parental behaviors correlated with a peer versus an adult orientation. Paternal directiveness, in contrast, was associated with negative social attributes, such as being socially withdrawn, seldom being sought out by other children, being hesitant with other children, and being a spectator in social activities. Moreover, an adult orientation, indexed by concern about adult approval and forming an attachment to the teacher, was positively correlated with paternal directiveness. For girls, paternal physical play was again associated with desirable social attributes such as high positive emotional expressiveness and clarity of communication as well as originality, novelty, and creativity. Maternal directiveness was associated with attraction to adults as well as some attributes that may facilitate peer acceptance, such as emotional expressiveness and social assertiveness (lack of hesitancy to engage others).

In summary, boys showed a consistent profile of positive characteristics being associated with paternal engagement and physical play and maternal verbal behavior. A negative array of attributes that were less likely to lead to peer acceptance was linked with paternal directiveness for boys. Girls who have physically playful fathers and to a lesser extent directive mothers showed a consistent set of positive social attributes as well as aspects of intellectual competence such as originality and creativity. The most robust finding concerned the ability of the parent and child to maintain physical playful interaction. For both boys and girls, physical play, especially father physical play was positively related to teacher ratings of the child's popularity. Second, the extent to which mothers and fathers elicited positive affect from the child during the course of play was also positively linked with peer popularity. For boys, the extent to which the mother verbally engaged her son was a significant correlate of peer popularity. Possibly, these boys learn verbal strategies that both help them in initiating and maintaining peer interaction. Another factor, directiveness, bears a more complex relationship with peer popularity, in part dependent on whether mother or father is being directive. While maternal directiveness is positively associated with popularity for girls, paternal directiveness for boys is negatively linked with popularity ratings. Others (Baumrind, 1968) have found a similar negative relationship between paternal directiveness (authoritarian style) and boys' social behavior with peers.

Although this study underscores the links across systems, many questions remain concerning both the style of parent-child interaction that most closely relates to peer competence and more specifically the processes that may mediate these links.

Parent-Child Control Strategies

Our strategy throughout our research program is to engage in partial replications across a series of studies. Although the sample sizes that we use in our studies are modest, by building in replications across independent studies, we can gain more confidence in the overall pattern of findings. Therefore the next step in our research program was to replicate and extend our earlier findings in several ways. Just as we had found the distinction between molecular and molar levels of coding useful in our studies of parent-infant play (Power & Parke, 1982), we (Burks, Carson, & Parke, 1987) again used this distinction in our analyses of parent play with their preschool-age children. To secure a more accurate measure of the duration of sustained play between children and their parents, the dyadic play session was divided into molar units called "bouts." A bout was defined as a play activity with a common theme and structure (e.g., chasing, tumbling).

The amount of time that the dyad was engaged in play was determined by totaling the length of all play bouts. This provided a more accurate measure of the duration of play than was available in the earlier study in which we relied on a time sampling strategy (MacDonald & Parke, 1984). To complement this molar level of analysis (bouts), a molecular coding strategy was employed involving second by second analysis that allowed the determination of differences in initiations to engage in a play bout, as well as responses to these initiatives and the success of these attempts as assessed by whether or not the dyad engaged in the activity. This allowed us to assess behavior at both molar and molecular levels. Second, in this work we utilized a current measure of sociometric status instead of the reliance on teacher ratings. This assessment is derived from earlier research that supports the value of a two-dimensional conceptualization of sociometric status, including the independent dimensions of being liked by peers and being disliked by peers (Coie, Dodge, & Coppotelli, 1982). Within this framework rejected children are considered to be highly disliked by peers and score low on being liked by peers while popular children are highly liked by their peers and are not actively disliked by them. One of the main advantages of using sociometric status is the fact that there has been previous research concerning the behavioral correlates of these status categories. Specifically, it has been found that peer interactions with popular children generally involve more engaged activities which are of longer duration than interactions involving rejected children (Dodge, 1983). Similarly, popular children tend to be less controlling and more willing to adapt to the activities of the group, while rejected children tend to be assertive and directive when they interact with peers (Coie & Dodge, 1983; Coie & Kupersmidt, 1983). One of our goals was to determine whether similar styles of interaction between children of different sociometric status and their peers are evident in their interactions with their parents as well. A second advantage of the use of an extreme group design is the heightened probability of detecting differences across groups of parent-child dyads.

Popular and rejected 3–5 year-old boys and girls participated (7 popular boys and 7 popular girls; 8 rejected boys and 5 rejected girls) in a laboratory playroom and were observed interacting with their mothers and fathers on separate occasions for a 5-minute warm up free play period as well as a 10-minute physical play session. Separate groups of sociometrically average boys and girls are being added to the design, but this phase is not yet completed.

Results indicated that dyads involving popular children and their parents engaged in play bouts for a longer period than dyads involving the rejected children and their parents, particularly when the popular children were with their fathers. Moreover the average length of a play bout tended to be longer for dyads involving popular children than for dyads involving rejected children. These results for the molar level of analysis are complemented by the molecular findings. The interaction strategies used varied by status of the child. As found in our earlier study, the degree of coerciveness of initiation tactics differed across the two groups. In this study, initiation tactics were assumed to vary in terms of their degree of control. Questions were least controlling, suggestions more controlling followed by directives; physical initiations were most controlling. This latter tactic occurs when one member of the dyad begins an activity without any verbal warning. Separate analyses were conducted for the initiation tactics of popular and rejected children, mothers and fathers of popular and rejected children and the dyad (mother-child and father-child combined).

In their use of the low-control tactic of questions, popular children with their fathers and dyads involving popular children tended to be higher than either rejected children with their fathers or dyads involving rejected children. In the case of the more controlling initiating tactics, such as suggesting, fathers of rejected children and rejected dyads were higher than popular fathers or dyads. In the case of directiveness, rejected children were more likely to use this initiating strategy than popular children, especially with their fathers. Finally, for the tactic of initiating an activity in a physical manner, rejected children, especially boys as well as rejected dyads, were more likely to use physical initiations than popular boys. Similarly, responses to initiations differed across the status groups. Dyads involving a rejected child were more likely to respond negatively—verbally or physically than popular dyads.

Of particular interest was the finding that in spite of the fact that rejected dyads respond negatively to their partners' initiations, the rate of success of popular and rejected dyads in engaging their partners in the activity did not differ. This suggests that even though there was initially a negative response the rejected children and their parents eventually engaged in the activity—an indication that coercive tactics were successful in achieving their interactional goals. Many of these patterns of coercive interchanges that were found in families of rejected children are similar to patterns of interactions between rejected children and their peers. This is clear confirmation of our hypothesis that styles of interaction across the family and peer systems are strikingly similar in many ways. In turn, this provides further support for the argument that these styles may possibly have their origins in family interactional experiences.

Social learning processes of observational learning as well as cognitive working models which are used to form expectations concerning the ways in which people behave in social situations and in turn how one ought to behave are both viable explanatory candidates for explaining these findings (Main, Kaplan, & Cassidy, 1985; Parke, MacDonald, Burks, Carson, Bhavnagri, Barth, & Beitel, 1989). A third explanatory candidate is available which flows more explicitly from our focus on physical play as an interaction context. In the following section we turn to an analysis of how emotional regulation may contribute to explaining the linkage between family and peer systems. Our shift to a focus on explanatory processes represents the other half of a two-pronged approach. The studies described earlier from the infancy period through the preschool years are largely descriptive in nature. The second underlying concern of our research program is to isolate processes that may account for some of the observed effects of variations in mother and father play interaction on children's social behavior.

Emotion Regulation Processes

Throughout our work the focus has been primarily on the context of parent-child physical play; this choice was made, in part, because successful parent-child physical play involves the regulation of affectively arousing stimulation, a process thought to be central to social competence in infancy as well as among older children (Stern, 1977, 1985; Sroufe, Schork, Motti, Lawroski, & LaFreniere, 1984). Parent-child physical play requires complex and subtle ability on the part of the parent to help keep stimulation within an optimal range. Overstimulation of the child by the parent and approach-withdrawal behaviors on the part of the child are common and both parent and child may be seen as regulating the child's affective display during these bouts. To evaluate directly the ways in which these arousal regulatory strategies are utilized in the case of parent-child play by parents of children of different sociometric statuses was the goal of the recent study by MacDonald (1987).

As in our other studies 3- to 5-year-olds were subjects, but in this investigation only boys were included. Children were selected on the basis of their sociometric status using the aforementioned Coie et al. (1982) method and 12 rejected, 12 popular, and in this case, 12 neglected children were included as well. Twenty-minute videotaped observations of parent-child interaction were made in the home (10 minutes free play and 10 minutes of physical play). Mother-son and father-son sessions were conducted on separate home visits.

The results indicated that popular children engage in higher levels of physical play and express more positive affect than rejected children especially during the physical play sessions. Moreover parents tend to be more directive with rejected children. These findings are consistent with earlier investigations (Burks et al., 1987; MacDonald & Parke, 1984; Puttalaz, 1987).

Despite the indication that popular children engage in more physical play and show more positive affective expressiveness than rejected children the data indicated that the play sessions of rejected children are characterized by more overstimulation and avoidance of stimulation than is the case of popular children and their parents. The interactions of the rejected children were characterized by alternatively approaching the source of stimulation and then withdrawing from stimulation. Moreover the rejected children were characterized by higher levels of overstimulation (i.e.—child became overaroused during physical play and screamed or showed a negative affective response to stimulation). Because the rejected children were characterized by higher levels of overstimulation than the other groups and because withdrawal from stimulation often coincided with expressions of overstimulation on the part of the child, it suggests that withdrawal from stimulation was motivated by the child being overstimulated. This, in turn, may account for the reduced amount of positive affect in the sessions of the rejected children in comparison to their popular counterparts. These findings underscore the regulation of affectively arousing stimulation as an important social process. Moreover the differences that were found in the regulation of arousal in the dyads of parents with popular and rejected children may, in fact, be evident in peer-peer interactions as well. If this hypothesis is correct deficits in arousal-regulating ability may be another factor associated with the lowered acceptance of rejected children. Although the current work cannot confirm that this skill is learned in parent-child interactive contexts, it is a viable possibility and provides a further clue concerning potential ways that parents may contribute to children's different social competence with their peers. Next, we turn to a further refinement of the arousal regulatory hypothesis by exploring the possible role that the ability to encode and decode emotional signals may play in this regulatory process.

The Relationship Between Emotional Decoding and Encoding Abilities and Sociometric Status

One set of possible skills that are of relevance to successful peer-peer interaction and may, in part, be acquired in the context of parent-child play especially affectively arousing physical play is the ability to decode others' emotional states and to clearly encode their own emotional signals. In other words, *through physically playful interaction with their parents, especially fathers, children may be learning the social communicative value of their own affective displays as well as how to use these emotional signals to regulate the social behavior of others. In addition, they may learn to accurately decode the social and affective signals of other social partners.*

In the next section, two studies are described that provide evaluations of these hypotheses, namely that decoding and encoding skills are related to peer competence. Then a preliminary evaluation of the relationship between these skills and parent-child play is presented.

Decoding and Peer Status

To determine the role that the ability to decode affective cues may play in mediating peer relationships, we conducted a further study (Beitel & Parke, 1985). Children were asked to correctly identify facial expressions depicting the following emotional states: happy, sad, scared, angry, or neutral. To determine the relationship between emotional deciding ability and children's peer relationships, the teacher popularity rating (Connolly & Doyle, 1981) was secured as well as two measures of sociometric status. One hundred and fifty-eight 3- and 4-year-olds were shown pictures of their classmates. In one procedure, they were asked to indicate their degree of liking on a 3-point scale using pictures of happy (like a lot) to sad (don't like) schematic faces (Asher, Singleton, Tinsley, & Hymel, 1979). In a second approach, they were asked to choose the classmate they liked best using a paired comparison procedure (Cohen & Van Tassel, 1978).

The results indicate that there are significant relationships between emotional decoding ability and various measures of children's sociometric status as well as teacher ratings of popularity. For boys these relationships are evident even after age of child, a strong correlate of emotional decoding ability, is controlled; in contrast, for girls the effect is less evident after controlling for age. This finding of a link between emotional decoding and social status is consistent with other investigators (Field & Walden, 1982; Edwards, Manstead, & MacDonald, 1984), who found evidence that preschoolers' sociometric status was positively related to children's ability to correctly identify facial expressions of emotion. Together this evidence suggests that one component of peer acceptance may be a child's ability to correctly identify the emotional states, as indexed by their facial expressions, of other children. It is assumed that this emotional identification skill would permit a child to more adequately and sensitively regulate his social interactions with other children; in turn, this could contribute to his greater acceptance by his peers.

Encoding and Peer Status

Evidence suggests that not only is emotional decoding linked with children's social status with their peers, but emotional encoding ability is a correlate as well. A number of investigators (Buck, 1975, 1977; Field & Walden, 1982) have found positive relationships between children's ability to accurately encode specific emotional expressions and children's popularity with peers. The goal of a recent study in our laboratory (Carson, Burks, & Parke, 1987) was to extend earlier work by examining how sociometric status is related to emotional production and recognition skills within the family. In contrast to other procedures where children and adults view posed photographs of different facial expressions, we devised a procedure by which adults and children generated live emotional expressions for one another.

The same children who varied in their sociometric status (i.e., popular or rejected) described above (Burks et al., 1987) participated in this study as well. In our paradigm parent-child dyads (mother-child or father-child) were seated facing one another. Each member of the dyad was given a set of headphones so that the experimenter could communicate with each subject independently. Subjects were asked to "play a game" in which they had to recognize each other's facial productions of emotional expressions. The 7 faces used were: happy, sad, mad, scared, surprise, neutral, and disgust. The child would then have to guess which face had been produced by the parent. After the parent had made 7 faces the game would be switched such that the child would then produce faces for the parent to identify. The labels "nothing" and "yuk" were substituted for neutral and disgust. The parent and child alternated making 7 faces each, so that each parent and child produced a total of 14 faces. The order of the faces was scrambled over the 14 total productions so that each subject made 2 productions of each of the 7 faces.

There were no sociometric status related differences in either parents' ability to recognize the faces of their children or in children's abilities to recognize their parents' faces. The parents of rejected children were as competent at recognizing their children's facial expressions as the parents of popular children and popular children were no better than rejected children at recognizing their parents' facial expressions. This finding would indicate that *within the family,* children and parents, regardless of sociometric status, can recognize each other's productions of facial expressions. This finding contrasts with the earlier results which indicated that children of different sociometric status vary in their ability to recognize expressions of unfamiliar individuals. Perhaps recognition of the expressions of family members who are more familiar is an easier task than recognition of unfamiliar individuals.

Although the emotional expressions produced by popular and rejected children and their parents are understandable within the family, it is not clear that these productions of emotional expressions by either parents or children can be discriminated by individuals outside of the family. Some families may utilize idiosyncratic affective cues that are not recognizable in interactions outside of the family. Their communications may reflect a "familycentric" bias.

As a test of this hypothesis, we showed videotapes of the childrens' and parents' facial productions to 150 undergraduates. Undergraduate subjects were separated into groups who saw the 14 expressions of eight different family subjects. The eight family subjects that they saw were scrambled from the total pool of family subjects by status, sex, and age (children vs. parents). Thus one set of undergraduate subjects might first see the 14 emotional expressions of a rejected boy with his father, then see the expressions of the mother of a popular girl, then the expressions of the father of a rejected girl, and so on.

We found that there was a significant sociometric status difference in undergraduates' ability to accurately decode the children's facial productions. The undergraduates were significantly better able to decode the emotional expressions of the popular children than those of the rejected children. We did not find any status differences in the undergraduates ability to decode the emotional expressions of parents.

Remember, *within the family* we found no status differences in family members' ability to recognize each others' emotional expressions. However, attempts to recognize emotional expressions by non-family members, in this case undergraduates, revealed that the emotional expressions of popular children were clearer than those of rejected children. This finding suggests that the emotional production skills of popular children are greater than those of rejected children.

Also, while rejected children may have difficulty providing facial expressions that are recognizable to observers *outside the family*, they remain successful at producing affective communications that are clear to individual *within the family*.

This pattern of findings suggests that the rejected children are learning a unique or different set of emotional expressions than popular children. These children do not show a deficit, but rather a difference, just as children in different social classes may learn unique language codes. Just as lower class children's language is most profitably viewed as unique rather than deficient, so rejected children's emotional productions may most usefully be viewed as unique or family-centric rather than deficient. Further evaluation of this issue is continuing by exploring whether objective raters outside the family are as competent at recognizing emotional expressions as raters within the family, in two ways. First, we are repeating the methodology used with the undergraduates with a sample of preschoolers, thus providing us with a "peer perspective" of the quality of emotional expression encoding. Second, we are coding each emotional expression using a standardized objective coding system (Ekman and Friesen's EMFACS). In this way we hope to obtain an objective rating of the production skills of popular and rejected children.

Together these studies provide further support for links between children's emotional encoding and decoding skills and children's sociometric status. Next we turn to the question that, in part, motivated this search namely the role of parent-child play in the development of these emotional detection and production skills.

The Relationship Between Parental Play and Emotional Decoding and Encoding Abilities

The aim of another phase of our project was to assess the relationship between affect decoding ability and parent-child interaction. In this study, Beitel and Parke (1985) utilized a set of procedures similar to those used in the previous studies (MacDonald & Parke, 1984) to assess parent-child play. In addition, children's ability to decode or recognize emotional expressions were secured using the same methodology described earlier (Beitel & Parke, 1985), namely the use of slides of the emotional expressions of unfamiliar individuals. This permitted an examination of the links between measures of parent-child play, and emotional decoding ability.

An analysis of this sample (N = 39; 20 boys and 19 girls) provides some support for our hypothesis that children's emotional decoding ability is related to physical play experience with their parents. Specifically, there were positive correlations (r = +.44; $p < .05$; r = +.58; $p < .01$; df = 18 for Sessions 1 and 2, respectively) between paternal physical play ratings and daughters' ability to correctly discriminate emotional states. However, there was only a trend between emotional decoding ability and paternal play patterns for boys (r = +.21;

$p < .18$; NS for Session 1). There was no significant relationship between maternal physical play and children's emotional decoding ability. It was clear that more work was needed to unravel the complexities of how parent-child interaction patterns relate to children's abilities to decode faces of unfamiliar people. We were encouraged that we were on the right track but the puzzle remained unsolved. Therefore a further investigation was undertaken to examine this issue.

Stronger support for the hypothesized links between parent-child interaction and decoding and encoding skills comes from a recent study by Muth, Burks, Carson, and Parke (1988). Decoding abilities was assessed during the facial production game that was described earlier (Carson et al., 1987). Briefly, 4–5 year-old popular or rejected children were asked to identify facial expressions of different emotions produced by their mothers and fathers in separate sessions. In support of the relationship between parent-child play and children's emotional decoding or recognition skill, it was found that the longer the length of the father-child and mother-child bouts (see earlier description of Burks et al., 1987 for details of coding), the better the child was at accurately decoding the parents' emotional expressions. ($r = 37$; $p < .05$; $r = .36$; $p = .06$ for father-child and mother child sessions respectively). This pattern is consistent with the Beitel–Parke (1985) findings in spite of the fact that parental emotional productions instead of a standard set of emotional displays was used. Moreover, in the present study a similar pattern was evident for both mothers and fathers.

The ability to encode emotions accurately was evaluated in a manner described earlier (see p. 176 for details). Briefly, children's productions of emotional expressions were shown to undergraduate raters who attempted to correctly identify the emotional expressions. The parent-child play assessments were already described in the Burks et al. (1987) study. In support of the hypothesized link between parent-child play and encoding ability, it was found that as the length of the play bouts between children and their fathers increased— a sign of competent play interaction—the more easily the undergraduate raters were able to correctly identify the childrens' productions. More specifically, the longer the play bouts of fathers and children the better the level of recognition by undergraduate observers of the facial productions that the children made with their fathers ($r = .62$; $p < .01$). Similarly the longer the mother-child play bouts, the better the level of identification by undergrad raters of emotional facial productions that the children made with their mothers ($r = .42$; $p < .05$). These data provide support for the link between the level of parent-child play engagement—as assessed by the length of the play bouts—and the children's ability to accurately encode emotional expressions.

Together, these findings provide support for the importance of parent-child play as a potential context for either learning and/or for refining and rehearsing emotional encoding and decoding skills—a set of skills that, in turn, appear to play a role in the successful management of peer social relationships.

Establishment of covariation among these factors represents only one further step in the evaluation of this hypothesis. Our hypothesis is not a static one, but a dynamic one, and a more adequate test involves the examination of the extent to which the child is able to adequately decode emotional signals of an interactive partner. Our assumption is that the ability may be acquired in the context of parent-child play interaction, especially father-child interaction, which in turn may generalize to other social encounters including peer-peer exchanges. This requires further analysis of the interactive exchanges between parents and children during play with specific attention to the extent to which children recognize and respond appropriately to the emotional signals of the parent-play partner. Similarly, the children's ability to utilize emotional signals to regulate social interaction can be assessed by examining the degree to which parents recognize and respond to their children's emotional cues during the course of play interaction.

Remaining Issues in Parent-Child Interaction Studies

Although our focus has been on nonverbal aspects of communication in light of its relative neglect by earlier investigators, it should be stressed that other aspects of communicative competence, such as verbal skills, may be acquired in the context of parent-child play, especially in the context of the mother-child dyad.

This series of studies illustrates one avenue through which families and peers may be linked, namely through the quality of parent-child play. Social lessons, which are valuable for regulating social behavior in other contexts, such as the peer group, may be learned in the course of parent-child play. However, this indirect path is only one avenue through which parents can influence their children's social relations outside the family. Parents directly influence their children's peer relationships as well through such activities as direct teaching of social skills and by the provision of opportunities for contact with other children (Parke & Bhavnagri, 1989; Rubin & Sloman, 1984). In our recent studies we have begun to expand our conceptual framework of the ways in which familial and peer systems relate to incorporate both indirect and direct paths of influence. (See Parke & Bhavnagri, 1989; Parke, MacDonald, Beitel, & Bhavnagri, 1988 for overviews.) However, this represents the beginning of a new research tangent, but one that has evolved directly from our earlier concerns about father and mother roles. It is a story that is only beginning to unfold at the present time.

FINAL REFLECTIONS

In this closing section, I offer some reflections on the past, some caveats, and some speculations about the future. First, some caveats are in order. This represents a personal perspective on the field of father research. I have chosen to focus my attention on a few strands of the larger research enterprise that is represented by this aspect of family research. Many other themes have been of interest to both myself and my coworkers as well as to other father researchers. One of the major themes that we have not examined in detail in this chapter is the determinants of father involvement. This has been a major area of father research and a wide range of determinants, including personality, familial and structural factors have been uncovered. Several reviews of this issue are available (Belsky, 1981, 1984; Lamb, 1981, 1986; Parke, 1979b, 1981; Parke & Tinsley, 1984, 1987; Russell, 1983). My approach to this issue has been to examine how father involvement shifts as a result of changes in either the medical sphere (e.g., rise of C-section births; increase in survival rates of preterm infants) or the social and work arenas (e.g., shifts in work patterns; changes in the timing of onset of parenthood including both earlier and delayed onset). (See Parke, Power, & Fisher, 1980; Parke & Nevelle, 1987; Parke & Tinsley, 1984; Sawin & Parke, 1976 for reviews.) One of our major efforts in this domain has been our ongoing longitudinal study of how the role of the father changes in response to a preterm in contrast to a full-term infant. Our findings indicate that the usual paternal physical play patterns are modified with preterm babies—an indication of both the plasticity of father roles and the noninevitability of some patterns of father-infant interaction (see Parke & Anderson, 1987; Parke & Tinsley, 1982 for reviews).

A second strand of investigation is the examination of how delayed parenthood affect father-child involvement and father's style of interaction. Earlier interview research suggests that older fathers are more involved with their children (Daniels & Weingarten, 1982) and shift their style of play toward less physical modes (MacDonald & Parke, 1986). In collaboration with Nevelle, we are currently observing late-timed fathers with their children to determine more clearly how timing of onset alters both the level and style of father-child interaction.

Second, can we definitively answer our recent questions concerning how interactional experiences that mothers and fathers offer their infants and children facilitate the development of social skills by reliance on nonexperimental strategies alone? I view it as unlikely. Instead a wide range of strategies including experimental approaches ought to be more heavily utilized. The use of these experimental strategies will help illuminate one of the major issues in the area namely the direction of effects. By experimentally modifying either the type of paternal behavior or level of father involvement further conclusions concerning the direct causative role that fathers play in their children's development will be possible. In our own work we have developed an experimental intervention in which we have shown that the amount of father involvement with their infants can be increased by exposure to a modeling film in the early postnatal period in the hospital (Parke, Hymel, Power, & Tinsley, 1980). Others have utilized related strategies for experimentally modifying either father play or caregiving behavior (Zelazo, Kotelchuck, Barber, & David, 1977; Dickie & Carnaham, 1980; see Parke & Beitel, 1986 for a review). By extending these studies to include measures of infant social and cognitive development, these intervention efforts could usefully serve to evaluate shifts in specific aspects of fathering behavior on infant and child development.

This advocacy of more experimentation does not imply an abandonment of our field based observational approach; instead it is a renewed call for methodological pluralism in which nonexperimental and experimental approaches are used together at different points in an ongoing research enterprise (Parke, 1979a, 1979b). I remain convinced that our early decisions to suspend our lab-oriented experimental approach for a field-based descriptive strategy was still a wise one. Particularly in the early stages of investigation of a relatively uncharted area, a descriptive strategy is an appropriate one. After the domain is better defined and the key processes and questions come into sharper focus the use of other more specifically directed strategies such as experimental manipulation for testing our theoretical notions become more appropriate (Parke, 1979a, 1979b).

In an ironic way, the research has come back to the beginning in two senses. First, it is clear to me that we need to go back to infancy, begin again and trace the development of parent-infant interaction and the emergence of subsequent social skills in children longitudinally. Only by tracing the emergence of social skills over time in the context of father and mother interactions with their infants and children can we begin to address some of central questions about the impact of the early father-infant relationship on later child development outcomes. Second, we began by studying triads and it is clear that we need to study units beyond the dyad again if we are to fully understand the ways in which families— not just individuals or dyads-relate to other social institutions such as the peer group. In our current conceptualization of fathers, they are viewed as part of the family system, and a full understanding of fathers needs to treat them as part of the context of other relationships among family members (Belsky, 1981; Parke, 1981; Parke & Tinsley, 1987; Sigel & Parke, 1987). In our own lab, several recent and ongoing studies reflect this family systems orientation. Our research on the impact of the marital relationship on father-infant communication in a social referencing situation (Dickstein & Parke, 1988) as well as our ongoing investigation of the role of maternal gatekeeping in determining father involvement (Beitel, 1989) both reflect this theoretical viewpoint. Moreover, we are in a better position to investigate fathers in family contexts than we were at the beginning of our research program, since we have better ways of both conceptualizing and measuring units at different levels of analyses (Barrett & Hinde, 1988; Parke, Power, & Gottman, 1979).

Developmental issues need to be addressed more fully. Again, the meaning of development has changed since we began. Although development traditionally has meant change in the individual child, it is clear that this is no longer satisfactory. Adults, as well as children continue to develop across time and the tracing of the development of adults is crucial (Parke, 1988; Parke & Tinsley, 1984). Consider two examples. First, we (MacDonald & Parke, 1986) found that fathers (and mothers) engage in less physical play as they grow older—even after controlling for child's age. This robust form of activity is more difficult for older than younger parents. What are the implications of growing up in a home where there is less focus on this type of play? Particularly in view of the trend toward later timing of the onset of parenthood, it is an important question (Parke & Tinsley, 1984). Nor are adult developmental effects restricted to fathers; timing of the onset of grandfatherhood is an important determinant of this type of cross-generational fathering activity as well. Tinsley and I (Tinsley & Parke, 1987, 1988) found that grandfathers who assume this role either early or late were less involved with their grandchildren than "on-time" grandfathers. Clearly, adult developmental as well as child developmental trajectories need to be considered in our studies of fathers.

As argued elsewhere (Parke, 1988), it is insufficient to trace only the individual—whether parent or child; it is also necessary to trace the development of dyads (mother-child; father-child as well as the husband-wife dyad), and larger units, such as families over time. Each of these units may show a partially independent trajectory and the interplay across the trajectories of different units (individual, dyad and family) provides a more complete picture of the context in which the individual of interest is embedded. Our earlier attempts that rely on additive models of family interaction are useful (Parke, Power, & Gottman, 1979) but it is necessary to move beyond these additive approaches if we are to capture the ways in which the family operates as a small group. Advances in this area are dependent on sophisticated modeling at the family level of analysis (Boss, 1980; Reiss, 1981)—a task that developmental psychologists have only begun to address conceptually and empirically.

Finally, I believe that a fuller appreciation of fathers and families will come from a historical perspective on these issues. We often assume that any recently documented discoveries about fathers are a departure from the roles that fathers played in the past. It is important to determine whether or not these recent assessments represent shifts or are more continuous and consistent with prior portraits of fathers. A number of recent researchers, including ourselves (Lewis, 1986; Parke & Stearns, in press) are expressing caution concerning the amount of change in fathering roles that has occurred over the past few decades.

Moreover the study of historical trends in fathering is analogous to the use of natural experiments; in this historical case, past social and economic conditions can be evaluated to determine their impact on patterns of fathers' roles in the family over time. By a careful examination of historical periods, we may begin to compare past and present processes underlying father and family relationships, in order to assess the historical generality of our assumptions. Similarly cross-cultural research on fathering is valuable in this regard, as a further means of testing the limits of fathering behavior within the contexts of differing social, economic and cultural conditions (see Lamb, 1986, for a review of cross-cultural studies on fathering).

It is clear that my search for the definition of the father's role and the impact of his role on children's development is far from over. It has not only been an interesting intellectual journey, but a fulfilling personal one as well. Finally, watching my own children's development and experiencing my own development as a father has been an integral part of this enterprise. Hopefully this report of my odyssey will serve as an invitation to join the search.

ACKNOWLEDGMENT

The preparation of this chapter and the research reported were supported in part by National Institute of Child Health & Human Development Grant No. HD05951 and by National Institute of Child Health & Human Development Training Grant No. HD07205. I am grateful to my father Horace D. Parke and my children Gillian, Timothy, Megan, Sarah & Jennifer for providing me with the cherished opportunity to learn about fathering first hand. Thanks to Barbara J. Tinsley for her helpful comments on this chapter and for sharing in this research enterprise. Finally thanks to Terry Sturdyvin and Ginny Ragle for their assistance in the preparation of the manuscript.

REFERENCES

Ainsworth, M. D. (1967). *Infancy in Uganda: Infant care and the growth of love*. Baltimore: Johns Hopkins.

Ainsworth, M. D. (1973). The development of infant-mother attachment. In B. M. Caldwell & H. N. Ricciuti (Eds.), *Review of child development research III*. Chicago: University of Chicago Press.

Asher, S. R., Singleton, L. C., Tinsley, B. R., & Hymel, S. (1979). A reliable sociometric sociometric measure for preschool children. *Developmental Psychology, 15,* 443–444.

Baldwin, A. (1967). *Theories of child development*. New York: Wiley.

Bandura, A., & Walters, R. H. (1963). *Social learning and personality development*. New York: Holt, Rinehart and Winston.

Baumrind, D. (1968). *Manual for the preschool behavior Q-sort*. Berkeley: Institute of Human Development, University of California.

Barrett, J., & Hinde, R. A. (1988). Triadic interactions: mother-firstborn-second born. In R. Hinde & J. Stevenson-Hinde (Eds.), *Towards understanding families*. Oxford, England: Oxford University Press.

Beitel, A. (1989). *The role of maternal gatekeeping in determining the level of father-infant involvement*. Unpublished doctoral dissertation, University of Illinois.

Beitel, A., & Parke, R. D. (1985). *Relationships between preschoolers' sociometric status, parent-child interaction and emotional decoding ability*. Unpublished manuscript, University of Illinois.

Bell, R. Q. (1968). A reinterpretation of the direction of effects in studies of socialization. *Psychological Review, 75,* 81–95.

Belsky, J. (1979). Mother-father-infant interaction: A naturalistic observational study. *Developmental Psychology, 15*, 601–607.

Belsky, J. (1981). Early human experience: A family perspective. *Developmental Psychology, 17*, 3–23.

Belsky, J. (1984). Determinants of parenting: A process model. *Child Development, 55*, 83–96.

Boss, P. G. (1980). Normative family stress: Family boundary changes across the life span. *Family Relations, 42*, 541–549.

Bowlby, J. (1969). *Attachment and loss, Vol. 1, Attachment.* New York: Basic Books.

Brackbill, Y. (1958). Extinction of the smiling response in infants as a function of reinforcement schedule. *Child Development, 29*, 1–12.

Bronfenbrenner, U. (1974). Developmental research, public policy and the ecology of childhood. *Child Development, 45*, 1–5.

Bronfenbrenner, U. (1979). *The ecology of human development.* Cambridge, MA: Harvard University Press.

Buck, R. (1975). Nonverbal communication of affect in children. *Journal of Personality and Social Psychology, 31*, 644–653.

Buck, R. (1977). Nonverbal communication of affect in preschool children: Relationships with personality and skin conductance. *Journal of Personality and Social Psychology, 35*, 225–236.

Burks, V., Carson, J., & Parke, R. D. (1987). *Parent-child interactional styles of popular and rejected children.* Unpublished manuscript, University of Illinois.

Cairns, R. B., & Green, J. A. (1979). How to assess personality and social patterns: Observations or ratings? In R. B. Cairns (Ed.), *The analysis of social interactions: Methods, issues, and illustrations.* Hillsdale, NJ: Lawrence Erlbaum Associates.

Carson, J., Burks, V., & Parke, R. D. (1987). *Emotional encoding and decoding skills of parents and children of varying sociometric status.* Unpublished manuscript, University of Illinois.

Clarke-Stewart, K. A. (1978). And daddy makes three: The father's impact on mother and young child. *Child Development, 49*, 466–478.

Cohen, A. S., & Van Tassel, E. (1978). Comparison of partial and complete paired comparisons in sociometric measurement of preschool groups. *Applied Psychological Measurement, 2*, No. 1, 31–40.

Coie, J. D., & Dodge, K. A. (1983). Continuities and changes in children's social status: A five year longitudinal study. *Merrill-Palmer Quarterly, 29*, 261–281.

Coie, J. D., Dodge, K. A., & Coppotelli, H. (1982). Dimensions and types of social status: A cross-age perspective. *Developmental Psychology, 18*, 557–570.

Coie, J. D., & Kupersmidt, J. B. (1983). A behavioral analysis of emerging social status in boys' groups. *Child Development, 54*, 1400–1416.

Connolly, J., & Doyle, A. (1981). Assessment of social competence in preschoolers: Teachers versus peers. *Developmental Psychology, 17*, 50–58.

Cowan, C., Cowan, P. A., Coie, L., & Coie, J. D. (1978). Becoming a family: The impact of a first child's birth on the couple's relationship. In L. Newman & W. Miller (Eds.), *The first child and family formation.* Carolina Population Center, The University of North Carolina at Chapel Hill.

Daniels, P., & Weingarten, K. (1982). *Sooner or later; The timing of parenthood in adult lives.* New York: Norton.

Dickie, J., & Carnahan, S. (1980). Training in social competence: The effect on mothers, fathers and infants. *Child Development, 51*, 1248–1251.

Dickstein, S., & Parke, R. D. (1988). Social referencing: A glance at fathers and marriage. *Child Development, 59*, 506–511.

Dodge, K. A. (1983). Behavioral antecedents of peer social status. *Child Development, 54*, 1386–1399.

Edwards, R., Manstead, A. S. R., & MacDonald, C. J. (1984). The relationship between children's sociometric status and ability to recognize facial expressions of emotion. *European Journal of Social Psychology, 14,* 235–238.

Field, T. M., & Walden, T. A. (1982). Production and discrimination of facial expressions by preschool children. *Child Development, 53,* 1299–1311.

Harlow, H. F. (1958). The nature of love. *American Psychologist, 13,* 673–685.

Hartup, W. W. (1973). Social learning, social interaction and social development. In P. J. Elich (Ed.), *Social learning.* Bellingham: Western Washington Press.

Hartup, W. W. (1979). Levels of analysis in the study of social interaction: An historical perspective. In M. E. Lamb, S. J. Suomi, & G. R. Stephenson (Eds.), *Social interaction analysis: Methodological issues.* Madison: The University of Wisconsin Press.

Hertzog, E., & Sudia, C. (1973). Children in fatherless families. In B. M. Caldwell & H. N. Ricciuti (Eds.), *Review of child development research* (Vol. 3). Chicago: University of Chicago Press.

Hetherington, E. M., & Deur, J. (1971). The effects of father absence on child development. In W. W. Hartup & S. Moore (Eds.), *The young child* (Vol. 1). Washington: NAEYC.

Hinde, R. A. (1976). On describing relationships. *Journal of Child Psychology and Psychiatry, 17,* 1–19.

Hunt, J. McV. (1961). *Intelligence and experience.* New York: Ronald.

Kotelchuck, M. (1976). The infant's relationship to the father: Experimental evidence. In M. E. Lamb (Ed.), *The role of the father in child development* (pp. 329–344). New York: Wiley.

Lamb, M. E. (1979). The effects of social context on dyadic social interaction. In M. E. Lamb, S. T. Suomi, & G. R. Stephenson (Eds.), *Social interaction analysis: Methodological issues.* Madison: University of Wisconsin Press.

Lamb, M. E. (Ed.). (1981). *The role of the father in child development* (2nd edition). New York: Wiley.

Lamb, M. E. (Ed.). (1986). *The father's role: Cross cultural perspectives.* New York: Wiley.

Lewis, C. (1986). *Becoming a father.* Philadelphia: Milton Keynes.

Main, M., Kaplan, N., & Cassidy, J. (1985). Security in infancy, childhood and adulthood: A move to the level of representation. In I. Bretherton & E. Waters (Eds.), Growing points of attachment theory and research. *Monographs of the Society for Research in Child Development, 50*(1–2) (Serial No. 209).

MacDonald, K. B. (1987). Parent-child physical play with rejected, neglected and popular boys. *Developmental Psychology, 23,* 705–711.

MacDonald, K. B., & Parke, R. D. (1984). Bridging the gap: parent-child play interaction and peer interactive competence. *Child Development, 55,* 1265–1277.

MacDonald, K. B., & Parke, R. D. (1986). Parent-child physical play: The effects of sex and age of children and parents. *Sex Roles, 7–8,* 367–378.

Muth, S., Burks, V., Carson, J., & Parke, R. D. (1988). *Peer competence: Parent-child interaction and emotional communication skills.* Unpublished manuscript, University of Illinois.

Parke, R. D. (1967). Nurturance, nurturance withdrawal and resistance to deviation. *Child Development, 38,* 1101–1110.

Parke, R. D. (1969). Effectiveness of punishment as an interaction of intensity, timing, agent nurturance and cognitive structure. *Child Development, 40,* 213–235.

Parke, R. D. (1970). The role of punishment in the socialization process. In R. A. Hoppe, G. A. Milton, & E. C. Simmel (Eds.), *Early experiences and the processes of socialization* (pp. 81–108). New York: Academic Press.

Parke, R. D. (1972). The socialization process: A social learning perspective. In S. B. Sells & R. G. Demaree (Eds.), *U.S. Office of Education: Child socialization task force report.* Washington, DC.

Parke, R. D. (1976). Social cues, social control and ecological validity. *Merrill-Palmer Quarterly, 22,* 111–123.

Parke, R. D. (1978a). Children's home environments: Social and cognitive effects. In I. Altman & J. R. Wohlwill (Eds.), *Children and the environment*. New York: Plenum.

Parke, R. D. (1978b). Parent-infant interaction: Progress, paradigms and problems. In G. P. Sackett (Ed.), *Observing behavior: Vol. 1. Theory and applications in mental retardation*. Baltimore: University Park Press.

Parke, R. D. (1981). *Fathers*. Cambridge, MA: Harvard University Press.

Parke, R. D. (1979a). Interactional designs. In R. B. Cairns (Ed.), *The analysis of social interactions*. Hillsdale, NJ: Lawrence Erlbaum Associates.

Parke, R. D. (1979b). Perspectives of father-infant interaction. In J. Osofsky (Ed.), *A handbook of infant development*. New York: Wiley.

Parke, R. D. (1988). Families in life-span perspective: A multi-level developmental approach. In E. M. Hetherington, R. M. Lerner & M. Perlmutter (Eds.), *Child development in life span perspective* (pp. 159–190). Hillsdale, NJ: Lawrence Erlbaum Associates.

Parke, R. D., & Anderson, E. (1987). Fathers and at-risk infants: Empirical and conceptual analyses. In P. Berman & F. Pedersen (Eds.), *Men's transition to parenthood: Longitudinal studies of early family experiences* (pp. 197–215). Hillsdale, NJ: Lawrence Erlbaum Associates.

Parke, R. D., & Beitel, A. (1986). Hospital based interventions for fathers. In M. E. Lamb (Ed.), *Fatherhood: Applied perspectives*. New York: Wiley.

Parke, R. D., & Bhavnagri, N. P. (1989). Parents as managers of children's peer relationships. In D. Belle (Ed.), *Children's social networks and social supports*. New York: Wiley.

Parke, R. D., Hymel, S., Power, T. G., & Tinsley, B. R. (1980). Fathers and risk: A hospital based model intervention. In D. B. Sawin, R. C. Hawkins, L. O. Walker, & J. H. Penticuff (Eds.), *Psychosocial risks in infant-environment transactions*. New York: Bruner-Mazel.

Parke, R. D., MacDonald, K. D., Beitel, A., & Bhavnagri, N. (1988). The role of the family in the development of peer relationships. In R. Dev. Peters & R. J. McMahan (Eds.), *Marriages and families: Behavioral treatments and processes*. New York: Bruner-Mazel.

Parke, R. D., MacDonald, K. D., Burks, V., Carson, J., Bhavnagri, N., Barth, J. M., & Beitel, A. (1989). Family and peer systems: In search of the linkages. In K. Kreppner and R. M. Lerner (Eds.), Family systems and life-span development. Hillsdale, NJ: Lawrence Erlbaum Associates.

Parke, R. D., & Nevelle, B. (1987). The male adolescent's role in adolescent pregnancy and childrearing. In S. Hoffreth & C. Hayes (Eds.), *Risking the future* (Vol. 2). Washington: National Academy Press.

Parke, R. D., O'Leary, S. E., & West, S. (1972). Mother-father-newborn interactions: Effects of maternal medication, labor and sex of infant. *Proceedings of the American Psychological Association, 85–86.*

Parke, R. D., & O'Leary, S. E. (1976). Father-mother-infant interaction in the newborn period: Some findings, some observations and some unresolved issues. In K. Riegel & J. Meacham (Eds.), *The developing individual in a changing world, Vol. II, Social and environmental issues*. The Hague: Mouton.

Parke, R. D., Power, T. G., & Fisher, T. (1980). The adolescent father's impact on the mother and child. *Journal of Social Issues, 36*, 88–106.

Parke, R. D., Power, T. G., & Gottman, J. (1979). Conceptualizing and quantifying influence patterns in the family triad. In M. E. Lamb, S. J. Suomi, & G. R. Stephenson (Eds.), *The study of social interaction: Methodological issues*. Madison: University of Wisconsin.

Parke, R. D., & Sawin, D. B. (1975, April). *Infant characteristics and behavior as elicitors of maternal and paternal responsibility in the newborn period*. Paper presented at the biennial meeting of the Society for Research in Child Development, Denver.

Parke, R. D., & Sawin, D. B. (1976). The father's role in infancy: A reevaluation. *The Family Coordinator, 25*, 365–371.

Parke, R. D., & Sawin, D. B. (1977, March). *The family in early infancy: Social interactional and attitudinal analyses.* Paper presented to the Society for Research in Child Development, New Orleans.

Parke, R. D., & Sawin, D. B. (1980). The family in early infancy: Social interactional and attitudinal analyses. In F. A. Pedersen (Ed.), *The father-infant relationship: Observational studies in the family setting.* New York: Praeger.

Parke, R. D., & Stearns, P. (in press). Fathers and childrearing in historical perspective. In G. Elder, J. Modell, & R. D. Parke (Eds.), *Children of their times: Developmental and historical perspectives.* New York: Cambridge University Press.

Parke, R. D., & Tinsley, B. R. (1981). The father's role in infancy: Determinants of involvement in caregiving and play. In M. E. Lamb (Ed.), *The role of the father in child development* (2nd ed.). New York: Wiley.

Parke, R. D., & Tinsley, B. R. (1982). The early environment of the at-risk infant: Expanding the social context. In D. Bricker (Ed.), *Intervention with at-risk and handicapped infants: From research to application.* Baltimore: University Park Press.

Parke, R. D., & Tinsley, B. R. (1984). Fatherhood: Historical and contemporary perspectives. In K. McCluskey & H. Reese (Eds.), *Life span development: Historical and generational effects.* New York: Academic.

Parke, R. D., & Tinsley, B. J. (1987). Family interaction in infancy. In J. Osofsky (Ed.), *Handbook of infant development* (2nd ed.). New York: Wiley.

Patterson, G. R., & Moore, D. (1979). Interactive patterns as units of behavior. In M. E. Lamb, S. J. Suomi, & G. R. Stephenson (Eds.), *Social interaction analysis: Methodological issues.* Madison: University of Wisconsin Press.

Pedersen, F. A. (1976). Does research on children reared in father-absent families yield information on father influences. *The Family Coordinator, 25,* 459–464.

Pedersen, F. A., Anderson, B. J., & Cain, R. L., Jr. (1980). Parent-infant and husband-wife interactions observed at age five months. In F. A. Pedersen (Ed.), *The father-infant relationship.* New York: Praeger.

Power, T. G., & Parke, R. D. (1982). Play as a context for early learning: lab and home analyses. In I. E. Sigel & L. M. Laosa (Eds.), *Families as learning environments for children* (pp. 147–178). New York: Plenum.

Power, T. G., & Parke, R. D. (1983). Patterns of mother and father play with their 8-month old infants: a multiple analyses approach. *Infant Behavior and Development, 6,* 453–459.

Power, T. G., & Parke, R. D. (1986). Patterns of early socialization: mother and father-infant interaction in the home. *International Journal of Behavioral Development, 9,* 331–341.

Putallaz, M. (1987). Maternal behavior and children's sociometric status. *Child Development, 58,* 32–340.

Reiss, D. (1981). *The family's construction of reality.* Cambridge, MA: Harvard University Press.

Rheingold, H. L. (1956). The modification of social responsiveness in institutional babies. *Monographs of the Society for Research in Child Development, 21*(63).

Rubin, Z., & Sloman, J. (1984). How parents influence their children's friendships. In M. Lewis (Ed.) *Beyond the dyad.* New York: Plenum.

Russell, G. (1983). *The changing role of fathers?* St. Lucia; Queensland: University of Queensland Press.

Sackett, G. P. (1978). Measurement in observational research. In G. P. Sackett (Ed.), *Observing behavior* (Vol. 2). Baltimore: University Park Press.

Sackett, G. P. (1979). The lag sequential analysis of contingency and cyclicity in behavioral interaction research. In J. D. Osofsky (Ed.), *Handbook of infant development.* New York: Wiley.

Sawin, D. B., & Parke, R. D. (1976). Adolescent fathers: Some implications from recent research on parental roles. *Educational Horizons, 55,* 38–43.

Schaffer, H. R., & Emerson, P. E. (1964). The development of social attachments in infancy. *Monographs of the Society for Research in Child Development, 29*(3, Whole No. 94).

Sears, R. R. (1975). Your ancients revisited: A history of child development. In E. M. Hethering-ton (Ed.), *Review of child development research* (Vol. 5). Chicago: University of Chicago Press.

Sears, R. R., Maccoby, E. E., & Levin, H. (1957). *Patterns of child-rearing.* Evanston: Row, Petersen.

Sigel, I. E., & Parke, R. D. (1987). Conceptual models of family interaction. *Journal of Applied Developmental Psychology, 8,* 123–137.

Sroufe, L. A., Schork, E., Motti, F., Lawroski, N., & LaFrieniere, P. (1984). The role of affect in social competence. In C. E. Izartd, J. Kagan, & R. B. Zajonc (Eds.), *Emotions, cognition and behavior.* New York: Cambridge University Press.

Sroufe, L. A., & Waters, E. (1977). Attachment as an organizational construct. *Child Development, 48,* 1184–1199.

Stern, D. (1977). *The first relationship.* Cambridge, MA: Harvard University Press.

Stern, D. N. (1985). *The interpersonal world of the infant.* New York: Basic Books.

Suomi, S. J., & Harlow, H. F. (1971). Abnormal social behavior in young monkeys. In J. Helmuth (Eds.), *Exceptional infant: Studies in abnormality* (Vol. 2, pp. 483–529). New York: Bruner Mazel.

Tasch, R. J. (1952). The role of the father in the family. *Journal of Experimental Education, 20,* 319–361.

Tinsley, B. J., & Parke, R. D. (1987). Grandparents as interactive and social support agents for families with young infants. *International Journal of Aging and Human Development, 25,* 261–279.

Tinsley, B. J., & Parke, R. D. (1988). The contemporary role of grandfathers in young families. In P. Bronstein & C. P. Cowan (Eds.), *Fatherhood to-day: Men's changing role in the family.* New York: Wiley.

Walters, R. H., & Parke, R. D. (1965). The role of the distance receptors in the development of social responsiveness. In L. P. Lipsitt & C. Spiker (Eds.), *Advances in child development and behavior* (Vol. 2). New York: Academic Press.

White, R. W. (1959). Motivation reconsidered: The concept of competence. *Psychological Review, 66,* 297–333.

Yarrow, M. R., Campbell, J. D., & Burton, R. (1968). *Child-rearing: an inquiry into research and methods.* San Francisco: Jossey-Bass.

Zelazo, P. R., Kotelchuck, M., Barber, L., & David, J. (1977, March). *Fathers and sons: An experimental facilitation of attachment behaviors.* Paper presented at the biennial meeting of the Society for Research in Child Development, New Orleans.

6 Sibling Relationships

Gene H. Brody
Zolinda Stoneman
University of Georgia

Before we discuss our work on sibling relations, we briefly describe some experiences from our graduate school training that foreshadowed our interests. We were both involved in conducting intervention research projects, albeit on different populations and in different parts of the country. These intervention programs proved successful; however, we probably learned as much from the children who did not benefit from them as we did from those who were more successful. First, in a majority of families, older siblings were expected to assume much of the responsibility for the care and nurturing of younger children; this was as true for older boys as it was for girls. As we independently reflected upon what we were learning about families, especially those with school-aged children, we concluded that little information about sibling relationships and their contributions to development was available. Second, we both formed impressions that the fathers of several children who did not benefit from the intervention program did not appreciate unfamiliar persons coming into their homes in a "teacher" role and changing normal routines. These impressions sensitized us to the ways in which intervention intended for one family subsystem (parent-child) can be supported or compromised by other family subsystems (spouse). We concluded that families are complex systems, therefore an intervention intended for one subsystem may have implications for relationships in others. These experiences played an important role in forming our interest in sibling relations as well as in subsequent theory development.

We began our research on sibling relationships by hypothesizing that development is facilitated by interaction with persons who occupy a variety of roles. In learning and practicing a role, a child learns not only his or her own role but also the complementary roles. Theoretically, the role asymmetries that siblings display with each other can be advantageous to development, particularly for older siblings. These children have the opportunity to practice dominant roles associated with such behaviors as teaching, caregiving, managing, and helping. Based on this hypothesis we initiated a series of studies on sibling interaction, employing a common behavioral coding system. We proposed that sibling interactions are related to the characteristics of the ecological context in which they take place. In this approach we assume that siblings' perceptions, attitudes, and behaviors cannot be understood without examining the contexts in which they occur: physical setting or an activity, the presence or absence of specific persons, or a combination of settings and persons. We further assume that siblings both adapt to existing contexts and contribute to the creation of new contexts through their own thoughts and actions. These biases in examining the sibling relationships of school-aged children are evident in all of our observational research in this area.

Several themes underlie our research program, one of which is our continuing interest in studying sibling relations within the context of the family. Just as researchers realized, a decade and a half ago, the limitations of unidirectional models of socialization, today they recognize the limitations of studying socialization in isolation from the larger family context. Researchers and clinicians alike now recognize that families contain several subsystems (i.e., spousal or marital, parent-child, and siblings), each of which affects and is affected by events that occur in the other subsystems. In particular, this transactional or systems approach to socialization suggests that parenting both influences and is influenced by the child; in addition, the quality of parenting is influenced by the marital relationship. The complex social and system processes that we have studied therefore allow for interaction between developmental, social, and social-cognitive functioning.

A second, and emerging theme in our research has been a focus on individual differences. The tremendous diversity in the personality and temperamental styles of individuals within families is particularly salient to family and individual functioning. The study of individual differences among family members has traditionally been the domain of sociology. Even the most skilled sociologists, however, recognized the limitations of the survey or self-report approach, which could at best provide only a general idea of the contributions of individual differences to individual and family functioning. By contrast, in our analysis of individual differences we have examined the combination of children's temperaments to form diverse sibling relationships, as well as their combination with individual differences in parental personal and psychological resources to form diverse parent-child relationships. These themes, as well as the methodological decisions they occasioned in our research programs, are discussed further in a later section. First, we present a brief summary of the major conceptual and methodological issues that define the study of sibling relationships.

MAJOR CONCEPTUAL ISSUES AND RESEARCH METHODS IN THE STUDY OF SIBLING RELATIONSHIPS

Research designed to further our understanding of sibling relationships reflects several conceptual issues: characteristics of sibling relationships, developmental changes they display, between-family differences in sibling relations, and differences between siblings in the same family. These issues are independent of studies of family constellation effects. A number of family constellation variables, including birth order, the size of the spacing interval between children, and the gender of the older and younger siblings, have been studied as possible influences on various aspects of children's development. Typically, family constellation data have been collected from college students in a group testing context. The psychological variables examined in the light of family constellation parameters range from psychiatric deviations to intellectual performance.

Family constellation has often been used as a proxy for sibling relationships. Instead of sampling relationship processes, a great deal of energy has been devoted to examining persons whose social experiences within the family are presumed to be different because of their birth order, spacing, gender, and so forth. It is fair to say that findings on the relationship between family constellation parameters and developmental outcomes have been inconsistent, and that most of this body of research has not been grounded in theory. Where relationships have been observed, the functional psychological variables underlying these associations remain a matter of speculation. We agree with Sutton-Smith (1983), believing that only after a rich foundation of research describing the day-to-day interactions and environments that siblings experience has been completed can the "variables worthy of quantifiable attention" for predictive research be selected and operationalized. We will not, therefore, consider studies that use family constellation parameters as proxies for family processes.

What Are Sibling Relationships Like?

Research on the nature of sibling relationships have been approached from survey research, self-report, and observational methodologies. Steinmetz's (1977) book includes a chapter on the frequency of sibling conflict and violence, notable for its nationally representative sample of 733 families who were surveyed about the occurrence of family violence, including that among siblings. The survey sampling technology eliminates plausible rival hypothesis associated with selection biases that occur when a restricted range of families volunteer to participate in research. Using this approach, Steinmetz found that 75% of her sample reported the occurrence of physical violence between siblings in 1 year. A more detailed analysis of 49 families from the larger sample revealed that 60% of male siblings and 49% of female siblings directed violent acts toward one another during a period of 1 week. Another survey research study found comparable results. Straus, Gelles, and Steinmetz (1980) conducted family interviews that revealed that more violent episodes occurred between siblings than between other family members. Because Steinmetz and her colleagues were investigating family violence, one could conclude that sibling relations are primarily conflict-ridden; such an inference, however, may not be accurate.

An acknowledged limitation of survey research approaches is their lack of concern with psychometric properties such as reliability and validity. Few self-report instruments that have established these properties have been developed to assess the nature of sibling relationships. The work of Furman and Buhrmeister (1985) is an exception. They conducted in-depth interviews with 49 5th- and 6th-grade-children concerning their relationships with their siblings. From the content analyses of these interviews, a questionnaire was developed and administered to 198 5th and 6th graders. This survey demonstrated that elementary school-aged siblings report a mixture of positive and negative qualities in their sibling relationships, with the former outweighing the latter. From a research perspective, this instrument is useful as both a dependent and an independent variable. As a dependent measure, it can be used to test the associations between children's perceptions of their sibling relationships and the processes hypothesized to affect their quality. As an independent variable, differences in the reported quality of sibling relations can be used to predict developmental outcomes.

During the past decade research on the qualitative nature of sibling relationships has more commonly been based on observational assessments of sibling behavior. In general, this research base consistently demonstrates that conflict between siblings is a fairly common occurrence; however, they also indicate that sibling interactions involve the use of either neutral or positive behaviors more often than negative behaviors. These conclusions are drawn from studies that have been conducted with subjects of different ages who were observed in different interactional contexts and whose behavior was coded using different observational systems.

Observational studies of infant-preschool age sibling pairs or two preschool-aged siblings can be divided into two groups, depending on whether or not the observation categories were aggregated across discrete behaviors to form broader categories (i.e., prosocial behavior). Aggregation of the measures implies that the investigator believes the summary measures to be more stable over time than individual behaviors, that they are a more accurate index of the sibling relationship, and that the likelihood of spurious results is reduced. The work of Dunn and her colleagues (Dunn & Kendrick, 1980, 1981a; Dunn, Kendrick, & Mac-Namee, 1981; Dunn & Munn, 1985; Kendrick & Dunn, 1980, 1983) and Abramovitch and her colleagues (Abramovitch, Corter, & Lando, 1979; Abramovitch, Corter, & Pepler, 1980; Abramovitch, Corter, Pepler, & Stanhope,

1986; Corter, Pepler, & Abramovitch, 1983) exemplify this approach to quantifying sibling interactions with relatively young sibling pairs. These investigations shared the bias that observations of sibling relationships should be obtained without any structuring of the interactions per se. This approach to data collection lends itself to the aggregation of data on both conceptual and practical grounds. Naturalistic interactions allow siblings to choose whether or not to interact; therefore, the frequency of any given behavior is typically lower than would be obtained if siblings were placed in a structured or semistructured context and asked to interact. One advantage of aggregating behaviors into molar classes from naturalistic sibling interactions is the opportunity to group low frequency behaviors that are conceptually related into a larger generic category. This strategy may not be as necessary with structured contexts because they occasion relatively high frequencies of sibling behavior.

Studies of preschool-aged siblings in structured or semistructured contexts have yielded similar results to those obtained by Dunn and Abramovitch. Generally, these studies describe sibling interactions as dominated by neutral to positive behaviors, with occasional struggles over objects and bouts of interpersonal antagonism thrown in for good measure (Berndt & Bulleit, 1985; Lamb, 1978a, 1978b; Stewart, 1983). These results are derived from analyses of individual behavioral categories that tap a gamut of behaviors ranging from looking, smiling, striking, and touching, to onlooking. In these studies, as well as those of Dunn and Abramovitch, there is considerable variability from family to family in the quality of sibling interactions during the preschool years. The extant research has not in our opinion provided insight into why this diversity exists.

Observational research on sibling interactions with school-aged children have used both naturalistic and structured observations. Using an observation system adapted from one developed by Patterson, Ray, Shaw, and Cobb (1970), Baskett and Johnson (1982) compared children's interactions with their parents and siblings. Behaviors directed to parents were more frequently positive, while most of those directed to siblings were more frequently negative. With their parent, the target children alternated between positive social interactions and attention-demanding behavior, and with their siblings, between quiet play and arguing. Aggression toward parents was more frequently expressed indirectly through tantrums and destructiveness, whereas toward siblings it was more frequently expressed directly through negative physical contact. Although in both cases the undesirable behavior was highly intense, it occurred infrequently.

These naturalistic observations demonstrate that interactions between school-aged siblings are qualitatively different from those between parents and children. Research from our laboratory, which is discussed in more detail later, and from others (Bryant & Crockenberg, 1980; Cicirelli, 1976) also describe sibling relations during middle childhood as distinct from both parent-child and peer relationships. In structured laboratory investigations Bryant and Crockenberg (1980) and Cicirelli (1976) studied sibling prosocial behavior and teaching competence, respectively. These studies demonstrated that school-age siblings possess the necessary competencies to engage in these behaviors in structured laboratory contexts. They do not indicate, however, whether these children spontaneously display similar styles of behavior in less structured contexts. A portion of Bryant and Crockenberg's data speaks indirectly to this point. When mothers ignored their daughters' requests for help and attention, their lack of response was likely to stimulate prosocial interaction between the girls simply by creating the opportunity. If a child did not get a response from her mother, she often turned to her sibling for help, and the data suggest she frequently received it.

Taken as a whole, these studies reveal variability across families in the quality of sibling relationships. Although conflict between siblings is common during the school-aged years, it is not the modal response that defines sibling interactions. Playful, solitary, and prosocial responses are far more common than conflicted ones. The reasons for variation in these responses among siblings in different families has been the topic of theoretical speculation without much empirical validation.

Little is actually known about sibling relationships beyond the middle childhood years. It is surprising that the study of sibling relationships during adolescence has been ignored, given the influence that older adolescent siblings may have on their younger siblings' adoption of values, attitudes, and beliefs. In the next section we present data to consider whether sibling relationships display any developmental changes across the lifespan.

Do Sibling Relationships Display Developmental Changes?

No data sets directly address the quality and intensity of sibling relationships across the lifespan. The available information includes observational studies of sibling interactions during the preschool and school-aged years, self-reports of sibling relations during the college years, and retrospective self-reports from middle-aged and older adults. From a methodological perspective, the lack of any semblance of standardization in the data gathering strategies make it difficult if not impossible to draw clear conclusions about sibling relationships across the lifespan. The researchers who gathered this data, however, did not intend to address questions relating to the developmental trajectories of sibling relationships.

Results from the short-term longitudinal studies of Dunn and Kendrick (1982) and Abramovitch et al. (1986) indicate that the affective quality of the sibling relationship remains fairly consistent over a three year period. These conclusions were drawn from observations of sibling interactions. Self-report data obtained from parents with school-aged and early adolescent children (Steinmetz, 1977; Straus et al., 1980) college students (Felson, 1983), and adults (Allan, 1977) suggest that overt conflict decreases with age. These studies did not, however, address sibling attachment which from our perspective is more germane to the quality of sibling relations over the lifespan.

As we have noted, sibling relationships during the preschool and school-aged years could be labeled ambivalent; evidence suggests that these feelings may persist into adulthood. Cicirelli (1980) presented questionnaire data that indicated that middle-aged adults felt close to their siblings, yet they would not use them as sounding boards for important life decisions. Further evidence of this is found in the interview studies of Ross and Milgram (1982) and Ross, Dalton, and Milgram (1981). Rivalrous feelings between siblings persisted well into adulthood and were associated with unresolved felings about siblings that remained from childhood, perceptions of parental favoritism, and relative life success vis-à-vis siblings. The respondents also reported that positive feelings toward a sibling rarely emerged later in life when their childhood relationships were characterized by anger and conflict.

What Accounts for Between-Family Differences in Sibling Relationships?

Attention recently has been directed toward determining the factors that differentiate conflicted from harmonious sibling dyads. In general, two approaches have been used, the first of which can be termed the individual difference method. In these studies, the independent variable of interest is a behavioral or cognitive characteristic of one or both members of a sibling dyad, which is then correlated with observational assessments of sibling behavior. Studies that fall into this category have assessed the association between hyperactivity (Mash & Johnson, 1983), undercontrolled behavior patterns (Patterson, 1980), highly active or emotionally intense temperaments (Brody, Stoneman, & Burke, 1987), perspective-taking abilities (Stewart, 1983; Stewart & Marvin, 1984) and sibling behavior. The subjects from the Mash and Johnson (1983) and Patterson (1980) studies were drawn from clinical populations whereas the Brody et al. (1987) and Stewart (Stewart, 1983; Stewart & Marvin, 1984) subjects were drawn from a nonclinic population. Children in dyads that included a hyperactive sibling or one with an externalizing behavior problem displayed higher rates of negative behavior and conflict than did controls. These findings were extended to nonclinic children by demonstrating that those children with a highly active or emotionally intense sibling experienced more conflicted interactions (Brody et al., 1987). In the two studies that assessed the association between perspective-taking skills and comfort giving between a preschool-aged and toddler sibling, the data revealed weak associations that were mediated by maternal behavior. The older siblings rarely engaged in spontaneous caregiving; rather, they were usually directed to do so by the mother.

The second approach to understanding between-family variability in sibling interactions has involved assessments of the impact of parenting behavior or family interactions on dyadic sibling behavior. Dunn and Kendrick (1982), for example, found that preschool-aged children whose mothers discussed care of a newborn baby and encouraged their efforts at such care exchanged more pro-social behavior with their younger siblings when the babies were 14 months old. The results of studies with families of preschool-aged and school-aged children indicate that maternal rearing practices featuring consistent use of nonpunitive control techniques are related to lower levels of agonistic behavior and higher levels of prosocial behavior, particularly among older siblings (Brody, Stone-man, & MacKinnon, 1986). They also reveal that maternal responsiveness to a daughter's expressed needs is associated with higher levels of prosocial behavior and lower levels of antisocial behavior among sisters (Bryant & Crockenberg, 1980). Other observational assessments of maternal differential behavior toward the younger sibling and subsequent sibling interactions generally indicated lower rates of verbal interaction and prosocial and agonistic behavior directed by sib-lings to one another suggesting a general decrease in behavior or "numbing" of sibling interactions (Brody et al., 1987).

Why Are Children in the Same Family Often Different From One Another?

A growing body of research has begun to illustrate how different children who grow up in the same family can be in terms of their personalities, adjustment levels, and interests (Plomin & Daniels, 1987). These data suggest that children in the same households experience different rather than similar family environ-ments, partially due to differential treatment from parents, differential interac-tions with each other, and the distinctive characteristics of their peer groups. Properly conducted examinations of within-family processes will provide insight into the origins and maintenance of a range of developmental and adjustment outcomes. By obtaining refined assessments of each child's family environment, the antecedents of differences or similarities in the developmental trajectories that children in the same family experience will become evident. Development of this approach to research is just beginning.

In a series of studies Daniels and her colleagues found that young adults believed that they had experienced different within-family environments than their siblings in a wide variety of areas (Daniels & Plomin, 1985); they also found that parents perceive differences in their treatment of siblings (Daniels, Dunn, Furstenberg, & Plomin, 1985). These data were obtained using a psycho-metrically sound self-report instrument that was administered to adolescents and their parents. It is not currently known how these perceptions of within-family processes compare with actual treatment of children in the same family. It is known that during triadic mother-sibling interactions mothers direct more overall behavior to younger siblings than to older siblings. This differential behavior in turn was associated with the quality of dyadic sibling interactions (Brody et al., 1987; Bryant & Crockenberg, 1980).

Another theoretical and methodological approach to understanding differential development of children in the same family deals with deidentification processes. Schachter and her colleagues have described the ways in which parents and children themselves label siblings as different (Schachter, 1982; Schachter, Gilutz, Shore, & Adler, 1978; Schachter, Shore, Feldman-Rotman, Marquis, & Campbell, 1976; Schachter & Stone, 1985). These data are obtained using Likert rating scales that address similarities or differences among children in the same family. The consistency of this data is impressive and could be even more compelling if it were combined with research methods that objectively describe actual family interactions.

The next section of the chapter details how we go about "our business." We recount the decisions we have made in developing our research designs and methods, many of which represent an evolution in methods and procedures that capture the development of sibling relationships.

RESEARCH DESIGNS AND METHODOLOGY

This section describes the research methodology we have used in describing and understanding sibling relations, overviewing both the methodological decisions and the empirical findings. This two-part section reviews descriptive research on sibling relationships, and preliminary data derived from a transactional model of sibling relationships.

Descriptive Research

Here, we present the methodologies and results of several studies that were designed to address the following contextual issues: (1) How are sibling interaction patterns different from peer interaction patterns? (2) How do person parameters, such as age, gender composition, and maternal childrearing practices, influence sibling interactions? (3) What kind of activities do siblings self-select, and do sibling interactions vary as a function of different activities?

Subject Selection. One of our first decisions when we began this research program was whom we were going to study. We decided to concentrate our efforts on young school-aged sibling pairs, a decision that was guided by our interest in studying children who were old enough to self-select a variety of activities that could create differences in sibling interaction. We also chose this age group because we presumed that these children were in the process of establishing important peer relationships. Further, we believed that the competency levels of young school-aged sibling pairs would be far less discrepant than would those of preschoolers. The disadvantage of selecting children of this age is that a history to which we have little access exists between the siblings. At times we felt as though we had walked into the middle of a movie and were not able to figure out the beginning. We have accepted this limitation in order to enjoy describing the interactions of two relatively competent children.

We have standardized the age ranges of the sibling pairs across several studies. Our criterion for inclusion in several studies has been that older siblings be 7–9 years-old and younger siblings were at least 2 but not more than 3 years younger than the older sibling. This decision has advantages and disadvantages. The advantage is control of siblings' ages and spacing as potential rival explanations for our observations; the disadvantage involves the narrowness of the sibling relationships described. With the control we achieved through age restriction, we lose the opportunity to generalize our research to siblings who are older or younger than those in our sample, or who are more closely or further spaced. Although the inclusions of such subjects would make our data more generalizable, our research in this area was not funded at the time we initiated it and we did not have sufficient resources to support the increased staffing that an increase in sample size would require.

In all but one of our descriptive studies we chose to include only same-sex sibling pairs; in each case, half of the sample were males and the other half were females. Again, this restriction was imposed for the sake of the control that has limited the external validity of our research. Even with this control for gender, the external validity has been further narrowed because we have found distinct interaction patterns that characterize male and female sibling pairs. To deal with the gender-based specificity of our results, we executed one study that included both same- and cross-gender sibling pairs (Stoneman, Brody, & MacKinnon, 1987); these results helped us to understand some of the observations we obtained when we examined same-sex sibling pairs only.

Subject recruitment is an important issue in the study of sibling relationships. We have always relied on what we call a "snowballing recruitment strategy," which involves finding sibling pairs in the community through contacts such as friends, teachers, scout leaders, coaches, etc., and by telephoning mothers to explain the purpose and procedures of the study. Also, upon completion of a family's participation in our project, we ask the mother whether she knows other sibling pairs who are similar in age to her children. If so, we ask her if she would be comfortable providing us with their mother's name and phone number. One reason for the success we have had with this technique has been the emphasis that our research team places upon establishing rapport with the mothers and siblings. The importance of establishing such supportive relationships with families cannot be underestimated, for a negative "snowballing" effect can also occur when families have a bad research experience and tell others about it.

Our subject recruitment technique fits well into our research plan because it provides sibling pairs who are similar to one another in age and social class background; however, it also has disadvantages. Although it maximizes the likelihood that sibling pairs will be similar to one another, it has limited the diversity of families that have participated in our research. We are also unable to assess the extent to which recruitment is affected by some unassessed parameter (i.e., sociability of the mother) that may be systematically influencing our results.

Research Contexts. The second decision with which we were confronted involved obtaining samples of sibling behavior. This proved to be a difficult decision and one we believe we have not adequately resolved. Part of the difficulty arose from a lack of knowledge about gathering interactional data with children who are beyond the preschool years. In many respects it is much easier to study preschool and toddler-aged children because they have a relatively limited set of activities and interests. Because the research literature provided us with little guidance, we decided to ask children what they do with their brothers and sisters; these interviews gave us several clues in determining which contexts could and could not reasonably be used in our research. We finally decided to obtain data from in-home structured observations as well as naturalistic ones. By presenting siblings with structured tasks that produced interaction, we were assured of obtaining the high rates of behavior that would require long periods of naturalistic observations to capture. The naturalistic observations allowed us to examine the self-selected contexts in which siblings interact; further, they afforded us the opportunity to obtain data on siblings who choose not to interact with each other and allowed us to determine whether the interaction patterns we obtained in the structured contexts were specific to those contexts or generalized to naturalistic interactions.

To date, we have used two structured tasks as interactional contexts, taking care to avoid tasks that were preferred by either males or females during structured or naturalistic observations. The first task is a board game ("Trouble," from Gilbert Industries) that both younger and older siblings enjoy. This game has rules for appropriate play and introduces a competitive quality by producing a winner and a loser. A construction toy (Legos) is the second structured task, selected because it is less structured than the board game and it allows the children to be as creative as they wish. Both tasks were familiar to the children in our studies; therefore, we were fairly confident that our results with these tasks were not affected by the tasks' unfamiliarity.

Our naturalistic observations of sibling behavior were straightforward. Siblings were requested to do whatever they wanted, except bicycle riding. This restriction was imposed following our first naturalistic study in which some of our research assistants found themselves running after children on bicycles while they were time-sampling behavior! As the following paragraphs illustrate, the structured and naturalistic research contexts provided different insights into sibling relationships.

In the first study (Brody et al., 1982), in the descriptive phase of our sibling research we observed school-aged children, their younger siblings, and their best friends while playing Trouble. The descriptive analyses of the sibling interaction revealed clear asymmetries in the roles that older and younger siblings assume. Older siblings and friends, however, generally assumed each role equally when they played together. The results of this study were embellished in a subsequent project designed to contrast sibling interactions in three frequently occurring contexts—Trouble, Legos, and television-viewing (Brody et al., 1986). As expected, the types of activities available to the siblings influenced their role relationships and behavior. Television viewing generally reduced the number of sibling exchanges, whereas the nature of sibling interactions during the board game and construction task closely followed the predictions derived from the work of Quilitch and Risley (1973). The construction task, which does not require the cooperation of two persons, occasioned more passive interaction patterns characterized by more observing and information seeking. The board game, as expected, occasioned more managing, teaching, and helping from the older sibling and more agonistic behavior from both siblings.

A discussion of the importance of contextual activities to the study of sibling relations must take into account both the self-selection of different activities by various sibling pairs and the functional relationships between certain activities and sibling behavior. Each of these is considered in turn.

Siblings help shape their own environments by choosing to participate in certain activities and not in others, as well as by selecting certain toys and games for play and ignoring others. Stoneman, Brody, and MacKinnon (1984) found that the patterns of activities peers and siblings selected provided some insight into the ways in which children accommodate their activities to the competencies of the other children present. Girls and boys both displayed these accommodation processes, but their form differed by gender. Boys engaged in fewer competitive activities with their younger brothers than they did with their peers, whereas girls used doll play as a means of involving children of differing competencies in the same activity. When older siblings and peers did not select activities that accommodated the competencies of the younger siblings, the younger siblings often left the group to play by themselves. Female peers selected activities in which the younger siblings could participate more often than did male peers.

Thus, it appears that children respond to their perceptions of the cognitive and behavioral competencies of their siblings and friends by agreeing to engage in different activities depending on the relative competencies of the social agents in their presence. It further appears that sibling gender constellations influence children's activity selections. This finding supports Parke's (1978) suggestion that siblings and peers often serve as mediators of the environment through the selection of toys as mediators in social interaction.

Despite the fact that siblings share at least 50% of a common gene pool, they often behave very differently (Scarr & McCartney, 1983). To explain these differences, behavior geneticists have recommended that researchers examine the direct influence of siblings on one another, differential treatment by parents, and sibling self-selection of different environments within the home. Accordingly, we have examined the interaction among siblings and their selection of interactional contexts.

The literature amply suggests that interactional contexts for same-sex siblings differ from those of opposite-sex children. Stoneman, Brody, and MacKinnon (1987) examined the possibility that sibling gender composition creates interactional contexts that may exert both direct and indirect effects. For example, the ecology of younger male siblings' rooms varied according to the sex of the older sibling. Boys with older brothers had more masculine items and decorations in their room than did boys with older sisters. Similarly, boys with older brothers engaged in a greater proportion of male sex-typed activities, as well as proportionally fewer cross-sex activities, when playing with their siblings than did boys with older sisters. This pattern of engaging in own-sex stereotyped activities carried over into times when the younger brother played alone. Similarly, girls with older brothers engaged in more opposite sex-typed activities than did girls with older sisters, both during times when the siblings were playing together and during times when they were playing alone. Thus, the gender of the older siblings not only affected the activities in which younger boys and girls engaged while playing with their siblings, but also carried over into times when the younger siblings were playing by themselves.

The results of the aforementioned studies were summarized to illustrate the importance of decisions about the contexts that are selected when observational research strategies are used. The structured contexts allowed us to observe fairly high rates of behavior in short periods of time, and the naturalistic contexts permitted us to content analyze the activities that mediate the quantity and quality of sibling interactions.

Observational Measures. The third major research decision we confronted was choosing the behaviors to observe when siblings interact. At the time we started this research few established observational systems for use with school-aged children or observational studies of peer interactions were available; therefore, we decided to create our own observational system. Because of a lack of guidelines on this subject in the developmental psychological literature, we turned to the anthropological literature on sibling relations. This literature describes in ethnographic accounts the roles that siblings assume vis-à-vis one another in different societies. These cross-cultural accounts suggested that siblings serve as socialization agents by directing behavior (manager role) and promoting cognitive growth (teacher role), as well as caregiving (helper role) (Weisner & Gallimore, 1977). Compliance with managing, teaching, and helping attempts by one sibling represented the acceptance of the complementary managee, learner, and helpee roles. Our observational system for quantifying sibling interactions included these roles as well as categories for a playmate role, solitary, and prosocial and agonistic behaviors. This coding scheme enabled us to assess the function of sibling behavior via the roles, the extent to which siblings choose not to interact with one another via solitary behavior, and the affective quality of the interactions via the prosocial and agonistic behavior categories.

The categories in our coding system are composed of composites of behaviors. On a continuum ranging from molecular to molar codes, our system would be properly classified as molar. Our decision to use several behaviors as examples of any of the behavior categories stems from our belief that conceptually related behaviors are not as meaningful as individual entities as they are important in representing the intention of the behavior. For example, when an older sibling provides new information about labels, objects, or events, or models a novel task, the older sibling is trying to teach the younger sibling. With our system, we are trying to determine the function that drives each child's behavior.

One could argue that we have made an inferential leap by suggesting that conceptually related composites of behaviors all serve the same function. Several pieces of information, however, suggest that our coding scheme reliably taps the interpersonal role relationships and affective qualities that siblings display. Similar role relationships and levels of prosocial and agonistic behavior have been coded during structured in-home observations of sibling behavior (Brody et al., 1982) and free-flowing, naturalistic sibling interactions (Stoneman et al., 1984). The observational scheme was subsequently scrutinized for its ability to detect developmental changes in sibling interactions (Brody et al., 1985). To do this, we used it in a comparison of free-flowing naturalistic interactions among preschool-aged and school-aged siblings. We discovered that several of the role relationships and behavioral differences found in previous studies of either preschool-age or school-age sibling pairs were specific to one age group. For example, preschool-age male siblings directed more agonistic behavior toward one another and school-age female siblings exchanged more prosocial behavior. Both of these results replicate findings from studies that observed either preschool or school-age siblings only (Abramovitch et al., 1979, 1980; Brody et al., 1982; Stoneman et al., 1984).

We also found that preschool-age female siblings played with each other less than preschool-age male siblings, whereas school-age female siblings played with each other more than school-age male siblings. The latter finding replicates previous research (Stoneman et al., 1984). One of the reasons that female siblings appear to interact with one another more as they develop, whereas male siblings appear to do the opposite, may involve the willingness of the older female sibling to accommodate her behavior to the competencies of her younger sister.

Older female school-age siblings assumed the teacher role more often than any sibling group × gender combination. Similarly, younger school-age female siblings accepted teaching attempts from their older sisters more often than did their male counterparts, thus spending more time in the learner role than any sibling group × gender × person combination. These results corroborate previous research conducted in structured laboratory contexts (Cicirelli, 1973, 1976).

The earlier studies did not focus on the ability of our coding scheme to detect relationships between sibling interactions and events that transpire within the larger family system. The purpose of the Brody et al. (1986) study was to examine the relations between maternal child-rearing practices and sibling interaction patterns. A transactional or systems approach to socialization suggests that events that occur in the parent-child subsystem influence the sibling subsystem. From this perspective, rearing practices are assumed to directly influence the behavior of each child and indirectly influence the behavior of the siblings with one another. We hypothesized that supportive, nonpunitive parenting practices would be related to supportive, nonpunitive sibling interactions. In addition, we speculated that the extent to which mothers reported they enjoyed the parental role and valued having an identity separate from the maternal role would be related to sibling behavior. We hypothesized that in families where the mothers enjoyed the maternal role, siblings would direct more prosocial and less agonistic behavior toward one another. In families where the mothers valued maintaining an identity separate from the maternal role, older siblings would be more accustomed to assuming caregiving functions and therefore would be more likely to display guidance and caregiving behaviors while interacting with their younger siblings.

Data on maternal childrearing practices were gathered using Block's (1965) childrearing Q Sort, a self-report measure that assesses each of the childrearing dimensions we investigated. We included this instrument because we were unsure whether our coding scheme was sensitive enough to correlate reliably with self-reported maternal rearing practices. This study was therefore an important test of the efficacy of our coding scheme; we were delighted when reliable associations emerged between maternal reports of rearing practices and observed sibling interaction patterns.

Roles that are widely ascribed to older siblings—such as, serving as a socialization agent by directing behavior (manager role) and caregiving (helper role)—were positively related to maternal childrearing practices that encouraged curiosity and openness and to the mother's valuing a life separate from her children. The performance of these roles was negatively related to maternal inconsistency and anxiety induction. These findings demonstrate that rearing practices which are associated with the development of prosocial behavior in individual children are related to the assumption of guidance and caretaking roles by older siblings. These data also suggest that older siblings may take on more socialization functions when their mothers have activities that they value outside the family. These results have implications for older siblings in families where the mother is employed full-time and in single-parent families, where role demands likely necessitate older siblings' assuming more caregiving responsibilities.

Maternal use of nonpunitive control techniques and enjoyment of her parental role were related respectively to less agonistic behavior and more prosocial behavior. The relationship involving the use of nonpunitive control techniques is consistent with other findings in the childrearing literature (Brody & Shaffer, 1982). These data suggest that some of the childrearing correlates of prosocial behavior in individual children also facilitate the development of prosocial behavior among siblings. It also follows that mothers who enjoy being parents are more likely to display prosocial behavior for their children to emulate in their absence.

A Transactional Model of Sibling Relationships: Decisions and Preliminary Empirical Results. Earlier, we discussed some experiences we had during our graduate careers that foreshadowed some of our research with siblings. These experiences taught us that family relationships and individual child adjustment could not be properly studied without a consideration of events that are occurring in other family subsystems; we therefore concluded the descriptive phase of our sibling research. Although there were other issues that we could have addressed, we wanted to move beyond the description of sibling relationships to focus more on the processes that account for the variability we observed in the amount of harmony or conflict they evince.

This transition has involved three steps, the first of which was the development of a theory to guide our work. In the beginning of the chapter, a transactional model of sibling relations was outlined briefly. This model is a product of the information we gleaned from the aforementioned descriptive studies and from our interest in examining the ways in which the individual characteristics of children and adults transact with family processes to produce different trajectories for individuals and family relationships. At the core of the model is the assumption that individual child temperaments place certain sibling dyads at risk for conflicted relations. This model further predicts that mothers' and fathers' employment of maladaptive sibling management strategies exacerbates children's at-risk status for conflicted sibling relations. These maladaptive sibling management strategies are more likely to occur in families in which the overall emotional climate is compromised (i.e., marital conflict) and parents have few emotional resources (i.e., high levels of depression).

The second step in this transition involved designing two studies to test the hypotheses suggested by the transactional model. In these studies, we decided to include sibling pairs of the same ages as those in our descriptive studies. We also decided to gather interactional data in the families' homes and to use the structured tasks that were described in the preceding section of the chapter. Finally, we decided to continue using our sibling interaction coding system making modifications when indicated by the research questions.

Our first study in this new sequence addressed two questions (1) Do sibling dyads evince higher rates of conflicted behavior when at least one child is highly active, emotionally intense, or low in persistence, as measured by maternal temperament ratings? and (2) Do sibling dyads display more agonistic and less prosocial behavior when maternal behaviors are unequally directed toward one child in the dyad? In examining these questions we were faced with two important measurement decisions; operationalizing temperament and differential behavior. We defined temperament as an early-developing personality trait that is both genetically and environmentally influenced. This definition concurs with recent research showing that both constitutional and environmental (particularly nonshared environmental) factors contribute unique amounts of variance to temperament assessments (Plomin, 1986).

We operationalized temperament using Martin's (1984) Temperament Assessment Battery. This instrument, a modified version of Thomas and Chess's (1977) Parent Temperament Questionnaire, is designed to measure temperament dimensions in children 3 through 9 years of age. The activity (motoric vigor), emotional intensity (amount of emotional energy or vigor that the child expresses in a variety of situations), and persistence (attention span and continuation of tasks despite obstacles) subscales were used, each of which contains eight items in a 7-point Likert format. The mothers required about 10 minutes to rate each child's temperament. We decided to use this particular instrument because it appeared psychometrically sound and displayed some interesting concurrent validity information. Children referred for a psychological evaluation because of reported behavior problems were rated as more active and emotionally intense, and less persistent, than a matched group of control children (Pfeffer & Martin, 1984). Furthermore, in Martin, Nagle, and Paget's (1983) study of the relation between temperament ratings and observed classroom behavior, the activity and emotional intensity subscales forecast lower levels of constructive and self-directed behavior, and higher levels of gross motor inappropriate behavior.

Maternal differential behavior was used as a proxy for maladaptive sibling management strategies. An association between maternal differential behavior and sibling relationship quality has been suggested in many psychological theories, such as the social learning (Bandura, 1977), psychoanalytic (Freud, 1916/1949), self-esteem maintenance (Tesser, 1980), and equity (Adams, 1965; Walster, Bercheid, & Walster, 1973) theories. Each of these supports the prediction that siblings will display more agonistic and less prosocial behavior when maternal behaviors are unequally directed toward one child in the dyad. Unfortunately, these theories do not specify the kind of maternal differential behavior that will affect sibling interactions. We therefore had to decide whether to observe mothers interacting with each child alone, or with both in a triad, to operationalize differential behavior. We decided on the latter because the opportunity for direct social comparison is greater in mother-sibling triadic interactional contexts than in mother-child dyadic contexts.

In order to examine the associations of sibling temperament and maternal differential behavior with the quantity and quality of sibling interactions, we observed mothers in triadic interactions with their two children and, on a separate occasion, the sibling dyad interacting in the same contexts as the mother-sibling triad. The order of these observations was counterbalanced in order to minimize confounds. The sibling dyadic and mother-sibling triadic interactions were quantified using a behavioral coding system designed to assess the amount of verbal interaction and prosocial and agonistic behaviors displayed by members of families with school-age children. The mothers provided temperament ratings of each of their children's levels of activity, emotional intensity, and persistence, and a measure of maternal differential treatment was derived from the mother-sibling triadic interactions. The results indicated that high activity, high emotional intensity, and low persistence levels in either the older or younger child were associated with increased agonisms between sisters, whereas high activity and low persistence levels in younger boys were associated with more agonistic behavior among brothers. An imbalance of maternal behavior that favored the younger child was generally associated with siblings' exchanging lower rates of verbalizations and prosocial and agonistic behavior.

A second study was designed (Brody, Stoneman, & Burke, 1987) to determine whether sibling relations feature more agonistic and less prosocial behavior in families characterized by higher levels of marital discord, greater maternal depression, and highly active child temperaments. In this study we observed school-age sibling pairs playing the Trouble board game and Legos construction task in their homes. Our observations focused on prosocial and agonistic behaviors because we considered them particularly relevant to a discussion of contemporaneous associations of family processes and individual child characteristics with conflicted/harmonious sibling relationships. We used three instruments to assess maternal marital quality and depression; the Dyadic Adjustment Scale (Spanier, 1976) as a proxy for marital satisfaction, the O'Leary-Porter Scale (Emery & O'Leary, 1982), assessed fighting between spouses in the children's presence, and the Beck Depression Inventory (BDI) (1967) measured depression. High active child temperaments were again assessed using Martin's (1984) Temperament Assessment Battery. The family process measures and the BDI were selected because they are psychometrically sound and each instrument provides concurrent and predictive validity data.

The study procedures were straightforward. While the siblings were being observed, their mothers were completing the aforementioned instruments presented to them in a random order. The results supported the hypothesized relations among sibling behavior, the marital subsystem, and individual children's temperamental characteristics. Observed levels of prosocial and agonistic behavior during sibling interactions were contemporaneously associated with maternal reports of marital quality, personal adjustment, and highly active child temperaments. For younger siblings, high rates of prosocial behavior were most strongly associated with low levels of interparental conflict and maternal depression, whereas for older siblings high marital quality most strongly predicted prosocial behavior. Low marital quality was most strongly related to agonistic behavior in both younger and older siblings; in addition, younger siblings displayed more agonistic behavior when the older sibling was reported to have a highly active temperament.

Younger siblings' behavior was hypothesized to display more sensitivity than that of older siblings to the family process variables examined in this study; this hypothesis was partially supported. The multiple regression analyses indicated that the predictor variables accounted for 32% of the variance in younger siblings' agonistic behavior, compared to 9% for older siblings. In addition to their ability to better understand family dynamics, the older siblings in this study were old enough to seek support elsewhere if the home situation was uncomfortable. Older children spend more time in other social settings, thus have more opportunities to find outside support systems that may buffer the deleterious effects of a discordant home. Such processes are an example of what Rowe and Plomin (1981) have termed nonshared environmental influences and serve as a reminder that events within families are often experienced very differently by members of the same family.

The third step in the development of our transactional model of sibling relationships was to write an extramural proposal to the National Institute of Mental Health, to test the hypothesized relations between individual child temperaments, parenting, family processes, and parental personal resources, and the quality of sibling relationships. A short-term longitudinal design was proposed to allow across-time predictions and avoid contemporaneous associations. This project was funded, and we hope it will provide insight into the determinants of the quality of sibling relationships.

Fine-Tuning Our Research Methods

Several aspects of our research methodology can be improved. The first issue we constantly confront is whether or not we are obtaining representative samples of sibling behavior. Initially, in our research program we alternated between observations of in-home structured interactions and naturalistic interactions. In our more recent studies we have observed structured interactions exclusively; fortunately, they correlate significantly with the child and family measures. We still wonder, though, whether there are more systematic ways of deciding how to gather representative samples of behavior. We are not alone in grappling with this issue. Family researchers in general have not investigated whether the behavioral samples collected in either naturalistic or laboratory contexts are actually representative of family behavior as it normally occurs for the subjects under investigation. An implicit assumption appears to be driving family process research; any context that elicits behavior from family members can be assumed to evoke behavior representative of the typical interaction patterns in that family. This assumption has led researchers to confuse the occurrence of behavior with its representativeness. To remedy this possible flaw, we recommend to others that they, as a standard step in the development of their research protocols, sample sibling behavior in various contexts and have the siblings themselves rate the representativeness of the interactions. Such a procedure would not be possible for preschool and toddler-age siblings; for these groups it would probably be beneficial to obtain parent ratings of representativeness.

Our observations of sibling interactions range from thirty minutes to one hour. Again, no empirically derived guides exist to inform us how much observation time is necessary to obtain representative samples of sibling behavior. Our naturalistic observations indicate that school-age siblings do not spend sustained amounts of time interacting around a given task. Younger children can be expected to spend even shorter periods of time on their interactions. We really do not know at this point whether two or three short (i.e., 15 minutes) interactions on different occasions would yield different conclusions about sibling relationships than one 30- or 45-minute observation session. Again, we encourage other researchers to sample different observational time periods to determine whether or not they are obtaining reliable samples of behavior.

Third, we need to put more emphasis on quantifying the different family environments that children in the same family experience. With the exception of one study (Brody et al., 1987), we have used between-family or across-family research approaches to account for variability in the quality of sibling relationships. It has been argued that behavior-environment relations found with the between-family research approach usually have been small and that most of the variance lies within, rather than between, families (Maccoby & Martin, 1983; Rowe & Plomin, 1981). Rather than focus on between-family differences in socialization techniques, the within-family or nonshared environment approach allows researchers to examine differences in the experiences that children in the same family encounter and associate these differences with variability in the amount of harmony or conflict that characterizes sibling relationships. A series of studies by Daniels and her colleagues showed that adolescents and young adults believed that they had experienced different within-family environments than their siblings in a wide variety of areas (Daniels & Plomin, 1985); in addition, they have found that parents perceive differences in the treatment of siblings (Daniels, Dunn, Furstenberg, & Plomin, 1985). Taken together, these data suggest that we should obtain both objective and subjective measures that index differential treatment and social comparison processes.

Finally, we have not obtained data from the siblings themselves. The conclusions we have drawn in our research program about the quality of sibling relationships have been based upon observational assessments to the exclusion of data on the children's perceptions and emotions. We have, for example, concluded that higher rates of agonistic behavior are indicative of a conflicted sibling relationship. It may be that high rates of agonistic behavior are simply normative for some siblings and should not be mistaken for a lack of closeness. We are taking steps to remedy this omission in our research methodology.

Careful investigation of how families go about socializing close or distant sibling relationships will have broad implications for understanding basic issues about family process, allowing both developmental and family researchers to better understand the different developmental trajectories that children in the same family pursue. Our goal in this chapter has been to raise empirical questions, to elucidate potentially useful research strategies, and to suggest guidelines for future research.

ACKNOWLEDGMENT

Preparation of this chapter was facilitated by support from NIMH grant 40704 and National Science Foundation Grant BNS 84-15505.

REFERENCES

Abramovitch, R., Corter, C., & Lando, B. (1979). Sibling interaction in the home. *Child Development, 50,* 997–1003.

Abramovitch, R., Corter, C., & Pepler, D. J. (1980). Observations of mixed sex sibling dyads. *Child Development, 51,* 1268–1271.

Abramovitch, R., Corter, C., Pepler, D. J., & Stanhope, L. (1986). Sibling and peer interaction: A final follow-up and a comparison. *Child Development, 57,* 217–229.

Adams, J. S. (1965). Inequity in social exchange. In L. Berkowitz (Ed.), *Advances in Experimental Social Psychology* (Vol 2, pp. 149–175). New York: Academic Press.

Allan, G. (1977). Sibling solidarity. *Journal of Marriage and the Family, 39,* 177–184.

Bandura, A. (1977). *Social learning theory.* Englewood Cliffs, NJ: Prentice-Hall.

Baskett, L. M., & Johnson, S. M. (1982). The young child's interactions with parents versus siblings: A behavioral analysis. *Child Development, 53,* 643–650.

Beck, A. T. (1967). *Depression: Causes and treatment.* University of Pennsylvania Press.

Berndt, T. J., & Bulleit, T. N. (1985). Effects of sibling relationships on preschools behavior at home and at school. *Developmental Psychology, 21,* 761–767.

Block, J. H. (1965). *The childrearing practices report.* Berkeley, CA: University of California, Institute of Human Development.

Brody, G. H., & Schaffer, D. R. (1982). Contributions of parents and peers to children's moral socialization. *Developmental Review, 2,* 31–75.

Brody, G. H., Stoneman, Z., & Burke, M. (1987). Child temperaments, maternal differential behavior, and sibling relationships. *Developmental Psychology, 23,* 354–362.

Brody, G. H., Stoneman, Z., & MacKinnon, C. E. (1982). Role asymmetries among school-aged children, their younger siblings, and their friends. *Child Development, 53,* 1364–1370.

Brody, G. H., Stoneman, Z., & MacKinnon, C. (1986). Contributions of maternal childrearing practices and interactional contexts to sibling interactions. *Journal of Applied Developmental Psychology, 7,* 225–236.

Brody, G. H., Stoneman, Z., MacKinnon, C., & MacKinnon, R. (1985). Role relationships and behavior between preschool-aged and school-aged sibling pairs. *Developmental Psychology, 21,* 124–129.

Bryant, B., & Crockenberg, S. (1980). Correlates and dimensions of prosocial behavior: A study of female siblings with their mothers. *Child Development, 43,* 282–287.

Cicirelli, V. G. (1973). Effects of sibling structure and interaction on children's categorization style. *Developmental Psychology, 9,* 132–139.

Cicirelli, V. G. (1976). Siblings helping siblings. In L. V. Allen (Ed.), *Children as teachers: Theory and research on tutoring.* New York: Academic Press.

Cicirelli, V. G. (1980). A comparison of college women's feelings toward their siblings and parents. *Journal of Marriage and the Family, 42,* 95–102.

Corter, C., Pepler, D. J., & Abramovitch, R. (1983). Effects of situation and sibling status on sibling interaction. *Canadian Journal of Behavioral Science, 14,* 380–392.

Daniels, D., Dunn, J., Furstenberg, F. F., Jr., & Plomin, R. (1985). Environmental differences within the family and adjustment differences within pairs of adolescent siblings. *Child Development, 56,* 764–774.

Daniels, D., & Plomin, R. (1985). Differential experience of siblings in the same family. *Developmental Psychology, 21,* 747–760.

Dunn, J., & Kendrick, C. (1980). The arrival of a sibling: Changes in patterns of interaction between mother and first-born child. *Journal of Child Psychology and Psychiatry, 21,* 119–132.

Dunn, J., & Kendrick, C. (1982). Siblings and their mothers: Developing relationships within the family. In M. E. Lamb & B. Sutton-Smith (Eds.), *Sibling relationships—Their nature and significance across the lifespan* (pp. 39–60). Hillsdale, NJ: Lawrence Erlbaum Associates.

Dunn, J., Kendrick, C., & MacNamee, R. (1981). The reaction of first-born children to the birth of a sibling: Mother's reports. *Journal of Child Psychology and Psychiatry and Allied Disciplines, 22,* 1–18.

Dunn, J., & Munn, P. (1985). Becoming a family member: Family conflict and the development of social understanding in the second year. *Child Development, 56,* 480–492.

Emery, R. E., & O'Leary, K. D. (1982). Children's perceptions of marital discord and behavior problems of boys and girls. *Journal of Abnormal Psychology, 10,* 11–24.

Felson, R. B. (1983). Aggression and violence between siblings. *Social Psychology Quarterly,* December.

Freud, S. (1949). *An outline of psychoanalysis.* New York: Norton. (Original work published 1916)

Furman, W., & Buhrmeister, D. (1985). Children's perceptions of the qualities of sibling relationships. *Child Development, 56,* 448–461.

Kendrick, C., & Dunn, J. (1980). Caring for a second baby and effects on interaction between mother and firstborn. *Developmental Psychology, 16,* 303–311.

Kendrick, C., & Dunn, J. (1983). Sibling quarrels and maternal responses. *Developmental Psychology, 19,* 62–70.

Lamb, M. E. (1978a). Interactions between eighteen month olds and their preschool-aged siblings. *Child Development, 49,* 51–59.

Lamb, M. E. (1978b). The development of sibling relations in infancy: A short-term longitudinal study. *Child Development, 49,* 1189–1196.

Maccoby, E. E., & Martin, J. A. (1983). Socialization in the context of family: Parent-child interaction. In P. H. Mussen (Series Ed.) & E. M. Hetherington (Vol. Ed.), *Handbook of child psychology: Vol. 4. Socialization, Personality, Social Development* (4th ed.). New York: Wiley.

Martin, R. P. (1984). *Manual for the temperament assessment battery.* Unpublished monograph, University of Georgia, Athens.

Martin, R. P., Nagle, R., & Paget, K. (1983). Relationships between temperament and classroom behavior, teacher attitudes, and academic achievement. *Journal of Psychoeducational Assessment, 1,* 377–386.

Mash, E. J., & Johnson, C. (1983). Sibling interactions of hyperactive and normal children and their relationships to reports of maternal stress and self-esteem. *Journal of Clinical Child Psychology, 12,* 91–99.

Parke, R. R. (1978). Children's home environments: Social and cognitive effects. In I. Altman & J. F. Wohwill (Eds.), *Children and the environment.* New York: Plenum.

Patterson, G. R. (1980). *Mothers: The unacknowledged victims.* Monograph of the Society for Research in Child Development, Serial No. 186, *45.*

Patterson, G. R., Ray, R. S., Shaw, D. A., & Cobb, J. A. (1970). *Manual for coding family interaction.* Unpublished manuscript, Oregon Research Institute, Eugene, Oregon.

Pfeffer, J., & Martin, R. P. (1984). Comparison of mothers' and fathers' temperament ratings of referred and nonreferred preschool children. *Journal of Clinical Psychology, 39,* 1013–1020.

Plomin, R. (1986). *Development, genetics, and psychology.* Hillsdale, NJ: Lawrence Erlbaum Associates.

Plomin, R., & Daniels, D. (1987). Why are children in the same family so different from one another? *Behavioral and Brain Sciences, 10,* 1–60.

Ross, H. G., Dalton, M. J., & Milgram, J. (1981). *Older adults perceptions of closeness in sibling relationships.* ERIC/CAPS, Document Service, Document ED 201903.

Quilitch, H. R., & Risley, T. R. (1973). The effects of play materials on social play. *Journal of Applied Behavior Analysis, 6,* 573–578.

Ross, H. G., & Milgram, J. (1982). Important variables in adult sibling relationships: A qualitative study. In M. E. Lamb & B. Sutton-Smith (Eds.), *Sibling relationships: Their nature and significance over the lifespan* (pp. 225–247). Hillsdale, NJ: Erlbaum.

Rowe, D. C., & Plomin, R. (1981). The importance of nonshared environmental influences in behavior development. *Developmental Psychology, 17,* 517–531.

Scarr, S., & McCartney, K. (1983). How people make their own environments: A theory of genotype environment effects. *Child Development, 54,* 424–435.

Schachter, F. F. (1982). Sibling deidentification and split-parent identification. A family tetrad. In M. E. Lamb & B. Sutton-Smith (Eds.), *Sibling relationships: Their nature and significance across the lifespan.* Hillsdale, NJ: Lawrence Erlbaum Associates.

Schachter, F. F., Gilutz, G., Shore, E., & Adler, M. (1978). Sibling deidentification judged by mothers: Cross-validation and developmental studies. *Child Development, 49,* 543–546.

Schachter, F. F., Shore, E., Feldman-Rotman, S., Marquis, R. E., & Campbell, S. (1976). Sibling deidentification. *Developmental Psychology, 12,* 418–427.

Schachter, F. F., & Stone, R. K. (1985). Difficult sibling, easy sibling: Temperament and the within-family environment. *Child Development, 56,* 1335–1344.

Spanier, G. B. (1976). Measuring dyadic adjustment. *Journal of Marriage and the Family, 38,* 15–28.

Steinmetz, S. K. (1977). *The cycle of violence: Assertive, aggressive, and abusive family interaction.* New York: Praeger Publishers.

Stewart, R. B., Jr. (1983). Sibling interaction: The role of the older child as teacher for the younger. *Merrill Palmer Quarterly, 29,* 47–68.

Stewart, R. B., & Marvin, R. (1984). Sibling relations: The role of conceptual perspective taking in the ontogeny of sibling caregiving. *Child Development, 55,* 1322–1332.

Stoneman, Z., Brody, G. H., & MacKinnon, C. E. (1987). Same-sex and cross-sex siblings: Activity choices, roles, and gender stereotypes. *Sex Roles, 11,* 317–328.

Stoneman, Z., Brody, G. H., & MacKinnon, C. (1984). Naturalistic observations of children's activities and roles while playing with their siblings and friends. *Child Development, 55,* 617–627.

Straus, M. R., Gelles, P., Steinmetz, S. (1980). *Behind closed doors.* New York: Doubleday.

Sutton-Smith, B. (1983). Birth order and sibling status effects. In Lamb, M. E. & Sutton-Smith, B. (Eds.), *Sibling Relationships*. Hillsdale, NJ: Lawrence Erlbaum Associates.

Tessor, A. (1980). Self-esteem maintenance in family dynamics, *Journal of Personality & Social Psychology, 39,* 77–91.

Thomas, A., & Chess, S. (1977). *Temperament and development.* New York: Bruner Mazel.

Walster, E., Berscheid, E., & Walster, G. W. (1973). New directions in equity research. *Journal of Personality and Social Psychology, 25,* 151–176.

Weisner, T. S., & Gallimore, R. (1977). "My brother's keeper": Child and sibling caretaking. *Current Anthropology, 18*(2), 169–190.

7

Adolescents as Daughters and as Mothers: A Developmental Perspective

J. Brooks-Gunn
Educational Testing Service
Russell Sage Foundation

Perhaps it is not surprising that a developmental psychologist would portray her research as a life course journey. While I characterize my research trajectory as fairly continuous, others sometimes perceive it as disjunctive, perhaps because I have conducted research on young children and their families as well as with adolescents and their families.

The stimuli for studying adolescents as daughters and mothers were experiences, both professional and personal, embedded in the context of attending graduate school in the late 1960s and early 1970s. These events led me to ask a series of questions which, while changing in form over the last 15 to 20 years, retained the same functions, namely to understand (a) how girls experience the social and biological changes that occur as they become reproductively mature, (b) what this experience means to them and to others, (c) how this experience alters self-definitions and relationships, and (d) how the experience sets the stage for subsequent development in a variety of domains. Indeed, while on the surface my research looks quite different today, lending credence to those espousing a disjunctive research line, the underlying themes are not.

At the same time, many events occurred that altered my research journey in interesting and sometimes unexpected ways. As with any life course, events that may be termed "fortuitous" happened (Bandura, 1982). Opportunities arose whose links with previous research were not always obvious to others. The challenge was to enter new research situations that did not neatly fit with past research, but which extended it in conceptually compelling ways. Drawing on these opportunities, integrating them into current frameworks, and using them as a springboard to expand our understanding of girls' development have enriched my research considerably. Part of what would be subsumed under the rubric of "fortuitous events" involves my collaborations with individuals from a variety

213

of disciplines—endocrinology, pediatrics, epidemiology, sociology, gyne-cology, and social, clinical, and educational psychology. Cross-disciplinary col-laborations are hard: We so often speak entirely different languages, and we often do not have the time or patience to understand each other's perspective. I feel the keys to successful cross-disciplinary endeavors are respect and humor: Never assume that your discipline is superior, more conceptual, more policy-oriented, closer to the data (and by inference, less biased), or more useful than another. At the same time, I have never agreed on everything (nor even on the majority of matters) with my collaborators; such disagreements are usually not highlighted in articles. Collaborations are like family relationships, they have a life of their own, they ebb and flow, and they require negotiations. I am indebted to my collaborators who have shared ideas and frustrations with me, urged me to extend the boundaries of research paradigms, have introduced me to previously unknown bodies of literature, and have pointed out ways in which literature outside of developmental psychology may relate to my research questions. My mentors, colleagues, and students have all influenced me profoundly, and I thank them.

In this chapter, the conceptual, pragmatic, and opportunistic links between my past and present research relating to adolescents as daughters and mothers are discussed. As this is a reconstruction of over 15 years as a developmental psychologist, the account probably is more linear, or at least neater, than initially anticipated. The debate about how science progresses (Kuhn, 1970) is not often applied to individual research trajectories. Typically, individual journeys pro-gress through fits and starts. Often, intrigued with a new set of questions, I would go off on a somewhat different tack. However tangential it seemed to others, the research usually told me something about girls' development.[1] My research on adolescents is made up of several converging themes, including the study of (a) reproductive events (in particular puberty, sexual behavior, and pregnancy), (b) biological and social events associated with transitional life phases (in particular early adolescence, early adulthood, and parenthood), (c)

---

[1]As an example, Warren and I focused part of our collaborative research on the antecedents and consequences of delayed puberty. We used two samples of girls, one in which delayed puberty is very common (national company ballet students) and one in which it is less common (nonathletic adolescents). Not only did we learn a great deal about how delayed puberty, in conjunction with other factors, presages the emergence of skeletal problems, but the comparisons of ballet students and nonathletic girls gave us insights into how family processes contribute to eating problems and depressive affect (Attie & Brooks-Gunn, 1989; Warren, Brooks-Gunn, Hamilton, Hamilton, & Warren, 1986; Brooks-Gunn & Warren, 1988a; Brooks-Gunn, 1988). Specifically, we have dis-covered that family relationships play a larger role in the expression of eating problems in nonathletic samples than ballet students. This finding provided clues about why and how eating problems may be more likely in particular contexts and in particular families (Attie & Brooks-Gunn, 1987). Another insight from this line of work was that late puberty is a particularly enhancing experience for ballet students, as demands for dating may be delayed, allowing girls more freedom to pursue other goals (Gargiulo et al., 1987).

self-definitional and family relational changes occurring at the time of puberty, pregnancy, and early parenthood, and (d) gender-role divergencies as they emerge during transitional life phases. In this chapter, the transition from more specific reproductive events to a general life-span framework, the emergence of the study of adolescent girls as daughters embedded in a family context, the beginning of work on adolescent girls as mothers, and the recent rumblings of a family systems approach encompassing research on both adolescents as daughters and mothers, is documented.

TRANSITION FROM SPECIFIC REPRODUCTIVE EVENTS TO A GENERAL FRAMEWORK

The transition from a more limited to a more inclusive perspective was gradual, involving the natural progression of my reproductive research. From the meaning of menstruation, I moved to research on menarche, then to puberty, then to pregnancy and early parenthood, and finally to a general framework emphasizing reproductive events across the life span.

Menstruation

Very early in my career I became intrigued with the meaning of women's reproductive events. I was disturbed by two somewhat orthogonal premises. The first involved the beliefs (a) that (almost) all women experience menstrual symptoms, (b) that these symptoms are wide ranging, including affective, cognitive, and performance decrements, and (c) that these symptoms are severe, as most women are debilitated by them. Experience told me that many women did not experience severe symptoms, that those who did were not reporting a wide range of symptoms, that very few had their life disrupted, and that I could not detect behavioral changes in my friends' behavior. At the same time, a small minority of women, including myself, experienced severe dysmenorrhea, resulting in being incapacitated for several hours. Even with fairly severe symptoms and trips to emergency rooms to receive medication, I was often told by family and friends that "cramps are all in your head; just ignore them." The research literature was not much help in reconciling these two opposing viewpoints. While biological substrates were believed to result in severe, ubiquitous and debilitating symptoms, some research also emphasized the fact that cycle-related behavior was due in part to neurotic or hypochondriacal personality characteristics.

As a graduate student teaching sex–role development at the University of Pennsylvania in the early 1970s, discussions about these opposing views were lively. I began to require that my undergraduates keep daily records of symptoms in order to chart possible menstrual cycle-related alterations in affective expression and behavior. Few reported cycle effects, even though students had definite and strong beliefs about the existence of cycle-related symptoms (even in the absence of confirmatory evidence). By the time my graduate work was completed in 1975, a profitable and satisfying collaboration and friendship with Diane Ruble was formed; she had made similar observations in her classes at Princeton University. We decided to examine the premise that while some menstrual symptoms may exist, they were not as ubiquitous as the literature suggested. We wished to promulgate a more differentiated view of menstrual symptoms, seeing some symptoms as more biologically mediated and others as more socially mediated. Additionally, we believed that some symptoms may not exist at all but are thought to, given the ways in which social expectations, beliefs, and social cognitions all converge to predispose individuals to make cause and effect attributions. With funding from NSF and NIMH in the late 1970s, we combined social, cognitive, cultural, and contextual perspectives to study menstrual-related phenomenon. This led to a general interest in the salience and meaning of reproductive events other than menstruation, specifically menarche (Brooks-Gunn & Ruble, 1980, 1982a, 1983), and pregnancy (Deutsch, Ruble, Fleming, Brooks-Gunn, & Stangor, 1988).

Our first collaborative endeavor was really a reaction to the biological determinism seen in the literature and a curiosity about how reproductive events are integrated into women's lives. Our menstrual research became a more general paradigm for studying such integration, especially the biological, social, and cultural aspects of reproductive events, the interaction of biological and social events, and the effects of such events on self-definitions and relationships.

In our first set of reproductive studies, we reviewed a corpus of prospective studies, finding that even marginally significant differences across cycle phases were not found for the vast majority of symptoms believed to vary as a function of menstrual phase (except abdominal pain and tender breasts, the former in part verifying my experience). However, in studies involving retrospective reports, cycle-phase differences were large and significant (Ruble & Brooks-Gunn, 1979). Findings from retrospective studies were identical to those of general knowledge and stereotyping studies (Brooks-Gunn & Ruble, 1980).

We then asked two questions: where do these beliefs originate, and how are they maintained in the face of contradictory evidence? In a cross-sectional study, we found that premenarcheal girls as young as 10-years-of-age held similar beliefs about symptoms as postmenarcheal girls, adolescents, and adult women (Brooks-Gunn & Ruble, 1982b). These similarities suggested to us (a) that a set of cultural beliefs exists regardless of actual cycle changes, and (b) that the direct knowledge of menstrual and premenstrual symptoms cannot fully account for reports of cyclic fluctuations (Ruble & Brooks-Gunn, 1979, 1987). Such data do not mean that biological mechanisms may not be operating, but that a set of beliefs exists and that these beliefs go beyond the knowledge base of direct experience of symptoms. In order to understand these phenomenon, we decided to tackle the problem from several social cognitive, individual difference, and cross-cultural perspectives.

From a social cognitive perspective, we examined the question of what could account for the development and persistence of such beliefs; biases in the way people process information when making judgments was one focus. The thesis was that the perceptions of cyclicity may be acquired and maintained by information processing errors (Ruble & Brooks-Gunn, 1979). In addition, we began to analyze individual differences in menstrual symptom reports, arguing that factors such as culture, religion, age, and gender affect how individuals perceive and experience menstruation (Brooks-Gunn, 1985; Brooks-Gunn & Ruble, 1982b; Ruble, Boggiano, & Brooks-Gunn, 1982).

One of my worries during this time was that I had moved too far away from possible biological underpinnings of reproductive behavior. Our work was sometimes interpreted as supporting a totally environmental view of symptoms, which was not as balanced as I would have liked. After all, a few symptoms emerged from our review of prospective studies as being cycle-linked, and I still had severe dysmenorrhea.[2] Therefore, I was pleased when the opportunity arose to collaborate with an endocrinologist. I had felt, from the beginning, that the best way to understand reproductive behavior was to look at the interaction of biological and environmental events; indeed, the most exciting developmental research seemed to be at this intersect (Bronfenbrenner, 1979, 1989). Being cast as a strict environmentalist was never a comfortable position for me.

Menarche

In an effort to understand how complicated social, psychological, and physiological factors interacted to influence symptom perceptions, Ruble and I turned to the adolescent experience of menarche as an exemplar. Menarche became the focus of study because it is a discrete event whose experience could be interpreted in terms of previous socialization instead of direct experience. We expected that information gleaned from media sources, the mother, and girlfriends would all be important in explaining the meaning of menarche to individual girls. A series of studies were conducted comparing premenarcheal and postmenarcheal girls with respect to menstrual symptom reports, sources of information about menstruation, and the psychological significance of menarche. Additionally, we examined changes in self-definitions occurring at the time of menarche, specifically aspects related to body image and self-consciousness. Finally, mothers' attitudes about menstruation and menstrual symptoms were

---

[2]Subsequent research resulted in a discovery that prostoglandin secretions were linked with severe dysmenorrhea; double blind crossover studies indicated that dysmenorrhea could be reduced by the provision of anti-prostoglandin medication; (Klein & Litt, 1983; Budoff, 1979).

examined in an effort to see whether these were associated with the experiences of their daughters (Brooks-Gunn, 1984, 1987; Brooks-Gunn & Ruble, 1982a, 1982b, 1983).

Reading the literature on menarche was a particularly pivotal experience. In the early 1970s, menarche was perceived as a normative crisis for the pubertal girl (only much later did I start thinking of the effect of menarche on the mother as well as on the daughter). The crisis model was based on retrospective reports of adults' recollections of their pubertal experience, rather than on prospective studies of girls themselves. Additionally, the focus was on negative consequences, not normative aspects, in a sense contradicting the appellation "normative crisis." Perhaps this reflected the psychodynamic, medical, and adult patient perspectives of most of the extant literature. As in the menstrual literature, the primary focus on negative aspects of menarche seemed puzzling. After all, it was an indication of becoming an adult female. Was this necessarily negative? Did all girls resist growing up? Weren't there self-enhancing aspects of becoming mature? We reframed the crisis model into an examination of the *meaning* of menarche to girls, and into a normative transition rather than on a normative crisis framework.

Another set of questions arose for me. Why was puberty seen as negative for girls, but no mention of a similar crisis was found for boys, who, after all, also experience puberty? For boys, puberty was seen as expanding role possibilities into the realm of work and achievement; for girls, roles were believed to be truncated. In Chodorow's (1978) terms, boys are characterized "doing" and girls "being." These distinctions, while believed to exist prior to puberty due to socialization, were thought to become pronounced at puberty, when gender role divisions became apparent (because of reproductive differences; Hill & Lynch, 1983). However, little research existed to substantiate or refute these claims. Does gender intensification occur at puberty, and do girls really redefine themselves primarily in terms of reproductive roles while boys do not? If so, what are the processes underlying such self-definitional changes and how do parents and peers contribute to this redefinition? Much of my subsequent research addresses these sets of questions in one way or another.

Returning to the question of normative crisis, our literature review indicated that the adult psychoanalytic literature most often characterized menarche as anxiety-producing and distressing (Brooks-Gunn & Ruble, 1980; Deutsch, 1944; Thompson, 1942). Our research, along with that of others, examined how tramatic menarche actually was for girls, rather than relying on retrospective reports from clinical adult samples (see Brooks-Gunn, 1984; Grief & Ulman, 1982 for reviews of this literature). Generally, these studies suggest that girls experience an array of feelings—positive, negative, and ambivalent. When we interviewed girls about how they felt right after menarche occurred (within 2 to 3 months), 20% gave only positive, 20% only negative, and 20% mixed emotions such as "felt same" or "felt funny" (Ruble & Brooks-Gunn, 1982). The others experienced a combination of positive and negative feelings. About 60% were somewhat scared or upset although the intensity of these feelings were mild.

Possible ambivalence about menarche also was demonstrated by the fact that in our longitudinal study, girls were reluctant to tell others for about 3- to 6-months after the event that they had begun to menstruate. What we termed the "secretive phase" may indicate either ambivalence, self-consciousness, or both. Indeed, heightened awareness of the body and self-consciousness increases after menarche (Koff, Reirdan, & Jacobson, 1981; Ruble & Brooks-Gunn, 1982).

With regard to our initial questions about the emergence of menstrual-related beliefs, we found that girls construct a definition of the menstrual experience from various sources of information, of which direct knowledge of symptoms is only one. Girls' symptom reports are correlated with their own premenarcheal expectations, suggesting that the direct experience of menstruation is interpreted in terms of previously formed expectations (Brooks-Gunn & Ruble, 1982b). Moreover, individual differences in symptom reports can be predicted from the context in which self-definitions are initially formed (Ruble & Brooks-Gunn, 1982). Negative reports of symptoms in postmenarcheal 7th- to 12th-grade girls are associated with being unprepared for menarche, being early to mature, and receiving information from sources perceived as negative. The definitions established during menarche may be difficult to change; for example, subsequent menstrual experiences are perceived in terms of, and may be instituted by, this definition. Thus, perceptions of and information received about the menstrual experience during menarche and shortly thereafter may have long-lasting impact, as we saw in our 11th- and 12th-grade girls.

In this research, our focus on socialization led to the discovery that comfort discussing menarche was lowest at early adolescence, compared to later adolescence phases. While almost all girls do discuss menarche with their mothers, the content seems focused on practical concerns and symptoms, not feelings. Girls may be more likely to discuss feelings about menarche with girlfriends, a possible concomitant of the rises in same-sex friendships reported for girls during early adolescence (Berndt, 1982; Brooks-Gunn, Samelson, Warren, & Fox, 1986). Later on, I return more specifically to the issue of parent-daughter communication about and during puberty.

Puberty

Given these findings about informational sources and how prepared girls felt for menarche, I initiated discussions with staff at the Johnson & Johnson Company regarding pubertal health education. It was clear that appropriate and timely information seemed to lessen a girl's negative perception about menarche and menstruation. The vast majority of American girls received such information from pamphlets and films used in health classes and produced by the feminine products industry. The Johnson & Johnson Company was enthusiastic about funding a conference for those few researchers who were studying menarche. A successful conference in 1981 led to an edited volume (Brooks-Gunn & Petersen, 1983), a friendship and collaboration, and the formation of an informal small working group of researchers including Dale Blyth, Paula Duke, Bettye Hamburg, John Hill, Iris Litt, Karen Paige, Larry Steinberg, Jacqueline Eccles, and Roberta Simmons, as well as Anne Petersen and myself (Petersen, 1988).[3] In order to embed menarche into a larger framework, Petersen and I entitled our book *Girls at Puberty* rather than *Girls at Menarche,* and dedicated it to Bettye Hamburg.

At the conclusion of the conference, it was clear to me (a) that pubertal events other than menarche are imbued with psychological meaning, (b) that these events may also alter self-definitions and expectancies, and (c) that they were virtually overlooked in almost all of the developmental research. Indeed, there almost seemed to be a taboo against discussing puberty outside of medical and health education circles.[4] Also, discussions with our more biologically oriented colleagues and the presentation of data on the prostaglandin-dysmenorrhea link at the conference convinced me that I had to look at the interface between biological and environmental contributions to development during early adolescence, rather than only focusing on the latter. I especially wanted to examine possible hormonal contributions to behavior and to contrast the effects of biological events with or without social stimulus value to others (i.e., breast development vs. hormonal changes). As others before me (i.e., Maccoby & Jacklin, 1974), I did not want to leave the interpretation of biological effects to those who did not take an interactive perspective.

At the same time, the other highly salient and quite fortuitous event was the introduction of Michelle Warren and myself by Louis Cooper, Chief of Pediatrics at St. Luke's-Roosevelt Hospital Center. As Cooper suspected, Warren, a reproductive endocrinologist at Columbia University, and I had overlapping interests. Here was a highly respected gynecologist who had been studying behavior as well as physical consequences of hormonal dysfunction and was as excited to conduct bio-behavioral collaborative research as I was. We set about preparing a research agenda and obtaining funds to initiate it, an endeavor that took almost 2 years (lest anyone think that new collaborations and projects are quick, all of my new initiatives have taken several years to get off the ground). By 1983 we began the Adolescent Study Program with the generous support of

---

[3]Three additional conferences on pubertal issues (Brooks-Gunn, Petersen, & Eichorn, 1985; Brooks-Gunn & Duke-Duncan, 1985; Petersen & Brooks-Gunn, in press), as well as numerous symposia opportunities at the Society for Research in Child Development and at the newly formed Society for Research in Adolescence, have promoted continuity of collegial interchanges and expansion of the "puberty" network.

[4]A problem for all social scientists studying puberty has been obtaining school permission to see students; the ways in which my colleagues and I have alleviated the worries of adults, many of whom think that pubertal children do not think or talk about these changes, is discussed in a later section. Suffice it to say that it has *not* been easy.

the W. T. Grant Foundation; Robert Haggerty, President of the Foundation, has been intellectually and emotionally as well as financially supportive of our attempts at interdisciplinary collaborative research. What is particularly important is that he allowed us to explore various ways of conceptualizing our research program. It gave us freedom at a time when the two of us were working out our collaboration and finding out how to mesh our interests into mutually agreed upon conceptual frameworks. We designed a series of studies, ultimately conducting two longitudinal studies and several cross-sectional ones. By conducting a series of studies, we did not put all our "eggs in one longitudinal basket," which was important since so little was known about bio-behavioral links during early adolescence. It also allowed flexibility. We were able to address different questions more or less simultaneously and to add different groups to our cross-sectional cohorts. For example, in our work on the antecedents and consequences of delayed puberty, adolescent ballet students and nonathletic students were seen first (Brooks-Gunn & Warren, 1985). Two additional groups of athletes, swimmers and figure skaters, were added later on. This allowed us to compare the behavior of adolescents engaging in sports varying in terms of energy expended and weight demands (Brooks-Gunn, Burrow, & Warren, 1988).[5]

The overarching themes of our research program, as it evolved in the first 2 years, had to do with (a) the biological (hormonal and secondary sexual characteristic development) and environmental contributions to adolescent girls' behavior, (b) the antecedents and consequences of delayed puberty, (c) emergence of specific forms of developmental psychopathology during adolescence, (d) the formation of gender identity and changes in self-definition, and (e) the meaning and salience of pubertal events. Girls across the adolescent years were drawn both from school populations as well as populations known to have a high incidence of delayed puberty with ballet dancers as a primary "clinical" comparison group (Brooks-Gunn, 1987; Warren, 1980).[6] We initially used the ballet

---

[5]Dancing requires low weight and has a relatively low caloric expenditure per hour of exercise. Figure skating requires low weight but has a higher caloric expenditure than dance. Swimming does not require a particular weight and has a relatively high caloric expenditure per hour of exercise. As expected, girls in sports with thin body ideals (dancers and skaters) weighed less and were more likely to be late maturers than girls in a sport with no body size demand (swimmers). Of interest from a behavioral perspective is the fact that the dancers engaged in more dieting behavior in order to maintain their low weights than did the figure skaters. We believe the former's eating patterns were a direct response to the fact that their energy expenditure is less than the skaters; in order to conform to the demands of their context, dancers are more likely to engage in dieting and purging (Brooks-Gunn et al., 1988). Indeed, the "press" for a particular body shape in the absence of large caloric expenditure in part may explain the relatively high incidence of severe eating problems seen in elite adult dancers (Hamilton et al., 1985).

[6]Our work has been greatly facilitated and enriched by several graduate and postgraduate students and colleagues, in particular, Ilana Attie, Janine Gargiulo, Martha Hennessey, Janet Carey, Carolyn Burrow, Linda Hamilton, Denise Newman, Marion Samelson, Cynthia Lancelot, Claire Holderness, Nazei Baydar, Elizabeth Schnur, Roberta Paikoff, Marta Zahaykevich, and Lindsay Chase-Lansdale.

students to examine contextual features influencing behavior. It was a short step to enlarging this paradigm to study (a) the reproductive and social events simultaneously, (b) the interaction of person and environmental characteristics, and (c) the goodness of fit between a child's physical characteristics and aspirations. This research took several paths which moved me closer to the study of family systems. During the beginning of the Adolescent Study Program, my focus changed from examining contextual features of reproductive events to considering such events as embedded in a life phase in which other events co-occurred (leaving aside for the moment the issue of causal links among events). Indeed, I have defined early adolescence in terms of transitional events (Brooks-Gunn, 1988a; Brooks-Gunn & Petersen, 1984). Examining sequences of events, however, does not mean that their temporal ordering is invariant across individuals nor within individuals, as examples from the literature on the progression of pubertal events demonstrate. The timing and sequencing of events that mark the progression toward adulthood are now seen as critical in the definition of this particular life phase and in our understanding of how the individual adapts to life change. As a consequence, we began to focus on the study of different events simultaneously, the interaction of person and environmental characteristics and the goodness of fit between a child's physical characteristics and aspirations.

Meaning of Pubertal Events to Girls and their Parents.   In examining the meaning of pubertal events other than menarche, we found that the onset of breast development was associated with enhanced peer relationships, behavioral adjustment, and positive body image, but pubic hair development was not (Brooks-Gunn, 1984; Brooks-Gunn & Warren, 1988b). The reasons for such alterations had not been studied previously. However, we hypothesized that these findings were due in part to the social stimulus value of pubertal change to others as well as to the self. Since breast growth is a normative event signaling the onset of maturity, the exhibition of signs of "adulthood" may confer enhanced status to young adolescents. Comparisons with others, while probably covert, are common; 5th- to 7th-grade girls had no difficulty categorizing classmates with regard to their stage of pubertal development (Brooks-Gunn et al., 1986). If the onset of puberty is valued by the peer group, which we are positing, physical comparisons that girls make are akin to the processes discussed in the social cognitive and social comparison literature (Ruble, 1983). Girls may initiate more frequent and more positive contacts and will elicit more peer interaction during the onset of physical development.

Goodness of Fit Between Physical Characteristics and Expectations.   The importance of contextual features (in this case, early maturation and being unprepared for menarche) upon a girl's self-definitions regarding menstruation and body image in the early menarche studies led to a consideration of other contextual features in the Adolescent Study Program.

This work was couched in terms of contextual mediation of behavior exhibited by on-time and late maturing girls. We wished to see whether the demands of a specific context and individual characteristic predisposed a girl to adapt to that context. In one of our studies we explored how maturational timing relates to adaptation within different social contexts. Specifically, girls in dance company schools were compared with girls in nondance schools in order to examine the goodness of fit between the requirements of a particular social context and a person's physical and behavioral characteristics. With respect to dancers, the demands are clear: Maintain a low body weight in order to conform to professional standards and devote a great deal of time to practice. With regard to maturation, dancers are more likely to be late maturers than are nondancers (Frisch, Wyashak, & Vincent, 1980; Frisch et al., 1981; Warren, 1980). Timing of maturation was expected to affect girls in the two contexts differently. Being a late maturer may be particularly advantageous for dancers, even though it is not always so for nondancers (Baydar, Brooks-Gunn, & Warren, 1989; Simmons, Blyth, & McKinney, 1983; Petersen & Crockett, 1985; Faust, 1960; Peskin, 1967). Because dancers are more likely to be late maturers than are girls not participating in dance (Frisch et al., 1980, 1981; Malina, 1983; Warren, 1980), being late may be normative in the dance world. In addition, being late may be a positive attribute: Late maturing dancers may be more likely to enter national companies after adolescence than are on-time maturers (Hamilton, Brooks-Gunn, & Warren, 1985).

The dance students weighed less and were leaner than the comparison sample and had higher eating problem and lower family relationship scores. The on-time dancers had higher psychopathology, perfection, and bulimia scores, and lower body-image scores than did the later maturing dancers. These findings suggest that the requirements of a particular social context and a person's physical and behavioral characteristics must be considered when interpreting timing effects. Also, they raised questions as to how interactions with parents and peers may be affected by both context and maturational timing (Brooks-Gunn & Warren, 1985).

Interaction Between Environment and Physical Characteristics.   The research just discussed was based on premises about the "goodness of fit," defined as the consequences of certain demands on body size upon girls' adaptation, especially when these demands were difficult to maintain (i.e., caloric expenditure was not high) or were not matched to body type (i.e., being an early maturer when a sport favors the body build associated with late maturation). We broadened this perspective following Bronfenbrenner's view that development is a function of the interaction of person and environmental characteristics (Bronfenbrenner, 1989; Bronfenbrenner & Crouter, 1983).

If behavioral correlates of puberty are studied in different environmental contexts, then it is possible to investigate physical characteristic-environment interactions in at least three ways. First, personal characteristics may influence behavior differently depending on the environment in which they occur, given differences in expectations or demands that characterize a particular social milieu. An example are the findings of Simmons and her colleagues that being an early maturing 6th-grade girl influences body image as a function of attendance at an elementary or middle school, (Blyth, Simmons, & Zakin, 1985; Simmons et al., 1983). Second, an individual who possesses certain physical characteristics may actively seek or reject a certain social milieu. The work by Magnusson and his colleagues in Sweden is a case in point. While early maturing girls were more likely to drink and to be sexually active than later maturers, the effect was due to those early maturing girls who had older friends, a phenomenon that was more prevalent in the early than later maturers (Magnusson, Strattin, & Allen, 1985). Presumably, early maturers actively sought, or were sought by, older adolescents as friends. From Hill's work, one might hypothesize that early maturing adolescents actively avoid spending time with their parents (Hill, Holmbeck, Marlow, Green, & Lynch, 1985). These data fit nicely the active or evocative genotype-environment effects described by Scarr and McCartney (1983).

Finally, pubertal children may have chosen environmental contexts that become inappropriate as their bodies grow (in contradistinction to the first example where contexts are not actively chosen; i.e., grade in which the transition to middle school occurs). In this instance, the match between individual and environment is altered as a function of changes beyond the control of the individual. The most obvious example of mismatches involves activities in which body shape and size are critical, as in athletics or modeling. An example is the influence of context and maturation upon dating in 7th- to 9th-grade girls, some of whom were enrolled in national ballet company schools and some who were not. Dating was not related to menarcheal status in nondancers, but was in dancers as premenarcheal dancers dated less than postmenarcheal dancers (Gargiulo, Attie, Brooks-Gunn, & Warren, 1987). It was hypothesized that in a context such as dancing that negatively values a particular characteristic, such as pubertal growth, individuals who develop that characteristic may be more affected than similar individuals who are in a context that does not negatively value a particular characteristic. We wondered whether contexts other than school, peer group, and athletic endeavor, specifically those having to do with family functioning, might also influence behavior differently as a function of puberty. Later on, we had the opportunity to examine this question.

Pregnancy

Pregnancy was the final reproductive event to be added to my research program. Three studies with different collaborators began almost simultaneously in the early 1980s. Diane Ruble and I, in collaboration with Alison Fleming, began a large cross-sectional investigation of prepregnant, pregnant, and postpartum women in order to examine (a) the process by which women define themselves as mothers, (b) information-seeking about pregnancy and motherhood, (c) expectations and experiences of pregnancy symptoms, (d) contextual factors influencing symptom reports, and (e) definitions of motherhood (Deutsch et al., 1988). Ruble and Fleming also began two longitudinal studies in Toronto (Fleming, Ruble, Flett, & Shaul, 1988; Ruble, Fleming, Hackel, & Sangor, in press). The conceptual links with our earlier work on menstruation and menarche are obvious.

About the same time, I was invited to a meeting at the Commonwealth Fund to discuss problems in the antenatal care of disadvantaged women. Especially troubling was the late entry of poor pregnant women into the health care system. Some of the lessons learned about providing menarcheal information to adolescents seemed *apropos*. While I had almost no first-hand experience with disadvantaged women, I was interested in the interaction of biological and environmental factors in influencing child outcomes from my infant work with Michael Lewis. A collaboration emerged from the initial meeting with two pediatric researchers, Margaret Heagarty of Harlem Hospital and Columbia University and Marie McCormick of Harvard University. We were a diverse team, with very different disciplinary approaches to the problem of women's reproductive health behavior. However, we were also quite pragmatic and not particularly daunted (when perhaps we should have been) by the improbability of conducting an intervention program in a large city hospital. Not only did I learn about how health care services actually are provided, but found out a great deal about women's behavior during pregnancy, the meaning of pregnancy to them, the usefulness and limits of outreach programs, the differences in how program providers and evaluators perceive and implement programs, and the limits of applying techniques developed by middle class professionals within communities with different value systems and experiences (Brooks-Gunn et al., 1988, 1989; McCormick et al., 1989). Of relevance here was that the Harlem study brought an increased awareness of how families may operate in very different ways than what is considered the ''norm'' in middle class communities, and of how such arrangements may be very adaptive in terms of providing necessary social and emotional support to pregnant women, mothers, and their children.

Finally, I met Frank Furstenberg at an Aspen Institute Conference in 1982. Orville Brim, then president of the Foundation for Child Development, suggested that we collaborate on a follow-up of the Baltimore study participants, given Furstenberg's interest in teenage pregnancy and my interest in reproductive events and adolescent development. This exciting collaboration and friendship has led to three follow-up studies, in which four generations of 300 families have been seen over a 20-year period (Furstenberg, Brooks-Gunn, & Morgan, 1987). This experience solidified my interest in how families structure their lives, how variability in family systems may promote healthy functioning in children and adolescents, and how parental life-course decisions influence child development. Additionally, a chance meeting with Lindsay Chase-Lansdale at the first Society for Research in Adolescent meetings led to a terrific collaboration. Issues such as how individuals overcome obstacles in their lives (in this case, an early, unplanned pregnancy in the context of a disadvantaged family, neighborhood and school), and how adaptable family systems are to changes in demographic trends (in this case, the high rate of out-of-wedlock births to teen parents and the frequent unavailability of the father for emotional and financial support) have become of increasing interest to us.

Life-Span Approach

Work on reproductive events began early, the year of my doctorate degree (1975), only a few years after my serious emersion into the field of early childhood. The two research programs remained separate, from a practical standpoint, until the early 1980s when I began the pregnancy studies and was introduced to a more life-span approach to development. It would be impossible to have done as much early childhood research as I had done and not make the obvious backward leap to pregnancy, a move facilitated by the support and encouragement of Margaret Mahoney and Thomas Moloney of the Commonwealth Fund (both the Harlem and Baltimore Studies were funded by them). The Harlem Study was directly concerned with outcomes of inadequate prenatal care and adverse maternal health behavior, both for the mother and the young child. And the Baltimore Study focused on longer-term consequences of early parenthood upon the mother, the child, and the family.

Additionally, attendance at a Social Science Research Council meeting and an Aspen Institute meeting was important. Paul Baltes, Orville Brim, Richard Lerner, and Glen Elder urged me to examine the sequencing and timing of life events, and to examine whether similar or different mechanisms account for changes seen in various transitional life phases, rather than to focus on a specific age group. This perspective led to the examination of how the life courses of parents and children intersect and how decisions made by parents may influence their children differently during early childhood and adolescence. Not surprisingly, my work with teenage mothers and pubertal adolescents was affected; however, I even found the perspective to be useful for studying the salience of menstruation and the behavior of different female athletes (Brooks-Gunn, 1985; Brooks-Gunn et al., 1988).

ADOLESCENTS AS DAUGHTERS

As a graduate student working with Michael Lewis, my attention was focused on the emergence of self in young children. This exciting and meaningful menteeship led to the identification of critical dimensions of the self that emerge in the first 3 or 4 years of life and the social cognitive processes underlying the development of these dimensions (Lewis & Brooks-Gunn, 1979). Social dimensions such as gender, race, and age, as well as affective dimensions such as self-worth and self-consciousness, are used to define oneself, to define others, and to mark the boundaries between self and other. Indeed, many social scientists and epistemologists assert that the sense of selfhood only develops in the context of the social system, or in relation to others (Cooley, 1909; Mead, 1934; Merleau-Ponty, 1964).

The work on menarche and puberty occurred in temporal tandem to the early childhood work and a social cognitive perspective informed both research programs. It was hypothesized that transitional life phases or critical life events resulted in an active search for information to construct self-definitions (Brooks-Gunn, 1988a; Deutsch et al., 1988; Ruble, 1983; Ruble & Brooks-Gunn, 1987). Most recently, I have begun thinking about how self-definitional changes dovetail with the relational changes that often seem to occur during transitional life phases, hearkening back to my infatuation with Cooley, Mead, and Merleu-Ponty. Not only may relationships be altered or at least redefined during important transitions (thinking of Hinde, 1979, and Hartup, 1989 greatly influenced me), but they are an essential aspect of one's self-definition. The individual does not engage in social cognitive processes and self-definition alterations in a vacuum. Individuals facing or experiencing an important life event or transitional life phase are embedded in relational systems. Persons in these systems may react to an important life event, even if the event is not being directly experienced by them. Indeed, others in the individual's relational system also may be experiencing a redefinition of their role vis-à-vis that individual. Specifically, I am looking at alterations in parent-child relationships during early adolescence with Marta Zayhaykevich and during the transition to teenage parenthood with Lindsay Chase-Lansdale (Brooks-Gunn & Zahaykevich, 1988, in press; Chase-Lansdale, Brooks-Gunn, & Reiss, 1988). Specific questions related to studying adolescents as daughters emerged from the work on mother-daughter and father-daughter communication about puberty. In addition, I began to think about the link between self-definitional changes and relationships that led to the following three questions and subsequent studies.

Parents and Puberty

Parental Communication Patterns and the Pubertal Experience. The first direct foray into how puberty may influence perceptions of one's parents came from the menarche studies, where we were interested in information transmission

227

and socialization. Girls were more uncomfortable discussing menarche during early adolescence compared to middle and late adolescence and were most uneasy when talking to their fathers. Very few girls, for example, told their fathers about their menarche. About one-half of the girls reported that their mothers told their fathers immediately following menarche. This family openness, as I termed it, may have positive value. Eleventh- and 12th-grade girls who reported their fathers knew about their menarche early (usually from the mother) had less negative attitudes about their bodies and menstruation than girls whose fathers were reported as not knowing (Brooks-Gunn, 1987).

These findings, while in retrospect not surprising, led me to speculate on how mothers, fathers, and daughters as a unit might construct the meaning of pubertal events. For example, when girls are asked if they have been teased about breast growth, the most frequently mentioned teasers are parents and the primary feeling reported is anger (Brooks-Gunn, 1984). We decided to explore girls' perceptions of interactions among the triadic system by using a TAT format. Girls were asked to tell stories about a picture of an adult woman showing a girl and an adult male a bra that she has just taken out of a shopping bag. Fifth- to 9th-grade girls' responses to this picture, the disclosure of the buying of a bra to the "father" reflect negative affect and discomfort. Embarrassment about the "father's" presence and anger at the "mother" for showing the bra to the father are common. Interestingly, in these stories, the causes of the uneasiness are attributed to the parent, particularly the mother, who is not perceived as being sensitive to the girl's desire for secrecy (Brooks-Gunn, Newman, & Warren, 1984).

It is my premise that early adolescent girls' communication patterns are altered, in large part because of pubertal changes and their feelings about them. Whether this is the stimulus for decreased sharing of other experiences with the mother via self-definitional changes, enhanced realization of separateness from parents in a physical sense, inability to consider one's own sexuality and parental sexuality simultaneously, or other factors, withholding of feelings from parents does not seem to increase thereafter. Thus, discomfort in discussing certain issues could exacerbate distancing and possibly conflict. Indeed, Montemayor (1982) reports that the most frequent response to parent-young adolescent conflict is *not* discussion, but walking away from the situation.

Parental Relationships and Their Effect on Depressive Affect During Puberty. Enlarging upon the theme of parental communication patterns and using a life events paradigm focusing on the timing and sequencing of events, we have studied the possible effects of social and biological events upon the expression of depressive affect in 120 early adolescent girls has recently been studied (Brooks-Gunn, Warren, & Rosso, 1987). The occurrence of positive and negative events in the family, with peers, and at school was considered separately. Negative family and school events, but not negative friend events, were correlated with depressive affect. Effects of familial disruption upon problem behavior are well-documented (Hetherington, 1987). Pubertal changes had no direct effect on problem behavior, but had a mediated effect. Less physically developed girls had lower depressive affect scores than more physically developed girls; however, this was true only in the absence of negative family life events. When undesirable events occurred, the association between physical status and problems was altered; one might go so far as to characterize pubertal growth as a protective factor in the face of negative family events.

Why might this be the case? Although speculative, it is possible that physical maturity, with its high social stimulus value, brings increased internal resources to manage undesirable events. For example, the increases in social maturity, peer prestige, self-esteem, and awareness of the body associated with menarche and breast development may enhance self-definitions in some as of yet unspecified way (Collins, 1988). At the same time, pubertal growth has high social stimulus value. More physically mature girls may elicit more freedom from parents (and probably request it from them), making it more likely that they will engage in dating, spend more time with girlfriends, and "distance" themselves from their parents (Hill et al., 1985; Simmons et al., 1983; Steinberg, 1987). Friends also may respond to the girl's more mature body: Boys may be more likely to ask them out on dates and girls may gravitate toward more mature girlfriends (Magnusson et al., 1985). Finally, friendships may become more intimate during puberty as girls discuss these developments with their best friends. These changes may result in more independence, especially from the family, which may be particularly protective if stressful events involve the family. In brief, a more mature body may facilitate the growth of internal coping skills as well as offer an "arena of comfort" as described by Simmons, Burgeson, and Reef (1988). In our study, peers may act as such an arena, being a refuge from stressful events occurring in the family or in school. This aforementioned premise is partially confirmed by the finding that the adolescent's vulnerability to negative events is partially offset by the availability of resources, in this case positive and supportive relationships with peers. Having one arena of comfort may make it easier to negotiate the other anticipated and unanticipated life changes occurring during early adolescence, especially those occurring within the family (Simmons et al., 1988).

Vulnerability to negative events may in part be due to the unavailability of personal and social resources needed. Indeed, less developed girls may have less resources, or may perceive their resources differently. In support of this possibility, premarcheal girls with less positive parent relationships had higher depressive affect scores than premarcheal girls with more positive relationships. This association is independent of the occurrence of negative and positive family events, making it unlikely that the relation is due to girls with less positive parent relationships having had more negative events occur. Such findings support the premise that social support may buffer the young person from untoward consequences of the occurrence of negative life events, in this case events occurring in the family (Thoits, 1983).

Parental Relationships and Eating Problems.   We also examined the effects of pubertal events and parental relationships upon eating problems. Eating problems are most likely to emerge at two different points—around the time of the pubertal transition and during the passage towards young adulthood. Ilana Attie and I have hypothesized that the onset of puberty may herald sometimes overwhelming developmental challenges for the vulnerable adolescent, who may have difficulty coping with all the simultaneous changes of early adolescence (Attie & Brooks-Gunn, 1989; in press). One possible factor predisposing the young adolescent toward eating problems is family functioning. Adolescents with frank eating disorders often live in families characterized by enmeshment, overprotectiveness, rigidity, lack of conflict resolution, and unresolved marital conflict (Minuchin, Rosman, & Baker, 1978; Sargent, Liebmen, & Silver, 1985). However, in the absence of controlled prospective and comparative studies of family process, it is difficult to identify predisposing factors, and to distinguish these from those which insure following the onset of these disorders. Attie's excellent followup of about 300 girls from middle to senior high school, gives a partial answer to this question, since any family dysfunction is not due to the existence of a clinical disorder in this school-based sample. In keeping with the clinical literature just cited, low scores on family cohesion, expressiveness, and organization, as reported by mothers, were related to adolescents' self-reported dieting and binging behavior (Attie & Brooks-Gunn, 1989).

Reproductive Events as They Influence Daughter-Mother Relationships. These intriguing findings led me to consider (a) possible changes in family relationships occurring at the time of early adolescence, (b) how such changes might manifest themselves, and (c) what effects upon girls' psychological adaptation such changes might have. At this time, Marta Zahaykevich was a postdoctoral fellow working with Irving Sigel. Sigel's work on the processes by which parental beliefs become translated into parental behavior and the ways in which behavior and beliefs may influence children's development (Sigel, this volume; Zahaykevich, Sigel, & Rock, 1985) was very important to me as was his friendship. Zahaykevich's work on disclosure theory (Zahaykevich, 1985) was quite relevant to the study of young adolescents and their mothers.

A quick reading of the literature leaves no doubt that parent-child relationships during early adolescence are often characterized as conflictual or as becoming more distant (Hill et al., 1985; Steinberg, 1987). While relational change has been characterized in terms of renegotiation from unilateral authority to mutuality (Youniss, 1985), or from a more vertical to a more horizontal relationship (Hartup, 1987), research has focused on the distancing of the parent and child from one another and increases in conflict and assertiveness. Only recently has the nature of the conflict been studied, as a window onto the salient developmental tasks and the type of renegotiation required (Zahaykevich, Sirey, & Brooks-Gunn, 1989) as well as the social cognitive processes underlying renegotiations (Smetana, 1988).

Although research has documented the nature of early adolescent relationships, discussion is sparse on actual developmental changes and on the processes underlying such change. We have begun to think about both, using a framework stressing the possibility that parent-daughter relationships may be influenced not only by changes in the child (i.e., pubertal events, subsequent self-definitional changes), but that the familial setting or parents themselves also change during early adolescence. The larger question being asked has to do with how girls' gender identity formation is influenced by interactions with the mother and how mothers encourage or discourage individuation. These issues are particularly important since the developmental course of girls may be different than boys, with the former being relationally focused and less autonomous (Chodorow, 1978; Gilligan, 1982).

We have looked at conflict in order to ask questions about how girls individuate from their mothers and how mothers respond to their developmental task of promoting individuation and gender identity development. Discourse analysis was used to define the arguments and counterarguments used in dyadic discussions (Zahaykevich et al., 1988). We found that girls tend to be critical of their mothers and use this criticality as an early means of individuating from her. Josselson describes this early practicing phase of individuation as one in which preadolescents assert a willful autonomy and oppose parental authority while still being internally dependent on the parent. As such, perhaps this kind of criticality is experienced by mothers as somewhat superficial and as not threatening their control. Mothers of premenarcheal girls exhibit a high level of other-centered recognition of their daughters and do not appear to withhold their recognition when daughters are oppositional.

In congruence with the findings from Hill's work (1988), signs of greater conflict seem to appear between mothers and postmenarcheal 7th-grade daughters, despite the fact that daughters in this phase significantly decrease their criticality of the mother. Daughters in this group begin to claim more autonomy in the sphere of friends and academics and increase in their passive resistance to the mother, while mothers increase in projective control and decrease in other-centered recognition of their daughters. This overall pattern may fit descriptively the portrait of ambivalence that clinicians paint of adolescents in the early rapprochement phase. In this phase, as girls demand more autonomy and resist maternal control, their renewed need for the mother's recognition and support may explain their decrease in criticality of the mother. In contrast to premenarcheal girls, these postmenarcheal girls may be perceived by their mothers as beginning to effect their first real separation from the mother. Thus, they may evoke in mothers the tendency to reinforce an undifferentiated closeness by exerting projective control and decreasing the recognition that is so important for daughters in this early phase of rapproachement.

The shift in mothers toward greater projective control of daughters following menarche supports Chodorow's thesis that mothers act to restrict their daughter's individuation in order to maintain the closeness and continuity of the relationship. Thus, maternal projection possibly may be a highly effective form of control of girls. This finding supports Mahler's and Josselson's positions that argue for the importance of maternal support of adolescent autonomy strivings in order for individuation to be possible. When mothers may continue to control daughters by imposing their own needs on them, daughters may yield to maternal control and abandon argumentation for their own claims. Thus, unlike the boys studied by Steinberg and Hill (1978), girls may stop opposing maternal control and yield to the mother after puberty, offering perhaps a partial explanation for the gender differences in autonomy. We are currently examining how these processes relate to personality development, to answer more directly the question of identity formation.

Methodological Considerations

In designing and carrying out the studies on menarche, puberty, and early adolescence, many decisions had to be made. Some of the methodological and recruitment issues that were, in my opinion, critical to the research questions under investigation are briefly presented.

Recruitment. Obtaining samples of girls for pubertal studies is extremely difficult. Because our objective has been to chart the course of girls' development, we did not wish to use clinic or medical practice "convenience" samples, but to contact girls within communities. Schools were the obvious choice for young adolescents. But many school administrators were wary about asking questions on pubertal development. The concerns seem to stem from adults' own discomfort discussing puberty and from their belief that teenagers do not discuss such changes (Brooks-Gunn, 1988b). In our menarche studies, conducted in the mid-1970s, principals in two central New Jersey school districts approved our protocol (with two other school districts declining our invitation). To augment the sample, we finally turned to the Central New Jersey Girl Scouts, whose support and enthusiasm were deeply appreciated. Although not the "perfect" sample in terms of representativeness, no discernible differences surfaced between the school and Girl Scout samples. Generally, we discovered that male school administrators and staff were much more wary about the research than their female counterparts, highlighting the discomfort reported by fathers and daughters in talking about puberty.[7]

---

[7]This uneasiness may extend to the discussion of male pubertal events. In a small study of boys' reactions to spermarche, of the five schools contacted, the only one who chose to participate had a headmistress, not a headmaster (Brooks-Gunn, 1989; Gaddis & Brooks-Gunn, 1985).

In the 1980s, through the Adolescent Study Program, we expanded our protocol to include questions on breast and pubic hair development, the growth and weight spurt, feelings about such pubertal changes, and others' responses to such changes. In addition, we needed Tanner ratings of physical development completed. It was clear that these topics were considered far more sensitive than menarche and the attitudes and feelings associated with it. Indeed, no one even questioned the appropriateness of asking about menarche (either adult attitudes had changed or, given the context, menarche was considered the least sensitive pubertal event in our protocol). Given our previous experience, we first contacted schools that had a high likelihood of having females running them and that were committed to girls' education: These were single-sex private schools. Later on, we included coeducational private schools, with no recruitment difficulties (although, of course, by this time we had a "track record" and a host of references). Our strategy was as follows: We emphasized the more medically oriented aspects of our research program (made possible by my collaboration with a gynecologist/reproductive endocrinologist and the questions we were asking); provided some (parental) feedback as to the existence of several problems if they occurred (i.e., scoliosis, eating disorders); asked for staff and teacher input in designing questionnaires; gave lecture series at the school; conducted a summer intern program for seniors from participating schools for 6 years; provided research reprints to parents and their daughters; and generally made ourselves available to staff at participating schools. We have found that our collaboration with the schools has enriched our research, given the thoughtful comments and suggestions made by the staff. Four schools were the "core" of our program, with several others participating in various studies. All were private, were concerned about the difficulties that girls have today with growing up, and were sympathetic and supportive of the need for pubertal research. Although our samples are not representative of a cross-section of youth, it is no different from samples drawn from primarily White, middle- to upper-middle class suburbs (such as Petersen's Chicago suburb sample, 1984). This may be due to the fact that the "core" schools are in Manhattan, where almost all professional families send their children to private schools.

As presented earlier, several athlete samples were seen to address specific research questions concerning the antecedents and consequences of variations in maturational timing, the emergence of eating problems, and the goodness of fit between a girl's developing body and the athletic context that she has chosen. Most of our work has focused on ballet dancers, because of the stringent weight requirements placed on them. In general, the dance world has been reluctant about research, especially that with a psychological cast. This is probably due to the negative portrayals of national ballet companies (Vincent, 1981). Our entre was the fact that Warren had worked with the national companies before (Warren, 1980) and had a number of dancers in her gynecological practice. In addition, a friend, colleague, and ultimately collaborator, William Hamilton, was the orthopedic specialist for several of the national ballet companies; he also helped us with our initial inquiries. Finally, a dancer who had been with the New York City Ballet since the age of 12, in contemplating life after the relatively early retirement of athletes, was just completing her undergraduate work at Fordham University. She had decided to become a psychologist and was eager to learn about research; conducting studies of dancers was ideal. Linda Hamilton is the secret of our success in recruiting dancers, since having dance company permission is no guarantee that individuals actually will participate. As a collaborator, Hamilton worked on several studies with us over the past 6 years, as is obvious from her coauthor and first author status. Now having completed her Ph.D. in clinical psychology, she is continuing to do research on dancers.

Samples of figure skaters and swimmers were recruited later on; Warren's reputation in sports medicine and our joint work on dancers made entré fairly easy (but time-consuming). Several students and research assistants were dogged in their pursuit of coaches, including Janine Gargiulo, Carolyn Burrow, Janet Carey, and Ann Elliott.

Design.   The design of the menarche studies was fairly straightforward. In order to examine, on a broad scale, developmental changes in symptom reports and expectations and in attitudes and feelings associated with menarche, a large cross-sectional study was conducted, including late elementary school, junior high, senior high, and college students. Then, to look at changes occurring at the time of menarche, over 100 premenarcheal 5th and 6th graders were followed and were seen after they had had their first menstruation. A matched comparison sample of still premenarcheal girls was used to control for repeated testing and time dependent changes (a same-aged premenarcheal girl was drawn from the longitudinal pool for each menarcheal girl; both girls were reinterviewed in the same time period). Thus, menarche, not age, grade in school, or time interval, was the "anchor point" in this study, given our interest in changes that might be a function of this specific pubertal event. Few studies have employed this design (see menarcheal literature reviews by Brooks-Gunn, 1984; Brooks-Gunn & Ruble, 1980; Grief & Ulman, 1982), even though it is common in studies of pregnancy, early motherhood, marriage, and divorce, all events that may occur at various times in a women's life. Given how little was known about puberty, we also wished to examine the "large picture" in the Adolescent Study Program, that is, differences as a function of age and pubertal status, and maturational timing. Therefore, 5th through 12th graders were included in our cross-sectional samples of dancers and nonathletic girls.

To examine change, we of course employed longitudinal designs. In the first study, 11- to 15-year-old girls were seen, given our interest in puberty. However, unlike the previous menarche longitudinal study, grade-in-school, not pubertal status, was used to define the timing of visits. This strategy was chosen since our design (a) required four test points, not two as before (in order to cover the time period in which pubertal change occurs), (b) called for multiple measures of puberty (so that using any one as an "anchor" point would be problematic), (c) could not enroll all girls prior to pubertal change (given the schools' requirement that all girls had to be in the spring of 5th grade, many girls already had begun the pubertal process), and (d) used ballet students as well as nonathletic girls (making it necessary to include 7th graders at the first test point, given that so many dancers are late maturers and exhibit intraindividual variability). Therefore, girls were tested each spring/summer, with grade-in school being the "anchor point."[8] All of the girls recruited for this study had been in the original cross-sectional study, making it possible to compare those who did and did not choose to participate a nice design feature.

In the second longitudinal study, girls from the cross-sectional study who were in 7th, 8th, and 9th grades were contacted 2 years later; this study, designed by Attie for her thesis, targeted the middle- to late-adolescent transition, given our interest in eating problems. Previous research suggested that such problems may occur at the time of most rapid weight gain (between Tanner Stages 3 and 5), which naturally led to a focus on the 13- to 15-year-old.

Girls' Reactions.   Given that many adults find puberty to be a sensitive topic, one might expect a similar reluctance in the girls themselves and in their mothers. In the early adolescent studies, we have had no one ask to have questions skipped in interviews and very few omit items on the self-report questionnaire (although girls are reminded repeatedly throughout our questionnaires that they may skip items, in accordance with NIH and ETS guidelines). From a clinical perspective, several girls do seem a bit embarrassed, in the Tanner staging examination (i.e., about 10% to 15%). At the same time, they also are pleased when they have completed the examination and interview, as many seem to see it as a major milestone (in that such physical examinations are a part of recommended medical practice). In personal interviews, many girls seem eager to share their pubertal experiences; given the pervasiveness of such conversations with peers and the meagerness of such talks with parents, having an interested adult woman who is not judgmental may be comforting.

Whether embarrassment in discussing puberty prevents some girls from participating in similar studies is not known. At least in this study, girls who did and did not volunteer for the longitudinal study were most similar on aspects of self-image (body image, emotional tone, family relationships) and pubertal status. About one-fourth of girls who did not volunteer told us that they did not like having their blood drawn (this study included a hormonal work-up).

Measurement.   In terms of measures, we have used a multimethod approach, depending on the specific research question of interest. Self-reports were used in

---

[8]Parenthetically, testing was conducted in the spring and early summer for pragmatic, not theoretical reasons: Girls could travel to and from the research laboratory (after school) when it was still daylight, since most girls made the trip without their parents.

the cross-sectional studies, augmented with maternal reports for specific topics. For example, several of the schools did not want us to give the girls schematic drawings of the Tanner stages to rate, but felt comfortable having the mothers fill out the Tanner schematics for their daughters (however, girls were asked how much they had developed, with regard to breasts, hair, and growth, using a 4-point scale for each). We followed up the cross-sectional study with a smaller validity study to see how accurate mothers actually were (Brooks-Gunn, Warren, Rosso, & Gargiulo, 1987). Mothers also provided information on their own physical development and reactions to their daughter's development.

In the longitudinal studies, we have included structured and semistructured interviews to augment the self-report questionnaires. This has proven to be invaluable for understanding girls' reactions to pubertal events. For example, with regard to menarche, different approaches yield varying intensities of responses. Typically, girls describe both positive and negative feelings—excited and pleased, scared and upset; however, these feelings are not particularly intense (Whisnant & Zegans, 1975; Petersen, 1983). Less direct measures of emotional reactions elicit different responses. In our study, girls were asked what they would tell a sister their age in order to prepare her for the experience. Girls were quite pragmatic when it came to telling their "hypothetical sister" about menarche—giving her information about hygiene and supplies. Few girls mentioned negative aspects of menstruation. Rierdan and Koff (1985) gave a small sample of 7th and 8th graders a sentence completion task, starting with the phrase "Ann just got her period for the first time." Responses were almost all negative, unlike the findings just reported. Girls may be more reluctant to discuss negative feelings in interviews. At the same time, preojective techniques may elicit girls' feelings about the event in general, not their specific reaction to the event. For example, adult and adolescent females report that women in general experience more severe symptoms than they themselves experience (Parlee, 1972; Brooks, Ruble, & Clarke, 1977).

Similar findings are cropping up for pubertal events other than menarche. In collaboration with Denise Newman, we are examining 5th- to 9th-grade girls' responses to breast growth, using a semistructured format (e.g., "How do you feel about breast growth?" "What physical change do you feel is most important?" "Who have you talked to about physical changes?") and a TAT format (the bra picture discussed earlier). Reactions to the latter are more intense than to the former. I do not believe that the responses from one method are more valid, but that they represent different aspects of girls' experience of puberty (see Kagan, 1988, for a discussion of the meaning of results devised from different methods).

A final example of the usefulness of multimethod approaches in this series of studies comes from the longitudinal study of middle and high school girls. Attie and I found that maternal, but not daughter, ratings of the family environment (the Moss Family Environment Scale) were associated with girls' report of eating problems. The discrepancy between findings using mother and daughter ratings suggests differences in their perceptions of the family's functioning, or in mothers' and daughters' willingness to report them. Not only is denial a salient feature of adolescents with eating disorders (Fairburn, 1984), so is the tendency for family members to avoid conflict (Minuchin, Rosman, & Baker, 1978).

ADOLESCENTS AS MOTHERS

The fairly recent focus on pregnancy and parenthood has resulted in thinking of adolescents both as mothers and daughters and in adopting a more family systems approach. These perspectives originated with the Baltimore Study. Originally, the Baltimore Study was an evaluation of a comprehensive prenatal care program for pregnant adolescents who were primarily Black lower and working class young women. Interviews were first conducted with both the adolescents and their mothers during the adolescents' pregnancies in 1967. Follow-up interviews were conducted several times over the next 5 years on a wide range of sexual, social, and family issues (see Furstenberg, 1976). When the 5-year follow-up was concluded in 1972, no plans were made for any further contact. However, a decade later, when the children of the teenage mothers began to reach adolescence, the idea of seeing the families again was seriously entertained, as discussed earlier. In 1983 to 1984, the original teenage mothers and their children were interviewed. Three major findings emerged from the 17-year follow-up study: (a) significant variability and improvement in the life circumstances of the original teen mothers, (b) strikingly poor outcomes of their adolescent children, and (c) clear links between changes in the mothers' life courses and the developmental trajectories of their children (Furstenberg et al., 1987).

Mothers' Life Courses

The results of the 5-year follow-up in 1972 suggested that a certain amount of variation in the life courses of the women would be evident in the 17-year follow-up. However, the extent of diversity and the degree of improvement seen over time between 1972 and 1984 were totally unexpected by Furstenberg and me. What accounted for the diversity among the Generation II mothers' adaptation to early childbearing? Characteristics of both the teens' family of origin and of the teens themselves were significant predictors of economic success in later life. The important familial factors were educational status of the teenagers' parents, family of origin's size and welfare status. Teens whose parents had higher levels of education, smaller family sizes, and no welfare assistance were more likely to succeed as adults. In contrast, other familial factors, such as teenager's mothers' marital or employment status or age, did not relate to the teenager's long-term outcome.

Three characteristics of the teens themselves predicted economic success in later life: Educational attainment and ambition, family size, and marital status. Whether or not the adolescent had repeated a grade by the time of the pregnancy was a powerful determinant of her future economic position. Her educational ambitions also were predictive of later economic outcome, independent of parental education and her own grade repetition. Both the probability of receiving welfare and of achieving economic security were strongly influenced by the number of additional births that occurred in the 5-year period after the birth of the study child. An important additional pathway away from economic dependency for the teen mothers was stable marriage. Those women who were married at the time of the 5-year follow-up were much more likely to have succeeded economically, presumably because of their husbands' income, than those who had never married. In contrast, women who remained with their families of origin for at least 5 years after their first child was born were less likely to be economically secure and more likely to be on welfare in adulthood. Thus, while living with one's parents for the first year or two promoted school attendance and employment, such an arrangement over the long term posed obstacles to independence and self-sufficiency in adulthood (Brooks-Gunn & Furstenberg, 1986; Furstenberg et al., 1987).

Children's Life Course

The long-term costs of teenage motherhood to the women were considerably less than expected, even given the diversity of outcomes seen at the 5-year follow-up. However, the costs to the children were more than we had expected. The complexities of the mothers' lives, as they juggled childcare, schooling, jobs, and relationships with men, were mirrored in potentially significant events to their children. One-third of the children had been separated from their mothers at least once for 2 months or more (excluding summer vacation) during their lives. Many children (40%) had another adult as primary caretaker for them during early childhood, as their mothers finished school or worked. The high rate of marital dissolution, the relatively large number of women who never married, and the frequency of short-term cohabitation relationships translated into the fleeting and unpredictable presence of adult men for the children. With the exception of the 9% who had never lived with an adult male (father, stepfather, or boyfriend), all of the children had spent some time with a male figure in the household. However, only a handful (16%) were living with the biological father as teenagers.

Regarding the academic status of the teenagers, they were characterized by what may only be described as massive school failure. Half of the sample had repeated at least one grade during their school career—59% of the males and 39% of the females. Perhaps the greatest concern of the public and policymakers alike is the spector of "children of children" perpetuating the cycle of early childbearing. In the Baltimore Study, 78% of the teens were sexually active, with higher rates for boys than girls (84 versus 69%). In brief, the mothers' struggle to avoid poverty levied a cost on their children, as measured by academic achievement and management of sexuality. The amount of time the teenage mother had available, the need for complex childcare arrangements, the absence of the father, lowered educational attainment, and in some cases, reduced economic circumstances, all are part of the adolescent mothers' experience. Even with the help of family and friends in childrearing, these obstacles could not be totally overcome (Brooks-Gunn & Furstenberg, 1987).

Changes in the Mothers' Life Courses and Children's Outcome

The 17-year follow-up provided the opportunity to examine whether variability in the children's outcomes could be understood in terms of the timing and sequencing of maternal life events. What types of changes at what points in time affected child outcome? Effects of changes depended upon specific maternal characteristics, specific child outcomes, and specific ages. For academic performance as an outcome, mothers' change in welfare status (i.e., moving off welfare after the child's preschool years) significantly reduced the likelihood of the child's subsequent grade failure. Similarly, mothers who entered a stable marriage and advanced their educational standing by the time of their children's adolescence had teens with superior school performance than teens whose mothers had not brought about these improvements. In contrast, mothers' early fertility behavior negatively affected preschoolers' performance, but later fertility did not affect adolescents' school achievement. Rapidly increasing family size during the child's early years may have had negative effects because of the intensity of childrearing demands in the first years of life. Births occurring later seemed not to affect adolescent performance, perhaps because the childrearing demands are spaced out over time.

Family Systems: Grandmothers, Teen Mothers, and Toddlers

Building upon how changing maternal life circumstances affect child development, Chase-Lansdale and I decided to go beyond static measures of child outcome and examine ways in which family interaction patterns may link maternal socioeconomic status and child outcome. Furthermore, we believed that not enough attention had been paid to the family structures and caregiving patterns seen with very young mothers. Questions emerged as to the complementary and competing roles that teenage mothers and the other significant adult—her mother—played in a young child's life.

To date, a family process perspective has been virtually absent in studies of young mothers. Most of the research has focused solely on the attributes and behavior of the teenage mother herself, and any acknowledgement of the role of other family members has been at the level of documenting their presence or absence. Chase-Lansdale and I examine the families of young mothers as a triadic family system, comprised of mother, grandmother, and child.[9] In order to predict child outcome, it is necessary to measure the quality of the three main subsystems (mother-grandmother, mother-child, and grandmother-child), as well as the functioning of the triad as a whole. We are examining such triads in the Baltimore Study sample, focusing on the children of the original teen mothers who are now adolescent parents themselves; approximately one-third of the first-born girls are now parents. They are seen in their homes when their child is 30- to 36-months-of-age. Mother-child, grandmother-child, mother-grandmother, and triadic interactions are videotaped. Quality of parenting and of mother-grand-mother relationships is assessed. Based on findings from the earlier generations in the Baltimore Study, we expect that at least 75% of the current teenage mothers and children will be living with the grandmother, and those who live apart will typically have frequent contact with one another. In addition, there was considerable variability among the original teenage mother families as to who was the primary caretaker of the child; similar patterns are expected in this new study.

Specific questions to be asked include the following: How does shared care-giving between mother and grandmother affect the child? Do mothers and grand-mothers differ in their parental practices toward the child? Is the provision of high quality parenting by one adult, usually the grandmother, sufficient for toddler development? Additionally, we wish to know about the characteristics of the emotional relationship between mother and grandmother, involving such qualities as closeness, conflict, self-disclosure, and hostility? Does the quality of this relationship set the emotional tone of the family, and how does this influence the development of the adolescent mother and of the grandchild?

Currently, we are struggling with how to conceptualize the development of the children of teenage mothers from the perspective of the larger family system influences. We have been helped immensely by our discussions with David Reiss and Mavis Hetherington (Chase-Lansdale was initially a postdoctoral fellow in the NIMH-funded Family Consortium with Reiss and Hetherington when we met and is now a Research Scientist at George Washington University Medical School). With Reiss, we are examining research from other family structures and on other relationships to see how they might help us to understand both the teenage mother as a parent and as a child and her influence upon her toddler. Examples include husband-wife interactions, sibling research, findings on single mothers, and studies of teenage girls and their mothers (Chase-Lansdale, Brooks-Gunn, & Reiss, 1988).

---

[9]While we realize that in many situations the family system is more complex than a triad, our primary interest is still in the relationships of the two adults most likely to be providing support and care to the toddler—mother and grandmother.

Methodological Considerations

As in the pubertal work, a variety of methodological considerations dictated the direction of the pregnancy work (Brooks-Gunn & Furstenberg, 1989). Recruitment, design, and reactions to the "sensitive" nature of the subject will be presented, albeit quite briefly.

Recruitment. Generally, recruitment for the pregnancy studies has occurred with relative ease. In part, this is (a) because the community-based institution from which women are recruited is the hospital or clinic, not the school, (b) since once a pregnancy is a *fact accompli,* parents have little difficulty with their daughters answering reproductive questions, and (c) since in many of our studies, parental consent was not necessary, given the age of the pregnant women. In the Harlem and Baltimore studies, staff associated with the medical center approached all women entering the prenatal clinic. In both of these urban, relatively poor settings, the vast majority of women receive care via neighborhood and hospital clinics, not from private physicians. Additionally, all but 8% to 12% receive some care prior to the delivery (although poor pregnancy women enter the health care system much later than is recommended), making it likely that those enrolled in the studies are representative of most pregnant women in that community (those that receive no care are more likely to be recent immigrants, and women with little or no social support; McCormick et al., 1989). Given the sensitivity of community outreach workers and hospital staff, high proportions of women have entered our studies (e.g., 75% to 80% of those contacted).

In the Toronto-New Jersey studies focusing on middle class married women, private physicians and organizations providing services to such families (La Maze, YWCA, and La Leche classes) had to be contacted, given that service delivery patterns for the middle and lower class are quite different. Like all developmental research not using the school or other fairly universal institutions (i.e., the bulk of infancy and early childhood as well as the pregnancy and early parenthood studies), this sample may or may not be representative of middle class populations. However, the demographics are similar to those in most studies of this kind (i.e., focusing on pregnant or postpartum middle class White women).

Design. Like the menarche studies, the event under investigation, pregnancy, was used as the anchor point in the Harlem and Baltimore studies as well as in the Toronto-New Jersey longitudinal studies. As pregnancy may occur across a very large age range, unlike menarche, we have used different strategies to limit the sample depending on the primary research question. In the Baltimore Study, the interest was in teenagers, originally in whether a special prenatal program helped these young women make the transition to motherhood smoothly (i.e., use of health services, contraceptive use, parenting behavior). In subse-

241

quent follow-ups, time of testing was still tied to the birth of the child, in order to keep the interval constant across individuals. By the 5-year follow-up, maternal age made no difference in outcomes. The Harlem study also was initiated as a program evaluation; therefore, all women enrolling at one of five Harlem Hospital clinics during a specific time period were invited to participate. Age was not a determining factor; this sample is fairly representative of pregnant women in Central Harlem (McCormick et al., 1987).

In the Toronto-New Jersey studies, we wished to examine the pregnancy and postpartum experience of first time mothers who were married or living with a partner. In order to look at developmental change, a large cross-sectional sample was recruited, including three groups—prepregnant (i.e., planning to become pregnant in the next few years), pregnant (1st, 2nd, and 3rd trimester), and postpartum (1 and 3 months). This is akin to the strategy employed in the menarche and puberty research. More specific longitudinal studies have been conducted in Toronto by Fleming and Ruble.

Women's Reactions.   While I am often asked if recruitment or interviewing is difficult because of the "sensitivity" of the topics, it seems that the issue is more in the eye of the beholder than in pregnant women themselves. The pregnancy experience is fascinating, one that most women are eager to discuss. This is true for teenagers as well as adults. Questions on sexual and contraceptive behavior also are answered readily, even in our samples of nonpregnant teenagers (i.e., the first borns of the Baltimore young mothers who, at the 17-year follow-up were between 16- and 17-years-of-age).

CONCLUSION

I continue to alter and hopefully to broaden my perspective on how to study the experience of the adolescent in the throes of physical and reproductive growth, of the emergence of initiation of sexual behavior, of the control of fertility and sometimes, of the onset of parenthood. How the girls make sense of these events, how they incorporate them into their self-definition as adults (and women), and how they alter their relationships with others are my current primary focus. Additionally, I am interested in (a) how others, especially parent and peers, perceive and respond to these events, (b) what relational changes occur as a consequence of self- and other- perspectives, and (c) whether such changes translate into particular modes of adaptation, with a particular interest in those associated with gender role identity. While not always neat and tidy, my research has always been compelling, fascinating, and fun.

ACKNOWLEDGMENT

The writing of this chapter was supported by grants from the National Institutes of Health and the Office of Adolescent Pregnancy, whose support is greatly appreciated. The W. T. Grant Foundation and the Commonwealth Fund also are to be thanked for their support of research contributing to this chapter. The assistance of R. Deibler, M. Cohen, and F. Kelly, who prepared the manuscript, is acknowledged. I. Sigel's thoughtful comments on earlier drafts were greatly appreciated. Portions of the chapter were written while I was a Visiting Scholar at the Russell Sage Foundation. Requests for additional information may be addressed to Dr. Brooks-Gunn, Educational Testing Service, Princeton, NJ 08541.

REFERENCES

Attie, I., & Brooks-Gunn, J. (1987). Weight-related concerns in women: A response to or a cause of stress? In R. C. Barnett, L. Bierner, & G. K. Baruch (Eds.), *Gender and stress* (pp. 218–254). New York: Free Press.

Attie, I., & Brooks-Gunn, J. (1989). The development of eating problems in adolescent girls: A longitudinal study. *Developmental Psychology, 25*(1) 70–79.

Attie, I., & Brooks-Gunn, J. (in press). The emergence of eating disorders and eating problems in adolescence: A developmental perspective. *Journal of Child Psychology and Psychiatry.*

Bandura, A. (1982). The psychology of chance encounters and life paths. *American Psychologist, 37*(7), 747–755.

Baydar, N., Brooks-Gunnm, J., & Warren, M. P. (1989). *Determinants of depressive symptoms in adolescent girls: A four year longitudinal study.* Unpublished manuscript.

Berndt, T. J. (1982). The features and effects of friendship in early adolescence. *Child Development, 53,* 1947–1960.

Blyth, D. A., Simmons, R. G., & Zakin, D. F. (1985). Satisfaction with body-image for the impact of pubertal timing within different school environments. *Journal of Youth and Adolescence, 14* (3), 207–225.

Bronfenbrenner, U. (1979). *The ecology of human development.* Cambridge, MA: Harvard University Press.

Bronfenbrenner, U. (1989). Interacting systems in human development research paradigms: Present and future. In N. Bolger, A. Caspi, G. Downey, & M. Moorehouse (Eds.), *Persons in context: Developmental processes.* New York: Cambridge University Press.

Bronfenbrenner, U., & Crouter, A. C. (1983). The evolution of environmental models in developmental research. In P. H. Mussen (Ed.), *Handbook of child psychology: Vol. 1* (W. Kessen, Volume Editor; pp. 357–414). New York: Wiley.

Brooks, J., Ruble, D. N., & Clarke, A. (1977). College women's attitudes and expectations concerning menstrual-related changes. *Psychosomatic Medicine, 39,* 288–298.

Brooks-Gunn, J. (1984). The psychological significance of different pubertal events to young girls. *Journal of Early Adolescence, 4*(4), 315–327.

Brooks-Gunn, J. (1985). The salience and timing of the menstrual flow. *Psychosomatic Medicine, 47*(4), 363–371.

Brooks-Gunn, J. (1987). Pubertal processes and girls' psychological adaptation. In R. Lerner & T. T. Foch (Eds.), *Biological-psychosocial interactions in early adolescence: A life-span perspective* (pp. 123–153). Hillsdale, NJ: Lawrence Erlbaum Associates.

Brooks-Gunn, J. (1988). The psychological significance of secondary sexual characteristics in 9- to 11-year-old girls. *Child Development, 59,* 161–169.

Brooks-Gunn, J. (1988a). Transition to early adolescence. In M. Gunnar & W. A. Collins (Eds.), *Development during transition to adolescence: Minnesota symposia on child psychology, Vol. 21* (pp. 189–208). Hillsdale, NJ: Lawrence Erlbaum Associates.

Brooks-Gunn, J. (1988b). Antecedents and consequences of variations in girls' maturational timing. *Journal of Adolescent Health Care, 9*(5), 1–9.

Brooks-Gunn, J. (1989). Barriers and impediments to conducting research with young adolescents. *Journal of Youth and Adolescence.*

Brooks-Gunn, J., Burrow, C., & Warren, M. P. (1988). Attitudes toward eating and body weight in different groups of female adolescent athletes. *International Journal of Eating Disorders, 7*(6), 749–758.

Brooks-Gunn, J., & Duke-Duncan, P. (1985, August). Co-Chairs of a symposium on *"Growing Up Female and Liking It"* sponsored by the Personal Products Company (Johnson & Johnson), Washington.

Brooks-Gunn, J., & Furstenberg, F. F., Jr. (1986). The children of adolescent mothers: Physical, academic and psychological outcomes. *Developmental Review, 6,* 224–251.

Brooks-Gunn, J., & Furstenberg, F. F., Jr. (1987). Continuity and change in the context of poverty: Adolescent mothers and their children. In J. J. Gallagher & C. T. Ramey (Eds.), *The malleability of children* (pp. 171–188). Baltimore, MD: Brookes Publishing.

Brooks-Gunn, J., & Furstenberg, F. F., Jr. (1989). Adolescent sexual behavior. *American Psychologist, 44*(2), 249–257.

Brooks-Gunn, J., Newman, D., & Warren, M. P. (1989). *Significance of breast growth.* Unpublished manuscript.

Brooks-Gunn, J., McCormick, M. C., Gunn, R. W., Shorter, T., Wallace, C. Y., Heagarty, M. C. (1989). Outreach as casefinding: The process of locating low income pregnant women. *Medical Care, 27*(2), 95–102.

Brooks-Gunn, J., McCormick, M. C., & Heagarty, M. C. (1988). Preventing infant mortality and morbidity: Developmental perspectives. *American Journal of Orthopsychiatry, 58*(2), 288–296.

Brooks-Gunn, J., & Petersen, A. C. (Eds.). (1983). *Girls at puberty: Biological and psychosocial perspectives.* New York: Plenum Press.

Brooks-Gunn, J., & Petersen, A. C. (1984). Problems in studying and defining pubertal events. *Journal of Youth and Adolescence, 13*(3), 181–196.

Brooks-Gunn, J., & Petersen, A. C. (in press). Special issue. The emergence of depression in adolescence. *Journal of Youth and Adolescence.*

Brooks-Gunn, J., Petersen, A. C., & Eichorn, D. (1985). Special Issue: The study of maturational timing effects in adolescence. *Journal of Youth and Adolescence, 14*(3/4).

Brooks-Gunn, J., & Ruble, D. N. (1980). Menarche: The interaction of physiology, cultural and social factors. In A. J. Dan, E. A. Graham, & C. P. Beecher (Eds.), *The menstrual cycle: A synthesis of interdisciplinary research* (pp. 141–159). New York: Springer.

Brooks-Gunn, J., & Ruble, D. N. (1982a). Developmental processes in the experience of menarche. In A. Baum & J. E. Singer (Eds.), *Handbook of psychology and health, Vol. 2* (pp. 117–147). Hillsdale, NJ: Lawrence Erlbaum Associates.

Brooks-Gunn, J., & Ruble, D. N. (1982b). The development of menstrual-related beliefs and behaviors during early adolescence. *Child Development, 53,* 1567–1577.

Brooks-Gunn, J., & Ruble, D. N. (1983). The experience of menarche from a developmental perspective. In J. Brooks-Gunn & A. C. Petersen (Eds.), *Girls at puberty: Biological and psychosocial perspectives* (pp. 155–177). New York: Plenum Press.

Brooks-Gunn, J., Samelson, M., Warren, M. P., & Fox, R. (1986). Physical similarity of and disclosure of menarcheal status to friends: Effects of age and pubertal status. *Journal of Early Adolescence, 6*(1), 3–14.

Brooks-Gunn, J., & Warren, M. P. (1985). Effects of delayed menarche in different contexts: Dance and nondance students. *Journal of Youth and Adolescence, 14*(4), 285–300.

Brooks-Gunn, J., & Warren, M. P. (1988a). Mother-daughter differences in menarcheal age in adolescent dancers and nondancers. *Annals of Human Biology, 15*(1), 35–43.

Brooks-Gunn, J., & Warren, M. P. (1988b). The psychological significance of secondary sexual characteristics in 9- to 11-year-old girls. *Child Development, 59,* 1061–1069.

Brooks-Gunn, J., Warren, M. P., & Rosso, J. T. (1987, April). *The impact of pubertal and social events upon girls' problem behavior.* Paper presented at a symposium entitled "The development of depressive affect in adolescence," Society for Research in Child Development meetings, Baltimore.

Brooks-Gunn, J., Warren, M. P., Rosso, J., & Gargiulo, J. (1987). Validity of self-report measures of girls' pubertal status. *Child Development, 58,* 829–841.

Brooks-Gunn, J., & Zahaykevich, M. (1989). Parent-child relationships in early adolescence: A developmental perspective. In K. Kreppner & R. M. Lerner (Eds.), *Family systems and life-span development.* Hillsdale, NJ: Lawrence Erlbaum Associates.

Budoff, P. W. (1979). Use of mefanamio acid in the treatment of primary dysmenorrhea. *Journal of the American Medical Association, 241,* 2713–2717.

Chase-Lansdale, P. L., Brooks-Gunn, J., & Reiss, D. (1988, March). *Emotional experience of children of adolescent mothers: The family context.* Symposium presentation at the Society for Research in Adolescent meetings, Alexandria, VA.

Chodorow, N. (1978). *The reproduction of mothering: Psychoanalysis and sociology of gender.* Berkeley: University of California Press.

Collins, W. A. (1988). Developmental theories in research on the transition to adolescence. In M. R. Gunnar & W. A. Collins (Eds.), *Development during transition to adolescence: Minnesota symposia on child psychology, Vol. 21* (pp. 1–15). Hillsdale, NJ: Lawrence Erlbaum Associates.

Cooley, C. H. (1909). *Social organization: A study of the larger mind.* New York: Schochen.

Deutsch, H. (1944). *The psychology of women, Vol 1.* New York: Grune & Stratton.

Deutsch, F. M., Ruble, D. N., Fleming, A., Brooks-Gunn, J., & Stangor, C. (1988). Information-seeking and self-definition during the transition to motherhood. *Journal of Personality and Social Psychology, 55*(3), 420–431.

Fairburn, C. G. (1984). Bulimia: Its epidemiology and management. In A. J. Stunkard & E. Stellar (Eds.), *Eating and its disorders* (pp. 235–258). New York: Raven Press.

Faust, M. S. (1960). Developmental maturity as a determinant in prestige of adolescent girls. *Child Development, 31,* 173–186.

Fleming, A. S., Ruble, D. N., Flett, G. L., & Shaul, D. L. (1988). Postpartum adjustment in first-time mothers: Relations between mood, maternal attitudes, and mother-infant interactions. *Developmental Psychology, 24*(1), 71–81.

Frisch, R. E., Gotz-Welbergen, A. V., McArthur, J. W., Albright, T., Witschi, J., Bullen, B., Birnholz, J., Reed, R. B., & Hermann, H. (1981). Delayed menarche and amenorrhea of college athletes in relation to age of onset of training. *Journal of the American Medical Association, 246,* 1559–1563.

Frisch, R. E., Wyashak, G., & Vincent, L. (1980). Delayed menarche and amenorrhea and ballet dancers. *New England Journal of Medicine, 303,* 18–19.

Furstenberg, F. F., Jr. (1976). *Unplanned parenthood: The social consequences of teenage child-bearing.* New York: The Free Press.

Furstenberg, F. F., Jr., Brooks-Gunn, J., & Morgan, P. (1987). *Adolescent mothers in later life.* New York: Cambridge University Press.

Gaddis, A., & Brooks-Gunn, J. (1985). The male experience of pubertal change. *Journal of Youth and Adolescence, 14*(1), 61–69.

Gargiulo, J., Attie, I., Brooks-Gunn, J., & Warren, M. P. (1987). Dating in middle school girls: Effects of social context, maturation, and grade. *Developmental Psychology, 23*(5), 730–737.

Gilligan, C. (1982). *In a different voice.* Cambridge, MA: Harvard University Press.

Grief, E. B., & Ulman, K. J. (1982). The psychological impact of menarche on early adolescent females: A review of the literature. *Child Development, 53,* 1413–1430.

Hamilton, L. H., Brooks-Gunn, J., & Warren, M. P. (1985). Sociocultural influences on eating disorders in female professional dancers. *International Journal of Eating Disorders, 4*(4), 465–477.

Hartup, W. W. (1989, in press). Relationships and the growth of social competence. *American Psychologist, 44*(2), 120–126.

Hetherington, E. M. (1987). Family relations six years after divorce. In K. Pasley & M. Ihinger-Tallman (Eds.), *Remarriage and stepparenting: Current research and theory* (pp. 185–205). New York: Guilford Press.

Hill, J. P. (1988). The role of conflict in familial adaptation to biological change. In M. R. Gunnar & W. A. Collins (Eds.), *Development during transition to adolescence: Minnesota symposia on child psychology, Vol. 21* (pp. 43–77). Hillsdale, NJ: Lawrence Erlbaum Associates.

Hill, J. P., Holmbeck, G. N., Marlow, L., Green, T. M., & Lynch, M. E. (1985). Menarcheal status and parent-child relations in families of seventh-grade girls. *Journal of Youth and Adolescence, 14*(4), 301–316.

Hill, J. P., & Lynch, M. E. (1983). The intensification of gender-related role expectations during early adolescence. In J. Brooks-Gunn & A. C. Petersen (Eds.), *Girls at puberty: Biological and psychosocial perspectives* (pp. 201–228). New York: Plenum Press.

Hinde, R. A. (1979). *Toward understanding relationships.* London: Academic Press.

Kagan, J. (1988). The meaning of personality predicates. *American Psychologist, 43*(8), 614–620.

Klein, J. R., & Litt, I. F. (1983). Menarcheal dysmenorrhea. In J. Brooks-Gunn & A. C. Petersen (Eds.), *Girls at puberty: Biological and psychosocial perspectives* (pp. 73–88). New York: Plenum Press.

Koff, E., Rierdan, J., & Jacobson, S. (1981). The personal and interpersonal significance of menarche. *Journal of the American Academy of Child Psychiatry, 20,* 148–158.

Kuhn, T. (1970). *The structure of scientific revolutions* (2nd ed.). Chicago: University of Chicago Press.

Lewis, M., & Brooks-Gunn, J. (1979). *Social cognition and the acquisition of self.* New York: Plenum Press.

Maccoby, E. E., & Jacklin, C. N. (1974). *The psychology of sex differences.* Stanford CA: Stanford University Press.

Magnusson, D., Strattin, H., & Allen, V. L. (1985). A longitudinal study of some adjustment processes from mid-adolescence to adulthood. *Journal of Youth and Adolescence, 14*(4), 267–283.

Malina, R. M. (1983). Menarche in athletes: A synthesis and hypothesis. *Annals of Human Biology, 10*(1), 1–24.

McCormick, M. C., Brooks-Gunn, J., Shorter, T., Wallace, C. Y., Holmes, J. H., & Heagarty, M. C. (1987). The planning of pregnancy among low-income women in central harlem. *American Journal of Obstetrics and Gynecology, 156*(1), 145–149.

McCormick, M. C., Brooks-Gunn, J., Shorter, T., Holmes, J. H., Wallace, C. Y., & Heagarty, M. C. (1989). Outreach as casefinding: Its effect on enrollment in prenatal care. *Medical Care, 27*(2), 95–102.

Mead, G. H. (1934). *Mind, self, and society: From the standpoint of a social behaviorist.* Chicago: University of Chicago Press.

Merleau-Ponty, M. (1964).*Primacy of perception.* J. Eddie (Ed.) & W. Cobb (trans.). Evanston, IL: Northwestern University Press.

Minuchin, J., Rosman, B. L., & Baker, L. (1978). *Psychosomatic families: Anorexia nervosa in context.* Cambridge, MA: Harvard University Press.

Montemayor, R. (1982). The relationship between parent-adolescent conflict and the amount of time adolescents spend alone and with parents and peers. *Child Development, 53,* 1512–1519.

Paikoff, R. L., & Brooks-Gunn, J. (1989, in press). Biological processes during early adolescence:

What role do they play in social-emotional development? In R. Montemayer, G. Adams, & T. Gullotta (Eds.), *Advances in adolescent development: Vol. 2. The transitions from childhood to adolescence.* Beverly Hills, CA: Sage.

Parlee, M. B. (1972). The premenstrual syndrome. *Psychology Bulletin, 80*(6), 454–465.

Peskin, H. (1967). Pubertal onset and ego functioning. *Journal of Abnormal Psychology, 72,* 1–15.

Peterson, A. C. (1983). Menarche: Meaning of measures and measuring meaning (pp. 63–76). In S. Golub (Eds.), *Menarche.* Lexington, MA: Lexington.

Petersen, A. C. (1984). The early adolescent study: An overview. *Journal of Early Adolescence, 4* (10), 3–106.

Petersen, A. C. (1988). Adolescent development. *Annual Review of Psychology, 39,* 583–607.

Petersen, A. C., & Brooks-Gunn, J. (in press). Transition to puberty. In A. L. Greene & A. M. Boxer (Eds.), *Transitions through adolescence: Research and theory in life-span perspective.* Hillsdale, NJ: Lawrence Erlbaum Associates.

Petersen, A. C., & Crockett, L. (1985). Pubertal timing and grade effects on adjustment. *Journal of Youth and Adolescence, 14*(3), 191–206.

Rierdan, J., & Koff, E. (1985). Timing of menarche and initial menstrual experience. *Journal of Youth and Adolescence, 14*(3), 237–244.

Ruble, D. N. (1983). The development of social comparison processes and their role in achievement-related self-socialization. In E. T. Higgins, D. N. Ruble, & W. W. Hartup (Eds.), *Social cognition and social development: A sociocultural perspective* (pp. 3–12). New York: Cambridge University Press.

Ruble, D. N., Boggiano, A., & Brooks-Gunn, J. (1982). Men's and women's evaluations of menstrual-related excuses. *Sex Roles, 8*(6), 625–638.

Ruble, D. N., & Brooks-Gunn, J. (1979). Menstrual symptoms: A social cognitive analysis. *Journal of Behavioral Medicine, 2,* 171–194.

Ruble, D. N., & Brooks-Gunn, J. (1982). The experience of menarche. *Child Development, 53,* 1557–1566.

Ruble, D. N., & Brooks-Gunn, J. (1987). Perceptions of menstrual and premenstrual symptoms: Self definitional processes at menarche. In B. E. Ginsberg & B. F. Carter (Eds.), *The premenstrual syndrome* (pp. 237–251). New York: Plenum Press.

Ruble, D. N., Fleming, A. S., Hackel, L. S., & Stangor, C. (in press). Changes in the marital relationship during the transition to first-time motherhood: Effects of violated expectations concerning division of household labor. *Journal of Personality and Social Psychology.*

Sargent, J., Liebman, R., & Silver, M. (1985). Family therapy for anorexia nervosa. In D. M. Garner & P. E. Garfinkel (Eds.), *Handbook of psychotherapy for anorexia nervosa and bulimia* (pp. 257–279). New York: Guilford Press.

Scarr, S., & McCartney, K. (1983). How people make their own environments: A theory of genotype-environment effects. *Child Development, 54,* 424–435.

Simmons, R. G., Blyth, D. A., & McKinney, K. L. (1983). The social and psychological effects of puberty on white females. In J. Brooks-Gunn & A. C. Petersen (Eds.), *Girls at puberty: Biological and psychosocial perspectives* (pp. 229–272). New York: Plenum Press.

Simmons, R. G., Burgeson, R., & Reef, M. J. (1988). Cumulative change at entry to adolescence. In M. Gunnar & W. A. Collins (Eds.), *Development during transition to adolescence: Minnesota symposia on child psychology, Vol. 21* (pp. 123–150). Hillsdale, NJ: Lawrence Erlbaum Associates.

Smetana, J. G. (1988). Concepts of self and social convention: Adolescents' and parents' reasoning about hypothetical and actual family conflicts. In M. Gunnar & W. A. Collins (Eds.), *Development during transition to adolescence: Minnesota symposia on child psychology, Vol. 21* (pp. 79–122). Hillsdale, NJ: Lawrence Erlbaum Associates.

Steinberg, L. D. (1987). The impact of puberty on family relations: Effects of pubertal status and pubertal timing. *Developmental Psychology, 23,* 451–460.

Steinberg, L. D., & Hill, J. P. (1978). Patterns of family interaction as a function of age, the onset of puberty, and formal thinking. *Developmental Psychology, 14,* 683–684.

Thoits, P. A. (1983). Dimensions of life events that influence psychological distress: An evaluation and synthesis of the literature. In H. P. Kaplan (Ed.), *Psychosocial stress: Trends in theory and research* (pp. 33–103). New York: Academic Press.

Thompson, C. (1942). Cultural pressures in the psychology of women. *Psychiatry, 5,* 331–339.

Vincent, L. M. (1981). *Competing with the Sylph: Dancers and the pursuit of the ideal body.* Kansas City, KS: Andrews & McMeel.

Warren, M. P. (1980). The effects of exercise on pubertal progression and reproductive function in girls. *Journal of Clinical Endocrinology and Metabolism, 51*(5), 1150–1157.

Warren, M. P., Brooks-Gunn, J., Hamilton, L. H., Hamilton, W. G., & Warren, L. F. (1986). Scoliosis and fractures in young ballet dancers: Relationship to delayed menarcheal age and secondary amenorrhea. *New England Journal of Medicine, 314*(21), 1348–1353.

Whisnant, L., & Zegans, L. (1975). A study of attitudes toward menarche in White middle-class American adolescent girls. *American Journal of Psychiatry, 132,* 809–814.

Youniss, J. (1985). *Adolescent relations with mothers, fathers and friends.* Chicago: University of Chicago Press.

Zahaykevich, M. (1985). *The discursive basis of socio-moral actions.* Unpublished manuscript, Teacher's College, Columbia University, New York.

Zahaykevich, M., Sigel, I. E., & Rock, D. A. (1985). *A model of parental speech acts and child cognitive development.* Unpublished manuscript, Educational Testing Service, Princeton, NJ.

Zahaykevich, M., Sirey, J. A., & Brooks-Gunn, J. (1989). *Mother-daughter individuation during early adolescence.* Unpublished manuscript, Educational Testing Service, Princeton, New Jersey.

8 Finding The Laws of Close Personal Relationships

John M. Gottman
University of Washington

HISTORICAL CONTEXT

I have been asked to write an historical account of my own research. I do so reluctantly because this seems like an undertaking that must involve hubris, and therefore it must be bad luck. I hope that I can respond to Irving Sigel's request with humility. I am an ordinary, hard working, and honest scientist, and I hope that as a representative of active research workers this chapter will prove interesting to read. I plan to be honest and brief in the hopes that the chart of my progress may be interesting to young researchers who choose a similar course.

Becoming an Ethologist

When I began teaching, my interests were not substantive but methodological. My advisor, Richard McFall, suggested that I select a research problem of some interest to me rather than sticking with primarily methodological and statistical questions. After a lot of soul searching, I decided that I would study marriage, and social isolation in children. Frankly, I selected these two areas of inquiry because they had been the source of considerable pain in my own personal life. I had been essentially an isolate in high school, but not before that or after that. Nonetheless, the experience had left its scars. Fortunately, I had made one good lifelong friend in high school, and I was certain that that fact had saved me a lot of later trouble. So for that reason I decided to study both friendship and socially isolated children. I also really enjoyed working with children. Unhappy marriage had also been something I had experienced both personally and as a clinician, and wanted to understand. I was interested in the more positive sides of life than the deeply pathological, so I began studying happy as well as unhappy marriages and close and more distant friendships.

After some extensive reading, I realized that there was an incredible oversight in the research literature on marriage and children's peer relationships. I concluded that scientists had basically skipped that phase of scientific investigation that involves *description*. Instead they had leapt immediately to the theorizing and testing of hypotheses. Perhaps this notion of the need for description itself is unclear. What I mean by it is that there is an initial need to understand patterns of behavior that characterize a problem. For example, no one seemed to know what socially isolated children are like, how they act, and what is different (compared to nonisolated children) about their behavior. From my strong background in physics as an undergraduate, I was convinced that this was bad science. The development of physics was based on some very accurate charting of the motions of stars and planets. Tycho Brahe's data is what made it possible for Johannes Kepler to deduce his principles of planetary motion, which then led Newton to develop a theory of gravitation that had something to explain. The first phase was good description, the second phase was the discovery of pattern or phenomena. Once one has a phenomenon, the next step is to ask why this happens, and this leads to theory construction. My heroes in graduate school had included ethologists like von Frisch, whose work on bees is a model for scientific investigation.

I expected that an initial stage of description would be a brief excursion that would lead back quickly to my main interest in understanding process, which I believed could only come from intervention. I gradually reversed my ideas about this. I found that little was ever learned by intervention research because there was an enormous confusion between intervention for the purpose of understanding and intervention for the purpose of helping. Interventions are always very complex and the search for the active ingredients of any change have been remarkably elusive. This would not be the case if one could do only a few, admittedly inadequate things in a clinical trial and then precisely assess the inadequacy of the trial; but this approach is unlikely in the current Zeitgeist of what is ethical in clinical psychological research. Never the twain between clinical intervention and research shall meet, is my sad conclusion. Although it was a very good idea, I have not seen the ''Boulder Model'' in clinical psychology work well. Also, the process of description turned out to be extremely interesting and absorbing. It led to great surprises, and it revealed a picture in every case that displayed a marvelous organization and order.

To discover this order it was necessary for me to return to my methodological interests and work on sequential and time-series analyses. Initially I had become interested in time-series analysis as a means for evaluating change in individuals, without the use of control groups, but employing the person's past behavior as a control. The problem turned out to be solveable, and it led to collaboration on a book with Gene Glass and Victor Willson. I did not think of applying time-series analysis to the study of interaction until I attended an important conference in Lake Wilderness, Washington, which was organized by Gene Sackett. It was at that 1976 conference that I met Roger Bakeman, who also became interested in the problems of sequential analysis. Sackett not only introduced the problem, but with his usual uncanny intuition, he outlined most of the solution. Fortunately these kinds of analyses are now quite feasible, even with personal computers, and scientists may someday think of using them. At the time of this writing the use of sequential analyses is still rare, although interest seems to be picking up.

At first the analysis of interactional data was really pure "dust bowl empiricism." I did not view this as bad. In fact, in graduate school at the University of Wisconsin's Regional Primate Laboratory, Harry Harlow had placed a bowl of dirt outside the library with a brass plaque that read "This is the Center of Midwest Dustbowl Empiricism." I thought that Dust Bowl Empiricism was precisely what was needed. Indeed, it was hard to know a-priori if a particular sequence would (in Sackett's terminology) "do work" as a useful descriptive variable. Better not to leave anything out.

When I say "empiricism" I do not mean to imply that one begins observing without any idea of what to look for. The categories that we began using for describing married couples' interaction was, of course, motivated by the ideas that seemed exciting at the time. These notions came primarily from the study of group conflict (Bales, for example), the study of interaction in classrooms, and the orientation to communication provided by the family systems theorists. Nonetheless, the process of developing useful observational coding systems was painstaking, but over the years there was progress in the use of the same observational category system within the context of a series of programmatic studies. The coding systems actually evolved. One learned from the micro-sequences to code at a more "macro" level. The codes began as microanalytic codes, but eventually it was possible to code for specific sequences (for examples of this see Gottman, 1983; and Gottman & Parker, 1986). I still think that this is The Way to develop macro codes, from the micro. Without this painstaking step you never really know what you are measuring. This is the dilemma that besets attachment research, in my view, and also the Type A/B personality research in cardiovascular disease. Something important is being measured in each field, but what is it? Neither field will know without getting reliability of the precise behaviors that they purport to assess.

What was I searching for? I was firmly convinced after a while that it was possible to discover laws of close relationships that had cross-cultural universality and that held for all time as characteristic of the human species. That's what I am trying to discover. I think that close relationships follow lawful patterns. I was not always convinced of this. What convinced me was replication of results. The second study we did on marriage, with an entirely different sample and different interaction tasks (but with the same observational coding system) gave us results discriminating satisfied from dissatisfied couples that differed from the first study only in the second decimal place. Since then many laboratories have done research on the same question and obtained essentially the same results (see Gottman & Levenson, 1986).

Becoming a Developmental Psychologist

The research on children's friendship led me to try to become a "real" developmental psychologist. By this I mean a psychologist who is truly interested in transformation and change. I needed help and guidance in this growth and there are very few people who knew how to think that way. I was again fortunate to have as a very close friend a superb theoretical thinker in the area of development, Ross Parke. The process of understanding how Ross thought about development and being able to apply this thinking to my own data took many years. It was an extremely pleasant process and many of the peak moments took place by the side of the University of Illinois swimming pool in what we called our "poolside chats." The fruits of this learning are in my book called "Conversations of Friends."

In the data on children's most intimate conversations with their best friends one could see what General Systems theorists called "second-order change." Here one could see the *reorganization* of social processes in the service of a particular task of development. It was a really beautiful pattern, and at each age group one could gain an appreciation of each phase of development and its beauty (see Gottman & Parker, 1986). In the conversations that best friends have at various ages one can ask where the energy and affect is, that is, what the children are most preoccupied with. What emerges from asking this question is a set of concerns the children have at each of three developmental periods that I have studied so far. From these concerns one can ask how the specific social processes I chose to study are organized to serve the pursuit of the concerns. A very interesting pattern emerges in answering these questions.

Becoming an Emotion Researcher

Inexorably all of my data led in one direction. *What mattered was emotion,* emotional communication, emotional responsiveness or emotional withdrawal, or emotional regulation. Usually the result was that it was particularly *negative* emotions (anger, fear, sadness, contempt) that were doing the work discriminating unhappily married from happily married couples. I am convinced that this is a real effect because it seems that marriages need to be very rich sources of positive events for most people to find them even tolerable. Happy marriages are extremely positive. This suggests that the negative strongly outweighs the positive in marriages. I think that this is a phenomenon worth understanding. In fact, Levenson and I have a hypothesis about gender differences that tries to explain this phenomenon. The hypothesis is that it takes males longer than females to recover from autonomic arousal. The hypothesis is interesting because it organizes all the results that I know of about gender differences in marital interaction. For example, in unhappy marriages wives complain that their husbands are too emotionally withdrawn while men complain that their wives are too engaging of conflict. For detail on this hypothesis, see Gottman and Levenson (1988).

However, I am also convinced that we have not studied positive affective events very well. Once these are understood, we will understand the dynamics of intimacy and attachment in close relationships. Nonetheless, it is my reading of the research that all the consistencies pointed toward affect as central.

In terms of identifying consistent patterns, the first 10 years of observational research on marriage have been quite encouraging. At the 1983 meeting of the Association for the Advancement of Behavior Therapy those of us who do observational research with couples met with an awareness that laboratories in California (G. Margolin), Oregon (R. Weiss; H. Hops), Washington (N. Jacobson), New Jersey (S. Ting-Toomey), Massachusetts (H. Raush), Washington, D.C. (C. Notarius), Colorado (H. Markman), Texas (J. Vincent), Holland (C. Schaap), Germany (K. Halweg, D. Revenstorf), and Australia (P. Noller) were observing similar differences between satisfied and dissatisfied couples. This was so despite wide variations in interactional tasks, recruitment procedures, ways of grouping couples and defining marital distress, and observational coding systems (for a review of the specific findings from these laboratories see Gottman, 1979; Schaap, 1982).

Three patterns can be identified as the most consistent results across laboratories. First, there is more negative affect in dissatisfied couples than in satisfied couples. Findings concerning positive affect are much less consistent. Second, there is greater reciprocity of negative affect in dissatisfied couples than in satisfied couples. This means that sequential analyses of the stream of behavior reveal that if one spouse expresses negative affect, the other spouse is more likely than baserate to respond with negative affect in a dissatisfied marriage than in a satisfied one. Third, the interactions of dissatisfied couples show a higher degree of structure, i.e., more predictability of one spouse's behaviors from those of the other, and less statistical independence than is found in the interactions of satisfied couples (see Gottman, 1979, for a review of evidence for greater temporal predictability in the interactions of dissatisfied couples). Across laboratories these patterns account for about 30% of the variance in marital satisfaction, which is greater than that found in the sociological studies using questionnaires. Further, the observational studies do not suffer from the problem of common method variance that has plagued the questionnaire studies. I actually think that if researchers use detailed coding schemes and sequential analytic techniques there would be consistency on the importance of specific sequences (such as the midreading to disagreement sequence) I identified in my 1979 book on marital interaction. Unfortunately, most studies with detailed coding schemes like the Marital Interaction Coding Scheme (MICS) eventually collapse codes into only a few for analysis, and they usually avoid sequential patterns. I hope that this is now changing. Robert Weiss provides a service of coding people's marital interaction tapes with the MICS and he provides them with first-order Markov matrices if they so desire. I hope more people will ask for this output.

Just think of the accomplishments of careful observational research! Originally the very idea that one would observe consistent patterns in the study of interacting systems like families when it had not been possible in the study of individuals seemed totally absurd. Some writers argued that if it took N variables to describe an individual, it would take at least $N \times N$ variables to describe a marriage. But they were wrong. To be sure the task was not easy. The first 20 years of research on families from the General Systems Theory perspective failed to empirically find consistent patterns that discriminated clinical from nonclinical families. Not a single hypothesis originally proposed has held, nor have any new ones emerged to take the place of the failed old ones. In contrast, the observational work on marriage has been incredibly productive from a scientific standpoint. I think this is so because we have learned how to measure things better (I refer here to our three Macbeth witches of Meaning, Reliability, and Validity) and we have learned how and what to observe. I should mention that it is remarkable how much consistency observational research on marriage has found. Across laboratories, with different subject selection procedures, different tasks, different observational coding systems, across regions within the U.S.A. and cross-nationally, similar patterns have emerged. Almost all of that consistency can be understood in terms of emotional behavior.

In 1979 I published a book on marital interaction that summarized a series of studies that I had done with several graduate students (primarily Howard Markman and Cliff Notarius) and I sent a copy of this book to Paul Ekman. He responded positively to the book, but he argued with me about the observation of emotion. I visited his laboratory in May, 1980 and he and I and Wallace Friesen went over two videotapes that I had coded and analyzed. They would occasionally stop the tape and replay a moment in slow motion. I saw very little of what they did on my tapes. Even though I considered myself to be a sensitive observer, I really had to admit that I did not know how to read faces. So I learned how to code with the Facial Action Coding System (FACS). Every student in my lab must learn to FACS code. I do not agree with Ekman about how to code emotion in interaction. I remain convinced that emotional communication needs to be coded in a manner far more complex than the FACS suggests. While we need to know which specific acts go into our judgments about emotional communication (the micro to macro issue again), it seems clear to me that emotion is communicated in conversational interaction by a gestalt of cues that include verbal and nonverbal channels of information, organized in nonadditive ways. This means that, for example, you cannot electronically filter out the words and hope to code emotion just in the voice. Which words are stressed, to take only one paralinguistic cue, can change the entire meaning of a sentence, and without even knowing the words, there is not a chance of being able to code emotion; this is an example of how what is considered state of the art in the study of emotion may be misleading (for more discussion of this point, see Gottman & Levenson, 1986). There needs to be a continual dialectic between detailed observational systems and ones that have a more distal perspective.

The scientific study of marriage was essentially the exclusive province of sociologists until about 1973, when psychologists began employing observational methods to systematically study marital interaction. The sociological tradition, initiated by Terman and colleagues (Terman, Buttenweiser, Ferguson, Johnson, & Wilson, 1938), had never employed observational techniques, choosing rather to utilize subjects' self-reports. What emerged from this sociological research were a number of good self-report measures of marital satisfaction.

Although sociologists rarely directly studied couples engaged in the process of making decisions and reaching agreements, an emergent theme in their research was the importance of consensual processes in marriage. Variables that tapped consensual dimensions of marriage consistently accounted for variation in marital satisfaction. For example, a demographic variable such as income might be unrelated to marital satisfaction, but the perception of the adequacy of the income would be related to marital satisfaction. What seemed to matter was precisely how couples managed the processes or inevitable disagreements that arise in close relationships. The sociological tradition was of little help in understanding these processes, and, in fact, this tradition appears to be relatively uninterested in questions of interactive processes in marriages. Nonetheless, despite all the problems of common method variance and multicollinearity that plagued this kind of questionnaire-based research, it provided some good clues as to where to look to find behavioral differences between satisfied and dissatisfied marriages. Since items that required spousal consensus were the best predictors of marital satisfaction, it suggested that the first place to look for differences in observable behavior would be when couples were attempting to reach consensus and agreement. Thus, when psychologists began to study marriage, processes of conflict resolution came in for careful scrutiny. So when I initially began studying couples, I videotaped them discussing high- and low-conflict tasks. We were able to refine these procedures across studies so that we now know how to construct situations that sample conflictual interaction.

From the beginning I was fascinated by the Thibaut and Kelley notions of exchange theory, which I took to be a *perceptual theory*. They stressed the payoffs and costs of behaviors exchanged in interaction, and I took this to mean perceived payoffs and costs. This was a departure from the mainstream of social psychology in which experimenters were actually manipulating costs and payoffs (e.g., with Prisoner's Dilemma games); a few studies of families with the externally manipulated games found no differences between distressed and nondistressed families, so it had to be the wrong track. Instead, we built a "talk-table" in which we had people rate the "intent" of the messages they sent and the "impact" of messages received during interaction. This turned out to be a very profitable way of operationalizing Thibaut and Kelley's ideas. We now use the rating dial with a video recall procedure and it also gives us very valuable information about people's perceptions of their interaction. I am convinced that we must integrate thought and behavior in any complete model of relationships.

It is interesting to note that, even in its early heyday, observational methodology in psychology included the study of marriage. Barker's (1963) classic book, *The stream of behavior* included a chapter by Soskin and John, which analyzed the interaction of a married couple on vacation. The couple wore backpacks with wireless transmitters that broadcast their every word (16-hours a day) to a receiving station. Although these researchers knew very little about what to examine in marital interaction, the study is a fascinating piece of scientific history. By 1973, a body of observational research on marriage began appearing in print. The first observational systems were very crude, particularly in their assessment of nonverbal behavior and emotion. In the ensuing decade, we have made considerable progress in making these kinds of assessments, and in developing methods for generating samples of marital interaction to observe. Previously I mentioned that the early attempts at observational description were quite crude, particularly in the extremely central area of describing emotion. This is understandable when we consider that it is only in the past 6 years that we have had the basic tools for such essential tasks as measuring the anatomical basis of emotion facial expressions (Ekman & Friesen, 1978). With tools such as the FACS, we can now describe what faces do, and this is a first step. It is my continuing belief that progress will be made by precision in measurement.

The major research question in the early observational studies of marriage was the same question posed by Terman, namely, how are satisfied and dissatisfied marriages fundamentally different? There were serious problems in the way this question was pursued, but the fact that systematic observation was employed at all turned out to be a major contribution of psychologists in the historical development of marriage research.

To deal with the problem of task selection, I empirically derived two tasks that produce conflict in both satisfied and dissatisfied couples. One task was derived by interviewing 60 couples and identifying those situations that induced conflict in both kinds of couples (e.g., issues concerning in-laws, sex, and money). This led to a set of "generic" conflicts that could be improvised or role played by both satisfied and dissatisfied couples. The second task was more "marriage specific." Here, each couple completed a problem inventory on which they rated the severity and duration of a number of problem areas in their marriage. The couple was then interviewed to sharpen and focus the conflict area (the "play-by-play" interview; Gottman, 1979). After preparing the subjects by using the problem inventory and the play-by-play interview to isolate an existing area of disagreement, the couple was asked to try to come to a resolution of this disagreement. Although this procedure was not always successful, in most couples it produced comparable samples of conflict resolution behavior that could be examined for specific differences in the way satisfied and dissatisfied couples resolve conflict.

For the past 9 years we have been using a third task in which couples talk about the events of their day after having been apart for at least 8 hours. This task is not viewed as a conflict resolution task (although it does sometimes induce conflict in dissatisfied couples), but provides a format in which other kinds of interactive behaviors can be studied in both satisfied and dissatisfied couples (e.g., information exchange, planning, empathic listening, support). The interactions of both kinds of couples seem quite natural on this task.

Collaboration with Levenson

In 1979 Robert Levenson and I began a collaboration on the study of emotion in marital interaction. I must admit that the basis of this collaboration was our friendship, the pleasure and joy that the two of us had in working together. This has always been the basis of what has become a long and satisfying collaboration. Fortunately, both of us had become interested in emotion, and Bob was interested in two lines of research, one that was basic emotion research, and one that studied how emotion works in social interaction. So, we designed a laboratory that collected synchronized physiological, self-report, and interactional (videotape) information. All of this was designed to focus on the study of emotion within the context of interaction. I will refer to our initial study briefly because it illustrates a turning point in my own research.

In 1983, we completed a longitudinal follow-up study of the 30 couples who had participated in the 1980 study, successfully locating 21 of these couples and having them complete questionnaires concerning their current levels of marital satisfaction. We then computed a simple change score that indicated the amount and direction of change in marital satisfaction that had occurred between 1980 and 1983. Using partial correlations (to control for initial levels of marital satisfaction), we determined which of the affective and physiological variables measured in 1980 were predictive of changes in marital satisfaction that had occurred during the ensuing 3 years. Two strong findings emerged. First, negative affect reciprocity was a strong predictor of change in relationship satisfaction. And second, physiological arousal (in all measures) was highly predictive of declines in levels of marital satisfaction. The sizes of these correlations were quite encouraging; for example, the correlation between the husband's heart rate during the conflict discussion and decline in marital satisfaction was .92.

Becoming a Psychophysiologist

What Levenson and I had discovered in our follow-up study was that we could account for most of the variance in change in marital satisfaction over 3 years with one pattern: The more autonomically aroused couples were in 1980, the more their marriages deteriorated over a 3-year period; also the more quiescent in 1980, the more their marriages *improved* over a 3-year period. Couples changed enormously over a 3-year period in our data, and we could account for most of the changes with one simple statement.

Why should this be the case? The answer lay in understanding the interface between social and biological processes. Since 1983 I have been educating myself in physiology, including endocrinology and immunology. Results are now emerging that suggest that the endocrine and immune systems are also connected to emotional processes in predictable ways. Data we obtained from our study of the ANS, in addition to being a source of dependent variables, can also be useful theoretically. We have recently theorized (Gottman & Levenson, in press) that many commonly noted sex differences in relationships can be derived from a hypothesis about sex differences in ANS reactivity. This admittedly controversial hypothesis is that males show a larger ANS response to stress, respond more readily, and recover more slowly than females. Our review of the literature on sex differences in physiological responses to stress provided some support for this hypothesis. If this sex difference is true, and if chronic ANS activation is considered to be harmful, unpleasant, and undesirable, then men might be more inclined than women to avoid situations that would be associated with repeated high levels of ANS activation. Taking this argument a step further, if intense negative affect is seen as activating high levels of ANS activation (especially in men), then men may try to manage the level of negative affect they are exposed to. They may try to create a rational as opposed to an emotional climate in relationships (which can be a major source of repeated high level negative emotions and of concomitant high levels of ANS activation); they may become more conciliatory and less conflict-engaging than females; and they may try to terminate negative affect encounters by withdrawing. In this new paper, we present instances from the marriage research literature that show that each of these behavioral characteristics has been ascribed to men. In direct contrast, women in this literature have been described as being less conciliatory, more conflict-engaging, and less likely to withdraw from negative affect.

I must admit that at first I had no intention of learning psychophysiology. I was motivated by a major goal in my life, avoiding humiliation. I gave a talk once on my work with Bob, and was asked questions about physiology that I could not answer. I gave the usual answer that Bob took care of this aspect of our work, but the questioner would not let me off the hook until he had tried to make me look the fool. After that talk I asked Bob to give me a lecture about our measures. Fortunately for me, Bob is a gifted teacher, and I really enjoyed learning about psychophysiology. Eventually I began reading introductory books. I also had a wonderful colleague at Illinois, Steve Porges, and he too guided me in my learning. Porges' theorizing has become very important in my current work on emotional development and emotional regulation in young children.

Brief Aside: The Autonomic Nervous System

In this section I briefly review a few facts about the autonomic nervous system that have been useful in our research.

Anatomy.   Peripheral physiological measures are selected to provide various information about the autonomic nervous system (ANS), which has two anatomically and functionally distinct subsystems, the parasympathetic branch (PNS) and the sympathetic branch (SNS). Both subsystems are characterized by a two-neuron linkage from the brain or spinal cord. The first preganglionic neuron is joined to a second neuron that innervates the target organ. In the SNS the neural fibers leave the spinal cord from the chest and saddle regions (thoracocolumbar) and in the PNS the fibers leave the spinal cord from the brain stem and tail regions (craniosacral). In the SNS the two-neuron chain is short preganaglioic and long postganglionic, whereas in the PNS the anatomy is reversed, long fibers from the spinal cord to the vicinity of the target organ, and then short fibers into the target organ. In the SNS the short preganglionic fibers go from the spinal cord to a chain (called the sympathetic ganglia) that runs alongside the spinal cord. One implication of these different anatomical features is that there is lots of potential for the mixing of sympathetic ganglia and possibly more "cross talk," which implies that the SNS is capable of diffuse action. For the PNS, on the other hand, the anatomy appears to be designed for little mixing and thus fairly specific action.

While there are no main SNS nerves due to the amount of SNS mixing, there are two main nerves of the PNS and the organs it serves. The first is the *vagus nerve* (Xth cranial nerve), which serves the heart, bronchioles of the lung, stomach, small intestine, liver, pancreas, and the large intestine. The second is the pelvic (Sacral nerves 2, 3, and 4), which serves the colon, kidney, bladder, the sex organs, and the exterior genitalia. PNS fibers are also found in the following cranial nerves: oculomotor (III), facial (VII), and glossopharyngeal IX).

Chemistry.   The stimulation chemistry of the two branches of the ANS are also different. Preganglionic fibers in both systems stimulate postganglionic targets using *acetylcholine* (ACh) released at the synapse. However, in the SNS the primary neurotransmitter from postganglioic fibers to target organs is *norepinephrine* (NE), whereas in the PNS it is *acetylcholine*. Two exceptions are: (1) the SNS innervation of the adrenal medulla, which is stimulated by SNS *pre*ganglionic fibers and hence ACh and, (2) the sweat glands, which are stimulated by SNS postganglioic fibers, but the neurotransmitter is ACh. Hence, sweat gland activity, which in the emotionally responsive *eccrine* glands is still SNS innervated has a different stimulation chemistry that, for example, SNS innervation of the heart.

Function.   The two branches of the ANS usually act in reciprocal and contrasting fashion throughout the body. However, there are a few well-established gross functional differences that can be described, albeit with some qualifications:

1. The SNS is a fight/flight system and it acts in an energy-expending or *catabolic* fashion, while the PNS acts in an energy conserving, or *anabolic* fashion. For example, while the SNS is responsible for converting the carbohydrate glycogen stored in the liver to glucose for energy, the PNS is responsible for the conversion of glucose to glycogen.

2. The SNS generally acts *diffusely,* while the action of the PNS is usually *specific.*

3. The SNS has a slow onset of the order of 2 seconds, while the PNS has a more rapid onset, of the order of 0.5 seconds.

4. The action of the SNS is longer lasting than the action of the PNS because NE is not degraded as readily by body tissue, whereas ACh is. The time for recovery of some effects of the SNS (for example on left ventricle contractility, see Berne & Levy, 1981) can be long, for example of the order of 2 to 3 minutes.

5. In the cardiovascular system the main effect of the PNS is on heart rate, while the main effect of the SNS is on myocardial contractility (actually both branches affect both aspects of cardiac function; see, for example, Levy, 1983).

These general contrasts have to be qualified in some major ways. First, the effects of the two branches of the ANS are usually reciprocal, so that, for example, it is tricky to tell whether a heart rate increase resulted from less PNS activity or more SNS activity. This problem holds throughout. Second, the SNS is quite capable of *specific* functioning. For example, in the human sexual response there is a temporal orchestration of PNS and SNS responding. The excitement phases that regulate the engorgement and lubrication of sexual tissue are usually controlled by the PNS; SNS activation during these phases of the sexual response will result in sexual dysfunction. However, orgasm and ejaculation are regulated by the SNS. It is as if the SNS were the cymbalist who came in at the conductor's signal only at the crescendo and in very specific fashion. Another example concerns the functioning of the PNS and SNS during pure emotions (Ekman, Levenson, & Friesen, 1983). Nonetheless, these general and gross contrasts are useful. Notions of *arousal* are quite old in psychophysiology and their history is quite confused, but on the basis of some new results it seems to be the case that the ANS is capable of specific or diffuse activation. In our own work this notion of diffuse physiological arousal is the one that seems most useful; we think that it is an aversive state that is usually a result of blends of negative affects.

Defining a New Field: Family Psychophysiology

In the past several years my student Lynn Fainsilber and I have begun to bring the research on marriage and the research on peer relationships together in a single series of studies, in a laboratory at the University of Washington that we call the "Family Psychophysiology Laboratory." In this work we have been focusing on the transfer of marital discord to the child and its effect on children when they are in a stage of learning the skills of emotional regulation. We are particularly interested in this research in the effects on the child's relationships with a best friend.

New Directions: The Apartment Laboratory

I am currently designing a laboratory that is an apartment in which families and couples will be able to live and carry on many of the tasks of everyday life, but under the scrutiny of camera and biotelemetered physiology. In this context it may be possible to collect moments of major importance to couples and families that we ordinarily do not observe in the laboratory. One of these kinds of moments we call "escape conditioning moments," and they are good theoretical candidates for what may be considered natural change moments in relationships.

Escape Conditioning Model. A phenomenon Levenson and I sought to explain is the greater rigidity, predictability, and stereotypy of behavior in dissatisfied marriages as compared to satisfied marriages. In our efforts to explain this phenomenon we have developed an *escape conditioning model* of marriages, which links the reduction of physiological arousal with the reinforcement of behavior sequences. This model has turned out to be two-edged. It may be able to explain both how marriages become more *and* less satisfying. We are examining "escape moments" during marital interaction, which are defined as occurring when both spouses make the transition from high levels of ANS arousal ("upset") to low levels of ANS arousal ("calm"). We expect that the behavior patterns that accompany these escape moments will be reinforced and increase both in unconditional probability and in conditional probability (i.e., given ANS arousal).

The escape conditioning model can be applied to the analysis of any relationship, and its theoretical contributions may be broad. For example, the escape conditioning model contributes to Patterson's (1982) negative reinforcement theory of coercive families by putting the chain of reinforcement in people's bodies. This removes an inherent circularity in the Patterson model pointed out by

Knutson's (1982) critique. Knutson noted that negative reinforcement *must* occur as soon as aversive interactions terminate; because these negative interactions do not continue indefinitely, he argued, negative reinforcement always occurs. The escape conditioning model eliminates this inherent circularity in negative reinforcement as an explanatory mechanism for the establishment of a particular (coercive) pattern. Escape only occurs if the diffuse physiological arousal decreases in the parent who starts the coercive chain. The escape conditioning model also would suggest that what changes is the conditional probability of coercion, given ANS arousal. This fits nicely with Patterson's idea in his 1982 book.

To return to the question of why dissatisfied marriages show greater stereotypy of behavior, it seems likely that in unhappy marriages, there will be many instances of upset over unresolved issues, and thus there will be many conditioning trials over which to strengthen the association that links a specific kind of upset with a specific behavior that serves to reduce that upset. In satisfied marriages, there will be fewer moments of upset, and thus fewer conditioning trials to establish rigid response patterns.

The escape conditioning model can also be used as a model for how relationships could improve over time. What makes people feel better and restores calm could just as easily be an empathic, loving response as the anger response seen in the previous example. Then, according to the model, this empathic, loving response should become more likely in the couple's repertoire as the response to upset. In nondistressed couples this happens about 70% of the time, mostly with neutral affect and with the positive affects being affection and humor. this happens even in the context of upset. I suspect that what accompanies this process of soothing are self-statements that reaffirm the love and empathy that underlies the relationship. Whatever the mechanisms of this process of soothing, it is likely that these are natural change moments in relationships. We do not know if this is what happens in couples whose marital satisfaction increases over time, but we are investigating this possibility.

ACKNOWLEDGMENT

This research was supported by NIMH grant MH29910 and NIMH Research Scientist Development Award K2-00257 to the author.

REFERENCES

Berne, R. M., & Levy, M. N. (1981). *Cardiovascular physiology*. St. Louis: C. V. Mosby.
Ekman, P., & Friesen, W. V. (1978). *Facial Action Coding System*. Palo Alto, CA: Consulting Psychologist Press.

Ekman, P., Levenson, R. W., & Friesen, W. V. (1983). Autonomic nervous system activity distinguishes among emotions. *Science, 221,* 1208–1210.

Gottman, J. M. (1979). *Marital interaction: Experimental investigation.* New York: Academic Press.

Gottman, J. (1983). *How children become friends, Monographs of the society for Research in Child Development,* Serial #201, Vol. 48 #2.

Gottman, J. M., & Levenson, R. W. (1986). Assessing the role of emotion in marriage. *Behavioral Assessment, 8,* 31–48.

Gottman, J. M., & Levenson, R. W. (1988). The social psychophysiology of marriage. In P. Noller & M. A. Fitzpatrick (Eds.), *Perspectives on marital interaction.* Philadelphia: Multilingual Matters, LTD.

Gottman, J., & Parker, J. (Eds.). (1986). *Conversations of friends: Speculations on affective development.* New York: Cambridge University Press.

Knutson, J. (1982). *Perspectives on Chapter 7.* In G. Patterson, *Coercive family process.* Eugene, OR: Castalia Press.

Levy, M. N. (1983). Hunting the wild vagus. *The Physiologist, 26,* 115–118.

Patterson, G. R. (1982). *Coercive family process.* Eugene, OR: Castalia Press.

Schaap, C. (1982). *Communication and adjustment in marriage.* The Netherlands: Swets & Feitlinger.

Terman, L. M., Buttenweiser, P., Ferguson, L. W., Johnson, W. B., & Wilson, D. P. (1938). *Psychological factors in marital happiness.* New York: McGraw Hill.

9 Cross-Cultural Collaboration in Studies of Family Effects on School Achievement

Robert D. Hess
Stanford University

Hiroshi Azuma
Shirayuri College, Japan

METHODOLOGICAL PROBLEMS IN CROSS-CULTURAL STUDIES OF FAMILIES

In this chapter we describe our experience in a longitudinal study of family influence on preschoolers' readiness for school and on their later achievement. This account is necessarily (and by invitation) autobiographical. Because it consists of personal recollection of events, we include some of the behind-the-scenes episodes of the study—the circumstances that shape outcomes of research projects but are usually omitted from published reports. Every project has such a history, of course, but cross-cultural studies are especially vulnerable to unexpected events and unintended circumstances.

We worked with mothers and their 4-year-old preschool children—58 families from Japan and 67 from the U.S. Data were gathered in both countries when the children were 4, 5, and 6 years-of-age and at a follow-up study when children in Japan were 11 (grade 5) and when they were age 12 (grade 6) in the U.S. Mothers were interviewed, children were given a variety of techniques to elicit performance relevant to performance in school. At the first round of the study, mothers and children worked together on three separate tasks—an unstructured situation, a block-sorting problem, and a referential communication game. At the follow-up period, mothers and children were interviewed on their beliefs about the reasons why children did well or did not do well in school, particularly in mathematics. At this time, children were administered tests of skill in mathematics.

Cross-national studies of family effects on children's behavior are, of course, ventures into two overlapping methodological quagmires. It is not our purpose in this chapter to discuss formal methodological problems in cross-cultural or family research. These are described in many other sources. However, the major issues deserve mention.

In family studies, ethical considerations preclude experimental manipulations and attempts to create experimental conditions are often so contrived as to be suspect. It is difficult to get valid data that represent the full range of significant events in the family's daily life. For some data, we must rely on the biased technique of self-report. Family interaction changes as children pass through their developmental phases so that even a true picture may represent a transitional stage. Each family develops its own culture, and routine activities carry private, unique meanings of which the researcher is often unaware. Unusual financial support and time are required to explore adequately the nuances of family interaction.

Cultural comparisons face equally serious methodological problems. Research techniques that require internal frames of reference are suspect because they draw on disparate experiences—"very important" of "often" is not likely to mean the same thing to Japanese and American mothers. Translation of instruments is an obvious problem, especially in languages as different as Japanese and English, and even exact translation does not always produce psychologically equivalent instruments. Sometimes attaining cultural equivalence is impossible—the concepts or behavior in one of the two countries are not found in the other.

Family roles and interaction are obviously dissimilar. Matching research groups across countries is often impossible: The experience of a college education or the occupation of an office manager are clearly not similar in Japan and the U.S. Research groups in detailed studies of family interaction are usually too small to represent a culture or country in a statistical sense.

Nonetheless, studies of diverse cultures offer a certain appeal if only because of the possibility that new insights may come from examining the unknown and unfamiliar. Research on family influences is compelling because of the primacy and intensity of the effects that families have upon their members. Despite changes in composition of families and roles of parents (especially in the U.S.), families continue to be a major influence on the behavior of children, including performance in school, and this influence needs to be more completely understood. Families represent the culture to the child and so are particularly rich environments in which to examine cultural differences.

Cultural contrasts offer unusual opportunities for reexamination of familiar problems and assumptions. They offer opportunities for replication in differing social contexts. They may provide a wider range of parental behavior on variables of interest. The data reveal behavior and relationships not present in one's own country and so require reconceptualization of once-accepted findings from other studies. Staff members from each country meet colleagues that they may work with later in their careers. There is, perhaps, a heightened sense of caution in subsequent research.

In describing our work in this study, we draw from several themes:

1. the importance of equal status of researchers from the two countries;
2. the influence of culture on the research behavior of the two staffs;
3. the effort to achieve cultural and psychological equivalence in the research plan; and
4. the insights gained from unexpected findings and even from methodological difficulties encountered in the study.

HOW THINGS GOT STARTED: THE ORIGINS OF THE STUDY

The occasion that led to collaboration was a conference organized to examine research dealing with family effects on children's school achievement. This meeting was sponsored and funded by the Social Science Research Council and convened at the Center for Advanced Study in Behavioral Sciences at Stanford, California in 1971. Although held in the U.S., it was the Japanese participants who proposed the conference and obtained funding for participants from Japan from the Japan Society for the Promotion of Science. They also nominated participants from the U.S. Hiroshi Azuma from the University of Tokyo headed the Japanese group. Robert Hess, who had recently moved from the University of Chicago to Stanford University, was invited to chair the delegation from the U.S.

Both Azuma and Hess had reasons to be interested in cross-national research. Azuma came to the conference with a perspective on cross-national research gained during his stay as a graduate student at the University of Illinois. Hess had been involved in research on cultural influences on children's performance on intelligence tests and on ethnic and national differences in school-relevant skills.

The prospect of examining cultural contrasts between Japan and the U.S. was particularly appealing. Both countries were industrialized societies that valued achievement and had instituted universal compulsory schooling but which differed sharply in language, family patterns, sex roles, and religion. These circumstances moved the focus to analysis of family processes, and away from attempts to explain differences in levels of achievement in school.

A conference makes it easy for colleagues to discuss their research interests and activities, particularly when the collaborative work is on the agenda. In the discussion, questions arose about several issues in both cultural and family influences on children's performance in school. The exchange about a topic that was receiving attention at the time—Basil Bernstein's views about the consequences of using restricted and elaborated linguistic codes—was especially significant. The Japanese group questioned the applicability of these concepts to

Japanese society. Bernstein's writings described relationships between school-relevant behavior and the linguistic modes observed in certain social contexts, including informal social interaction and ritualistic behavior. The tendency to use restricted codes seemed to be related to educational and socioeconomic background.

Although Bernstein's ideas seemed to be relevant to some studies of family influences on school-relevant behavior in families from different social backgrounds, the Japanese were not convinced that Bernstein's theories applied to Japanese society. Their arguments ran something like this: In Bernstein's definition of restricted codes, the speaker's (e.g., mother's) use of some restricted codes—contextbound, implicit, indirect, and unindividualized ritualistic approaches—are pooled with her use of other types of restricted codes—authoritarian, inhibiting, and harsh forms. A distinction was not made between these two types of restricted speech or between the purpose and intent of such linguistic forms. In Bernstein's reports of speech in Britain and in the U.S., such restricted codes are predominant in families with less than average education.[1] The Japanese members of the conference took the view that these separate types of restricted code were not usually found together in the same way in Japanese society. Indeed, socialization practices in sophisticated families in Japan include suppressing excessive explicitness and encouraging moderate vagueness of verbal expression. Admittedly, this happens in many cultures to some extent, but the sense of Bernstein's description was to define such linguistic forms as typical of socioeconomically disadvantaged groups. This, in the eyes of the Japanese, was a distinctly Western view. To be sure, ritualism is often a sign of modest respect for social custom and reinforces confidence in the stability of social forms. Again, this is true in any culture, but the threshold is different in Japan, where individual expressiveness is highly suppressed in formal occasions. To wrap one's individuality almost completely under the routine of ritualistic expression is often appreciated as a sign of self control among the well-educated class.

Characteristics of speech that may seem to fit the definition of "restricted code" thus have very different functions in Japan. On the other hand, some other characteristics of this code, such as harsh authoritarianism and disregard for the feelings of the child, are seen as clearly inappropriate, unless the demands of the situation are urgent. The two different behavioral characteristics of mothers, which tend to be associated in the West, are split into at least two relatively independent clusters in Japanese culture.

Curiously, this issue, which took such a prominent place in early conversations about what might be learned from a joint study, did not recur often during the course of the study. Bernstein's concepts soon seemed so clearly inappropri-

---

[1]Bernstein's writings stimulated considerable discussions and restatements of his position. We do not attempt here to review the issues but to recall the context of our discussions.

ate as to rob the issue of intellectual interest, although they often served a useful heuristic purpose in conversations about the findings. The issue of restricted linguistic codes served more as a catalyst for initiating the study than a basis for planning and analysis.

The Japanese also wanted to examine more general aspects of family influences on children's academic achievement. They were interested in getting more experience with research procedures that were popular in the social sciences in the United States. The Japanese have followed developments in psychology in the U.S., especially in the post World War II years. The APA has a large membership in Japan, and students from Japan often elect to do graduate work at universities in the United States.

The influences that brought the two groups together were thus a combination of professional interests, national history, and personal experience of the participants. These factors gave the collaboration a focus for the people responsible for the studies within each country.

THE CRUCIAL ROLE OF COLLABORATION IN CROSS-CULTURAL STUDIES

Collaboration as Separate and Equal Studies

Following the conference, Azuma and Hess each sought funds to support a study of family influences on school readiness. The Japan Society provided funds for the study in Japan; the Spencer Foundation supported the project in the U.S., under sponsorship of the Social Sciences Research Council. A follow-up study was also separately funded, by the National Science Foundation in the U.S. and the Japanese Science Foundation in Japan. Funds for the initial phase of the project were awarded in 1972.

It was decided at the outset to conduct the project on a fully collaborative basis: two studies to be administered as parallel but separate investigations. The conceptual frame, although loosely defined, was similar, and instruments were to be as nearly identical as possible. Similar criteria guided selection of the sample, including the range of family SES. The authority within each country lay in the hands of the director of that study; commitment to the concept of collaboration created the impetus for maintaining comparable plans.

This was not a typical cross-cultural administrative format. More often, the plan and funding of a study are the responsibility of an investigator in one country who may then seek colleagues in the country or countries that are to participate. These studies can be productive, of course, and the cooperation among scholars from the different countries can be smooth and rewarding. It is obvious that both cultures should be represented in a cross-cultural research group that designs the study, selects and develops tools, collects, analyzes, and reports the results. In the prevailing modes of research, this is difficult unless the two groups are financially independent. Otherwise the party that finances the study and is accountable to the funding agency will have much stronger influence upon decision makings at various stages. This is not a matter of personality or of scientific imperialism of the members of one research group. It is the way we have been trained to conduct research—with firm direction to see that errors are minimized and that scientific procedures are followed. Thus, unless the concerned people are extremely sensitive and careful, a study can become monocultural in all phases except that the data are collected from two cultures.

On the other hand, a collaborative arrangement lacks the formal sanctions to prevent either of the directors of the separate studies from departing from the agreed-upon plan. The motivation to work in parallel and to follow similar procedures comes from the intrinsic rewards of collaboration, including the opportunity to learn from one another and the benefits of following a design that is more likely to gain respect from the professional community. However, these are powerful forces. Although such an organizational plan may appear to be administratively less efficient than the formal sanctions inherent in a single source of authority and funding, it may facilitate more joint contribution by participants in the study.

When two independent cultural groups cooperate as we did, coordination requires a remarkable amount of work. The need for communication creates a need for careful organization. In our case, it incurred significant expenditures of money and effort. Written correspondence alone fills file drawers in each of our offices. There were numerous telephone calls across the Pacific. There were seven formal conferences, four in the U.S. and three in Japan, plus several informal conferences that took place whenever one of Japanese members visited the U.S. for various reasons. We were able to keep close contact, in part, because we liked and respected each other and enjoyed our personal as well as our professional interaction. In spite of such closeness, cross-cultural collaboration differed from cooperation with colleagues in our own countries. It gave us new experiences, unfamiliar challenges, additional insights, and, admittedly, occasional frustrations.

Collaboration in a parallel project in which there is formal separation of the two studies puts at least two requirements on the staff and directors of project. The first is a genuine need for full and prompt communication between the staffs, including frequent checking with one another to identify questions or issues that deserve discussion. Second is a willingness to compromise or accommodate where there may be conflicting preferences in instruments, methods of datagathering, analysis, and scheduling. Sometimes the best compromise is to select one instrument from the recommendations of each staff and to follow more than one line of analysis.

We believe that collaboration in cross-cultural studies demands that some members of the research staff have experience in both cultures. In our case, the

Japanese team represented this experience to a greater extent than the U.S. did. Hiroshi Azuma completed his graduate work at the University of Illinois (Urbana) in educational psychology and was familiar with research methods used by psychologists in the United States. He lived with his family, including two small children, in Urbana for several years. These experiences not only gave him a command of English but a knowledge of American ways. Family experience brought him into close contact with other families, giving him a perspective of the interaction between parents and small children in the U.S. Two other researchers of the Japanese group spent a sabbatical year in the U.S.—Keiko Kashiwagi at the University of Wisconsin and Kazuo Miyake at Harvard University. The Japanese team thus offered considerable bicultural experience that was directly relevant to the project.

The multicultural resources of the U.S. team were bolstered early in the life of the study by the addition of two staff members (Cathy Lewis and Kay Sandberg) who spoke Japanese and were familiar with Japanese culture. From time to time, the U.S. team also used colleagues at the University to help describe and interpret some of the social and cultural contexts of the research activities and findings in Japan. As an additional resource, the Associate Director of the U.S. team, W. Patrick Dickson, spent an academic year in Japan, working directly with the Japanese team. This strengthened another point of communication between the two staffs and gave Dickson additional opportunity to gain information about Japanese schools and families.

We had an opportunity early in the project to develop the personal relationships that are essential for successful collaborative studies. The XX International Congress of Psychology was held in Tokyo in 1972. Staff members from both national teams attended and used the occasion to discuss plans.

Personal affiliation enables participants to see one another's cultures and professional perspectives through each others' eyes. Friendship encourages sensitivity to nuances of communication, to differences in perspective that may be difficult to express explicitly. Trust makes it easier to propose ideas, raise questions, and offer counter proposals. Since one of the hazards of cross-cultural research is the probability that important cultural differences will go unnoticed or that their significance will be underestimated, this aspect of collaborative research is exceedingly important at all stages of the study. It facilitates cooperation on instrument design, definition of coding categories, analysis, and interpretation and write-up of findings.

Staffing: Structure, Interaction, and Productivity

The first thing we had to learn was that interactive styles of the research groups are themselves products of culture even when the staffs are working within a shared view of what constitutes scientific investigation. Each side had to learn something about the thinking, working, and communicating style of the other team and how to adapt to it.

One of the first lessons for the American team was to understand the readiness of the Japanese group to accept suggestions made in face-to-face conferences. Participants from the U.S. were at times a little surprised at such immediate agreement. They discovered, however, that Japanese colleagues might make suggestions for changes after the conference was over. The Americans soon realized that some of this initial acceptance was a culturally based desire not to show disagreement or disapproval in public without time to consider the ideas carefully. It also reflected some caution in interpreting the nuances of English, as used by Americans.

The Americans came to recognize such agreement as a contribution to the discussion and a wish to be helpful rather than as concurrence with specific proposals. To the Japanese, the apparently clear and well-phrased assertions that Americans made sounded like well-considered, final decisions to which a refutation was impolite and inappropriate. It took the Japanese team some time to understand that presenting proposals in this way was an invitation for discussion.

During conference times, as team directors, we soon discovered the value of taking time to talk together leisurely, perhaps over dinner, reviewing decisions and interpreting to each other the events of the day.

Staffing and flow of work on a project express cultural styles of administrative structures and practices. In the U.S. group, the project was housed at a single university, directed by a principal investigator and staffed by graduate students and staff hired to perform specific tasks. For the most part, the staff was paid, either by salary or through research assistantships that included stipends and tuition. Typically, the work of graduate students on projects of this sort is part of their training; they join a study at a time when their skills are developing and gain in experience and skill as the work proceeds. After they have earned their doctoral degrees, they typically move on to positions as faculty members at another university, often at a distance from the site of the original project.

The longitudinal nature of the study thus required that staff members who graduated be replaced. In some instances, graduate students working in a central way on the later stages of the study were not part of the initial effort; indeed sometimes they were not yet in graduate school when the work began. Maintaining a sense of the history and purpose of the study became an important task. Maintaining computer files and office records involved significant technical problems. It was possible in the U.S. only because of good fortune in being able to attract graduate students with remarkable talents to take administrative responsibility for important components of data gathering, analysis and management— Pat Dickson, Gary Price, Susan Holloway, and Teresa McDevitt.

In the U.S., a research team typically consists of one or two faculty members paid by university salary or/and mature researchers who are paid from the project funds, one or two senior graduate assistants who receive a stipend from the project during the duration of funding, and several graduate students who are employed as part time assistants. When the period of funding is over, associates and assistants leave the project to take positions elsewhere. This is in line with the American style of employment where people move from employer to employer and from job to job.

An analogy, although exaggerated, may make the contrast clear. The structure of the typical American research group resembles that of an efficient combat team. The director is the final authority who may consult with his members and may even yield to them, but nevertheless is the decision maker. Most other members are bound by contract to work for his project. Under this structure, the research plan can be more clearly designated from the beginning and can be executed without lengthy negotiations. In the early stages, central control is an advantage.

On the other hand, there is a cost at the other end, especially for cross-national studies. If the work is genuinely collaborative, data analysis, interpretation and writeup will reveal topics that deserve to be followed up in more detail. The complexity of cultural contrasts becomes more apparent. At this point, the staff is experienced and informed and at a peak of productivity in managing and analyzing the data. If funds are exhausted, some of these exciting leads cannot be pursued. Indeed, there is often a loss of experienced staff before the project reaches the final stages of analysis and reporting. Commitments of staff initially made through salaries and research assistantships begin to erode when funds are exhausted, not because of lack of interest so much as the press of new commitments in new jobs. The constraints of funding are thus poorly suited to cross-national studies.

The Japanese study followed a very different pattern of cooperation and staffing. Several faculty members from different universities and governmental agencies were involved. Students who worked on the study were also in residence at different universities. There was a larger central staff responsible for the conduct of the project in Japan with a stability that came from the fact that many of the participating faculty and students did not depend on external funding.

In Japan, research funds usually do not provide for the employment of personnel. A research team typically consists of people employed by various institutions who agree to contribute some of their time to the project. This reflects a Japanese tradition that the employee should be loyal to a single employer and that the employer should in return look after the employee. Even now the salary system itself curbs employment mobility. It is rare and difficult to employ a researcher full time or part time even for a limited period. Only temporary student helpers are employed by the project on an hourly basis.

In response to such cultural patterns, the structure of the research team in Japan is often much looser, and the control of the director is necessarily weaker because the team members are not employees. Rather, they are colleagues who devote spare time to the project without financial compensation but because of their own research interests. It is understood that they will accommodate their interests to the common goal of the project, but it was also necessary for the project to accommodate its purpose to their somewhat diverse interests if they are to continue to be part of the team. Under these circumstances, the team tends to move slowly, perhaps somewhat unevenly, at the beginning, seeking to establish consensus within the group. This can be a long and painstaking process because good researchers tend to be independent and uncompromising. Once some significant agreement as to purpose and roles has been reached, however, they are committed to work on the study. The end of funding does not mean the end of the project. Members will continue working if there are things left to be done.

Cultural Differences as Threats to Research Design

Administrative problems threaten comparability in studies of families and schools in different countries. For example, our study design called for using chronological age of children to set the testing schedules in the two countries in order to afford comparability. This worked reasonably well during the preschool years, but less efficiently when it came time to administer tests of school readiness prior to children's entry into the school system. The Japanese school year begins early in April, in contrast to the September opening of the school year in the United States. This created a slight disjunction in the timing of testing in the two countries. If pretests were given immediately before the children started school, the testing would be done at different times in the two countries. This did not necessarily distort results but presented scheduling concerns in analysis and discussion of data.

The procedures used in gathering data are less easily observed and thus less readily adjusted in collaborative studies. It may be that procedures were noncomparable in ways that we still do not recognize. We sought to reduce this possibility by sending tapes of instruments being administered, full instructions of words used in presenting a task to parents or children, and the like. Nonetheless, this aspect of research is less easy to monitor than, say, coding or rating, where reliability can be established. For example, the staff member who interviewed mothers in the United States was a woman, herself a mother, who presented to the families a person who understood the day-to-day demands, rewards, and frustrations of caring for young children. In Japan the interviewers were male graduate students. A consideration that prompted the decision to engage males as interviewers was that mothers might have felt it awkward to be interviewed by much younger girls who had not yet raised children. Males are outside this social hierarchy of women and would be accepted in a more neutral spirit. This contrast in interviewers escaped our attention until after the interviewing was completed.

Another disjunction arose while the project was underway. The U.S. group had an opportunity to include fathers in the study, offering the chance to compare the roles of fathers and mothers in preparing children for school. Although recruiting fathers to participate in research activities is not easy in the U.S., it is apparently even more difficult in Japan, and a comparable study was not feasible. Differential access to families across cultural groups thus presents methodological problems in cross-cultural studies.

At the follow-up study, differences between the two school systems created more significant obstacles. In Japan, a significant proportion of students take the entrance examination to private junior high schools at the end of the 6th grade and often carry extra work during that school year. Since we wanted to assess student performance in mathematics and language, it was important for the Japanese branch of the study to complete testing before the students started on these different curricular paths.

The decision to conduct a parallel follow-up study in the U.S. came too late to secure funds for the study while students were in the 5th grade, in part because of the 6-month difference in schedule of the school year. This created another disjunction between the plans of the two studies. This might be seen, perhaps, as part of the price of an attempt at collaboration. Given the distance and lag in communication that is involved in written correspondence, decisions can easily move ahead more quickly in one country than in another.

This emphasizes the importance of timing and decisiveness in communication between teams when separate projects are involved. In several aspects, the follow-up study suffered from distance and from lack of funds that would have enabled the groups to meet and plan the follow-up study together. By the time that such planning began, the original budgets had been used to complete analysis of the data from the preschool phase of the study. Conversations about the follow-up project took place when members of the teams met at conferences or en route to meetings. A specific cost in the follow-up study was that the instruments were less comparable than had been the case in the preschool phase of the project.

Selecting the Research Groups: Whom do they Represent?

Representativeness is particularly tricky in comparisons of Japan and the U.S. in part because the population of the United States is more heterogeneous than that of Japan. This presented us with a problem. Given that funding possibilities constrained the size of research groups, should we try to represent the several major ethnic/SES strands in the U.S., making intracountry analysis more difficult because of the small number in each subgroup, or select some part of a diverse population to represent American culture? Our decision was to include only caucasians, with the obvious limitations that such selectivity brings. Even in Japan, the staff encountered a similar problem. The initial plan included families from an agricultural section of the country. This group was dropped from the analysis because of marked differences that emerged between urban and rural

Japanese families in mother-child interaction styles. In many agricultural families, the principal caretaker, and hence the socializing agent, for the child was the grandmother and not the mother.

There is, of course, the additional question about using seemingly similar occupational (e.g., skilled workers) and educational levels (e.g., high school education) to draw relatively comparable research groups from the two countries. Despite obvious cultural differences in educational and occupational experiences, we used such indices of social status to assure a similar range of social backgrounds in the research groups. The distribution of SES was roughly comparable across professional/executive, white-collar, and skilled/unskilled workers in each country—about one third from each of these three backgrounds. Again, this is not the proportion of families in these occupational/educational segments within either Japan or the U.S. However, such a distribution provided an opportunity to examine relationships between SES and other variables within country.

Although the formal structure of families in the U.S. and Japan seems, on the surface, to be highly similar in that the nuclear family is a basic unit in both countries. There are important contrasts, however, in family roles and expectations. For example, more mothers of small children are in the labor force in the U.S., the divorce rate is higher, fathers participate more often in childrearing, the affective relationships and techniques of discipline are dissimilar in important ways. Although these discrepancies became useful points of interpretation, they also raised questions of comparability.

The solution to problems created by differences in demography is not necessarily to select strictly similar groups, e.g., use only intact families where mothers were not employed in both countries. This sort of matching would have altered to some degree the nature of the cultural differences between the two groups—that is, many mothers in the U.S. are employed outside the home; many children are brought up in one-parent homes. Our solution was to compromise, using procedures that can be explained, perhaps, more easily than they can be defended. As we indicated earlier, we selected only caucasians in the U.S. in an attempt to minimize cultural variation within country and give more confidence in within-country results. At the same time, we selected children who were first-born in order to hold constant the effect of birth order or number of children on mothers' responses and behavior.

In Japan, it was necessary to include a small number of second-born children. At the time the study began (1972), the majority of children in classes for 3-year-olds were second- or third-borns. Parents were hesitant to send their first-born to preschools as early as age 3. When the oldest sibling was in an older class, it was much easier for mothers to send their second or third children to school at this young age. The effect of this circumstance on selection of subjects was unavoidable. In a sense, it was parallel to the need to include children of single parents in the U.S. as we drew from participating preschool and day care centers.

There may be no way out of this sort of dilemma. Culture, family characteristics, and demographic patterns are confounded in the most basic sense—culture directly affects the other two types of variables. Problems of this kind illustrate two general principles: first, the importance of selecting groups that can be used to make within-country analyses, and second, the importance of using detailed qualitative analyses to describe and understand cultural differences in those processes that are of concern. These points are illustrated by specific findings that are described later.

THE SEARCH FOR CULTURAL AND PSYCHOLOGICAL EQUIVALENCE

The two research teams dealt with problems of equivalence directly in conferences held in Tokyo and at Stanford. The cross-cultural experience of the Japanese team helped with the task of translation of interviews and other instruments. We used the familiar technique of back-translation in instrument development in some instances but the bilingual competence of members of the Japanese team made it relatively easy to assure that the phrasing of items conveyed similar content.

However, translation was not the most formidable challenge in the search for cross-cultural equivalence. Less obvious, at least to the American team, but more troublesome was the cultural appropriateness of the instruments selected and the categories that were later developed for data analysis. The three mother–child interaction tasks provide examples of the cultural nature of data-gathering instruments.

Block Sort Task. In the initial stages, the overall research plan followed a general approach used by Hess and Shipman in a study of family influences on school-relevant skills in Chicago. The central instrument for eliciting interaction between mothers and children in that study was a block-sort task. In this task, the staff member showed mothers in the study how to sort 8 blocks by two characteristics—height of block and a mark (X or O) on top of the block. Other features of the blocks (e.g., color, shape) were obvious but irrelevant to the goal. A successful sort produced two short blocks each with an O on top, two tall blocks with X on top, and so on.

This task required that the staff member instruct the mother and that the mother give the child clear information about the problem, since it is not a task that occurs naturally in the daily routines of families. Indeed, block-sorting was selected to minimize the possibility that prior experience within families from a particular socioeconomic level would give some children in the research group an advantage. This sort of explicit instruction—what we sometimes called an instrumental approach—was well suited to the styles of mothers in the United States.

However, explicit teaching appears to be less compatible with the customary behavior of Japanese mothers. Mothers in Japan could, of course, follow the instructions, and the task produced some interesting comparative data (Hess et al., 1986). However, they appeared to have a goal in mind that differed from that of the American group. Mothers in Japan seemed to want to be certain that their children could perform the specific operations needed to sort the blocks correctly; mothers in the U.S. tended to encourage children to understand the principles involved and be able to explain them to the staff person involved. Japanese children made fewer errors; children from the U.S. could more often explain the principles on which the sort was made.

Referential Communication Task.   A second international task, developed by Pat Dickson (Dickson, Hess, Miyake, & Azuma, 1979), used an inverted notebook that presented the child with a series of pages on which were four similar abstract figures. One was the target; the mother was to describe this figure to the child who was then to push a button under the correct pattern.

During this game, the mother had to do two things. One was to describe the target, the other was to have her child push the button to indicate her or his choice. A staff member in Japan, who was fluent in English, pointed out to us that mothers in the U.S. tended to deal with both of these aspects explicitly while mothers in Japan often neglected to mention the button push request. This led to a more formal, explicit style in the U.S. For example, an American mother might say to her child, "Can you push the red button under the picture that looks like a triangle?" A Japanese mother might say, "I see a shape that looks like a crooked triangle. Do you see something that looks a little bit like a triangle?"

To Japanese ears, the request to push the button sounds a little too formal or explicit because what is clear in a situation is rarely verbalized in Japanese. Referring to the button was redundant.

The emphasis by mothers in the U.S. on the button push seemed to lead to false pushes—instances where the child pushed before the mother completed her description. In the Japanese group, however, the child was more likely to point to the picture before pushing the button, as if the emphasis were on analyzing the features of the figure rather than on a prompt physical response.

The two groups of mothers also responded to the child's button push in different ways. In the U.S., the mother's response was most often a signal of the correctness or incorrectness of the child's action—"Right," "OK," or "Fine." In Japan, however, the connotation was different. Mothers responded with "Atari," meaning "hit." While "Right" or "OK" refer to correctness, the Japanese term "Atari" seems to refer to the probabilistic chance of a correct response—efforts to reach a goal that one is approaching. A Japanese mother is thus treating the task as a game while the American mother is presenting it as a test. In defining the task as a game, the Japanese mothers subtly show their tendency to approve any response at some level—an attitude in keeping with the traditional Japanese view of children as "kami" or gods, who are allowed to do anything they like.

Responses of Japanese mothers were recorded as "No" in about the same proportion as those of mothers in the U.S. However, they carried different messages. In the U.S., "No" meant that the child was wrong; in Japan, a "No" meant a miss—an approximation that called for another attempt. Also, in Japan, a considerable number of Japanese mothers gave no feedback when the child was correct, except to say "Turn to the next page." This was enough to tell the child that he or she was correct, and at the same time it did not lead the child to be too concerned with the hit score.

Unstructured Game.   The Japanese team suggested an additional instrument for eliciting interaction between mothers and children. This task was much less structured than the other two; indeed, it came to be called the *Unstructured Game.* Two sets of peg-board with colored pegs were provided. The mother and child could use these in any way they liked—work separately, jointly, let the child take the initiative, or let the mother direct the activities. The instructions specified no outcomes; the pair made its own decisions. The staff member stated no goal, established no criteria for successful performance, gave no hint of what was expected. The mother and child set the rules.

The resulting interaction was more difficult to score and analyze than the block-sort task or communication game. It varied considerably among mother-child pairs. At one end were situations in which the mother set up a task and either taught or monitored the child's performance. At the other extreme, the child took the initiative, set the task, and directed his mother's behavior.

In the view of the Japanese team, this activity yielded data that were much more informative and faithful to the typical behavior of Japanese mothers than were the interactions in the block-sort game. The unstructured nature of the game made it possible for Japanese mothers to use subtle, indirect techniques of control that represented their everyday experience.

The preference of the Japanese team for the unstructured task became increasingly apparent to the American team as the data from the groups were analyzed. It became clear later that the Japanese team was aware early on of the need for an interaction task with relatively little structure.

Azuma (1981) has described his team's view of this task in these terms:

> The Japanese group members, however, doubted that it ⟨block-sort task⟩ was appropriate for Japanese subjects. We were not able to give an explicit reason, but the task was somehow incongruent with our image of mother-child interaction in Japan. We preferred less structured free play which seems to us to be more 'natural.' After an intensive debate, neither side of the two national groups yielded and our compromise was to administer both tests to both groups.

The data very clearly showed that the block-sort variables were more relevant ⟨to preschool cognitive test results⟩ in the U.S. while the free play variables were more relevant in Japan, and that each national group, unknowingly, favored the research tool which had higher relevance in its own culture.

A pos hoc thought is that the block-sort requires an analytical and structured approach on the side of the mother. As other results show, the Japanese mothers tend to be less analytical, more impressionistic and more feeling oriented in their communication with children. They want to avoid direct teaching when possible, and tend to model behavior rather than structure through verbal instruction. Therefore, for Japanese mothers, the block-sort situation was awkward. They tended to be more tense as compared to American mothers [in playing the block-sort game]. The free play game was not a teaching situation and thus more personal approach styles were observable, although well-specified coding of the variables had to be sacrificed to some extent.

It is significant that we [the Japanese team] felt this about free play vs. block sort but we did not have a clear grasp it at the planning stage of the study. We were not ready to be logically persuasive. If we had not been working together on equal grounds and did not have mutual respect for each other's intuitions as mature researchers, perhaps we would have ended up discarding free play since its coding had to be less objective. In doing so we would have lost have lost a set of predictor variables that were very suggestive in cross-cultural comparisons.[2]

A summary of the correlational data is shown in Table 9.1.

The lesson that we learned from this aspect of the project is that instruments themselves are culturally typed and that there exists a sort of culture–tool interaction. This makes cross-cultural comparisons difficult as it introduces the possibility of cultural bias that goes beyond linguistic issues. There was no linguistic problem for Japanese or American mothers in either of these interactional tasks. Rather, the issue turned out to be cultural congruence of the behavior required by the task. The problem presented for researchers comes from the fact that such

TABLE 9.1
Number of Significant Correlations Between Two Interactional
Tasks and Three Types of Child Performance Outcomes

| Interactional Task | | Child Outcomes | | |
| | | | Performance | |
		Verbal	Nonverbal	Task
Block sort	Japan	2	4	3
(Of 19 possible)	U.S.	9	7	10
Unstructured play	Japan	4	6	3
(Of 17 possible)	U.S.	2	0	0

[2]Quoted by permission.

cultural relevance may not be known when the design of the study is developed. Important features of relevant behavior may thus not be measured.

Another example of mismatch in cultural correspondence shows a more familiar problem—how linguistic issues may obscure the meaning of results. This example comes from an instrument designed to elicit mother's beliefs about the age at which children should master a number of developmental skills, such as "Be able to feed himself," "Answer the telephone," "Come or answer when called," and the like (Hess, Kashiwagi, Azuma, Price, & Dickson, 1980). The two teams selected two items to represent children's courtesy to adults. "Uses polite forms ('Please') to adults," and "Greets family courteously." On the basis of common knowledge about the two cultures, we expected that the Japanese mothers would want their children to show these behavioral skills at an earlier age than would mothers in the United States.

The item, "Greets family courteously," showed the expected difference, but mothers in the U.S. reported that they would expect children to say "Please" at an earlier age than did the Japanese group. As we discussed the item, it became apparent that terms expressing the concept of a polite request (e.g., "Please"), are linguistically quite complex in Japanese. Different forms are appropriate for different situations and for addressing persons of differing status and role. Children are not expected to master the nuances of this linguistic form at an early age only because the task requires more practice and experience.

Differences in cultural definitions can also appear in the categories developed for coding and summarizing data. An example of this kind of disparity emerged as the staff tried to construct categories to describe maternal behavior in disciplinary situations. The data came from a task that requested the mother to indicate what she would say to her child in each of several events in which maternal intervention often appears—e.g., if the child will not eat vegetables at dinner, if he or she makes marks on the bedroom wall, refused to brush teeth, and the like.

Several categories seemed applicable in both countries—use of appeals to maternal authority, appeals to feelings, or to rules, and appeals to consequences of the child's action. Another set of categories summarized the mother's tendency to insist on compliance. A description of what the staff member on the American team called "Persuasion" included the idea that the mother would try to get the child to comply, then abandon the effort if the child seemed intractable.

In the U.S., we saw this behavior as a relatively mild attempt to impose maternal wishes upon the child. It turned out, however, that in Japan, attempts at persuasion coupled with comments such as, "All right, then, you won't have to do it," can send the child a very powerful message. Comments seen in the U.S. as persuasive, in Japan may be understood as imperatives expressed as requests. As suggested by the writing of Doi (1973), the message carried this implication: "Well, I will not bother you or be concerned with you any longer. Our close relationship of interdependence, or *amae* will be terminated."

CULTURAL DIFFERENCES AS A SOURCE OF NEW INFORMATION ABOUT ONE'S OWN CULTURE

Cultural differences can be revealed by unexpected differences in performance that cannot be explained by lack of psychological equivalence of instruments or analytic categories. For example, when the children were first tested shortly before their fourth birthday, we administered Palmer's *Concept Familiarity Index* (Palmer, 1970). This test utilized concepts that children encounter in the every day physical environment—color, shape, number, quantity, size, position, direction and the like. It thus presumably presented concepts equally familiar to children in both countries.

However, contrary to our expectations, Japanese children performed less well on items asking about position and direction, such as *around, behind, through, over,* and the like. Although 80 to 90% of children in the U.S. group got the correct answer on these items, only about half of the children in Japan knew these concepts.

This difference seemed to be topic-specific as it did not appear in other areas of the test. Our speculation about the reason for this disparity is that Japanese language is less articulated than English with regard to directional concepts. In Japanese, words representing directions, are often equivocal. These prepositional concepts are often confounded with verbs, and their independent use was infrequent in the Japanese language, often being substituted by less specific indicators.

For example, "Place it *on* the shelf," rigorously translated is "tana no ue ni oite kudasai" in Japanese. Usually, however, from the underlined portion the word "no" and "ue" are dropped and only "ni" is left. But "ni" can be used in many other positional contexts. Examples: "Kage ni" means "in the shadow," Kochira ni," means "toward this way," and "shita ni" refers to "down under." This does not mean that the concepts themselves are vague or equivocal. "To jump over" is "tobikoeru," a verb commonly used in Japanese, the latter part of which means the act of going over and beyond. "To run between" is "hashirinukeru," the latter part of which is a verb representing an act of going through. Thus, in Japanese prepositions like "between" and "over" are often implied in the action verb and not stated independently. The difficulty of Japanese children could have been due to the difficulty in separating positional concepts from specific action concepts.

It is obviously unreasonable to conclude that Japanese children are inferior in mastery of positional concepts. It appears that the culture does not provide for verbal articulation such as is represented in English prepositions.

Another finding of the study that invites cultural interpretation but for which the explanation is less clear comes from the children's performance on three tests: (1) the Matching Familiar Figures Test; (2) a cross-modal instrument developed for the study; and (3) the Draw-A-Circle Task, a familiar technique in attempts to assess impulsivity.

The MFF presents the child with a line drawing of a familiar figure (e.g., kite, cat) on one page (the "standard"), and on a facing page shows an array of 5 similar drawings, only one of which is exactly like the standard. The staff member asks the child to select the figure that exactly corresponds to the standard. Performance is measured in two ways—first, by whether the figure selected is the correct one, and second, by the number of seconds that the child waits before making the first choice. In this test, American children, as a group, waited 57.5 (median) across the set of drawings and made 11.4 errors. Japanese children took much more time, waiting a median of 76.5 seconds. They also made fewer errors (9.9).

In the second task, children were shown a small box with a door covered by a dark cloth. The tester placed a small three-dimensional abstract wooden object inside the box. The child could feel the object with her or his hand but not see it. To the left was an array of objects similar to the target object in the box. Only one was identical in shape. The child's task was to explore the object in the box with his or her fingers and select the figure on the array that was identical. We scored performance by correctness of response and latency—time to first response. Again, the Japanese children took longer on this task—80.5 seconds—to first response than did the children from the U.S.—55.3 seconds. The Japanese children also made slightly fewer errors (4.8 vs. 4.4).

The third task—Draw-A-Circle—showed similar results in the time that children took to complete the task: 16.5 seconds for the Japanese group, 11.5 seconds for the children in the U.S.

These differences in performance thus occurred on tasks where getting the correct answer was probably within the competence of all the children. Discrepancies thus raise questions about cultural differences in experience and training in performing tasks. The tendency of Japanese children to use more time and to make fewer errors suggests a difference in problem-solving style. Although we do not know what went on in the heads of the children, it is easy to imagine that those that took longer were engaging in a simple form of "quality control," trying to be certain that their answers were correct or that they carried out the task in accord with instructions.

A more pronounced cultural distinctiveness appeared in the data obtained from what we called "control strategy" questions, described earlier. In administering this instrument, the staff member asked mothers what they would say in six hypothetical situations that elicit parental intervention. The form of the questions was "What would you say to (child's name) if you went into his room and found that [he had been writing on the wall? Imagine that he is here now. What would you say?" Several different situations are presented—refusing to eat vegetables at dinner, refusing to brush teeth, running around in a grocery market, and the like (Conroy, Hess, Azuma, & Kashiwagi, 1980).

The answers of the mothers were coded to yield nine categories indicating varying degree of flexibility in carrying out discipline or demands on the child (e.g., *imperatives,* on the one end, to *yielding* on the other). Another set of

categories represented seven types of maternal behavior that might have cognitive consequences for the child—*appeals to authority, appeals to rules, appeals to feelings, appeals to external consequences* (Conroy et al. 1980; Hess &
McDevitt, 1984).

There were dramatic differences between the Japanese and American mothers
in their responses to these situations (Conroy et al., 1980), with mothers from the
U.S. showing a much greater tendency to use appeals to authority and to rules
than did Japanese mothers, who more often used appeals to feelings and to
consequences. The emphasis of American mothers on their personal authority (as
mothers) and the low frequency of this category in Japan seems to contradict the
intuitive view that lines of authority are more significant in regulating human
interaction in Japan. This apparent contradiction led to the interpretation that in
the U.S. authority may be less stable and the mothers less confident that they will
be obeyed. Such lack of confidence might be expressed in overemphasis. Alternatively, it may be that Japanese socialization depends to a great extent on a
close affective identification that is communicated in nonverbal ways. Japanese
mothers, when less confident, were afraid of jeopardizing this relationship by a
directive verbal reprimand.

However, it is in the correlations between these variables and children's
cognitive measures that the most striking contrast appeared. The direction of
correlations seems to be reversed for the two countries, especially on the category "appeals to authority." This category represents an inflexible, authority
oriented approach (one characteristic, we note, of "restricted code" linguistic
forms). As a number of studies have shown in the U.S., the effects of overuse of
this type of behavior on children's cognitive performance and school achievement are predominantly negative (Hess & McDevitt, 1984). In Japan, on the
other hand, the correlations are consistently positive. Although the values are
low, the tendency reappeared in a replication in Japan with 80 more subjects.

In order to understand this apparent dilemma, we selected mothers who
scored high (that is, upper one third) in each control strategy variables in each
country. We then computed average standard scores on the behavioral measures
based on the observation during mother–child interaction. We find again a
striking U.S.–Japan contrast. Japanese mothers who were high in "status-based
control" showed the following characteristics:

* In the block-sort task, they were more permissive and used more positive
  evaluation;
* In communicating information, they were straightforward and tolerant to
  errors;
* In the unstructured task ("free play"), they did not interfere with the child
  and tended to accept the child's remarks.

The behavior of American mothers who are high on authority are almost
always in the opposite direction. The pattern shown by Japanese mothers who

were orientated toward "high authority" was a warm and confident attitude toward the child. The pattern of their American counterpart is completely opposite.

According to many observations, including our own, the modal tendencies of Japanese mothers' approach are indirect, feeling oriented, less explicit, and evasive of personal confrontation. The control situations, however, presented special conditions where confrontation was needed. Only members who are confident of their norms and their relationships with children dare to diverge from their modal pattern.

In the U.S., status hierarchy is probably less stable. For less confident mothers, any child behavior that needs to be controlled is seen as a direct threat to their authority. Therefore, they overreact and emphasize their authority.

These interpretations are speculative, of course. Nevertheless, the foregoing examples demonstrate that similar responses to a psychological instrument may take on entirely dissimilar meaning in different cultures.

WHAT SHOULD BE INFERRED FROM CULTURAL SIMILARITIES?

If differences in cultural views and practices can be more easily discerned in a genuinely collaborative study, does this mean that more significance can be placed on results that are similar across the two countries?

When faced with similar findings in the two countries, we felt more confident in the relationship shown by the data. There were a relatively large number of such findings. For example, maternal expectations for children's achievement, indicated by mothers' report of their occupational aspirations for the child and the years of schooling they thought the child would achieve, were positively correlated with school-relevant outcomes in both countries. The findings from the two countries on the referential communication game followed similar patterns (Dickson et al. 1979; McDevitt, Hess, Kashiwagi, Dickson, Miyake, & Azuma, 1987). In both countries, the measures of mental abilities or functioning at preschool were highly correlated with subsequent measures of performance in school. Mothers in the two countries showed similar profiles of priority assigned to several areas of children's behavior: independence, social skills, artistic talent, verbal abilities, and preschool reading skills. Similar findings thus serve as a form of replication. This is worthwhile in itself, but is especially important when two different cultures are involved. The "undetected effect" that appears when a variable, Z, although not measured, is responsible for a correlation between X and Y is less likely to appear in different social contexts. One gains confidence in the stability of the result.

SUMMARY

Several points can be summarized from our experience. They do not necessarily apply to other cross-national studies, but we think they are likely to be especially relevant in research on family interaction. Such studies focus on interpersonal relationships, perceptions of others, beliefs, and intent. In these areas of human behavior, cultural distinctions are particularly likely to be involved. These are the most general ideas to come from our experience with this project.

1. The administrative structure (parallel studies vs. a single principal investigator) is critical, not only in the conduct of the study (e.g., data-gathering procedures and schedules), but in the choice of instruments and interpretation of results.

2. Some of the staff of each team involved in the study should have experience in both cultures.

3. Frequent communication about procedures and findings helps identify discrepancies that, in turn, may reveal new areas for study.

4. Cultural and psychological equivalence applies not only to translations of instruments but to the cultural appropriateness of the instruments themselves. Research teams are themselves influenced by their cultural experience, even when they believe they are acting in accordance with strict scientific principles.

5. Unexpected findings, rather than being a source of frustration should be seen as leads to a deeper understanding of the data.

6. Cross-cultural comparisons may lead to revisions in the prevailing wisdom about one's own culture. This is most likely to occur when it is the *relationships* among variables that are being compared, rather than the data on individual variables themselves.

Such cross-cultural differences in the pattern of inter-relationships among observed variables are of primary importance. Describing differences on scales will not mean much unless we know how each variable is related to other behavior in each culture.

7. Because of the need to accommodate new information and to adjust the study to exploit new insights, projects should have considerable flexibility built into the research plan. Cross-national studies of family interaction benefit from loose rather than rigid planning.

In short, a cross cultural study must be cross cultural not only in data collection but in the development of instruments and categories for data analysis. The science of psychology, however, has developed in a predominantly Western tradition. Even non-Occidental researchers are acculturated to Western theories and concepts. The hazard is that strict adherence to traditional scientific ideas may result in missing or misinterpreting many important features of other cultures.

The contribution of cross-cultural research to psychology will probably not produce neat theories and clear explanations for some time, if ever. Perhaps the initial task is to reveal cultural reality and so expose both the limitations and cultural restrictions of our methods, concepts and theories. Hopefully, the cross-cultural contrasts that research can uncover will contribute to an even more productive view of human nature.

ACKNOWLEDGMENTS

This project was supported by grants from the Japanese Society for the Promotion of Science, the Spencer Foundation, through the Social Science Research Council, the Ministry of Education of Japan, and the National Science Foundation (Grant #NSF BNS 91-07542). Many individuals participated in some aspect of the study. Participants in Japan were Hiroshi Azuma, University of Tokyo; Ikuyo Hamana, Hokkaido University; Giyoo Hatano, Dyokkyo University; Kayoko Inagaki, Chiba University; Keiko Kashiwagi, Tokyo Christian Woman's College; Yoko Kuriyama, International Christian University; Kazuo Miyake, Hokkaido University; Naomi Miyake, Aoyama Gakuin Woman's Junior College; Shiegefumi Nagano, National Institute of Educational Research; Yuriko Oshima, University of Toronto, Nobumoto Tajima, Tokyo University of Foreign Studies; Hiroshi Usui, Hokkaido University of Education; Keiko Watanabe, Kanagawa University.

Research participants in the United States included Robert D. Hess, Stanford University, W. Patrick Dickson, Michigan State University; Susan Holloway, University of Maryland (College Park); Gary G. Price, University of Wisconsin; Teresa McDevitt, University of Northern Colorado; Mary Conroy, San Jose State University; Kay Sandberg, Stanford University, Deborah Leong, Metropolitan State College, Denver; Cathy Lewis, University of California at San Francisco; William Arsenio, Yeshiva University; Peggy Estrada, Stanford University; and Eleanor B. Worden, Stanford University.

REFERENCES

Azuma, H. (1981, April). A note on cross-cultural study. *The Quarterly Newsletter of the Laboratory of Comparative Human Cognition, 3*(2), 23–25.

Conroy, M., Hess, R. D., Azuma, H., & Kashiwagi, K. (1980). Maternal strategies for regulating children's behavior in Japanese and American families. *Journal of Cross-Cultural Psychology, 11*(2), 153–172.

Dickson, W. P., Hess, R. D., Miyake, N., & Azuma, H. (1979). Referential communication accuracy between mother and child as a predictor of cognitive development in the United States and Japan. *Child Development, 50,* 53–59.

Doi, L. T. (1973). *The anatomy of dependence.* Tokyo: Kodansha International Press.

Hess, R. D., Holloway, S. D., McDevitt, T. M., Azuma, H., Kashiwagi, K., Nagano, S., Miyake, K., Dickson, W. P., Price, G. G., & Hatano, G. (1986). Family influences on school readiness and achievement in Japan and the United States: An overview of a longitudinal study. In H.

Stevenson, K. Hakuta, & H. Azuma (Eds.), *Kodomo: Child development and education in Japan* (pp. 147–166). New York: Freeman.

Hess, R. D., Kashiwagi, K., Azuma, H., Price, G. G., & Dickson, W. P. (1980). Maternal expectations for mastery of developmental tasks in Japan and the United States. *International Journal of Psychology, 15,* 259–271.

Hess, R. D., & McDevitt, T. M. (1984). Some cognitive consequences of maternal intervention techniques: A longitudinal study. *Child Development, 55,* 2017–2030.

McDevitt, T. M., Hess, R. D., Kashiwagi, K., Dickson, W. P., Miyake, N., & Azuma, H. (1987). Referential communication accuracy of mother-child pairs and children's later scholastic achievement: A follow-up study. *Merrill Palmer Quarterly.*

Palmer, F. H. (1970). Socioeconomic status and intellective performance among Negro preschool boys. *Developmental Psychology, 3,* 1–9.

The Family as a System of Reciprocal Relations: Searching for a Developmental Lifespan Perspective

Frank H. Hooper
University of Wisconsin

Judith O. Hooper
Affiliated Counseling Services, Madison, WI

Humans are ecologically situated in many contexts, the most important of which is the family. . . . Its unique and massive effects, rooted in blood ties, not only have had past personality-forming influences but exercise powerful forces on one's current life and future destiny. The family shapes the fiber of people's beings in a way no other social force can begin to realize. Peer groups, work settings, friendship networks, social class, age, race, sex, nationality, and religion can only have glancing effects compared with that of the family. You reserve for your family the best and the worst that is in you; toward these intimates you will show your greatest cruelty, yet for them you will make your greatest sacrifices. Family members, in turn, can frustrate and hurt you the most because you want and expect more from them. . . . The family as a human institution is universal and has survived through history as the most workable kind of living unit for mediating the culture in preparing the young for the next generation. Families provide the deepest satisfactions of living and an emotional refuge from harsh external realities. Whatever is human in people in their capacity to relate beyond their narcissism and to love comes from their family relationships . . . family living can also paradoxically provide the context for tragedy and anguish of endless variety—the cruel rejections, marital discord or emptiness, murderous hostility, the child unloved or discriminated against . . . jealousy, hatred, unrealized fulfillments, and outrages against the human spirit. (Framo, 1979, p. 988)

INTRODUCTION

As we begin this chapter, we think it is important to make it clear that, in some respects, we really have no business writing it. Frank H. Hooper has conducted investigations of cognitive functioning in various specific age groups (Hooper, 1969; Hooper, Wanska, Peterson, & DeFrain, 1979) lifespan normative assessments using cross-sectional designs (Hooper, Sipple, Goldman, & Swinton, 1979; Muhs, Hooper, & Papalia-Finlay, 1979–80), and longitudinal studies of Piagetian logical concept abilities in young children (Hooper, Swinton, & Sipple, 1979; Hooper, Toniolo, & Sipple, 1978; Lawton, Hooper, Saunders, & Roth, 1984). Judith O. Hooper has conducted research on nontraditional aged students in university settings, focusing on demographic, cognitive and personality factors (Hooper, 1981; Hooper & March, 1980; Hooper & Traupmann, 1983). One research project (Hooper, 1979), was on familial reactions to adult women's return to school, and all members of the target student's family were interviewed and family aggregate data analyzed. Together we have investigated the personality and memory correlates of intellectual functioning in samples of young and middle-aged adults as well as elderly individuals (Hooper, Hooper, & Colbert, 1984; Hooper, Colbert, & McMahan, 1986). Neither of us, however, has done family/individual research of the particular type being considered in this volume.

We have, however, always been attracted to the possibility of integrating individual and family developmental issues in a coordinated theoretical model and related research design. Part of this interest comes from our frustrations with our own work, in which we have sometimes felt that one labors away at explaining more and more about less and less until one explains everything about nothing regarding the human condition. Having worked most of our professional lives in university departments called "Child and Family Studies" or their equivalents, we were in daily contact with specialists from both fields. The doctrine of interdisciplinary collaborative research was constantly heard (originating most of the time from university or college level administrators). Yet, it has been our experience that genuinely collaborative research endeavors were extremely rare—the family people continued to do family-type studies (mostly sociological in emphasis) while the human development staff studied individuals primarily from a psychological perspective. Thus, the goal of truly integrative research dealing with individuals and their families was seldom if ever seen. In addition, in recent years, Judith O. Hooper has worked full-time in clinical practice, and has found that her ignorance about human development and family functioning has grown even beyond that established by earlier reading and research. Indeed, both of us have found that most of our "insights" gained from the literature have been primarily negative. Thus, there are certainly a great many publications available that illustrate all too clearly how not to do research in this cross-linked area. There are, of course, a great many reasons why this is true. In this chapter, we highlight some of these reasons and the problems which we see in the literature and research attempting to interrelate the development of individuals and families (which is, after all, the way the real world is), and we point out some of the obvious and some of the subtle causes of these problems.

We conclude with a section on applications of a life-course perspective and offer some suggestions for future conceptualizing and research.

FROM PRAXIS TO LOGOS: THE EFFECTS OF PRACTICAL CONSTRAINTS ON THEORY AND RESEARCH

Academics are very fond of treating theory construction, research design and methodology, statistical analysis, and particular behavioral content as rather separate domains. They often write as if this were the case and thus teach separate college courses under distinctive titles for each of these areas. These domains are, of course, related and interdependent and professional researchers probably do each a conceptual disservice to isolate them and stress the unique idiosyncratic issues and problems associated with each. Of equal, if not greater, importance, each domain is effectively constrained and channeled by practical considerations once we turn to their actual employment as in a particular research project.

In the area of theory construction, for example, the dialectical/systems approach, with its block universe doctrine (Lapsley, 1985; Riegel, 1975), suggests that every component in our analysis interacts dynamically with each and every other component in simultaneous fashion. Indeed, we can analytically intervene and measure only in the most arbitrary fashion. If this fundamental assumption is valid then we are doomed to finding only successive approximations forever distanced from the original target phenomena—in this case the family and individual developmental dynamic. Yet as Reese (1982) has pointed out, the dialectical approach, as represented in dialectical materialism, does indeed permit abstract analysis. "Consequently, . . . parts can be studied separately from the whole and can be understood separately from the whole—although when separated from the whole their meanings change. For example, subatomic particles can be studied and understood separately from molecular particles, molecular particles separately from organisms, and organisms separately from societies" (p. 426). At some point we have to enter the real world of people, time, and place in order to conduct our observations, and it is precisely these observations which have to be the basis for altering our models or theories of human interaction and development—even at the possible expense of our more treasured theoretical axioms or postulates. When one's preferred theory and subsequent observations are at variance, it is the theory that must give way (Piaget, 1971b).

However, in the area of research design and associated methodology, we sometimes encounter the myth of the nonparticipant observer. This is the idea that one could obtain precise and valid measurements of the system or entity of interest without in any way disturbing the system or introducing observer bias— as in a truly nonobtrusive or nonreactive assessment procedure. Sometimes our handbooks and special journal issues seem to imply that this is possible, e.g., Brown and Kidwell (1982), Seitz (1984). Nevertheless, when we join a system in order to measure it (Hultsch & Hickey, 1978; Riegel, 1973, 1975) or to aid the members in a clinical sense (Whitaker, 1976) we run at least the implicit risk of altering the system as a direct function of our observations and so-called "helping" behaviors. Some writers, e.g., Boulding (1967) Labouvie (1975) and Whitaker (1976), claim that indeed we always alter the system. "All scientists are participant-observers in their own systems. . . . Hence the system changes as it is studied and because it is studied. There can be no myth of an unchanging universe with the scientist acquiring abstract knowledge about it" (Boulding, 1967, as quoted in Riegel, 1973, p. 16). This is a conundrum that is probably insoluble, and one with which we will have to learn to live. We can hope to develop theories of observed human development and interaction, but, probably, not of what goes on when "no one" (i.e., no one outside the family) is looking. This need not be a big blow to those who are searching for the elusive "truth" about individual development and family interaction. After all, there is, by definition, no unobserved interaction, interaction requiring as it does a minimum of two participants. Similarly, it is unlikely that any individual could develop in any sense whatsoever if totally isolated. We have found that individuals and families will, after an initial period of self-consciousness, adapt to the presence of one or more observers. Perhaps we can never know what they do when we're not there. In the meantime, as family clinicians have shown, we don't even know much about what they do when we are there. We persist in our observations nonetheless.

In a similar methodological vein, the practical stringencies and methodological constraints of large-scale repeated measurement designs over long time intervals are extremely demanding. In terms of the ideal random sampling and external validity assumptions in particular, it is questionable whether these admittedly superior lifespan longitudinal designs are realistic options for the typical investigator's patience and resource reserves. Furthermore, the grounding of social science in the academy has had a subtle effect on the types of research that are carried out. It might be argued that, generally speaking, only very young social scientists have the stamina, idealism, naivete and, dare one say, chutzpah, to attempt research on the large scale that is repeatedly called for in design and methodology textbooks. Yet these young people, even assuming they could get the necessary funding, are often effectively restrained by the demands of the tenure system. Most university professors have 5, possibly 6, years in which to prove their worth to the institution and to society. They simply cannot say, "Hold on while I analyze and report the data from my 5-year study," even though they may have been encouraged to write the proposal and praised for receiving the grant (Norman, 1986). Frequently, by the time the data are available, the tenure decision has been made. Beyond these considerations, since these designs are being questioned on both logical inferential grounds (Wohlwill, 1973) and in terms of pragmatic outcome differences (Horn, 1982) when compared to conventional cross-sectional assessments, we may need to find new methodologies which acknowledge the complexity and dialectical nature of individual/family development at the same time that they are actually do-able.

Recent advances in statistical analysis techniques have enhanced the study of individual/family development. Derivations of the basic correlational approach such as structural equation modeling and path analysis, time sequential and reciprocal interaction models, loglinear analysis, and confirmatory factor analyses (Brown and Kidwell, 1982; Green, 1988), often seem both conceptually and operationally distant from the overall theoretical models and associated process dynamics with which they are used. They also may be distant from the actual family or developmental process dynamics, at various levels of environmental impact, toward which we wish to generalize (Bronfenbrenner, 1986; Kaye, 1985). Sadly it seems to us that many of the recently published studies in the more prestigious family and developmental psychology journals, while noteworthy and perhaps innovative in terms of data analysis, are lacking in the fundamentals of logical design, address trivial developmental questions, and/or have little bearing on the everyday functioning of individuals and their families. Research and data analysis should not, we argue, be performed for their own sake (or for the sake of the rules of the academy). In the face of often painful familial and individual reality, the kind of research which glitters with numbers and words but sheds little light on the human condition is at best useless, and, at worst, arrogant, wasteful and obstructive. Of course, there are excellent investigations that are directed towards answering meaningful and functionally relevant questions, and many of these are university and foundation or federally supported endeavors. A selective list could include Patterson's and Reid's work on intervention with families at risk (e.g., Patterson, 1987; Patterson, Chamberlain, & Reid, 1982; Reid, 1983a, 1983b), Sigel's research on parental belief systems and the reciprocal interaction effects upon children's behavior and development (e.g, Sigel, 1986; see also the recent reviews by Goodnow, 1988, and Miller, 1988), Laosa's research on family effects on children's intellectual development (Laosa, 1982), recent investigations of adolescent puberty and family interaction (e.g., Anderson, Hetherington, & Clingempeel, 1986; Steinberg, 1988), McCubbin's work on family reactions and adjustment to stress and crisis (e.g., McCubbin & McCubbin, 1988), and, finally, the recent analyses of alternative family forms including divorce (Hetherington & Camara, 1984) and serial marriage (Brody, Neubaum, & Forehand, 1988). Other recent examples could no doubt be cited.

ORGANISMIC AND LIFE-COURSE APPROACHES TO FAMILY AND INDIVIDUAL DEVELOPMENT

In recent years we have noted an increasing awareness of the need to conceptually and operationally integrate family and individual studies (Hooper & Hooper, 1985). As professional developmental specialties, the work and writings of social gerontologists, home economists, and life span developmentalists have led the way here, although child development as a field has certainly demonstrated a clear and renewed commitment to family processes and family dynamics as a context for developmental analysis (e.g., Belsky, 1981; Kaye & Furstenberg, 1985; Lerner & Spanier, 1978; Maccoby & Martin, 1983; Parke, 1984; Sigel & Laosa, 1983). In parallel, family studies specialists have included the individual child, adolescent, or adult within their conceptual systems (e.g., Broderick & Pulliam-Krager, 1979; Hill & Mattessich, 1979; Troll & Bengston, 1979). Each of these can trace today's emphases to earlier scattered instances of mutual interdisciplinary concern (e.g., Dager, 1964; Hoffman & Lippitt, 1960) and to earlier traditions such as the Child Study Movement within developmental psychology (Bronfenbrenner, Kessel, Kessen, & White, 1986; Cairns, 1983; Lerner, 1983), the specialized area of parents and parenting (Alpert & Richardson, 1980; Clarke-Stewart, 1988; Gans, 1926; Schlossman, 1985), to the early history and continuing emphasis on cross discipline cooperation in the Society for Research in Child Development (Rheingold, 1985), and, finally, to the focus upon families as the setting for child care and socialization (Christensen, 1964; see also the following discussion of the Chicago School of sociological theory and research). We view these historical trends as fundamentally important, with the present volume as an example of a natural continuation of these mutual interdisciplinary concerns.

There are a number of differing possibilities open to the individual who wishes to "marry" (or at least attempt courtship between) family and developmental theories within a lifespan orientation. Historically, some approaches have had counterparts in the other domain. For example, behavioristic functional theories of human development, with their heavy emphasis on social learning and experential factors, have their counterpart in Parson's theory of family structure (structural-functional analysis) and in situational approaches (Stryker, 1964). The key term here is of course functionalism. Symbolic interactionism, which primarily came from the University of Chicago school of functional sociology led by W. I. Thomas, Robert E. Park, George Herbert Mead, and especially Ernest W. Burgess, and Willard Waller (Burns, 1980; Dubin, 1986; Elder, 1984), can in some respects be compared to Piaget's genetic structuralism (e.g., Piaget, 1977) and recent attempts to incorporate contextualism into lifespan developmental theory. Actually the eclecticism and pluralisms found within the general framework of symbolic interaction have produced less of a unified school as such but rather a broadly based manner of viewing man as a distinctly social animal functioning in a variety of cultural settings (Burr, Leigh, Day, & Constantine, 1979). The implicit generality of this approach suggests historical linkages to both its major counterpart in mainstream sociology, role theory, as well as a number of theories which have their own particular antecedents, e.g., social exchange theory (Bengston & Dowd, 1980); Lewinian field theory and phenomenology (Burr et al., 1979). The key term here is probably interaction rather than any reference to symbols and symbolization. As Elder (1984) has made clear, both the behavioral family analysis tradition of Burgess and Waller, and W. I. Thomas's emphasis upon the study of families reacting to the complex of larger social structures and institutions, share this commitment to an interactionist perspective. "For Thomas as well as Burgess, personalities and social interactions are part of family chemistry. Ideas of time and process inform their shared concept of family dynamics, which relates individual and family development" (pp. 100–101).

In our view the most important intellectual precursors are the writings of Burgess (e.g., Burgess, 1926; Burgess & Locke, 1945; and Burgess & Wallin, 1953) and Waller (e.g., Waller, 1930; 1951/1938). Burgess's dual focus on families and the individuals who constitute them is epitomized by his well known definition of family as a "unity of interacting personalities," Burgess (1926). From this perspective, what persons carry into social situations serves to codetermine the essential subsequent course of these ongoing relationships. Waller's contributions include a view of family solidarity as basically problematic (as a process and an outcome requiring explanation). From this perspective, and essential to clinical practice as well as family theory, family conflict is not necessarily a deviant response pattern but a naturally occurring event which may or may not have an adaptive function. Waller also suggested as early as 1938 a sequence of five family phases or stages, a concept which has obvious relevance to current life course models (Elder, 1984). Family stages, which are most commonly associated with Hill's developmental approach (Hill & Rogers, 1964), are also germane to systems theory applications to family functioning and development.

Where to Start: Family or Individual Models?

It is easy to see that both the general orientation and the specifics of any of the present research programs depend upon whether you begin with families and derive your questions regarding individual development secondarily, or if you begin with individuals (for example, the courting couple as representatives of two differing families of origin) and treat the new family collective as a type of outcome event. In logical or conceptual terms one may ask if either strategy is inherently superior? The answer here must either be No–or better yet–That is a spurious question which can never be answered on solely logical or theoretical grounds (Kaplan, 1967; Mayer, 1986; Piaget, 1971a, p. 368 and 1977, p. 146). This becomes immediately clear if one changes the question to—Which is fundamentally more important, sociology or psychology? In practical terms of course it does indeed make a difference which disciplinary perspective provides your point of departure. The point we emphasize is that because no single starting point is inherently superior, it is essentially arbitrary where we start. It is the

initial bias (and probably the earlier professional training) of the particular inves-
tigator(s) which determines any starting point and, further, constrains the choice
of general models and theories to be evaluated, the assessment or observational
techniques to be employed, and the data analyses used to confirm/disconfirm
predictions and design inferences (Baltes, Reese, & Nesselroade, 1977; Hooper,
1973).

Organismic and Systems/Dialectical/Contextual Approaches

Because it is essentially arbitrary, depending upon the investigators' personal
biases and training, where one begins a family and individual development
research study, we need only to state our biases. One of us (FHH) received his
undergraduate education at the University of Michigan majoring in psychology
and sociology with as many credits in history courses as he could manage. This
was followed by masters degree work in general experimental psychology (major
emphasis on Hullian inspired behaviorism and learning) and a doctoral degree in
cognitive processes from Wayne State University with a minor concentration in
child and family studies taken at the Merrill-Palmer Institute. Equally important
was an initial 3-year academic appointment in child development and life span
developmental psychology at West Virginia University. Almost all the earlier
and subsequent substantive research work dealing with cognitive functioning,
including educational intervention studies, could be described as Piagetian inspired within an organismic life span framework. The most recent special interest
areas have concerned the history of human development and child psychology as
professional fields (Hooper, 1988). The other author (J.O.H.) also received her
undergraduate education at Michigan majoring in English language and literature, with a teaching certificate in secondary education. This was followed by 5
years of teaching in middle schools in suburban Detroit. After a 3-year interval of
full-time parenting and homemaking, an instructive period in itself, there was a
return to school. This experience triggered an interest in the impact of family
functioning on adult development, and led finally to a doctoral dissertation topic.
In the meantime, masters degree work focused on human development over the
life span, and doctoral work on individual and family development. A 6-year
academic appointment at the University of Wisconsin crystallized an impatience
with theory and research for their own sake and fueled a determination to become
more personally involved with individuals and families.

The end result of all of this is that we have quite naturally come to view family
and individual developmental issues and research problems from a perspective
which joins the organismic theories of Piaget and, especially, Werner, to the
family approaches of symbolic interactionism and systems theory particularly the
latter. The individual developmental theories of Piaget and Werner are essentially particular applications of a dialectical model (Brent 1978; Hooper & Hoop-

er, 1985; Langer, 1969). The same holds true for systems approaches to the family (Broderick & Smith, 1979; Urban, 1978). Thus our views of both individual and family developmental processes and interactive outcomes share all the strengths and possible weaknesses of a dialectical approach (e.g., see our earlier comments on the block universe doctrine).

Even given the intuitive appeal of integrating the organismic model of human development with a systems approach to family functioning and development (Hill & Mattessich, 1979; Hooper & Hooper, 1985; Melito, 1985), we are left with a number of problems or issues. At the most general and "holistic" level the problem is to convert the organismic/structural network of relationships and the family system into a single interactive causal matrix. Here the underlying contrasts between descriptive and functional analytic approaches to developmental study are relevant. The descriptive or taxonomic task, as exemplified in the work of Darwin (Gould, 1986), Piaget (Sigel, 1979) or Werner (Langer, 1969), is no more or less important than the functional analysis designed to more directly demonstrate causal relationships among our target variables. Nonetheless, the goal of careful description is usually viewed as the initial prerequisite step to later functional or experimental analysis (Baltes, Reese, & Nesselroade, 1977). Descriptive analytic designs are known under a variety of labels including differential, structural, field, or observational approaches, but all are correlational and, in the classic developmental case, ipsative, and multivariate with repeated measurement over extended time spans. In the present sense, functional analytic designs denote experimental, laboratory or controlled investigations which are univariate and constrained to relatively short time intervals in the prototypical case. Both types of analysis are, of course, essential to developmental investigations (Cronbach, 1975; Labouvie, 1975; Wohlwill, 1973). Functional designs place a premium on internal validity and (by direct implication) causal inference while leaving external validity indeterminate (or at least of much less consequence). Descriptive/structural approaches, in contrast, take external validity as a given (assuming the usual space/time and person sampling restrictions) and are indeterminate regarding the causal relationship networks at issue (Hultsch & Hickey, 1978; Labouvie, 1975). Often, proponents of the descriptive approach deny the possibility (at this point in scientific cultural time) of true multiplicative-multidimensional causal analysis, claiming we lack the essential inference techniques. The relative strong points and appropriateness of each of these general approaches also suggest analogs to the contrasts between laboratory design based versus ecological or so called "natural" field studies of behaving and developing organisms (e.g., Bronfenbrenner, 1986; Sears, 1986). In our view both types of study are necessary, just as structural and functional analyses fundamentally complement one another, but it is unlikely that a single series of focused research studies could encompass all the essentials and caveats of each approach.

A related general issue concerns the task of functionally integrating clinical case study data with academic family and individual developmental analysis (cf. Grunebaum, 1988). Recently, Minuchin (1985) has written a thorough, clear, and compelling argument for both the importance and the feasibility of such an integration. She has pointed out several critical implications of clinical work for the study of human development. Among these are the necessity to recognize that

1. every important relationship is unique, requiring a focus on process rather than outcome;

2. relationships are unique because "All participants come to a new situation with their templates and repertoires, making each new system a fresh construction and the process of prediction complex at best" (p. 293);

3. developmental transitions may be a task of individual and/or family;

4. individuals live in many subsystems of varying sizes, and that research on subsystems realizes significantly more information than research on individuals; and

5. family living requires the "meshing of the psychological needs of family system members at different stages of the life cycle" (p. 296).

In her discussion of these issues, Minuchin makes what seems to us to be a crucial point about the failure of individual developmental psychology to do research on systems and interaction rather than on individuals and outcomes: "Since it is clear that people live in multiple subsystems of varying size, what accounts for the caution? Probably a mix of legitimate methodological difficulties and a tendency to protect prevailing scientific paradigms (Kuhn, 1962). Psychologist value elegant methodology, and triadic or larger units introduce a complexity greater than the sum of their parts. The temptation is to go with the established methodology and to avoid those structures we cannot handle. But complex systems are integral to the understanding of child [human] development, and what is not tackled will not yield" (p. 294).

We think that Minuchin is right, and that there are additional issues that contribute to the problem. Historically, clinical research has focused on outcomes in an attempt to evaluate clinical methodology (Bednar, Burlingame, & Masters, 1988; Goldstein, 1988; Gurman & Kniskert, 1978). Little attention has been paid to the dynamics of family or individual development *qua* development, or to developmental stage as a variable affecting outcomes of individuals in a given family. Furthermore, clinical populations have been widely viewed as deviant, and holding little that is instructive for nonclinical populations. However, the growth of family therapy theory has resulted in a change in clinical writing, such that interactional issues and the impact of given interactions on individual development, in both normal and pathological directions, are being more widely addressed (e.g., Wachtel, 1987). Nevertheless, while developmental psychologists have recognized that individuals, particularly children, live in families, the metaphor might be that of the diamond ring: The setting is of secondary importance, existing only to display the gem. In contrast, Framo (1979) has pointed out that "The family [therapy] approach was not just another form of therapy or body of techniques but a new theory and way of looking at experience and behavior" (p. 990). The family therapy emphasis on developing individuals in a bounded, yet developing, family system, represents a true paradigmatic shift from individual-oriented models.

A related problem is the fact that clinicians with training in individual development are somewhat rare. This lack can be a crucial handicap in working with certain clinical issues. Clinical practice is profoundly affected by the understanding that the impact of an event on an individual is mediated by the individual's developmental stage. For example, the egocentricity of children's cognition, as opposed to the more clinical view of egocentricism of personality, must be understood, and cannot be overemphasized, in working with adult children of alcoholics. The young child, believing that the parent's alcoholic rages are her fault because of some unknown shortcoming, strives to be perfect in the expectation that the drinking, and rages, will thereby stop. The drinking does not stop and child is ever-after stuck in the unresolved child's cognitively egocentric belief that self is bad or not good enough. Similarly, the developmental stage of the sexually abused child must be taken into account in working on that issue, whether at the time of the abuse, or much later in adult life. In my (JOH) clinical experience, the developmental stage of the child when the parental dysfunction (be it alcoholism or some other problem) begins is a crucial variable in determining the adult child's resultant psychological problems.

A final area of concern is the apparent lack of intermediate or transitional level constructs in many theories of individual and family functioning, including both organismic and systems approaches (cf. Baltes & Willis, 1977; Zigler, 1963). Here we are referring to the common void between the most general or global postulates of a theory and the actual specific task settings or interactional formats (in the usual cases of family theory application) which are the operational source of the data to be analyzed and from which the eventual inferences will be drawn. For example, the family system concepts of "transactional interchange," or "boundary maintenance," or the more general "input–throughput–output" patterns are seldom if ever linked directly to the operational measures employed to assess these events or processes in families. In similar fashion for the individual development case, the orthogenetic principle (Werner, 1957), or the structural model of a particular stage, e.g., concrete operational groupements for Piaget (Piaget, 1970), or "id–ego–superego" relationships during the latency stage for Freud (Rapaport, 1959), may bear only the most indirect relation to microgenetic outcome variables, conservation performances, or therapeutic outcomes, respectively. It seems that we clearly need to pay more attention to conceptualizing intermediate, intervening, or middle-range variables before our theory construction efforts are completed. Perhaps this should precede further collection of empirical research data?

What complicates thinking in these terms is the fact that each of the targets or developmental units in our analysis is undergoing simultaneous change over time, and at the same instant, altering and being altered by the other known (and unknown) units. Recognition of this demanded that we take a relativistic or dynamic view, i.e., one that carries a probabilistic version of statistical determinism as the proper medium of causal analysis (Featherman & Lerner, 1985; Heisenberg, 1958; Hooper & Hooper, 1985; Lerner, 1986). "Every conclusion drawn from our observation is, as a rule, premature, for behind the phenomenon which we see clearly are other phenomena that we see indistinctly, and perhaps behind these latter, yet others which we do not see at all" (Gustave Le Bon, La Psychologie Des Foules). Therefore, we will be forced to abandon any scientific dreams of simplistic causal reductionism or univariate antecedent-consequent determinism which may have been proposed for many microlevel processes in the developing organism and the family.

APPLICATIONS OF THE LIFE-COURSE PERSPECTIVE

Perhaps the general theme of this section could be stated as the integration of the institutional accounts of human behavior provided by history, sociology, and economics with the view of human development informed through psychology and biology. The sources for the life course perspective are many and varied, and include social and psychological gerontology (Hagestad & Neugarten, 1985), as well as more specialized subdisciplines concerned with society as an age-graded system (Riley, Johnson, & Foner, 1972).

Applications of the life-course perspective to individuals and families follows the original work of such writers as Clausen (1972), Elder (1979, 1984), Hagestad (1982) and Riley (e.g., Riley, 1985, 1986; Riley, Johnson, & Foner, 1972). We learned from our reading and experience that social structure goes beyond global conceptions of context, environmental influence, or ecology as aggregates of many diverse factors. Such a point of view seeks to disentangle cohort versus intergenerational analyses. Although authors often treated them as if they were synonymous or interchangeable, these are distinct albeit related constructs (Nydegger, 1981; Riley, 1985; Rosow, 1978). In the present context, age defined in terms of the birth year of the family head serves as a general locator for the life course of the family. In concert with kinship relations it operates to define and temporally locate the family life cycle and to anchor the lineal hierarchy of generational position distinctions (Elder, 1984). "Age and kinship distinctions currently represent key elements in a dynamic perspective on the life course of family and individual development. Both sets of factors indicate the range of possibilities for a life-course approach to the family in which time, process and context matter'' (Elder, 1984, p. 81).

Another source of influence on our thinking is our interest in history. Changes in Western modernization have not only altered our system as an institution but have affected individual life stages. This growing institutionalization of the life course has resulted in greater homogeneity (lesser interindividual variability), sharper time constraints for transition points between the life stages, and a redefinition of normative life events (Baltes, 1987; Kohli & Meyer, 1986; Meyer, 1985). For example, one could view the stages of formal schooling, working, and retirement as primarily state or institutionally defined and in so doing recognize that career cycles and family stages are nonexclusive event categories (Hareven, 1986). These emphases on structural and cultural indi- vidualization suggest that the ideal human life span trajectory is at least a joint function of intraindividual biopsychological factors and institutionally based so- cial structural variables (Baltes, 1987; Featherman & Lerner, 1985). Thus much of human development logic is, in reality, the logic of social structure and broadly based institutional patterns (Kohli & Meyer, 1986).

However, some of our most recent social change data suggests a deinstitu- tionalization trend and a loosening of the classic age-constrained model. Female role participation, for example, in terms of family membership and careers depends on both employment opportunities and fertility patterns as reciprocal influences. Employment status of women seems to depend on the birth of the first child since future nonworkers leave the labor force at this time and addi- tional births are unrelated to labor force participation (Waite, 1980). Age at first birth, in turn, depends on educational level but women do not quit school because of child birth; rather, ''. . . they legitimate the termination of education by having a baby'' (Held, 1986, p. 160). Held elaborates further by claiming (1) family roles and obligations are becoming detached from chronological age (median age at first marriage is increasing and, of greater import, greater vari- ability is present since some early marriages still occur in early adolescence; age at first childbirth shows similar trends), and (2) setting up new households can occur at any age and may not denote the starting of a new family. Thus the parenting role as a public identity must be viewed in a different perspective in accord with recent never-married, divorced, remarried, and alternative life style patterns. These patterns tend to be largely ''age irrelevant'' (Held, 1986; Reinke, Ellicott, Harris, & Hancock, 1985).

These facts bring to mind the more recent conceptualizations of family history as stressing the interactions among ''family time,'' ''individual time,'' and ''historical time'' (Hareven, 1985, 1986), and the importance of timing, syn- chronization, and the cumulative integrative effects of these variables for particu- lar individuals as family members. While timing of transitions through adulthood (leaving home, marriage, parenthood) have, over the past century, shown greater uniformity and more abrupt rapid transitions within cohorts, the most recent trends suggest a return to the late 19th-century patterns (where age was less crucial than family time dictated by economic needs). As may be expected, individual differences are evident with differential patterns for men (less syn-chronization of parenting and career roles over extended time) and women (more marked transitions keyed to family roles per se). These distinctions may be seen in a variety of areas including siblingship tasks and relationships (Goetting, 1986), elder adult caretaking (Cantor & Little, 1985), marriage and remarriage patterns (Hareven, 1985), and even grandparenthood (Bengston & Robertson, 1985). Hareven (1986) claims that the ". . . current trend toward specific age-related transitions is closely related to the decline in instrumental relations among kin over the past century and their replacement by an individualized and senti-mental orientation toward family relations. This trend has led to an increasing age segregation and isolation of the elderly in American society" (p. 177).

Although an extended kin network with three or more generations centered upon the nuclear family household is not, and probably never was a dominant Western institution, kin and sibling support systems remain very important to the family especially during the aging years (Goetting, 1986; Sussman, 1985). In many families today four or even five generations can be alive at the same time. Returning to the historical theme, family size limitation with greater age spacing of children, later ages at time of first marriage, and the nuclear family household structure itself actually preceded the industrial era. Perhaps the greatest historical changes due to industrialization concern family functions, values, and the timing of family transitions. Occupational, religious, and educational functions have been transferred to other social institutions. As a result, the family has ceased to be a center of production and has become, rather, a center for consumption and one whose major purpose is the procreation and nurturing of children. The overall result is a view of modern family life as privatized, nuclear, domestic, and child-centered with an emphasis on affective individualism for all the family members (Hareven, 1985).

Among the many possible topics germane to life-course applications to family and individual development we have selected three representative areas for more extended discussion. These are (1) Individuals and families as both producers and consumers of developmental change; (2) Integration of individual and family developmental "stages"; and (3) Definitions of developmental change and the time construct.

INDIVIDUALS AND FAMILIES AS BOTH PRODUCERS AND CONSUMERS OF DEVELOPMENTAL CHANGE

The sources for this conception are also many and varied, but most are of recent origin. Historically, this view can be traced to any theories of individual behav-ior, learning or development, as well as social organizations which make explicit provision for the needs, motivating drives and overall goals of the person. Examples of this conative theme (Hilgard, 1980) are common in European psychology, particularly among organismic writers such as Freud, Jung, Erikson, Piaget, Werner, and Buhler. In the area of cognition, at least, we can see this as one manifestation of the general issue of conscious intentionality as a special criterion for developmental progress. Here we find the emphasis on instrumental goal-directed activity and, in the special case of symbolically·mediated planful behavior, a unique characteristic of the higher primates (Langer, 1951). Viewed from a general life-course perspective, conscious striving and an awareness of the potential outcomes of one's own actions may be found during the years of infancy (Bower, 1982; Breuer, 1985; Piaget, 1953), childhood (Piaget, 1983; Vygotsky, 1978), as well as adulthood and later life (cf. Werner, 1957, on individuality, pp. 140–146.).

Most of the recent applications of these ideas have concerned the adult years (e.g., Baltes, 1987; Featherman & Lerner, 1985; Lerner & Busch-Rossnagel, 1981; Mayer, 1986) and have emphasized the consequential role of individual acts both in personal terms and as potential influences on other individuals and on larger social units including the family. In brief, individuals are not only the recipients of external influence over the course of their development, but each contributes uniquely to this developmental trajectory and to those of significant others, e.g., children, peers, parents, and grandparents. Much of the recent research on reciprocal interaction models in infancy (e.g., Kreppner, Paulsen, & Schuetze, 1982; Stevenson, Leavitt, Thompson, & Roach, 1988), childhood (e.g., Falbo & Polit, 1986; Mink & Nihira, 1986), adolescence (e.g., Grotevant & Cooper, 1986) and the aging years can be subsumed under this general orientation. Moreover, these individuals, viewed as developmental social collectives, can also mutually influence the larger social and institutional units of which they are a part. In addition to the psychological traditions described earlier, this position, as Featherman and Lerner (1985) point out, is quite consistent with the general symbolic interactionist tradition of G. H. Mead and C. H. Cooley, whereby voluntary action can affect or even create developmental sequences and related transitions (Deegan & Burger, 1978). These producer effects should be magnified as greater numbers of individuals and larger social units (especially families?) are involved in coordinated actions. The targets or developmental "products" of these actions could include bureaucratic organizations in government, education or the private sector, such as administrative agencies or legislators, local schools, employers, and health care provider agencies (Meyer, 1985). In general, the larger the organization or social collective, and the greater the degree of remoteness from the individual/family locus, the longer the time interval before significant change can be expected. This would be especially true for broadly defined social policy issues and would be maximal for the case of intergenerational adaptations (Brent, 1978), which involve "sleeper" or time lag effects over many years. In the latter cases, the particular cohort members who initiate the change activities may not survive long enough to experience the social changes they have advocated. The relationship of these changes as reflecting altruism and long-term cultural values or beliefs is self-evident (Rosenmayr, 1985; Skinner, 1971). At the very least, the concept of individuals and families as coproducers of biocultural change suggest a multidirectional causal pathway (as among parents and children, or grandparents and their lineal descendents) but also a means of effecting long-term change through enlightened collective self interest, social change, and selective genetic transmission (Brent, 1978; Featherman & Lerner, 1985). As Riley (1986) recently stated, "Thus, in its own way, each cohort exerts a collective force as it moves through the age-stratified society, pressing for normative adjustments in social roles and social values, changing the social structure. And changing social structures redirect the ways in which people develop and grow older" (p. 155).

INTEGRATION OF INDIVIDUAL AND FAMILY "STAGES"

Although they are sometimes used interchangeably, there are logical distinctions inherent in the terms "period," "phase," "level," and "stage" (Glaserfeld & Kelly, 1982). Specifically, stages, as distinct from these other concepts, are characterized as (1) relatively prolonged intervals of developmental time; (2) having form or structural constancy which may be described both in regards to things present and things absent, and (3) having differences vis a vis other points on the overall time continua which are not merely of a quantitative nature. Moreover, criteria for these qualitative differences are always questions of explanatory interpretation, not only descriptive observation (Flavell, 1985, pp. 291–295; Glaserfeld & Kelly, 1982, p. 156).

The use of concepts like stage, phase, and cycle in the family literature probably began with Roundtree's (1901) survey of laboring families in York, England (Elder, 1984). Willard Waller in 1938 proposed a set of five sequential phases—(1) Dependency in the Family of Origin; (2) Courtship; (3) First years of Marriage; (4) Parenthood; (5) Empty Nest. Paul Glick was the first to employ both age and kinship designations in his descriptions of the stages of the family life cycle (Glick, 1947), and this was followed by Lansing and Kish (1957) who found for a sample of younger versus older parents that a stage typology was a better predictor than chronological age (Elder, 1984). Perhaps the best known family stage model is that of Reuben Hill (1964) who suggested a more finely grained nine-stage model. The primary classificatory criteria were father's occupation, family size and composition, and major changes in the status of the youngest and oldest children. Thus, while ages of children were important, parents' ages and individual developmental life trajectories were not. As Elder (1984) makes clear, the Hill model represents a normative order of phases or stages in the reproductive cycle of the target couple. Children mature and leave home all in relation to "timeless" parents. Of course no subsequent life stage for these conventional couples is postparental so long as their children continue to survive. "Overall, the static nature of stage models yields 'snapshots' of family development which tell us little about the actual course of a family's history or experience. Families that march through an identical sequence of stages vary markedly in their respective life courses. Much of this variation is due to the variable timing, order, and duration of family events, as determined from age data" (Elder, 1984, p. 117). We have commented at some length on the latter versions of Hill's developmental model (cf. Hill & Mattessich, 1979; Hooper & Hooper, 1985) and agree with Elder that any comprehensive model of intergenerational cycles or stages requires at a minimum information regarding age, sex, and family role functioning (see also Klein, Jorgensen, & Miller, 1978, and Nock, 1979).

This leads to the general issue of how to handle the individual participant's developmental stage status within a family life-cycle model. This individual stage data could assume a variety of forms depending upon the theorist, the age ranges, and the behavioral content one chooses to employ. While a great number of writers have used stage models (cf. Cavanaugh, 1981) the currently better known cases include Piaget's infancy stages, Erikson's extensions of psychoanalytic theory to adolescence and adulthood, Levinson's stages of male midlife, and special content stage models such as Kohlberg's moral development scale and the Kubler-Ross stage theory of death and dying. Obviously great variability exists regarding the degree of structural complexity and detail found in each of these stage typologies (cf. Wohlwill, 1973, pp. 190–239), but in principle any of them could be used in conjunction with a general life course perspective to family development.

These considerations raise the conceptual and developmental process issue: How exactly could an investigator recognize both family and individual stage designations at one and the same time? In a strictly logical sense alone, the matrix of intersecting or interacting time-constrained stages could include all the extended family members (viewed in intergenerational terms) and the family system as a continuing developmental unit. In terms of behavior, this approach would yield an overall stage location or intersection matrix which would at least be operationally complex and probably very cumbersome to implement. Viewed conceptually, this type of forced integration of stage typologies would yield such a nonparsimonious picture of developmental trajectories as to defeat the original descriptive and explanatory purposes of stage usage. It would be better to select one circumscribed set of individuals, i.e., the marital pair, and use their behavioral stage descriptions as anchoring reference points against which the other family members' (earlier and later generations, for example) developmental states could be compared. Baseline information from these two sources (target couple and other family members) would serve as the developmental coordinates for a fuller understanding of the family unit as it progresses in developmental time. If the family stage is taken as the primary reference point, we will need to have the essential individual difference data for the couple, and children, and the grandparents as a minimum condition. An example of what we have in mind here is provided by Nydegger (1981). For the limited case of two generations, the timing of fatherhood was examined through an interactive analysis of father's age, timing age (early, on time, and later parenthood), and the eldest children's age ranges. As the ages of some of the children are directly comparable across the sample design adjacent row diagonals (see Nydegger, 1981, Table III, p. 10), the fathers' relations with all the children in the family were studied. The latter comparisons added the variable of birth order to the design. Thus, classic variables from the developmental tradition tapping general experience (cohort membership), specific experience (chronological age), and current experience (time of testing) are combined with the counterpart experience factors from the sociologist's family stage or role timing model, i.e., general (father's C.A.), specific (timing of parenthood) and current (age of first born child). Ideally, the stages of family development should be viewed within the larger context of changing institutional patterns, e.g., school and educational system changes, social and economic conditions, governmental policy, and larger historical trends, all of which may be cohort or generationally specific. One outstanding example of this approach can be found in the work of Elder (1979, 1984). Work like that of Nydegger and Elder moves well beyond the linear, age-bound stage model of family development proposed by Hill (1964) and others. Hill was once asked by a graduate student how family development theory would handle all those families whose timing, make-up, ages, etc., do not fit the stage model. 'Those families,' replied Hill, 'the theory renders peripheral' (Hill, personal communication, 1977). And there, we feel, is the rub! And there, simply put, is our rationale for many of the suggestions and questions raised in this paper. If family development theory is to prove useful to family researchers and practitioners, as well as researchers in human development, it must render far fewer families peripheral than it now does.

DEFINITIONS OF DEVELOPMENTAL CHANGE AND THE TIME CONSTRUCT

One of the earliest recognized conceptual advantages of the organismic view of developmental change concerned the use of the time variable. For Piaget the form and sequence of the developmental progression was critical whereas the rate of change or movement along this sequence was not. For Werner both the defining characteristics of a developmental event, as designated by the nonempirical "orthogenetic principle," and the objectively observed developmental functions were essentially "timeless" or time irrelevant. In both cases, however, the concept of directionality in development was paramount. Development is always change toward something, i.e., formal operational thought or symbolic functioning, and thus an explicit teleology is present. This orientation has been of major value in clarifying just exactly what a valid developmental event is, especially if one wishes to concentrate upon qualitative structural changes. These structural changes are quite naturally (that is from an organismic/dialectical/systems perspective) the major defining criteria for stage designations. Time, as represented in the chronological age variable, is viewed in a noncausal sense and the emphasis is placed on questions of sequence and transition along the progressive developmental continua.

When notions of valid developmental change such as these are applied to life course analysis, the primary assistance lies in the proper identification of qualitative changes and associated transition points across the life span (bearing in mind that the actual assessment and subsequent statistical analysis of these events may be quite complex, cf., Wohlwill, 1973, for a general treatment of these issues and Hoem, 1986, for the single special case of longitudinal event-history analysis). Unfortunately there are a number of unresolved problems when the direction of development and the associated time construct are viewed in this manner (problems which many organistic proponents, certainly including Werner and Piaget, attempted to deal with). Even if one is comfortable with the explicitly teleological assumptions of this view, the possibility of general non-progressive change has to be dealt with and this often takes the form of including bidirectional and multidirectional options. More basically, the time variable reenters the picture as soon as one becomes concerned with questions of accurate developmental assessment, item sensitivity, diagnostic adequacy, and so forth. When an investigator is concerned with such questions as "what develops with what?" or "What develops before this?" or "Where and when in a developmental sequence is intervention apt to be optimal?" the nature of the time continuum or scale becomes critical. In the case of either individual or family development, these matters tend to direct our attention to consideration of the major defining characteristics of quantitative versus qualitative and continuous versus discontinuous event categories.

Recently, there have been attempts to deal with these admittedly complex issues from the perspective of dialectical contextualism (e.g., Featherman & Lerner, 1985; Lerner, 1984, 1986). Featherman and Lerner, for example, propose that the general concept of rates of change may be used to possibly disentangle developmental from nondevelopmental events, and to extend developmental analysis to include a wide range of psychological, biological, sociological, and historical event categories. Building upon the earlier views of Heinz Werner (cf. Werner, 1957, pp. 133–137), they distinguish quantitative continuous change characterized by "abruptness" from qualitative discontinuous change characterized by both abruptness and "gappiness" (or an absence of intermediate forms in the development sequence). The key feature of change rate is duration dependence which defines the amount of time a person or larger social or institutional unit (the family in the present context) has endured within the current state or level.'' . . . When the rate of change in the population of interest is non-constant, or non-stationary, aging or development is occurring; when the rate is constant (stationary) for the population of entities, the observed change is not developmental change. If the rate of change is duration-dependent, then persons in some developmental state (viz., in the process of leaving the state) are developing at different rates as a function of their "ages' or time spent in the state. . . . By contrast, if the rate is stationary, all elements of the population experience the same likelihood or pace of leaving the original state at any given moment without regard to their durations or 'waiting times' in that state'' (Featherman & Lerner, 1985, p. 667). The relative probability of change is considered in a nondeterministic sense although antecedent-consequent causal relationships are not excluded (see our earlier discussion of statistical determinism). The authors note further that this approach to defining valid developmental changes is particularly appropriate to life-course applications since change, in principle, can occur at any point along the life span and no restrictions as to age ranges or critical periods are necessary. It also points out the necessity of adopting a truly comparative perspective, for some individuals or some families may be changing while others (even those randomly drawn from the same population) are not. And the absence of significant change is sometimes of equal import, as in a clinical setting. One is alerted to changes in a variety of contexts at micro and macrolevels; changes, moreover, which may be simultaneous or concomitant, or sequentially related in a causal manner.

Viewing developmental change in this manner is only a start. While it does permit the possible integration of significant alterations in both individuals and family units within the same general framework, the explanations for these stable or nonstable patterns of alteration remain to be elucidated. Treating the time variable in this manner does permit the inclusion of both short and long-term event sequences and perhaps most importantly, allows personal time, family time, and historical/evolutionary time to enter into our analyses in an equal and coordinated fashion.

In brief, this view of the time concept allows for equal consideration for many of the topics and factors discussed earlier as relevant to individual and family developmental analysis. It may even suggest a common meeting ground for the essentially complementary sociological and psychological viewpoints from which we have woven the present discussion.

Having read all of this, the reader may well wonder what are the more personal views of the authors. One of us (FHH) is a born life-style optimist and I guess this naturally carries over to my professional activities. Having struggled for 35 years to become a university professor, and then joining the academic system to attain promotions, salary and professional respect, I resist the occasional suspicion that not very much was really accomplished. Resistance is easier because I am actively teaching and supervising graduate students who are often refreshingly naive and enthusiastic. (Without the students I believe the entire academic system would wind down in a sort of scholastic entropy.) In short, I simply can't admit that all this searching was futile and doomed to failure from the onset. So it is with my thinking about life-span developmental theories and family interaction research. The complexities within each domain make the search for a combined and superordinate model exceedingly difficult. For example, having been trained in experimental cognitive psychology, the temptation to ignore annoying and confounding social relations factors is very real. At another level, though, I know people don't develop (even cognitively) in a neat social vacuum. My reading and acquired sense of history tell me that (to choose only two individuals), both Freud and Piaget early recognized this. One chose to study the vicissitudes of irrational thought energized by social relationships while the other concentrated on the development of rational man governed by the classical principles of logical inference. The contributions of both were enormous and hindsight tells us that each was right in his own way. The task of integrating rational and irrational man remains. Similarly, to integrate family and individual development in a life-span perspective demands that we accept the constraints of each while stretching ourselves to expect much more. While the overall goal may indeed be beyond our immediate means (in terms of both theory and method) one can't afford the luxury of self-fulfilling despair. We keep struggling and searching for the elusive goal ever mindful of the possible detours and blind alleys. Even if, as Pooh and Piglet found, the goal may have Woozle-like qualities, the journey has been most informative and enjoyable. As it turns out, we may be on much safer ground regarding grand strategies and general research policy than we are regarding the preferred logistics and tactics to employ in our investigations of individual and family development over the life span.

REFERENCES

Alpert, J. S., & Richardson, M. S. (1980). *Parenting: In L. Poon (Ed.), Aging in the 1980's: Psychological Issues* (pp. 441–454). Washington, D.C.: American Psychological Association.

Anderson, E. R., Heatherington, E. M., & Clingempeel, W. G. (1986, April). *Pubertal status and its influence on the adaptation to remarriage.* Paper presented at the Society for Research on Adolescence Meeting, Madison, WI.

Baltes, P. B. (1987). Theoretical propositions of life-span developmental psychology: On the dynamics between growth and decline. *Developmental Psychology, 23*(5), 611–626.

Baltes, P. B., Reese, H. W., & Nesselroade, J. R. (1977). *Life-span developmental psychology: Introduction to research methods.* Monterey, CA: Brooks/Cole.

Baltes, P. B., & Willis, S. L. (1977). Toward psychological theories of aging and development: In J. E. Birren & K. W. Schaie (Eds.), *Handbook of the psychology of aging* (pp. 128–154). New York: Van Nostrand Reinhold.

Bednar, R. L., Burlingame, G. M., & Masters, K. S. (1988). Systems of family treatment: Substance or semantics? In M. Rosenzweig & L. Porter (Eds.), *Annual Review of Psychology* (pp. 401–434). Palo Alto, CA: Annual Reviews.

Belsky, J. (1981). Early human experience: A family perspective. *Developmental Psychology, 17*, 3–23.

Bengston, V. L., & Dowd, J. J. (1980). Sociological functionalism, exchange theory and life-cycle analysis: A call for more explicit theoretical bridges. *International Journal of Aging and Human Development, 12*, 55–73.

Bengston, V. L., & Robertson, J. F. (1985). *Grandparenthood*. Beverly Hills, CA: Sage.

Boulding, K. W. (1967). Dare we take the social sciences seriously? *American Psychologist, 22*, 879–888.

Bower, T. G. R. (1982). *Development in infancy*. San Francisco: Freeman.

Brent, S. B. (1978). Individual specialization, collective adaptation and rate of environmental change. *Human Development, 21*, 21–33.

Breuer, K. H. (1985). Intentionality of perception in early infancy. *Human Development, 28*, 71–83.

Broderick, C. B., & Pulliam-Krager, H. (1979). Family process and child outcomes. In W. Burr, R. Hill, F. I. Nye, & I. L. Reese (Eds.), *Contemporary theories about the family, Vol. I. Research-based theories* (pp. 604–614). New York: The Free Press.

Broderick, C. B., & Smith, J. (1979). The general systems approach to the family. In W. Burr, R. Hill, F. I. Nye & I. L. Reese (Eds.), *Contemporary theories about the family, Vol. 2, General theories/theoretical orientations* (pp. 112–129). New York: The Free Press.

Brody, G. H., Neubaum, E., & Forehand, R. (1988). Serial marriage: A heuristic analysis of an emerging family form. *Psychological Bulletin, 103*, 211–222.

Bronfenbrenner, U. (1986). Ecology of the family as a context for human development research perspectives. *Developmental Psychology, 22*, 723–742.

Bronfenbrenner, U., Kessel, F., Kessen, W., & White, S. (1986). Toward a critical social history of developmental psychology. *American Psychologist, 41*, 1218–1230.

Brown, L. H., & Kidwell, J. S. (Eds.). (1982). Methodology: The other side of caring. *Journal of Marriage and the Family, 44*, 827–1072.

Burgess, E. W. (1926). The family as a unity of interacting personalities. *Family, 7*, 3–9.

Burgess, E. W., & Locke, H. J. (1945).*The family: From institution to companionship*. New York: American Book.

Burgess, E. W., & Wallin, P. (1953). *Engagement and marriage*. New York: Lippincott.

Burns, L. R. (1980). The Chicago school and the study of organization-environment relations. *Journal of the History of the Behavioral Sciences, 16*, 342–358.

Burr, W. R., Leigh, G. K., Day, R. D., & Constantine, J. (1979). Symbolic interaction and the family. In W. R. Burr, R. Hill, F. I. Nye, & I. L. Reis (Eds.), *Contemporary theories about the family, Vol. II. General theories/theoretical orientations* (pp. 42–111). New York: Free Press.

Cairns, R. B. (1983). The emergence of developmental psychology: In W. Kessen (Ed.). Handbook of child psychology, Vol. I of P. H. Mussen (Ed.), *Handbook of child psychology* (4th ed., pp. 41–102.) New York: Wiley.

Cantor, M., & Little, V. (1985). Aging and social care. In R. H. Binstock & E. Shanas (Eds.), *Handbook of aging and the social sciences* (pp. 746–782). New York: Van Nostrand Reinhold.

Cavanaugh, J. C. (1981). Early developmental theories: A brief review of attempts to organize developmental data prior to 1925. *Journal of the History of the Behavioral Sciences, 17*, 38–47.

Christensen, H. T. (1964). Development of the family field of study. In H. T. Christensen (Ed.), *Handbook of marriage and the family* (pp. 3–32). Chicago: Rand McNally.

Clark-Steward, K. A. (1988). Parents' effects on children's development: A decade of progress? *Journal of Applied Developmental Psychology, 9*, 41–84.

Clausen, J. A. (1972). The life course of individuals. In M. W. Riley, M. Johnson, & A. Foner (Eds.), *Aging and society*. New York: Sage.

Cronbach, L. J. (1975). Beyond the two disciplines of scientific psychology. *American Psychologist, 30,* 116–227.

Dager, E. A. (1964). Socialization and personality development in the child. In H. T. Christensen (Ed.), *Handbook of marriage and the family* (pp. 740–781). Chicago: Rand McNally.

Deegan, M. J., & Burger, J. S. (1978). George Herbert Mead and social reform: His work and writings. *Journal of the History of the Behavioral Sciences, 14,* 362–373.

Dubin, R. (1986). Sociology at Chicago. *Journal of the History of the Behavioral Sciences, 22,* 215–219.

Elder, G. H., Jr. (1979). Historical change in life patterns and personality. In P. Baltes & O. Brim (Eds.), *Life-span development and behavior* (Vol. II, pp. 117–151). New York: Academic Press.

Elder, G. H., Jr. (1984). Families, kin, and the life course: A sociological perspective. In R. D. Parke (Ed.), *Review of child development research* (Vol. 7, pp. 80–136). Chicago: University of Chicago Press.

Falbo, T., & Polit, D. F. (1986). Quantitative review of the only child literature: Research evidence and theory development. *Psychological Bulletin, 100,* 176–189.

Featherman, D. L., & Lerner, R. M. (1985). Ontogenesis and sociogenesis: Problematics for theory and research about development and socialization across the lifespan. *American Sociological Review, 50,* 659–676.

Framo, J. L. (1979). Family theory and therapy. *American Psychologist, 34,* 988–992.

Flavell, J. H. (1985). *Cognitive development* (2nd ed.). Englewood Cliffs, NJ: Prentice-Hall.

Gans, B. S. (Ed.). (1926). *Concerning parents: A symposium on present day parenthood.* New York: New Republic.

Glaserfeld, E. von, & Kelly, M. F. (1982). On the concepts of period, phase, stage and level. *Human Development, 25,* 152–160.

Glick, P. C. (1947). The family cycle. *American Sociological Review, 12,* 164–174.

Goetting, A. (1986). The developmental tasks of siblingship over the life cycle. *Journal of Marriage and the Family, 48,* 703–714.

Goldstein, M. J. (1988). The family and psychopathology. In M. Rosenzweig & L. Porter (Eds.), *Annual Review of Psychology* (pp. 282–299). Palo Alto, CA: Annual Reviews.

Goodnow, J. J. (1988). Parents' ideas, actions and feelings: Models and methods from developmental and social psychology. *Child Development, 59,* 286–320.

Gould, S. J. (1986). Evolution and the triumph of homology, or why history matters. *American Scientist, 74,* 128–136.

Green, J. A. (1988). Loglinear analysis of cross-classified ordinal data: Applications in developmental research. *Child Development, 59,* 1–25.

Grotevant, H. D., & Cooper, C. R. (1986). Individuation in family relationships. *Human Development, 29,* 82–100.

Grunebaum, H. (1988). The relationship of family theory to family therapy. *Journal of Marital and Family Therapy, 14,* 1–14.

Gurman, A. S., & Kniskert, D. P. (1978). Research on marital and family therapy: Progress, perspective, and prospect. In S. L. Garfield & A. E. Bergin (Eds.), *Handbook of psychotherapy and behavior change: An empirical analysis.* New York: Wiley.

Hagestad, G. O. (1982). Parent and child: Generations in the family. In T. M. Field, H. C. Huston, L. T. Quay, & G. E. Finlay (Eds.), *Review of human development.* New York: Wiley.

Hagestad, G. O., & Neugarten, B. L. (1985). Age and the life course. In R. H. Binstock & E. Shanas (Eds.), *Handbook of aging and the social sciences* (2nd ed., pp. 35–61). New York: Van Nostrand Reinhold.

Hareven, T. (1985). Historical changes in the family and the life course: Implications for child development. In A. B. Smuts & J. W. Hagen (Eds.), *History and research in child development. Monographs of the Society for Research in Child Development,* Vol. 50, Serial No. 211, (pp. 8–23).

Hareven, T. (1986). Historical changes in the social construction of the life course. *Human Development, 13*, pp. 171–177.

Heisenberg, W. (1958). *The physicist's conception of nature.* New York: Harcourt, Brace & World.

Held, T. (1986). Institutionalization and deinstitutionalization of the life course. *Human Development, 29*, 157–162.

Hetherington, E. M., & Camara, K. A. (1984). Families in transition: The processes of dissolution and reconstitution. In R. Parke (Ed.), *Review of child development research* (Vol. 7, pp. 398–439).

Hilgard, E. R. (1980). The trilogy of mind: Cognition, affection, and conation. *Journal of the History of the Behavioral Sciences, 16*, 107–117.

Hill, R. (1964). Methodological issues in family development research. *Family Process, 3*, 186–206.

Hill, R., & Mattessich, P. (1979). Family development theory and life-span development. In P. B. Baltes & O. G. Brim, Jr. (Eds.), *Life-span development and behavior* (Vol. II, pp. 161–204). New York: Academic Press.

Hill, R., & Rogers, R. H. (1964). The developmental approach. In H. T. Christensen (Ed.), *Handbook of marriage and the family* (pp. 171–214). Chicago: Rand McNally.

Hoem, J. M. (1986). Briefly annotated reading list on event-history analysis. *Annotated bibliographies for longitudinal research methodologies.* Washington, DC: National Institute on Aging/National Institute of Mental Health.

Hoffman, L. W., & Lippitt, R. (1960). The measurement of family life variables. In P. H. Mussen (Ed.), *Handbook of research methods in child development* (pp. 945–1013). New York: Wiley.

Hooper, F. H. (1969). The Appalachian child's intellectual capabilities—deprivation or diversity? *Journal of Negro Education, 38*, 224–235.

Hooper, F. H. (1973). Cognitive assessment across the life-span: Methodological implications of the organismic approach. In J. R. Nesselroade & H. W. Reese (Eds.), *Life-span developmental psychology: Methodological issues* (pp. 299–316). New York: Academic Press.

Hooper, F. H. (1988). The history of child psychology as seen through handbook analysis. *Human Development, 31*, 176–184.

Hooper, F. H., Hooper, J. O., & Colbert, K. (1984). *Personality and memory correlates of intellectual functioning: Young adulthood to old age.* Basel/New York: Karger.

Hooper, F. H., Sipple, T. S., Goldman, J. A., & Swinton, S. S. (1979). A cross-sectional investigation of children's classificatory abilities. *Genetic Psychology Monographs, 99*, 41–89.

Hooper, F. H., Swinton, S. S., & Sipple, T. S. (1979). Logical reasoning in middle childhood: A study of the Piagetian concrete operations stage. In H. J. Klausmeier et al. (Eds.), *Cognitive learning and development: Information processing and Piagetian prospectives* (pp. 127–171). Cambridge, MA: Ballinger.

Hooper, F. H., Toniolo, T. A., & Sipple, T. S. (1978). A longitudinal analysis of logical reasoning relationships: Conservation and transitive inference. *Developmental Psychology, 14*, 674–682.

Hooper, F. H., Wanska, S. K., Peterson, G. W., & DeFrain, J. (1979). The efficacy of small group instructional activities for training Piagetian concrete operations. *Journal of Genetic Psychology, 134*, 281–297.

Hooper, J. O. (1979). Returning women students and their families: Support and conflict. *Journal of College Student Personnel, 20*, 145–152.

Hooper, J. O. (1981). Older adults earning university credits. *Educational Gerontology, 6*, 385–394.

Hooper, J. O., & Hooper, F. H. (1985). Family and individual developmental theories: Conceptual analysis and speculation. In J. A. Meacham (Ed.), *Family and individual development. Contributions to Human Development,* (Vol. 14). Basel/New York: Karger.

Hooper, J. O., Hooper, F. H., Colbert, K., & McMahan, R. (1986). Cognition, memory, and personality in elderly students. *Educational Gerontology, 12,* 219–229.

Hooper, J. O., & March, G. B. (1980). The female single parent in the university. *Journal of College Student Personnel, 21,* 141–146.

Hooper, J. O., & Traupmann, J. (1983). Older women, the student role, and mental health. *Educational Gerontology, 9,* 47–61.

Horn, J. L. (1982). The aging of human abilities. In B. B. Wolman (Ed.), *Handbook of developmental psychology* (pp. 847–870). Englewood Cliffs, NJ: Prentice-Hall.

Hultsch, D. F., & Hickey, T. (1978). External validity in the study of human development: Theoretical and methodological issues. *Human Development, 21,* 76–91.

Kaplan, B. (1967). Meditations on Genesis. *Human Development, 10,* 65–87.

Kaye, K. (1985). Family development. In K. Kaye & F. F. Furstenberg, Jr. (Eds.), Family development and the child. *Child Development, 56,* 279–280.

Kaye, K., & Furstenberg, F. F., Jr. (Eds.). (1985). Family development and the child. *Child Development, 56.*

Klein, D. M., Jorgensen, S. R., & Miller, B. C. (1978). Research methods and developmental reciprocity in families. In R. Lerner & B. Spanier (Eds.), *Child influences on marital and family interactions: A life-span perspective.* New York: Academic Press.

Kohli, M., & Mayer, J. (1986). Social structure and social construction of life stages. *Human Development, 29,* 145–180.

Kreppner, K., Paulsen, S., & Schuetze, Y. (1982). Infant and family development: From triads to tetrads. *Human Development, 25,* 373–391.

Kuhn, T. S. (1962). *The structure of scientific revolutions.* Chicago: University of Chicago Press.

Labouvie, E. (1975). The dialectical nature of measurement activities in the behavioral sciences. *Human Development, 18,* 396–403.

Langer, S. K. (1951). *Philosophy in a new key.* Cambridge, MA: Harvard University Press.

Langer, J. (1969). *Theories of development.* New York: Holt, Rinehart, & Winston.

Lansing, J. B., & Kish, L. (1957). Family life cycle as an independent variable. *American Sociological Review, 22,* 512–519.

Laosa, L. M. (1982). Families as facilitators of children's intellectual development at 3 years of age: A causal analysis. In L. Laosa & I. Sigel (Eds.), *Changing families* (pp. 79–135). New York: Plenum.

Lapsley, D. K. (1985). *On dialectics and developmental meta-theory: A critical appraisal.* Unpublished manuscript, University of Notre Dame.

Lawton, J. T., Hooper, F. H., Saunders, R. A., & Roth, P. (1984). A comparison of logical concept development in three preschool programmes. *Human Learning, 3,* 143–164.

Lerner, R. M. (Ed). (1983). *Developmental psychology: Historical and philosophical perspectives.* Hillsdale, NJ: Lawrence Erlbaum Associates.

Lerner, R. M. (1984). *On the nature of human plasticity.* New York: Cambridge University Press.

Lerner, R. M. (1986). *Concepts and theories of human development.* New York: Random House.

Lerner, R. M., & Busch-Rossnagel, N. A. (1981). *Individuals as producers of their development: A life span perspective.* New York: Academic Press.

Lerner, R. M., & Spanier, G. P. (1978). *Child influences on marital and family interactions.* New York: Academic Press.

Maccoby, E. E., & Martin, J. A. (1983). Socialization in the context of the family: Parent-child interaction. In E. M. Hetherington (Ed.), *Social and personality development* Vol. IV of P. H. Mussen (Ed.), *Handbook of child psychology* (4th ed., pp. 1–102). New York: Wiley.

Mayer, K. U. (1986). Structural constraints on the life course. *Human Development, 29,* 163–170.

McCubbin, M. A., & McCubbin, H. I. (1988). Typology model of family adjustments and adaptation: Framework for assessment, crisis intervention, and treatment. In C. Figley (Ed.), *Family stress and treatment.* New York: Brunner Mazel.

Melito, R. (1985). Adaptation in family systems: A developmental perspective. *Family Process*, *24*, 89–100.

Meyer, J. W. (1985). The institutionalization of the life course and its effect on the self. In A. Sorensen, F. Weinert, & L. Sherrod (Eds.), *Human development and the life course: Multidisciplinary perspectives*. Hillsdale, NJ: Lawrence Erlbaum Associates.

Miller, S. A. (1988). Parents' beliefs about children's cognitive development. *Child Development*, *59*, 259–285.

Mink, I. T., & Nihira, K. (1986). Family life-styles and child behaviors: A study of direction of effects. *Developmental Psychology*, *22*, 610–616.

Minuchin, P. (1985). Families and individual development: Provocations from the field of family therapy. In K. Kaye & F. F. Furstenberg, Jr. (Eds.), Family development and the child. *Child Development*, *56*, 289–302.

Muhs, P. J., Hooper, F. H., & Papalia-Finlay, D. E. (1979–80). Cross-sectional analysis of cognitive functioning across the life-span. *International Journal of Aging and Human Development*, *10*, 311–333.

Nock, S. L. (1979). The family life cycle: Empirical or conceptual tool. *Journal of Marriage and the Family*, *41*, 15–26.

Norman, K. L. (1986). Importance of factors in the review of grant proposals. *Journal of Applied Psychology*, *71*, 156–162.

Nydegger, C. N. (1981). On being caught up in time. *Human Development*, *24*, 1–12.

Parke, R. D. (Ed.). (1984). *Review of child development research. Vol. VII The family*. Chicago: University of Chicago Press.

Patterson, G. R. (1987). Three stages in a mother-child stress process. In F. R. Patterson (Ed.), *Family consortium series: I. Aggression and depression in families: Substantive and methodological issues*. Hillsdale, NJ: Lawrence Erlbaum Associates.

Patterson, G. R., Chamberlain, P., & Reid, J. B. (1982). A comparative evaluation of a parent training program. *Behavior Therapy*, *13*, 638–650.

Piaget, J. (1953). *The origins of intelligence in the child*. London: Routledge & Kegan Paul.

Piaget, J. (1970). *Structuralism*. New York: Basic Books.

Piaget, J. (1971a). *Biology and knowledge*. Chicago: University of Chicago Press.

Piaget, J. (1971b). *Insights and illusions of philosophy*. New York: New American Library.

Piaget, J. (1977). *Etudes sociologiques*. Geneva: Librairie Droz.

Piaget, J. (1983). Piaget's theory. In W. Kessen (Ed.), *History, theory, and methods*, Vol. I of P. H. Mussen (Ed.), *Handbook of child psychology*, (4th ed., pp. 103–128). New York: Wiley.

Rapaport, D. (1959). The structure of psychoanalytic theory: A systematizing attempt. In S. Koch (Ed.), *Psychology: A study of a science, Vol III. Formulations of the person and the social context* (pp. 51–183). New York: McGraw-Hill.

Reese, H. W. (1982). A comment on the meanings of "Dialectics". *Human Development*, *25*, 423–429.

Reid, J. B. (1983a). *Final Report: Child Abuse: Developmental factors and treatment*. Grant No. 7 RO1MH 37934, National Institute of Mental Health, United States Public Health Service.

Reid, J. B. (1983b). Social-interactional patterns in families of abused and nonabused children. In C. Waxler, M. Cummings, & M. Radke-Yarrow (Eds.), *Social and biological origins of altruism and aggression*. New York: Cambridge University Press.

Reinke, B. J., Ellicott, A. M., Harris, R. L., Hancock, E. (1985). Timing of psychosocial changes in women's lives. *Human Development*, *28*, 259–280.

Rheingold, H. L. (1985). The first twenty-five years of the Society for Research in Child Development. In A. Smuts & J. Hagen (Eds.), *History and research in child development, Monographs of the Society for Research in Child Development*, *50*, 126–140.

Riegel, K. F. (1973). Developmental psychology and society: Some historical and ethical considerations. In J. R. Nesselroade & H. W. Reese (Eds.), *Life-span developmental psychology: Methodological issues* (pp. 1–24). New York: Academic Press.

Riegel, K. F. (1975). Toward a dialectical theory of development. *Human Development, 18,* 50–64.

Riley, M. W. (1985). Age strata in social systems. In R. H. Binstock & E. Shanas, *Handbook of aging and the social sciences* (2nd. ed., pp. 369–411). New York: Van Nostrand Reinhold.

Riley, M. W. (1986). The dynamisms of life stages: Roles, people, and age. *Human Development, 29,* 150–156.

Riley, M. W., Johnson, M. E., & Foner, A. (Eds.). (1972). *Aging and society: A sociology of age stratification.* Vol. 3. New York: Sage.

Rosenmayr, L. (1985). Culture, behavior, and aging in the comparative perspective. In J. E. Birren & K. W. Schaie (Eds.), *Handbook on the psychology of aging* (2nd ed., pp. 190–215). New York: Van Nostrand Reinhold.

Rosow, I. (1978). What is a cohort and why? *Human Development, 21,* 65–75.

Schlossman, S. (1985). Perils of popularization: The founding of Parents' Magazine. In A. B. Smuts & J. W. Hagen (Eds.), *History and research in child development. Monographs of the Society for Research in Child Development,* Vol. 50, Serial No. 211, (pp. 65–77).

Sears, D. L. (1986). College sophomores in the laboratory: Influences of a narrow data base on social psychology's view of human nature. *Journal of Personality and Social Psychology, 51,* 515–530.

Seitz, V. (1984). Methodology. In M. H. Bornstein & M. E. Lamb (Eds.), *Developmental psychology: An advanced textbook* (pp. 493–531). Hillsdale, NJ: Lawrence Erlbaum Associates.

Sigel, I. E. (1979). A structuralist response to a skeptic. *Behavior and Brain Science, 2,* 148–149.

Sigel, I. E. (1986). Reflections on the belief-behavior connection: Lessons learned from a research program on parental belief systems and teaching strategies. In R. Ashmore & D. Brodzinsky (Eds.), *Thinking about the family: Views of parents and children* (pp. 35–65). Hillsdale, NJ: Lawrence Erlbaum Associates.

Sigel, I. E., & Laosa, L. M. (Eds.). (1983). *Changing families.* New York: Plenum.

Skinner, B. F. (1971). *Beyond freedom and dignity.* New York: Knopf.

Steinberg, L. (1988). Reciprocal relations between parent-child distance and pubertal maturation. *Developmental Psychology, 24,* 122–128.

Stevenson, M. B., Leavitt, L. A., Thompson, R. H., & Roach, M. A. (1988). A social relations model analysis of parent and child play. *Developmental Psychology, 24,* 101–108.

Stryker, S. (1964). The interactional and situational approaches. In H. T. Christenson (Ed.), *Handbook of marriage and the family* (pp. 125–170). Chicago: Rand McNally.

Sussman, M. B. (1985). The family life of old people. In R. H. Binstock & E. Shanas (Eds.), *Handbook of aging and the social sciences* (2nd ed., pp. 415–449). New York: Van Nostrand Reinhold.

Troll, L. E., & Bengston, V. (1979). Generations in the family. In W. R. Burr, R. Hill, F. I. Nye, and I. L. Reiss (Eds.), *Contemporary theories about the family, Vol. I, Research-based theories* (pp. 127–161). New York: Macmillan.

Urban, H. B. (1978). The concept of development from a systems perspective. In P. B. Baltes (Ed.), *Life-span development and behavior* (Vol. I, pp. 45–83). New York: Academic Press.

Vygotsky, L. S. (1978). *Mind in society: The development of higher psychological processes.* Cambridge, MA: Harvard University Press.

Wachtel, E. F. (1987). Family systems and the individual child. *Journal of Marital and Family Therapy, 13,* 15–25.

Waite, L. J. (1980). Working wives and the family life cycle. *American Sociological Review, 86,* 272–294.

Waller, W. (1930). *The old love and the new: Divorce and readjustment.* New York: Horace Liveright.

Waller, W. (1951). *The family: A dynamic interpretation* (rev. by R. Hill). New York: Dryden. (Originally published, 1938).

Werner, H. (1957). The concept of development from a comparative and organismic point of view. In D. B. Harris (Ed.), *The concept of development* (pp. 125–148). Minneapolis: University of Minnesota Press.

Whitaker, C. (1976). The hindrance of theory in clinical work. In P. J. Guerin (Ed.), *Family therapy: Theory and practice*. New York: Gardner Press.

Wohlwill, J. F. (1973). *The study of behavioral development*. New York: Academic Press.

Zigler, E. (1963). Metatheoretical issues in developmental psychology. In M. Marx (Ed.), *Theories in contemporary psychology*. New York: Macmillan.

Author Index

Numbers in italics indicate pages with complete bibliographic information.

Subject Index